SOUTH AFRICA
Limits to Change

The Political Economy of Transition

HEIN MARAIS

Zed Books Ltd
LONDON & NEW YORK

University of Cape Town Press
CAPE TOWN

South Africa: Limits to Change: The Political Economy of Transition was first published by UCT Press (Pty) Ltd, PO Box 14373, Kenwyn 7790, South Africa and Zed Books Ltd, 7 Cynthia Street, London N1 9JF, UK and 175 Fifth Avenue, New York, NY 10010, USA.

© Hein Marais 1998, 2001

Reprinted 1999
Second edition 2001

ISBN 1-919713-60-3 UCT Press, limp
ISBN 1 85649 967 7 Zed Books, limp

Cataloging-in-Publication Data is available from the British Library

US CIP has been applied for from the Library of Congress

Cover design: Simon Ford, University Estate 7925, South Africa
Typesetting and reproduction: RHT desktop publishing cc, Durbanville 7550, South Africa
Printing and binding: Creda Communications, Eliot Avenue, Epping II, Cape Town

Contents

Foreword

Commissioned by the Third World Forum, this book marks an important shift in analyses of the South African democratic breakthrough and the subsequent efforts to transform South Africa along progressive lines, as it locates the transformation critically in broader historical, political-economic and global contexts.

In the book, Marais demonstrates that the struggle for a just and equal society proceeds, but on terms and under conditions that by no means guarantee a happy outcome. In fact, South Africa has launched itself on a long and difficult trek to achieve a truly democratic, non-racist, progressive society. Not least among the dilemmas confronting it is its ambivalent place in the world system.

South Africa has always been hard to classify, in part because it represents a microcosm of the world capitalist system. There exists on its territory zones that correspond to all four constituent 'worlds' that make up the world system. There is the overwhelmingly white section of the population whose popular culture and standard of living seem to belong to the 'first' (advanced capitalist) world. A humorist would note, however, that the 'statist' policies of the former white rulers put the country in a category that used to include the so-called socialist countries of the 'second' world. Much of the urban black population belongs to the modern, industrializing 'third' world, while rural Africans do not differ much from their counterparts in 'fourth' world Africa.

Construction of this curious and exceptional situation began in the 17th century when Dutch settlers looked upon indigenous Africans much as the English settlers in North America regarded Amerindians or the Israelis the Palestinians. British Industrial imperialism, intent on exploiting the fabulous mineral riches discovered in the late 19th century, understood that black labour, if mobilized for that purpose, would present an effective solution to the problem of extraction. It was the British, therefore, and not the Afrikaners who invented apartheid.

They established the antecedents of the miserable homeland system – some within the boundaries of the Union, two as British 'protectorates' (Lesotho and Swaziland), all designed to supply cheap migrant labour for the mines.

In the aftermath of World War Two, the National Party took over responsibility for the overall running of the system under the aegis of an explicitly racist legitimating ideology.

The decades since then were characterized by industrialization in the peripheries of the global system. By nature uneven and unequal in its development, this industrialization split the old 'third' world into a new, industrializing 'third' world and a severely marginalized 'fourth' world, which has remained a producer and export of agricultural and mineral products.

South African capitalists developed within this framework a project aimed at moving up in the global system by means of an industrialization process that would be firmly protected and supported by the state. The apartheid system was perfectly rational in that context. Cheap productive labour does not necessarily create a problem of realizing surplus value when that demand can be stimulated by raising the incomes of the ruling minority and by expanding some exports. The claim that there existed a fundamental conflict between apartheid and capitalism misunderstood what was at stake.

The standard measure of success for a country of the periphery that has industrialized since World War Two is (in accordance with the globalization of capitalism) its ability to be 'competitive' on the world market. From this vantage point, countries can be classified into four groups:

- those which have industrialized and achieved 'competitiveness', or could do so with relatively minor adjustments (the countries of east Asia, with communist and capitalist political regimes, as well as most major Latin American countries);
- those which have industrialized but are clearly not competitive and require drastic restructuring to become so (South Africa and the industrialized Arab countries like Algeria and Egypt);
- those which have remained preindustrial but have succeeded in promoting 'traditional' agricultural, mineral or oil exports and, for that reason, may appear comparatively prosperous (the Gulf states, Gabon, Ivory Coast belong here); and
- those which have failed to promote 'traditional' exports (the majority of African countries).

Only the first group of countries constitutes the periphery of the global system. Their successes are routinely portrayed as evidence that they are progressing towards 'full development' and are 'catching up' with the Western capitalist states. The image is false. In the past, polarization was based on a clear distinction between the industrialized and non-industrialized countries, the latter constituting the periphery.

The polarization of the future will no longer be based on that distinction. The new centres will be those countries that control the global industrial system through their command of financial power and communications systems, their dominance in decision-making over the use of resources at the global level, and their monopolies of technology and weapons of mass destruction.

By these criteria, countries in the first of the four groups cannot belong to the 'first' world merely because they have successfully industrialized. They will constitute the 'third world' of the future while the other groups constitute the 'fourth' world.

Again, South Africa presents a peculiar case. Side-by-side within its national boundaries are zones whose characteristics assign them to the last three groups. Its industries have failed to achieve international 'competitiveness', while its industrial exports are negligible compared to those of South Korea, Mexico and Brazil, for example, and are absorbed mainly by captive markets in southern Africa. Moreover, South Africa's location in the world system is, in the main, that of an exporter of primary products. At the same time, its rural hinterlands remain among the poorest areas of the 'fourth' world and struggle to maintain even minimal levels of survival.

Now that formal apartheid has ended, the institutions of formal democracy have been introduced and the country is governed by a party of the majority, what are the chances that South Africa can break free of the patterns inscribed by its history? Contrary to the reality, the black majority is said to have inherited a magnificent country which, with the 'correct' adjustments, can ascend into the ranks of the world's industrialized success stories. Demanded of its workers and its poor are the standard sacrifices necessary for attaining 'competitiveness'. Were the irony not so vicious it would be laughable – for the working classes are now saddled with the task of achieving what capital, with the active support of the Western powers over several decades, failed to do. And, indeed, as Marais shows, that failure counted among the main factors that led to South Africa's political settlement.

The possibility of genuine democracy and progressive social change exists – if a start is made now. Even then it will be a long and painful process of change, one that will last several decades still. Some of the conditions for such progress are in place: a democratic political system, a progressive Constitution and a unitary state is needed for the redistribution of income socially and regionally as well as a geographical redistribution of investment. Other conditions still have to be struggled for. An immense effort is needed to develop the backward rural areas and achieve agrarian reform that can benefit the rural African population and create a bedrock for industrial development (as the east Asian countries showed). Also, a redistribution of income and social infrastructure (education, health, etc.) is required and will, inevitably, require a diminishing of the status of affluent whites (for it is a simple fact that the overall development of the country cannot support the 'first' world consumption levels of its most privileged layers). Finally, a gradual restructuring of industrial policy is essential and should be geared both at servicing needs and stimulating demand. This means more goods for popular consumption, improved productive capacity in the rural areas, more housing to meet the needs of people and less wasteful production to satisfy the desires of the white minority. In my opinion, these are some of the requirements for real democratization.

Marais' incisive analysis of the visions and strategies, and the political and social forces at work in South African society presents compelling perspectives on the questions raised here.

This book must be read – not only in South Africa but in Africa and beyond – by all who desire a fuller understanding of this country.

Samir Amin
Dakar, June 1997

Acknowledgements

This is the second edition of the book *South Africa: Limits to Change: The Political Economy of Transition* (1998), which began as a research project commissioned by Samir Amin and Bernard Founou for the Dakar-based Third World Forum Institute. It formed part of a pan-African investigation into the experiences of democratic transitions and structural adjustment on the continent. It was Amin and Founou's boundless support and encouragement that transformed that project into a book. This edition includes sections of that book but builds substantially on its analysis. It has been comprehensively updated and expanded to reflect post-1997 developments.

I am grateful to Vishnu Padayachee, Bill Freund, Dot Keet and Mike Morris whose discussions and notes were of inestimable value to me, particularly in my writing of the first half of the book. For their valuable comments, I am also indebted to John Sender (specifically Chapters 4 and 5) and David Everatt. Grateful thanks also to Sandile Dikeni, Monty Narsoo and Pierre Beaudet (for their intellectual camaraderie and courage), Alexander Cockburn, Colin Bundy and Eduardo Galeano (for being inspiring examples), Robert Molteno and Glenda Younge (for their perseverance and support), Vishwas Satgar, John Saul, Stephen Wright, Steve Friedman, Norah Brochu, Joan-Anne Nolan, Dennis Lewycky, Patrick Bond, Jeremy Cronin and Langa Zita. Most of all, my deepest thanks and respect go to Samir Amin, in whose work and person stand crystallized the ideals that underpin this volume.

Needless to say, the flaws and omissions are entirely mine.

This book is dedicated to Susan.

Acronyms

ANC	African National Congress
ANCYL	African National Congress Youth League
ASEAN	Association of Southeast Asian Nations
AZAPO	Azanian People's Organization
BC	Black Consciousness
BCM	Black Consciousness Movement
CASE	Community Agency for Social Enquiry
CBO	community-based organization
CCB	Civil Cooperation Bureau
CEO	chief executive officer
CONTRALESA	Congress of Traditional Leaders of South Africa
COSATU	Congress of South African Trade Unions
CP	Conservative Party
CPSA	Communist Party of South Africa (later SACP)
CST	colonialism of a special type
DAG	Development Action Group
DEP	Department of Economic Policy (of ANC)
DP	Democratic Party
ECC	End Conscription Campaign
FDI	foreign direct investment
FEDSAW	Federation of South African Women
FOSATU	Federation of South African Trade Unions
GATT	General Agreement on Tariffs and Trade
GDP	gross domestic product
GEAR	Growth, Employment and Redistribution
GNU	Government of National Unity
HDI	human development index
HSRC	Human Sciences Research Council
ICU	Industrial and Commercial Workers' Union
IDASA	Institute for a Democratic Alternative in South Africa
IDC	Industrial Development Corporation

IFP	Inkatha Freedom Party
ILO	International Labour Organization
IMF	International Monetary Fund
ISP	Industrial Strategy Project
IT	information technology
JSE	Johannesburg Stock Exchange
LDC	least developed country
MAI	Multilateral Agreement on Investment
MAWU	Metal and Allied Workers' Union
MDM	Mass Democratic Movement
MERG	Macro-Economic Research Group
MK	Umkhonto we Sizwe (armed wing of ANC)
NAFCOC	National African Federated Chambers of Commerce
NAFTA	North American Free Trade Accord
NEC	National Executive Committee (of ANC)
NECC	National Education Crisis Committee
NEDLAC	National Economic, Development and Labour Council
NEF	National Economic Forum
NEM	Normative Economic Model
NGO	non-governmental organization
NIC	newly industrialized country
NIEP	National Institute for Economic Policy
NIS	National Intelligence Service
NLC	National Land Committee
NP	National Party (later renamed New National Party, NNP)
NSMS	National Security Management System
NUM	National Union of Mineworkers
NUMSA	National Union of Metalworkers of South Africa
NUTW	National Union of Textile Workers
NWC	National Working Committee (of ANC)
ODA	overseas development aid
OECD	Organization for Economic Cooperation and Development
PAC	Pan-Africanist Congress
PCAS	Policy Co-ordination and Advisory Services
RDP	Reconstruction and Development Programme
SACOB	South African Chamber of Business
SACP	South African Communist Party
SACTU	South African Congress of Trade Unions
SADF	South African Defence Force (SANDF after 1994)
SALDRU	South African Labour and Development Research Unit
SANCO	South African National Civic Organization
SANDF	South African National Defence Force

SAP	South African Police (SAPS after 1994)
SAPS	South African Police Services
SASM	South African Students' Movement
SAYCO	South African Youth Congress
TGWU	Transport and General Workers' Union
TNC	transnational corporation
TRC	Truth and Reconciliation Commission
TUCSA	Trade Union Council of South Africa
UDF	United Democratic Front
UK	United Kingdom
UNCTAD	United Nations Conference on Trade and Development
UNDP	United Nations Development Programme
UP	United Party
US/USA	United States of America
USSR	Union of Soviet Socialist Republics
UWO	United Women's Organization
WTO	World Trade Organization

Introduction

More than six years have passed since South Africa earned its place among the 'miracles' of the twentieth century. In an epoch highlighted by the horrors erupting in the Balkans, the Rwandan genocide and the prolonged violence of the Israeli–Palestinian struggle, a seemingly intractable conflict at the tip of Africa ended in a political settlement that appeared to refute the rhythms of history. Not only was it achieved without the apocalyptic conflagration many had feared, but it seemed to spur a newfound sense of unity, conciliation and common purpose in a society that had become synonymous with terminal discord and division. It yielded a constitution bristling with features that justifiably earned the envy of people around the world. It produced spectacles of reconciliation that baffled even its own citizens. It set in motion not economic collapse but tentative recovery. It brought closer the prospect of change in the lives of millions.

Little wonder then that the bemused admiration of the world was matched by a sense of triumphant pride and hope among the majority of South Africans and the liberation organization, the African National Congress (ANC), they voted into power in 1994 and returned to office in 1999. A history marked by brutally enforced inequalities appeared to have been ruptured, enabling the black majority to pass through portals beyond which lay equality, dignity and freedom.[1] A benign and progressive path seemed to have been cleared. Along it, the devastation wrought under apartheid could be redressed.

As in the first edition, this book shares those hopes. Unfortunately, the likelihood of their fulfilment is hardly hale. This apprehension stems not from pessimism but from an analysis of the political economy of the South African transition, an inquiry that excavates the many, stout historical trends and continuities that, far from having been erased by the 'miracle' of 1994, persist. Some of them are plain to the eye, many others are rendered visible only by a more inquisitive gaze – before which South Africa stands revealed as an engrossing but perilous mix of the 'old' and the 'new'.

Most accounts of the transition have sought to dissect the post-1990 developments by focusing on the minutiae of political engagements and the personalities at their helm. These are valuable enquiries that, at their best, sketch a kind of psycho-political account of the transition. In doing so, however, they risk over-personalizing history and obscure the structural and other dynamics that shape South Africa's transition.

Some readers might feel that, in attempting to broaden this inquiry beyond the confines of political drama, it errs in the opposite direction – by laying undue stress on the economic. One hopes that such judgements would take into account the extent to which the South African struggle itself became defined by a political reductionism that collapsed the political economy of privilege and deprivation into the form of the apartheid state. Generated was an instrumentalist conception of state, one that regarded it as a site of concentrated power that, once captured, would become the central agent of transformation. Thus, the key objective of the liberation struggle became the seizure of state power in order to work its levers in the interests of the majority. Of course, this did not happen. Instead of seizing power, the democratic movement negotiated its partial transfer. Instead of taking over and transforming the state, the movement found itself assimilated into it. From there, it has steadily transformed the state, but in stunted and ambiguous ways. That alone, however, does not explain the apparently foreshortened horizons of change that now confound that movement. For in capitalist society, the circuits through which power and privilege are reproduced course not only through the state but also through civil society, which is dominated by the formations of capital. This requires an expansive understanding of the transition and the developments that presaged it.

The analysis that follows seeks to fill some of those vacuums by locating the transition in a historical and global context. This requires probing South Africa's political-economic undercarriage, the developments that led to the political settlement, the terms upon which the transition proceeds, the ideological and structural shifts (local and international) that accompany or drive it, and the relative strengths and weaknesses of the main forces contesting its outcome.

In doing so, the book argues that the transition be understood less as a miraculous historical rupture than as the (as yet inconclusive) outcome of a convergence of far-reaching attempts to resolve an ensemble of political, ideological and economic contradictions that had accumulated steadily since the 1970s. It departs, therefore, from the conventional narratives that gauge the transition in predominantly political terms. In doing so, it does not propose that the tilt towards seeking a negotiated settlement or the ensuing developments were *inevitable* – other, equally risky options existed. But it does concur with Stuart Hall's contention that:

... material circumstances are the net of constraints, the 'conditions of existence', for practical thought and calculation about society ... [and that] what is 'scientific' about the Marxist theory of politics is that it seeks to understand the *limits of political action* given by the terrain on which is operates.[2]

The basis for the transition lay in a historic deadlock achieved between the ruling bloc and the democratic opposition in the late 1980s. The impasse rested on the dire need to modernize and reinvigorate the processes of capital accumulation, on the apartheid state's simultaneous inability to manage the expansive forms of restructuring that were required, and on the democratic opposition's ability to challenge and veto the haphazard 'modernization' attempts of the state and capital. At the same time, though, the opposition was unable to force the capitulation of the old order.

The 1980s had been characterized by an increasingly aberrant mix of repression and reforms, the latter geared primarily at restructuring the social and economic basis for capital accumulation. They were responses to trends identified by Harry Oppenheimer, then chair of the Anglo American Corporation, as early as 1971:

We are approaching the stage where the full potential of the economy, as it is at present organized, will have been realized, so that if structural changes are not made, we will have to content ourselves with a much lower rate of growth.[3]

Partly because those reforms only marginally and ineffectively addressed the demands of the opposition, they failed to halt the surge of resistance and, instead, fuelled successive waves of popular action that climaxed in the uprisings of 1985–6. Subsequent state repression dismantled the movement's capacity to capitalize on the 'insurrectionary climate' it claimed prevailed at the time. Animated by visions of change that focused on the overthrow of the apartheid state, the democratic movement found its path at least temporarily blocked, while an ensemble of other local and international factors combined to consolidate the stand-off. Upon this hazardous impasse an ambitious and far-reaching attempt to restructure the political and ideological basis for the 'modernization' of South African capitalism would proceed.

A ruling bloc based on the political exclusion of the majority and revolving around a beleaguered minority political party had become a manifest liability. The rise of a well-organized and militant working class movement, politically allied with the excluded political opposition, and the spread of other popular organizations severely compounded the predicament. A negotiated political settlement would not resolve these difficulties but could serve as the gateway for an ongoing bid to revitalize South African capitalism. For the democratic forces, a settlement could usher in a transition that heralded – but did not guarantee – far-reaching adjustments aimed at undoing the patterns for the allocation of power, privilege and opportunities.

From the vantage point of capital, two salient and risky adjustments were required. The abandonment of the exclusionary political framework of apartheid and its replacement with a democratic system meant that the National Party (NP) would no longer function as the political axis of the ruling bloc. That role would befall the ANC albeit on terms, business hoped, that would inhibit its ability to advance the interests of the disadvantaged majority at the expense of the key prerogatives of capital. The fundamental importance of 1994, therefore, was not just the end of apartheid but the dissolution of the dominant alliance of social, economic and political forces in South Africa. The ANC's ascent to political power did not immediately fill the resultant vacuum. Rather, it recast and intensified a struggle to reshape state and capital relations, to determine which alliance of social forces would come to constitute a new ruling bloc and to establish the decisive terms of that alliance.

Those processes have advanced considerably since the mid-1990s, to the point where they have matured into a new dominant hegemonic project that answers, in the first instance, to the prerogatives of incumbent and aspirant élites, while at the same time (but to a lesser extent) servicing some of the needs and rights of the impoverished majority. They are expressed in a post-apartheid development path that, as this volume argues, is incorrectly understood as a *temporary* hybrid of progressive intent and more expansive concessions and 'aberrations'. In short, that path betrays not flux but the steady maturation of a modernized class project of considerable sophistication and likely longevity. Its outline is most visible in post-apartheid economic policies. Their evolution and outcomes are examined in Chapters 5 and 6.

The neoliberal features of the ANC government's macro-economic strategy, the supine postures struck before the demands of capital and the dogged bids to build a black 'patriotic bourgeoisie' are, in such a reading, not anomalies. Spurring these developments is the tendency to judge the possibilities of a more progressive development path on the basis of deeply conservative and empirically questionable interpretations of globalization, as Chapter 5 shows. With a few, valuable exceptions the new South Africa still confirms Ellen Meiksins Wood's lament that 'it is not only that we do not know how to *act* against capitalism but that we are forgetting how to *think* against it' (1995:11).

In sketching the rudiments of an alternative development path, Chapter 7 possibly does not rise to Wood's challenge, for it argues that in the short- to medium-term an alternative will have to remain grounded in the *mechanisms* of markets, while steadily challenging and superseding their *logic*. Many of the adjustments surveyed are eminently feasible, even if they necessarily require challenging powerful forces inside and beyond South Africa's borders.

At the same time, the prospects of an alternative project do not seem hardy – despite the energies expended in opposing some policies and in advancing possible alternatives. Chapter 8 seeks to explain this weakness by examining the manifold, imposing features and advantages of the ascendant hegemonic project in the ideological, political and economic spheres. It also identifies and tries to explain some of the main frailties of a more authentically popular project, foundering as it seemed to be at the turn of the century. Many of those shortcomings are shown to have sturdy roots in the theory and practice of the South African left. Others, however, are new and stem from structural changes that potently afflict the labour movement, while also reconfiguring the character and constituencies of other, traditional popular organizations, as Chapters 8 and 9 show.

Far from having dissolved into a fraternity of common purpose, tranquillized by the levelling language of nation-building, South Africa remains in the midst of an intense, renewed struggle that currently and demonstrably favours the most powerful and privileged sections of society. The defining trends of the transition are shaping a revised division of the society, with the current order stabilized around, at best, 30–40 per cent of the population. Entry into those ranks is increasingly being deracialized, even if the entrants remain socially and politically separated along racial lines – which complicates but does not contradict the bid to muster and reproduce sufficient social consent for the country's development path. For the rest (overwhelmingly young, female and African) the best hope is some trickle-down from a 'modernized' system.

None of this should detract from the sterling achievements registered since 1994. The admirable superstructural changes effected are visible in a democratic dispensation, in an armoury of new, mostly progressive legislation, and in the slow but ongoing transformation of the state. Too often overlooked or misread is the import of those changes in South Africans' lives. Unfairly given short thrift, too, are the socio-economic improvements achieved, many of which testify to the extraordinary determination of unsung bureaucrats operating in a hostile fiscal environment and in difficult institutional settings. Yet, they perform their work on terms that are structurally reinforcing the country's insider/outsider mould. Attributing this to a 'sell-out' or betrayal obscures the complex convergence of factors, pressures and inclinations that shape the relation of forces in post-apartheid South Africa – which this book tries to subject to critical scrutiny.

There is nothing inevitable about the outcome of these processes. But that ever-blue truism, while replenishing hope, is no substitute for a clinical examination of the balance of forces that is defining the new South Africa, and of the character of the resultant development path. Many of these aspects seemed tentative in 1997 when the first volume of this book was completed. Sadly, they have since ossified. The pages that follow do not pretend to offer compact answers to the trends and challenges they identify. They are presented as a contribution to what, hopefully, can become a growing body of critical leftist reflection, analysis and understanding. That alone cannot guarantee a society that finally does justice to its inhabitants. But without it, that quest surely shall remain unfulfilled.

Notes

1 South African realities unfortunately force a resort to racial categories. Thus 'African' refers to indigenous inhabitants whose ancestors' presence in the region pre-dated the arrival of European and other settlers; 'coloured' refers to people of mixed race origins; 'Indian' refers to descendants from South Asia; 'white' refers to descendants of European settlers; 'black' refers inclusively, in the manner of black consciousness (BC) tradition, to all South Africans who are not 'white'.

2 Stuart Hall, 'Marxism without guarantees', in Morley and Chen (1996:44–5). Emphasis added.

3 Harry Oppenheimer in his chairperson's address to Anglo American Corporation, cited in Gelb (1991:20).

CHAPTER ONE

Origins of a divided society

A wealthy country by continental standards, South Africa is also one of the most unequal societies on earth. By the World Bank's calculations, the poorest 40 per cent of its citizens earn less than 4 per cent of the income circulating in the economy. The wealthiest 10 per cent pocket more than 51 per cent of income.

That apartheid entrenched these features with grotesque fastidiousness and anti-human severity is a matter of painful historical record. Yet, tracing the lineages of this inequality strictly to the apartheid system obscures the profound political-economic contours of inequity that define South African society. It also confounds the efforts to forge a society that not only extols but realizes the dignity, desires and rights of its citizens. In many respects South Africans' visions of the future rest on foreshortened perspectives of the past. This applies centrally to the millions who engineered, administrated and savoured the complex of exploitative practices that penetrated every aspect of lived reality – few of whom will today admit to their authorship of, or moral culpability for, the devastation they achieved. Nor are they under much pressure to do so; their indifference is indulged, even encouraged, in the quest for reconciliation.

But an abbreviated and elliptical sense of the past is evident also, though in very different respects, within the democratic movement. The history of successful liberation projects tends to be rendered in terms that portray an unequivocal and linear advance towards triumph. History is cleansed of failure, ambivalence and blemish. And yet, left celebrated and uninterrogated, the past ferments discreetly in the present.

It is not unlikely, though by no means certain, that the transition will extend the accumulated continuities of South African history in ways that reinforce the inequities visited on the majority. Sadly, the signs pointing to a happier outcome are irresolute and dwarfed by more encompassing dynamics that fortify the sanctity of privilege against human need. The pages that follow have one purpose only: to render these less opaque.

The roots are sunk

The definitive origins of South Africa's status as a 'Two Nation' society – marked by the systematic and violent segregation between privilege and deprivation – lie in the late nineteenth century, when the development of capitalism accelerated rapidly after the beginning of diamond mining in 1867 and gold mining in 1886.[1]

Pockets of commercial and agricultural capitalism had been established in the coastal regions colonized by Britain. But the hinterland remained essentially pre-capitalist, with Boer *trekkers* engaged in rentier exploitation, living off rents in labour and in kind extracted from indigenous peoples whose land they had seized. Racial prejudice was already rampant, though by some accounts it was often overshadowed by class division and religious bigotry as the basis for systematic social polarization.[2] In large parts of the country an economically independent African peasantry survived.[3] In many cases these societies remained organized within their own social and political systems; in some cases they were militarily powerful enough to inflict bloody defeats on British colonial armies.

The discovery of gold and diamonds, however, upped the ante – transforming the territory, at least in the eyes of British colonialism, from a geopolitical asset (hence the focus on controlling coastal strips) into a potentially huge capital asset.

These discoveries set in train processes that would definitively shape South African history for the next century. A huge influx of foreign, mainly British, capital put the mining industry on the world map and spearheaded the highly centralized character of an industry which would remain at the centre of the South African economy for the next century. There was a rush of European immigrant labour, which supplied the semi-skilled and skilled labour required by the industry and boosted the numbers of white settlers beyond the levels typical in other African colonies.[4] Also generated was the need for a steady supply of cheap, unskilled labour. The dismantled African peasantry would become the chief source, while a range of measures would be applied to guarantee and regulate the supply of labour. Administrative measures were introduced to establish and police a racial division of labour separating skilled white (mainly European) labour from gangs of unskilled African labour. Organized white labour would lobby strongly (and act militantly) to entrench those measures. This established the basis for a political alliance between the capitalist class and white labour, which was to survive until the 1970s.

For the next 50 years, the accumulation strategy centred on mining and, to a lesser extent, agriculture, with manufacturing industry at best an incipient feature of the economy.

With the huge gold fields yielding low grade ore, the mining concerns were faced with two central needs: a hefty flow of capital to establish and run mines, and a reliable, cheap labour supply to keep the profit margin attractive.

The first requirement saw the integration of the 'South African'[5] economy into the world economy as a source of primary commodities (the value of which was set in the European metropoles) and a destination for investment capital. The second sketched the pattern of labour and social relations that would become the definitive feature of this society. Capital accumulation would be based on the exploitation of a low-wage, highly controlled, expendable African workforce which was to be reproduced in a system of 'native reserves' at minimal cost to capital. Importantly, this workforce would be recruited from the entire subcontinent: until the 1970s, the mining industry employed more non-South African than South African workers.[6]

This accumulation path seemed to correspond to those in other African colonies, with the important distinction that a large settler population, itself segmented culturally and socio-economically, soon became ascendant in the political, administrative and, later, economic realms. The resemblance would lead the South African Communist Party (SACP) to develop its theory of 'Colonialism of a Special Type'.[7]

The economic independence of the African peasantry was gradually removed through a barrage of administrative and punitive measures which transformed this surplus-producing peasantry into a pool of labour for the mines and emergent capitalist agriculture. The African peasantry dwindled from 2,5 million in 1936 to 832 000 people in 1946. A trio of factors drove this process: increased mechanization of agriculture, the crushing effects of the Depression and, centrally, state expropriation of land. A legislative climax was the mammoth expropriation effected by the 1913 Land Act which barred Africans from acquiring land outside 'native reserves' (7,3 per cent of the South African land area). That process was augmented by the 1936 Natives Land and Trust Act which doubled the land area 'set aside' for 'native reserves' in a bid to reverse the 'incapacity of the Native Reserves to provide even the minimum subsistence requirements', as one government report later put it.[8]

Accompanying the establishment of capitalist mining at the centre of the South African economy – and its incorporation into the world economy on terms that would remain relatively consistent over the next half century – was the introduction of some of the definitive, systematic divisions in society:

- There was a racial division of labour in urban centres between skilled white labour (both immigrant and domestic) and unskilled African labour (essentially 'economic refugees' fleeing the remnants of wrecked pre-capitalist zones). White workers imported the trade union tradition, organizing artisans and craftsmen, and vehemently defended their status against 'encroachment' by African workers when mining bosses, for instance, attempted to loosen the colour bar in a bid to lower wage costs by allowing black workers some upward mobility.[9]

■ There was an increasingly fierce marginalization of African societies, who were not only converted into reserve armies of labour but were also burdened with the principal costs of reproducing that labour supply. Deprived of their means of production – land – they were physically barricaded into 'native reserves' outside the mining and industrial zones, where they were denied access to the types of health, education, welfare and recreational networks introduced in the urban centres. Measures like the pass law system regulated the flow of labour into the cities and deflected the cost of reproducing labour to the periphery – thus laying the basis for a highly profitable cycle of capital accumulation. In essence, the 'native reserves' (and later the homelands) would subsidize capitalist growth in South Africa.

■ There was the proletarianization of large numbers of Africans, 'which distinguished the class structure of South Africa from the peasant economies of African colonies to the north' (Fine & Davis, 1990:14). By 1946, the number of urbanized African people had increased by 36 per cent over the previous decade. One third of them were women, suggesting long-term urbanization. But the urban/rural dichotomy was not rigid – hundreds of thousands of people *traversed* these zones. With the rise of an urban working class would come new forms of resistance: trade union organizing, strikes, boycotts and other mass protests.

■ Within white society, increased divisions were also materializing. Marked by the consolidation of large farms and their mechanization (a process accelerated by the 1929–32 Great Depression), the advance of capitalist agriculture drove thousands of Afrikaner settlers off the land and into the cities, which they entered at a disadvantage to European immigrant workers. A category of newly proletarianized 'poor whites', mainly Afrikaners, arose. Until the 1930s what passed for 'Afrikaner capital' was restricted mainly to the agricultural sector, which represented a tiny fraction of gross domestic product (GDP). This material marginalization combined with a history of enmity towards British imperialism (expressed explosively in the two Boer wars) and a hermetic cultural framework derived from apocalyptic readings of the Old Testament of the Bible – all of which aided the exposition of a 'distinct' Afrikaner identity, a process which, by the 1920s, would begin evolving into a political project, Afrikaner nationalism.

■ Significant tensions developed between mining capital, and agricultural and industrial capital. Internationalized in terms of markets and capital input, mining capital preferred 'free trade' policies. Agricultural and industrial capital was localized and required state intervention in the form of subsidies and protection, financed largely through taxes drawn from mining capital. The rudiments of different approaches to state–capital relations were taking form.

During this period a skewed, integrated regional economy was shaped, centred around migrant labour for the mines but extending also to trade, water supply, transport and capital investment patterns. As noted by Davies *et al.* (1993:14):

> ... the principal poles of accumulation came to be located in South Africa (and to a lesser extent in Zimbabwe) while the other territories were incorporated in subsidiary roles as labour reserves, markets for South African commodities, suppliers of certain services (such as transport) or providers of cheap and convenient resources (like water, electricity and some raw materials).

The rise of the working class

By the 1940s, manufacturing industry was growing in earnest, thanks to lavish state support in the form of protective measures and tariffs, subsidies and major infrastructure projects that facilitated its growth. The shift from artisinal to mechanized production was rapid, and the African proletariat swelled to number some 800 000 by 1939. Workers had become increasingly combative, with African and white workers (usually separately) staging strike actions.

In 1913 about 19 000 white miners and 10 000 African miners struck; a year later the state mobilized thousands of troops to crush a railway strike. In 1918 African miners won a wage increase after striking. Two years later 70 000 African miners struck for better pay, while in 1922 a white miners' strike was put down by 20 000 troops, killing 214 people. Five years later the black Industrial and Commercial Workers' Union (ICU) claimed a membership of 100 000.

The rise of an urban African working class raised the prospect of multi-racial industrial action which could evolve into a more forthright challenge against the system. This precipitated a political realignment which brought to power, in 1924, the Pact government, which strove to give white workers a bigger stake in the system. Heightened (racial) wage differentials, job reservation for whites and expanded social benefits all deepened white racism, and encouraged white workers to throw in their lot with a system constructed around a racist class alliance.

Evident was the hardening of the 'Two Nation' society. The trappings of a social welfare state were extended gradually to a tiny, racially defined minority, while the majority was expelled to the physical and socio-economic margins of the system, subsidizing the privilege of the 'insiders'. By the mid-1930s several related developments were afoot that would leave deep imprints on the future of the country.

Resistance and defeats

Strong economic growth after 1933 boosted the industrialization process, though the manufacturing sector remained relatively small (until the 1940s when it grew considerably during mobilization of production for the war effort). This in turn increased demands for African labour, some of it skilled. At the same time, the reserves into which Africans had been driven were becoming increasingly unsustainable, with overcrowding and resultant poor environmental management of marginal land rendering huge parts of the periphery economically unviable. The result was an accelerated urbanization process. In the urban areas, meanwhile, at least one generation of African workers had sunk its roots. These trends, the intense poverty and the violent manner in which labour relations were controlled spurred a healthy rise in trade union organization – from which sprang the first sustained cycle of modern, militant resistance in South Africa's history.[10]

These trends should not be exaggerated, however. Despite the rise of an African proletariat, the vast majority of Africans still survived in rural areas. Although in decline, the peasantry remained a social and economic force in rural South Africa. In addition, the urban African proletariat retained strong links with rural communities, due to the migratory character of African labour. The greatest concentration of African labour was to be found on the mines where, separated from broader society, they were subjected to fierce disciplinary regimes – thus limiting their role as an organic element of a 'wave of resistance' which, some historians have claimed, generated a crisis in the ruling bloc by the mid-1940s. The upshot was that the social weight of the working class during the 1930s and 1940s – and the threat it posed to the ruling forces – was actually less formidable than claimed in many left-wing historical accounts:[11]

> We have to abandon the simplified image of the organisation and combativity of black workers ever escalating in the 1940s and of the defeats inflicted on labour struggles ... serving only as a stimulus for yet more militancy from below (Fine & Davis, 1990:99).

The 1946 miners' strike is commonly portrayed as a landmark event, announcing a crisis in South African capitalism. In this view, worker militancy in support of higher wages and better working conditions challenged the basis of a system that pivoted on an abundant supply of very cheap, controlled labour. Common has been the view that:

> The violence of the state's response not only indicated the degree to which it felt threatened, but foreshadowed the extreme repression after 1948.[12]

The NP's victory at the polls became interpreted as a consequence of that trepidation and a mandate for the hardline solution to the crisis favoured by the NP.

The 1946 strike – with 70 000 miners and 6 000 iron and steel workers out on strike – surely was an impressive event, but honest appraisal has to take into account the ease with which it was smashed by state repression. Indeed, the strike was something of an anomaly: the number of black workers organized in trade unions as well as strike actions were in decline by 1946, suggesting rather that the 'miners' strike of 1946 represented the last gasp rather than the high point of the wartime strike wave'.[13] In 1947 only 2 000 workers would embark on strikes; by 1948 the number dropped to 1 500. Two years later, the African Mineworkers' Union (which had organized the 1946 miners' strike) had been reduced to barely a shadow of its former self and could claim only 700 members. According to government calculations, 66 trade unions became defunct between 1945 and 1951.[14]

More persuasive is a reading that links the rise of apartheid not to an alleged surge of sustained challenges from a militant working class, but rather (in part) to the telling defeats suffered by that class. Those defeats can be ascribed to several factors.

Firstly, the liberal wing within the ruling class (and with it the reform programme it was counselling) had been marginalized. Several of the reforms which would be introduced piecemeal fashion from the late 1970s onwards were already considered – and rejected – by the ruling bloc at this point. As Saul and Gelb reminded, several commissions had suggested nurturing a stable, semi-skilled labour force and accepting urban Africans as a given (1981:14). Secondly, state repression had a crushing effect on resistance. And thirdly, 'the lack of numbers, concentration and bargaining power of the black industrial proletariat' prevented the black working class from sustaining the threats it appeared to pose.[15]

A fourth, subjective, factor also needs to be considered. After the Nazi invasion of the USSR in 1941, the Communist Party of South Africa (CPSA)[16] abandoned its support for intensified class struggle and switched to a people's front policy which called for support for the Allied war effort and opposition to industrial action – putting CPSA and ANC policy on an accommodationist track.[17] This steered CPSA policy into (and deepened the ANC's commitment to) a 'liberal-democratic paradigm' which:

> ... presupposed that the rulers of South Africa were ready to reach an accommodation with the black working class and that the black working class had the social weight to force an accommodation on the rulers. On both counts the policy was mistaken. The state turned against consensual politics, directing its fire instead to extinguish the threat posed by black workers, while black workers themselves lacked the power to resist the attacks mounted on them (Fine & Davis, 1990:56).

The rise of African nationalism

After an impressive rise, black working class organizations had suffered a series of telling defeats, the effects of which were compounded by the sectarianism that plagued the Left. As a result, the late 1940s saw a drift away from class politics – preparing the stage for the dramatic rise of African nationalism which, although periodically challenged, would not only definitively shape the course of resistance strategies but eventually help establish the parameters of the accommodation reached with the ruling bloc in the 1990s. Portentous roots of the defeat of South African socialism are imbedded in these developments during the 1940s.

At the same time, the extreme hardships confronting the urban proletariat had spawned spontaneous community-based struggles which indicated a ferment of grassroots resistance that stood at an angle to the demonstrable failure of the policies followed by the ANC, and periodically shared by the CPSA. Still lodged on an accommodationist track, the ANC was unable to capitalize on those struggles and transform them from sporadic expressions of discontent into a challenge that threatened the ruling bloc.[18] State repression had confirmed the failure of the constitutionalist route trekked by the ANC since its inception in 1912.

Formed on 8 January 1912 as the South African Native National Congress, the ANC had functioned until the 1940s as a vehicle for the aspirations of the African middle classes. Initially built around a relatively privileged layer of independent African peasants, the organization followed a liberal trajectory, petitioning for the extension of voting and other rights to 'civilized' Africans. Its jaundiced view of so-called 'blanket' or 'uncivilized' Africans is unabashedly captured in leaders' statements and writing. As late as 1942, ANC president general Dr A. B. Xuma would write to General Jan Smuts, assuring him that:

> ... we are anxious not to embarrass the government ... We humbly and respectfully request the Prime Minister to receive a deputation from the ANC and CNETU [Council of Non-European Trade Unions] ... to assist you toward settlement of recent strikes and prevention of future strikes.[19]

By 1935, the CPSA's J. B. Marks would pronounce the ANC 'literally dead'. Its descent had been fuelled by its failure to register gains for its constituency and by the rapid erosion of its peasant social base, whose ranks had been seriously denuded during the Depression years. The ANC could not point to a single concession wrested from the state. Furthermore, the decline of the liberal wing of the ruling bloc removed any prospect of belated success for its policy. Less than ten years later, the CPSA would lament the fact that the 'African people have been frustrated by a Congress leadership which does not organize mass support nor carry on mass action

to improve their living standards'.[20] This assessment was hardly controversial, as ANC veteran Govan Mbeki has confirmed:

> [The ANC] was not in a position to go to the people with any plan of action,
> being top-heavy with very little support amongst the masses of people ... As
> a result, not only were the masses not provided with an effective leadership,
> but those who were at the head of the ANC felt helpless to do anything
> (1992:37).

It was into this vacuum that a new generation of more militant urban
African intellectuals stepped in the mid-1940s, organized within the newly-
formed ANC Youth League (ANCYL). Reacting to the moribund state of
the ANC – labelled as 'an organization of gentlemen with clean hands' by
A. P. Mda, president of the ANCYL[21] – the ANCYL fashioned a fierce
brand of African nationalism which drew heavily on the 'Africa for
Africans' philosophy popularized by the followers of Marcus Garvey. These
militants – mostly doctors, lawyers, teachers and clerks – scorned in equal
measure liberal ideology and class politics. They idealized an imagined past
of unity and harmony among Africans, and posited a liberation struggle
that would be led by the 'African nation' and a new society that would be
ruled by it. This would be achieved by reviving mass struggle under the
aegis of a reconstituted national movement in which the politics of African
nationalism would eclipse class politics as the driving dynamic of struggle.

By 1949 the African nationalists had established their authority in the
ANC, which had adopted key parts of the ANCYL's manifesto in its
Programme of Action. The focus would be on organizing mass struggle in
urban areas – along the lines of the subsequent 1952 Defiance Campaign.
However, the African nationalist upsurge was already diverging into two
currents. Eventually dominant within the ANC was a more moderate
stream which viewed South Africa as comprising four nations (African,
Indian, coloured and white), of which three were oppressed. Meanwhile, an
ultra-nationalist stream insisted that South Africa belonged to Africans
only; in 1959 it would split from the ANC and form the Pan-Africanist
Congress (PAC).

The historical developments that made this possible deserve emphasis.
Blame for the dramatic decline of the working class movement cannot fairly
be laid at the feet of the ascendant African nationalists. Instead, that decline
and the defeat of a socialist project in the mid-1940s enabled the rise of
African nationalism as the hegemonic force within a broad, evolving resistance movement. Certainly, later efforts (particularly during the 1950s and
1980s) to revive class politics would draw fierce reaction from the nationalists, but this should not cloud an understanding of the dynamics which
precipitated the conversion of the South African struggle from a potentially
class-based one to a nationalist one. Nevertheless, it was this historic turn in

the South African resistance struggle that not only made possible but made likely the class compromise which in the 1990s would underpin the transition. The class contradictions which determine the society's 'Two Nation' structure would become submerged within a discourse – African nationalism – which in the 1990s would prove unequal to the task of transforming a restructuring project led by capital into a transformatory project that could break South Africa's insider/outsider mould. Read in this context, post-1994 developments appear less than surprising.

The system hardens

South Africa's 'Two Nation' character hardened radically after the surprise victory of the white supremacist National Party (NP) in the 1948 election under the banner of Afrikaner nationalism.[22] The NP's margin of victory was a slim, five-seat parliamentary majority won with a minority of votes cast. But it immediately set about implementing a meticulously codified racist project. Henceforth, race would become the definitive criterion for South Africans' access to privilege and opportunity, further restricting the social and economic mobility of black South Africans through a battery of legislative and administrative measures. Hardest hit was the African population. Deprived of political rights and full citizenship of the nation, Africans would eventually be decreed to belong to specific 'nations' assigned homelands on the 13 per cent of land reserved for Africans.

However, the NP's policies did not rupture the country's historical continuum. While they fiercely intensified the levels of oppression inflicted on the majority, they proceeded along routes staked out over the preceding half century. Although deepened along much more explicit racial lines, the patterns of inclusion and exclusion from the productive and consumptive centres of a growing economy rested on trends already present.

Mainstream historical accounts have consistently overlooked this continuity, preferring to view the NP's apartheid policies as a *sui generis* programme generated strictly in fulfilment of the perceived needs of Afrikanerdom. Such accounts have tended to seek an understanding of the 'apartheid era' via ethnographic studies of a purportedly undifferentiated group. As O'Meara has shown, the NP would become viewed through the prism of ideology and cod psycho-politics. Thus, the NP victory would be 'taken to represent the triumph of the frontier over the forces of economic rationality – of ideology over economics'.[23] Hardline policies would be ascribed to Afrikaner 'intransigence', the '*laager* mentality' or an enduring 'frontier mentality'. Softened approaches would be attributed simply to the rise of 'modernizing' currents within the party. In such analyses the NP is made to float above history and society, its decisions determined solely by the dictates of the ideology of Afrikaner nationalism. The effect was to obscure the capitalist character of the apartheid state, leading to a fixation on the secretive, highly ideological *Broederbond* as the hand engineering apartheid state policies strictly in accordance with the interests of the Afrikaner *volk*. While the *Broederbond*'s importance within the NP is well documented, its enduring centrality to NP government policies must be questioned. Any analytical enterprise that rooted NP policies in the dictates of a hermetic ethnic cabal tasked with ensuring the well-being of the *volk* ran aground during the late 1980s. How was it that the *Broederbond* then suddenly lost its role as the NP's puppeteer, and receded into insignificance?

A secretive organization formed in the 1930s, the *Broederbond* comprised largely Afrikaner intellectuals and *petit bourgeois* figures. As O'Meara has shown, an understanding of the rise of the NP and its subsequent policies in government could not rest on an abstraction of Afrikaner nationalist ideology from 'the material conditions, contradictions and struggles in the development of capitalism in South Africa' (1983:3). As elaborated and pursued from the 1930s onwards, Afrikaner nationalism had at its core the ambitions of a layer of aspirant bourgeois Afrikaners, who assiduously articulated and promoted Afrikaner nationalism, 'the ideology through which Afrikaner capital developed' via an 'extensive network of cross-cutting organisations'.[24] One might conclude that the demise of the *Broederbond* reflected, simply, its *fulfilment* of that historic role.

The NP rode to power on the back of a nationalist class alliance, the rudiments of which had been established 30 years earlier. It included agricultural capitalists, white workers (especially newly proletarianized Afrikaners), a growing layer of the Afrikaner *petit bourgeoisie*, and fledgling manufacturing capital. The party pledged to advance the interests of these sectors by restructuring the economy in their favour – consequently, its 1948 election rhetoric reflected the ambiguous and often contradictory demands of these constituencies.[25] Of prime concern is the material context in which this occurred, primarily the emerging contradictions within the capitalist system of production (differentially affecting the branches of capital) and the state's temporary inability to resolve them.

Key to the development of South African capitalism was the dependency of capital accumulation in mining, agriculture and industry on a guaranteed supply of cheap, African migratory labour. Labour costs were suppressed by the reserve system, which by the 1930s had proved economically unsustainable. This, combined with the intense exploitation of labour-tenants by white farmers and increased mechanization of agriculture, led to an increased flow of African workers into urban areas, producing a growing, semi-permanent African proletariat. One result was a new cycle of urban resistance in shanty-towns and a rise in black trade union organizations and strike actions. The challenges posed by these developments, however, should not be exaggerated. For example, O'Meara's claim that 'the problem of political control over Africans became acute' seems unwarranted

(1983:229). As indicated, trade union organizing and action was in decline by the end of 1946, the ANC as a political organization was ailing (with its revitalization at the hand of the ANCYL's young turks still a work-in-progress), while the boycotts and other protests launched in the shanty-towns were sporadic and localized, lacking a political centre of gravity.

More tenable is the view that 'it was through the defeat of [black] resistance that apartheid was able to resolve the crisis of segregationism in its own racist and dictatorial fashion' (Fine & Davis, 1990:7). The 'crisis' which led to the rise of the NP and the application of the apartheid system can be framed more accurately as a set of growing disjunctures within the capitalist system and the state – as the branches of capitalist production sought different solutions to their dilemmas. Indeed, the harsh repression unleashed by the NP government had been prefigured by its predecessor's sharp turn to repression after the end of the Second World War.

Manufacturing production had risen sharply during the Second World War (the sector's share of GDP had topped that of mining by 1943). Manufacturers favoured reforms that would ensure a large, permanent urban labour supply which could be regulated through recognized trade unions and bargaining structures. They preferred the relaxation of influx control, pass laws and the job colour bar (to enable cheaper African labour to do semi-skilled and skilled work), as well as the extension of still limited labour rights to urban African workers.

Mining capital, on the other hand, reasoned that the collapse of the reserve system undermined their cheap migratory labour supply. Rather than turn to a stabilized but more expensive urban workforce, it sought to shore up the rural reservoirs of migrant workers. And agricultural capital (especially in the then Transvaal, Orange Free State and Natal) wanted influx control and the pass laws tightened so as to stem the outflow of African labour towards the cities and towns. O'Meara has captured this fission well:

> As the 1940s progressed, the differing forms of state policy demanded by various capitals came into increasing contradiction with each other, opening deep divisions within the capitalist class ... The ruling UP was no longer able to organise together the increasingly contradictory demands of the various capitals and act as the political representative of the entire capitalist class ... [this] gave rise to a gradual realignment in the party political organisation of class forces (1983:232).

The state of affairs described by O'Meara was not extraordinary or peculiar. Capitalism is constantly marked by shifting tensions between the different branches of production and the resultant contradictory demands placed on the state, which has to attempt to reconcile or resolve them. Under the United Party (UP) government, the state was unable to fulfil that task which, after 1948, befell the NP. Some of its anti-capitalist rhetoric invited concern, but it was geared mainly at marshalling the class alliance that would bring it to power. Indeed, history would show that 'apartheid was designed to secure labour for all capitals, not to deprive any employer of it' (O'Meara, 1983:237).

This is not to say that there existed a precise 'fit' between the imperatives of capital and apartheid state policy, nor that the racist ideology of Afrikaner nationalism was a mere shadow play.[26] But it is to argue for caution against the Poulantzian insistence on the 'autonomy of politics', a line of analysis that over-dramatizes the fact that in capitalist society the state and the political system retains a compromised 'relative autonomy' from the system of production.[27] Apartheid would spawn laws which prohibited sexual union between whites and blacks, or excluded blacks from 'white' buses and park benches – so-called 'petty apartheid', implemented and policed at considerable cost to the system. But these were hardly central elements of the accumulation strategy pursued by South Africa capital. The sweep, the vehemence and many of the details of the apartheid system disclosed the powerful hand exerted by Afrikaner nationalist ideology. It was around this cultural, historical and political mythos that a differentiated group was organized into a political and economic force. After 1948, it was this ideology (and its translation into practice) that preserved the political base of the NP. But this does not alter the fact that the apartheid system for almost 40 years remained functional to the needs of the capitalist class; had it not, the state would have been plunged into a genuine crisis.[28] Indeed, some aspects of 'petty apartheid' were functional to the aspirations of the white *petit bourgeoisie*. The average white supported the expulsion of Indian and African traders from 'white' urban zones on the basis of racial exclusivity. But the core function of these exclusions lay elsewhere: they were expropriations aimed at guaranteeing the entrance of white merchants into the market or the removal of competition from that market.[29]

The NP won subsequent 'white' elections by broadening the class alliance that constituted its core political base (by effectively implementing measures that advanced Afrikaner material and cultural interests) within a broader programme which intensified the rate of exploitation and profit in South Africa and which ensured that the benefits were dispensed intensively within the white community. Within white South Africa, formidable hegemony was achieved. The NP regime offered something for everyone, even if a tiny minority of whites would recoil from some of its excesses.

In short, from capital's point of view, the contradictions of the 1940s were resolved by the apartheid state with comparative ease and little disruption. The costs were visited upon the black, particularly African, majority.

Restructuring under an iron fist

The NP regime quickly introduced two key sets of interventions. Influx control of African labour and the pass law system were expanded and tightened, intensifying efforts to reduce the African population to a labour army serving capitalist industries and agriculture.[30] Organizations representing the interests of the African majority (especially trade unions and the CPSA, which was banned in 1950) came under sustained attack. One result was that African wages were dramatically driven down and continued to fall in real terms until 1958/9. Adjunct to these interventions was a gallery of racist measures which segmented every aspect of social and economic life along racial lines.

Central, too, was the notion of an 'activist' state (common internationally in the post-war years) which actively and often forcibly would intervene in social and economic affairs. The state's ability to 'manage' aspects of the economy – specifically the allocation and control of labour – was enhanced. Webs of administrative structures were set up, including the notorious Bantu Administration Boards, which managed the influx control system. The resultant increase in profitability led to a surge of foreign investment, much of it channelled into the manufacturing sector. In spite of the NP's earlier threats, it did not introduce any anti-monopoly legislation. On the contrary, 'tariff protection policies … and fiscal and taxation policies favourable to efficient firms, all encouraged the trend towards monopoly capitalism'.[31]

The state also intervened with vigour to aid the survival of marginal capitalist enterprises (particularly in agriculture) and assist the birth of new, mostly Afrikaner-owned, ones. Through a concerted affirmative action programme it augmented the Afrikaner capitalist class and advanced Afrikaners in all spheres of life. Government bank accounts were moved to an Afrikaner-controlled bank, government contracts were handed to Afrikaner-owned firms, Afrikaners were appointed to serve in and head scores of state departments, top bureaucratic and military posts, official boards and commissions. Cultural production by Afrikaners was encouraged and widely disseminated through a range of cultural bodies, festivals and publishers. History books were rewritten in accordance with the ideology of Afrikaner nationalism, and school curricula were altered accordingly. The contracts for new textbooks went to Afrikaner-owned publishers. The state bureaucracy was expanded and made to absorb huge numbers of Afrikaner workers who thereby gained access to soft loans, housing bonds and other benefits[32] – 'a parasitic layer' living directly off the state, and from which evolved rapidly an Afrikaner middle-class. Afrikaners, hitherto confined largely to the 'Third World', were propelled into the 'First World'. In all these respects, the achievement by the NP of state power stood at the hub of the Afrikaners' elevated status and roles in South Africa society.

The post-war accumulation strategy

Dramatic changes were also wrought within the capitalist class. In two decades, Afrikaner capitalists were propelled into the upper reaches of the economy and integrated into the steadily evolving web of conglomerates that would dominate the economy by the 1970s. Significant were the joint ventures launched by English monopolies with Afrikaner corporations: in one instance the Anglo American Corporation practically handed over its General Mining and Finance Corporation to a subsidiary of the Afrikaner-owned insurance giant Sanlam. The graduation of Afrikaner capital as a junior partner in the (still English-dominated) economy was in full swing.

Even more far-reaching were the restructurings applied in pursuit of a new accumulation strategy, which rested on two central pillars: an industrialization strategy based on import-substitution and the ongoing dependency on cheap African labour.

The strategy of import-substitution industrialization was selected as the route into the company of 'First World' industrialized economies. Like Chile, Argentina and Brazil, South Africa focused on developing basic industries (an emphasis not dissimilar to Soviet forms of industrialization), with strong state intervention to protect a burgeoning manufacturing sector against foreign imports. The expansion of mass production of consumer commodities was linked to the rising consumptive power of whites, especially white workers who enjoyed a dramatic rise in wages. A key element of the accumulation strategy, therefore, was 'racially structured', leading economist Stephen Gelb to describe the post-war growth model as 'racial Fordism' while noting that the foundation of this model 'was the expansion of exports of gold and other precious metals, and their stable prices on world markets' (1991:2).

Rather than adopt a 'hands-on' role throughout the economy in terms of a comprehensive economic strategy, the apartheid state tried to establish optimal conditions for capitalist growth to occur. It did so by erecting high tariff and non-tariff protective walls around vulnerable industries, setting up massive parastatal corporations (like the steel manufacturer Iscor, electricity supplier Eskom and energy supplier Sasol), and expanding and upgrading transport and telecommunications infrastructure. From this path emerged deep social transformation, a modern working class and pockets of relatively modern industrial capitalism marked by increasingly concentrated ownership patterns.

The strategy did not match the later example of East Asian Newly Industrialized Countries (NICs) which restructured capitalist production by intervening in investment and production decisions, research and development, and more, to move from the import-substitution stage to a primary export-substitution stage. The *export-substitution* paths adopted by Taiwan and South Korea centred on strong state intervention in the economy, with a focus on the production of non-durable, labour-intensive goods and the development of markets for them. This path addressed the problem of an urban influx of workers from ailing agricultural areas, by structuring the economy in ways that would absorb the labour surplus.

In contrast, South Africa chose to persist with an exclusionary regime of accumulation, barricading the labour surplus on a periphery which took economic, social, political and geographic forms.[33] Furthermore, the growth model favoured capital-intensive industry, which meant limited absorption of labour surplus, and an (increasingly mechanized) agricultural sector marked by very low wages and dismal working conditions.

Dependency on the reproduction and exploitation of cheap African labour increased, chiefly in the mining and agricultural sectors, thus elaborating and intensifying a process which had been integral to the development of capitalism in South Africa. The homeland system saw the insider/outsider division expressed geographically, enabling the state to deflect the social and economic costs of reproducing African labour and absorbing unemployment onto a literal periphery. Massive forced removals saw the labour tenant system replaced by a contract labour system. Between 1960 and 1982, 3,5 million people were forcibly removed by the state; almost half were Africans who had lived on white-owned farms or on their own land in African districts. About 700 000 more people were removed from urban areas declared 'white' (Surplus People Project, 1983). Most were removed to homelands. Influx control measures were tightened, preventing Africans from being physically present in urban ('white') areas without state permission (in the form of the notorious 'pass books'). The prime function of the homeland system was, to paraphrase Alain Lipietz, the production of an immense reserve army of children available for wage-labour as and when required (1987:149). As late as 1980 an apartheid think-tank would still propose that 'the problem of race relations' be solved through 'a system of separate political sovereignties' joined in 'economic cooperation' with 'white' South Africa.[34] However, one should guard against an economic reductionist reading of the homeland policy. Political factors were also to the fore, as apartheid administrators sought to deflect the post-war continental surge of nationalist liberation politics into barricaded political entities.

The popular forces fight back

Popular resistance, though still fragmented, quickly revived in reaction to the apartheid measures – in the form of sporadic strikes and consumer boycotts in towns and cities, and more militant (occasionally violent) action in rural areas.[35]

Goaded on by its newly-formed youth wing, the ANC emerged from its slumber. Its 1949 Programme of Action had incorporated several elements of the ANCYL's manifesto and signalled a turn to 'mass struggle' under the ambit of African nationalism. Although the ANC's core base had shifted to the urban African working class, the organization was by no means under working class leadership: its top ranks – including the rising stars of the ANCYL like Nelson Mandela, Oliver Tambo, Walter Sisulu and Joe Matthews – were still drawn from the African middle class.

The predominance of African nationalism within the resistance movement was not yet assured, however. Following a leftward turn by the CPSA after 1948, the party generated a scathing critique of African nationalism and the ANC. Its 1950 Central Committee report warned that 'the class conscious proletariat cannot rally under the "national" flag of the bourgeoisie', and lambasted the black middle class for failing to provide effective leadership to the masses.[36] However, Fine has argued that the central thrust of the report was less towards shifting resistance onto the track of socialist struggle than at radicalizing the nationalist struggle (Fine & Davis, 1990:113). The CPSA would continue to fight for socialism, but the immediate task was the struggle for national liberation under the leadership of a revolutionary organization. In essence, the framework for an alliance between the CPSA and ANC had been proffered. Relations between the two organizations were not tranquil, as shown by the fierce reaction from ANC conservatives to the joint May Day stayaway called by the CPSA and Transvaal ANC in 1950.[37] A month later, the CPSA dissolved, in anticipation of the promulgation of the Suppression of Communism Act by the NP government. Three years later it reconstituted itself as an underground organization, the South African Communist Party (SACP).

The first major resistance action organized by the ANC was the Defiance Campaign of 1952, in which African women – led by the example of figures like Dorothy Nyembe, Lilian Ngoyi and Annie Silinga – played a central role. The ANC Women's League, hitherto an ineffective group dominated by the wives of ANC leaders, was 'transformed into a fighting arm of the ANC' (Mbeki, 1992:73). The campaign also spawned joint actions with other political groups, a move that would lead to the formation of the multiracial Congress Alliance in 1955,[38] and the drafting of the Freedom Charter. At the height of the campaign, ANC membership rocketed from 4 000 to 100 000 (Mbeki, 1992:64).

Given the disparate nature of resistance and the earlier quiescence of the ANC, the Defiance Campaign was a landmark attempt to mount a co-ordinated challenge against the apartheid state. Again, though, official history tends to exaggerate the accomplishments. The campaign was aimed at forcing the NP government to repeal six sets of legislation introduced or reinforced since 1948[39] – which it failed to do. By early 1953, the flow of volunteers for civil disobedience actions had slowed to a trickle, and the government had responded with new repressive legislation outlawing political protest. By the end of the year, the ANC's membership surge had been reversed, dropping to 28 000. This prompted an anonymous ANC writer to complain that 'the building of the organisation did not correspond to the enthusiasm the campaign had aroused ... As a result we did not consolidate our gains'.[40]

Attempts to consolidate the fragmentary elements of popular resistance under the banner of African nationalism continued in earnest – including the creation of the Congress Alliance and its historic adoption of the Freedom Charter, and the launching of the ANC-aligned South African Congress of Trade Unions (SACTU). The Freedom Charter for the first time presented South Africans with the outline of a democratic alternative to apartheid. Its pronouncements were sweeping, but they pointed to a new order where liberal democratic rights could be combined with a welfarist socio-economic system. The Charter and its drafting process would, in decades following, become intensely mythologized: the Charter became the touchstone of ANC policy and assumed sacrosanct status as the product of the 'will of the people'. That status is perhaps controversial.[41] Nevertheless, the Charter acquired immense political utility – particularly as an instrument in the ANC's efforts to establish its hegemony amongst the anti-apartheid opposition. The state, meanwhile, used the Freedom Charter as the basis for laying charges of treason against 156 leaders of the Congress Alliance. All the accused were eventually acquitted, but the five-year Treason Trial effectively removed them from political activity.

Formed in 1955, the non-racial SACTU represented the trade union wing of the Congress. With 19 affiliate unions, its membership would more than double by 1961 and reach some 55 000. It was tasked with furthering 'political unionism', a conception that linked workers' struggles for better wages and working conditions to the broader struggle for national liberation. SACTU played a significant role in the rise of industrial militancy between 1955 and 1958. The number of strikes rose markedly between 1954 and 1958, and some historians have suggested that the reinvigorated militancy contributed to halting the steady decline in African wages by 1959.[42] The number of organized African workers was tiny, however, although some 300 000 Africans worked in factories, 150 000 in transport, 800 000 in services, and a million in agriculture by the end of the decade.[43]

By mid-1958, though, SACTU had experienced fully the suffocating weight of 'political unionism'. It had pushed for a national strike in support of demands for a minimum wage, shorter working hours and trade union recognition,[44] but ANC leaders were intent on launching a mass campaign to coincide with the whites-only election in April. In the end, a three-day stayaway was called, nominally including the union demands but, in reality, focusing on the election – as the slogan 'Defeat the Nats' made clear. It was called off after the first day, to the dismay of some union leaders,[45] while leftists blamed the ANC leadership for undermining the militancy of the masses. Great controversy still surrounds the election stayaway and the decisions taken around the earlier 1957 bus boycotts, when ANC leaders were also accused of restraining the apparent militancy of workers. Whatever the verdict, by the end of the decade, the working class movement was decidedly weak – in Fine's view, partly because of the 'internal fragmentation of the working class', its 'structural position' in production, and 'the lack of distinction of the working class as a party in its own right from other class forces' (Fine & Davis, 1990:153). More than ever before, its demands and aspirations were being refracted through the prisms of race and nation.

Meanwhile, tensions between the ANC mainstream and its Africanist elements had grown, producing the 1959 split when a breakaway group led by Robert Sobukwe formed the Pan-Africanist Congress (PAC) in April. It was the PAC that organized the anti-pass law campaign during which police shot dead 69 protestors in Sharpeville township and 17 in Langa outside Cape Town. Pretoria used the opportunity to declare a state of emergency, and banned both the ANC and PAC on 8 April 1960.

The swing to armed struggle

The banning of the ANC forced the organization underground and occasioned a dramatic shift away from its strategy of non-violent resistance. There remains some dispute about the manner in which the decision to launch an armed struggle was taken. Govan Mbeki has acknowledged that there was strong disagreement within Congress on the matter as late as June 1961 (1992:90), whilst other writers have asserted that the decision came about fitfully.[46] Nevertheless, an armed wing, Umkhonto we Sizwe (Spear of the Nation), or MK, was set up under a National High Command, comprising ANC and SACP leaders, and carried out its first bombings on 16 December. In its manifesto, MK declared:

> The time comes in the life of any nation when there remain only two choices: submit or fight. That time has now come to South Africa. We shall not submit and we have no choice but to hit back by all means within our power in defence of our people, our future and our freedom ... Refusal to resort to force has been interpreted by the Government as an invitation to use armed force against the people without fear of reprisals. The methods of Umkhonto We Sizwe mark a break with that past.[47]

The focus was to be on rural areas, where recent peasant uprisings (in Pondoland, Witzieshoek and Zeerust) seemed to indicate an untapped potential for a guerrilla war – an improbable enterprise in a countryside dominated by white-owned farms and white-run towns and lacking impenetrable natural features usually associated with such warfare.[48] Even more surprising is the fact that this strategic turn was taken by an organization whose major organized support base indisputably lay in the urban working class. Consequently, as historian Colin Bundy reminds, not all ANC and SACP leaders were convinced and strategists like Walter Sisulu and Bram Fischer slammed the decision as the 'unrealistic brainchild of some youthful and adventurous imagination'.

Left analysts (notably Harold Wolpe[49]) have, in varying ways, adopted a periodicization model for resistance strategies, segmenting it into distinct phases during which largely objective conditions purportedly prescribed certain forms of struggle. Thus, 1948–1960 saw legal, non-violent forms of mass resistance, 1961–1973 was a period of illegality and armed struggle in the form of guerrilla war, and post-1973 allowed for a synthesis of the two forms. The central determinant in each phase was the posture of the apartheid state. For instance, the state's decision after 1961 'to rule by force alone', thereby shutting out 'all lawful modes of opposition'[50] is typically presented as the singular rationale for the resort to armed struggle. But, in the view of Fine and Davis, that line of analysis ignores:

> ... the conscious, rational side of social movements; their capacity to make programmatic and operational choices, to learn from the past and from theory, to combine their own experience with the experience of other movements abroad, to question themselves through debate and criticism and to rebuild afresh (1985:25).

Armed struggle might have been the most attractive option but it was not the only viable one, despite the severity of the state's crackdown. In the aftermath of the Sharpeville and Langa massacres, protests erupted in the country's industrial heartland and in Cape Town, along with widespread strike action. The state's repressive capacities were strained as police reinforcements were shuttled frantically from flashpoint to flashpoint – it had not yet established a blanketing, systematic and co-ordinated repressive presence. In addition, local and foreign capital had grown markedly nervous. A strong outflow of capital commenced even before the Sharpeville massacre, and accelerated afterwards. Gold and foreign reserves dropped by 55 per cent, while the stock market and gold price plummeted. This amplified tensions in the ruling bloc: neither in the state nor the capitalist class was there unanimity about the appropriate response – indeed, acting prime minister P. O. Sauer openly supported reforms in key areas (pass laws, some political rights for Africans, improved wage levels), while five major business associations petitioned the government for policy reforms.[51]

Without exaggerating these developments, in theory all other strategic options had not been sealed off. Although very difficult under prevailing conditions,[52] a 'war of position' approach was perhaps available – by marshalling the militancy of African workers, women and other sectors of the urban African population. The fundamental question was whether such an option was *feasible*. An answer required an assessment of the comparative strengths and weaknesses of the popular sector, and the extent of disorientation and strategic heterogeneity in the ruling bloc. Instead, the movement's historians and strategists have bequeathed a version of history which denies the existence of any other strategic path.

Into the doldrums

The turn to armed struggle marked not only a major strategic shift, but also a critical paradigmatic shift.[53] Henceforth, reforming the system was declared impossible. The ANC and SACP adopted:

> ... an assumption that revolutionary armed struggle was not merely the means by which ultimately to contend for state power but also the principal means by which to progress in each phase of escalation towards that goal.[54]

This characterization would become dominant within the liberation movement, yielding an all or nothing approach that launched resistance struggles on a path of outright conflict with the state, and which rubbished bids to wrench reforms from the ruling class. SACP leader Joe Slovo's formulation of the strategy at a December 1960 SACP conference captured this thinking well. It would entail:

> ... a long-term, multi-staged campaign of disciplined violence in which a hard core of trained militants, supported by mass-based political activity and crucial external aid, *confront state power with the ultimate goal of seizing it*.[55]

As analyst Mike Morris has noted, 'a tendency was born which threatened to equate armed struggle with revolution and legal struggle with reformism'. The paradigmatic shift was immense. Removed from the range of options was any:

> ... conception for political activity [that] centred on open internal struggle, on taking advantage of fissures within the state, of incremental change, of operating within the system, of using existing institutions for organisational activity or policy work.[56]

Whilst rhetorically deemed an element of the new strategy, mass struggle was moved onto the backburner and armed struggle (based on *guerrilla* warfare) occupied the strategic centre-stage, thereby also fortifying the vanguardist and militarist tendencies in the movement. The urban masses – though demonstrably still capable of mounting telling resistance initiatives – were reduced to passivity, their return to the stage of history having become predicated on the materialization of a *deus ex machina*, guerrilla war, which would founder for the next two decades. If anything, the next 10 to 15 years would validate philosopher Paul Virilio's warning:

> The principle aim of any truly popular resistance is thus to oppose the establishment of a social situation based solely on the illegality of armed forces which reduces a population to the status of a movable slave, a commodity.[57]

These observations are hardly heterodox. Entrenched by the armed struggle was, by Slovo's own, later admission,

> ... an attitude both within the organisation and amongst the people that the fate of the struggle depended on the sophisticated actions of a professional elite. The importance of the masses was theoretically appreciated, but in practice mass political work was minimal.[58]

The ANC's 1969 Morogoro consultative conference endorsed the guerrilla warfare strategy but emphasized that it could not occur in a political vacuum. Political struggle had to be primary. Consequently, the decision was taken to build the ANC's underground structures inside South Africa. The advocates of guerrilla war held their ground until 1978, when a study tour to Vietnam persuaded many of the enthusiasts (Slovo included) that an armed struggle had to be based on and arise out of mass political support – 'therefore all military activities at all times had to be guided and determined by the need to generate political mobilisation, organisation and resistance' (Bundy, 1989:7).

This dominant paradigm of armed struggle would prefigure the strategic disorientation of the movement after the late 1980s. Henceforth, apartheid could 'not be reformed', it had to be destroyed – an 'all or nothing' approach would eventually yield the tenets of 'ungovernability' and 'non-collaboration', and generate the calls for 'insurrection' and a 'people's war'. Its legacies would haunt the movement long after the achievement of liberation.

In the medium-term it would usher the resistance movement into the 'dark decade' of the 1960s. 'By the end of 1962,' Govan Mbeki has recalled, 'most units could no longer operate since they did not have the materials to carry out their sabotage activities' (1992:94). During the early 1960s, most of the ANC leadership that had not been imprisoned, moved into exile and guerrilla training camps were set up in Tanzania. The ANC was cut off from its support base inside South Africa and turned its attention to mustering international support for its struggle. Conditions hardly favoured guerrilla warfare. South Africa was surrounded by a *cordon sanitaire* – the Portuguese colonies of Mozambique and Angola, white-ruled Rhodesia and South African-occupied South-West Africa. Internally, the country offered few of the geographic features associated with rural guerrilla warfare: large, secluded mountain ranges and forests. It was not until 1967 that a major effort would be made to launch a guerrilla war, when guerrillas tried to infiltrate into South Africa through the Wankie Game Reserve in Rhodesia –

apparently in response to growing disaffection among cadres in the training camps. The attempt failed when Rhodesian security forces intercepted the 80-man force, killing 30 guerrillas and capturing 20.[59] For the next decade, the armed struggle remained largely a strategy on the drawing board.

Meanwhile, the state was able to reorganize its repressive capacities, viciously crush any remnants of internal resistance, and resolve some of the main conjunctural sources of tension in the ruling bloc.[60]

Apartheid's harvest

The post-war accumulation strategy established for whites an affluent welfare state. White workers were guaranteed access to jobs, experienced rising wages and were cushioned by a wide-ranging social security system plus easy access to credit and loans. This increased their consumptive power, making them (and the ballooning middle class) the consumptive core of a growing economy. Vast resources were invested in education, health, cultural, recreational and sports infrastructure and services for whites. White trade unions won collective bargaining agreements for white workers and successively defended their privileges against some employers' attempts to cut wage costs by shifting the job colour bar upwards and elevating low-paid African labour into semi-skilled jobs. In sum, the class alliance that returned the NP to government in successive whites-only elections was shored up. As long as the claim by black South Africans to full political rights could be held in check, the political survival of the system could be ensured – or so it seemed.

In African communities, the effects were the reverse, with the great majority of Africans ruled out of these circuits of production, distribution and even consumption. Access to skilled jobs was heavily restricted, through discrimination in the workplace and an education system which, until the early 1970s, was explicitly designed to equip Africans only with the rudiments required for entry into the lower ranks of the labour market.

Class formation in African communities was curbed, flattening class differentiation in the townships. Some segmentation did occur within the African working class, as a semi-skilled urban layer emerged, but an African middle class remained a distant prospect. The state had closed off access to most accumulatory activities and continued to drive African businesspeople from the central business districts. Even the informal sector was closed down through a barrage of regulations, forcing African consumers to spend their money at white-owned businesses. Wages rose but, in the absence of a social security net and with destitution increasing in the homelands, they had to be distributed widely within extended family networks. The rate of savings was negligible, and disposable income remained too small to afford most items deemed 'essential' by whites.

At the same time, the weight of the apartheid system was distributed unevenly among blacks (i.e. Africans, coloureds and Indians), as state budget allocation to housing, education and health departments showed. Along with white workers, Indians and coloureds predominated in the expanding sectors of the economy and were accorded some mobility within and between jobs (Hindson, 1991:229). By the 1970s there had developed in both 'groups' a significant middle class, comprising mostly professionals and merchants. Although disenfranchised, these small minorities were deemed to be citizens of 'white' South Africa.[61]

The 'boom' years

The economy performed strongly, with GDP rising at an average rate of almost 6 per cent between 1960 and 1969.[62] This strong growth cycle continued until the early 1970s,[63] attracting large inflows of foreign capital, much of it route into the manufacturing sector. By the mid-1960s, the manufacturing sector was growing at almost 12 per cent annually, but much of the growth was capital intensive and did little to stem the chronic rise in unemployment.

Although performing impressively at first glance, the economy stood on shallow, rickety foundations. The manufacturing sector did not became export-oriented. Even though manufacturing's contribution to GDP in 1960 was almost double that of the mining and agricultural sectors combined, it comprised a small part of foreign earnings, which depended overwhelmingly on the export of primary products (with gold the biggest earner). By 1975, agriculture and mining accounted for three-quarters of merchandise exports with manufacturing relying on an almost saturated domestic market (Davies *et al.*, 1985:53); a decade later mining, whilst representing only 11 per cent of GDP, contributed 70 per cent of foreign exchange earnings. Also, the manufacturing sector did not possess a capital goods branch of any note. This meant that the capital intensive growth registered in manufacturing during the 1960s rested on a high rate of capital goods imports (destined both for the private manufacturing industry and the massive parastatal industries set up by the NP government) which strained foreign reserves.

The fortunes of the South Africa economy still hinged on two *external* factors: the gold price and access to foreign exchange. At this fundamental level, its location in the world system still resembled that of most 'Third World' countries.

The model falters

After the oil shock of 1973, the growth rate slowed demonstrably. Annual GDP growth dropped to 1,9 per cent until 1984 and to 1,5 per cent for the rest of that decade – signs that the post-war accumulation strategy had encountered serious difficulties. Orthodox economic analysis recoiled from diagnoses that detected the onset of a long-cycle crisis. Rather, the natural soundness of the economy was said to be distorted or undermined by inappropriate government policies and/or disruptions in the global economy. At the macro level, such analyses stressed the increasing dysfunctionality of the government's apartheid policies to the economy, policies which were said to limit the natural workings of the free market and to invite external distorting factors like sanctions. Thus, the economic difficulties were regarded as downswings occasioned by, among other factors, the oil-price increases following the oil shock of 1973, periods of capital flight and sanctions (particularly in 1976 and 1985), and drops in the price of gold.[64] But the problems that had congealed in the economy were too severe and cumulative to represent a mere cyclical downturn. Against the background of a global recession and post-1972 revival of working class organization and action, several chronic handicaps had emerged. In summary:

- Capital intensive growth prevented the economy from absorbing surplus labour.
- The manufacturing sector's dependency on imports and its failure to become a major exporter deepened the economy's vulnerability to external factors (such as world market prices for precious metals and currency fluctuations) and caused chronic balance of payment difficulties.
- Manufacturing investment had become tardy, betraying a tendency towards over-accumulation.
- The market had become too small to sustain manufacturing centred on luxury import-substitution.
- Productivity growth had slowed, partly because of a shortage of skilled black labour and the deliberate depreciation of social capital under the apartheid system.

As in other industrializing economies on the periphery, growth in the manufacturing sector depended on capital goods imports, which during periods of expansion grew at much quicker rates than export earnings. In addition, the effects of the slowdown in the advanced world economies 'were transmitted to the South African economy ... through a rise in the price level of imported machinery' (Gelb, 1991:20). Aggravating matters was the failure of the manufacturing sector to penetrate export markets (which would have relieved the economy's dependency on mineral exports for foreign exchange earnings), and the wild fluctuation of primary commodity export prices (notably gold prices) after 1971. Chronic balance of payment problems set in. South Africa's industrial development was being severely stunted and its essential status as a primary commodity exporter confirmed.

The boom had been financed by large foreign capital inflows that were contingent on sustained economic growth. But by mid-1976 – *before* the Soweto uprising – South Africa was experiencing a net outflow of capital, raising the spectre of a debt crisis. The economy lost a quarter of its foreign exchange reserves in the first three months of 1976, forcing resort to an emergency loan from the International Monetary Fund (IMF). Total invest-ment dropped by 13 per cent between 1975 and 1977 (Saul & Gelb, 1981: 23). In industry, productivity remained low, with manufacturing outputs dropping and production costs rising. The economy had entered a period of stagflation. Rising rates of inflation fuelled a revival in worker resistance in the early 1970s – signalling the breakdown of the disciplinary regime in the workplace.

The rigid racial structuring of production and consumption patterns made whites (and, to a much smaller extent, the coloured and Indian minorities) the core market for the manufacturing sector.[65] That market was now too small to sustain production growth. As the local chief executive of General Motors would put it in 1980: 'We need people to sell to' (cited in Saul & Gelb, 1981:27). This consumer shortage was deepened by the lack of infrastructure in African areas: consumers without electricity, for instance, were not going to buy electrical goods. Simply increasing wages would not solve this problem: the soaring unemployment rate and rising inflation meant that wage-earners' pay packets had to stretch further, since more people within extended families depended on them as breadwinners. Thus, even when wages increased (as they would in the 1980s), disposable income did not expand at the same pace.

Destitution in the homelands, increased mechanization in agriculture, and the expulsion of labour tenants from 'white' farms forced more of the huge labour surplus to seek salvation in the urban centres. The state contin-ued to apply influx control measures fiercely and introduced a variety of grandiose schemes (including very costly efforts to redirect these economic refugees into new 'economic growth zones' set up inside or on the borders of homelands). The idea of blockading Africans in literal peripheries was in crisis. The reality of an exponentially growing, permanent urbanized African population had become irreversible.

Meanwhile, it was not salvation that awaited Africans in the urban areas. Work was scarce, on the whole wages remained extremely low and the oppressive realities of diffuse racist state apparatuses continually confronted residents. The economy was experiencing a terminally high rate of black unemployment, despite the high growth rates achieved through the 1960s. In the lived experienced of Africans – and many coloureds and Indians – this ubiquitous, all-encompassing nature of oppression led to the struggle to sur-vive being couched more and more in political terms.

There remains enduring debate over whether the economic crisis was centred on the demand side or the supply side.[66] Demand side analyses have concentrated on the contradictions that arose between industry's need for expanding consumptive capacities and the restrictions imposed on black – particularly African – incomes. The state's attempts in the late 1970s to extend wage and other benefits to semi-skilled layers of the urban black working class partly seemed to respond to a demand-side conception.

More conventional Marxist analyses have characterized the crisis as one of overaccumulation of capital: '[A] situation in which goods cannot be brought to market profitably, leaving capital to pile up without being put back into new productive investment' (Bond, 1991a:27). This view seeks corroboration in the dramatic rise in speculative activity, the increase in mergers and takeovers since the late 1970s and declining industrial output. Certainly, capital became increasingly centralized with hosts of companies absorbed into seven massive conglomerates through merges and takeovers. By 1983 they controlled 80 per cent of the value of shares listed on the Johannesburg Stock Exchange (JSE) and straddled different sectors. Mining monopolies moved into the financial, industrial, property and agricultural sectors; insurance giants launched raids into the mining and industrial sectors.[67] In short, the overaccumulation thesis emphasized the terminal nature of the difficulties which, allegedly, could not be resolved within the capitalist system. What it did not explain was 'capitalism's mutability and continued survival through several crises' (Gelb, 1987:35).

Notes
1 For a terse account, see Colin Bundy's 'Development and inequality in historical perspective' in Schrire (1992:24–38).
2 According to Davies *et al.*, in the British-held Cape Colony, for instance, class position 'rather than outright racial discrimination determined the patterns of economic and political power' (1985:6).
3 An independent African peasantry survived in significant numbers until the early 1930s, when its dissolution was intensified by the Depression. See Bundy (1979). Until then this peasantry served as the main social base of the ANC. Its decline coincided with the ANC's slump during the 1930s and early 1940s.
4 With the exception of Algeria, where a similar pattern of settler domination occurred.
5 South Africa, of course, would only emerge as a geopolitical entity in 1910, with the establishment of the Union of South Africa.
6 For more, see Legassick and De Clerq (1978).
7 See *The Road of South African Freedom: Programme of the South African Communist Party* (adopted in 1962). Central to that theory was the notion of 'two South Africa's, which must be distinguished from the 'Two Nation' divide referred to in this book. The SACP's theory distinguishes between a 'White South Africa' with 'all the features of an advanced capitalist state in its final stage of imperialism' and a 'Non-White South Africa' with 'all the features of a colony'. Hence, the notion of 'internal colonialism'.
8 *Economic Planning Council Report No 9*, 1946, cited in Fine and Davis (1990:15). The intervention failed. Seven years later, the Lansdown Commission would conclude that 'reserve production [is] but a myth' (cited in O'Meara, 1983:230).
9 In one of many anomalies, white workers combined this racist chauvinism with militant action, under the banner of socialism, against capital. In 1922, a miners' strike mushroomed into the Rand Revolt – a bid to overthrow the state and replace it with a 'White Workers' Republic'.

10 The famous Bambata revolt of 1906 belonged to the pre-capitalist epoch. The 1922 white miners' strike ostensibly fitted the tradition of trade union militancy but was geared mainly at shoring up racial privileges. By 1945, however, about 40 per cent of African industrial workers were unionized, with some 119 trade unions fighting often fierce wage struggles (Davies *et al.*, 1985:12–16).

11 As argued, for instance, by Saul and Gelb (1981) and Davies *et al.* (1985).

12 Historian Dan O'Meara cited in Saul and Gelb (1981:14).

13 Fine and Davis (1990:12).

14 Botha Commission, cited in Fine and Davis (1990:11).

15 Fine and Davis, *op. cit.*, p. 18.

16 The CPSA was formed in 1921 out of the International Socialist League, which was founded in 1915 following a breakaway from the South African Labour Party.

17 Since 1935, CPSA policy had vacillated, largely in response to directives from Moscow. From 1936 to 1939, CPSA policy centred on mustering a popular front based on opposition to 'imperialism, fascism and war'. The 1939 Hitler–Stalin pact precipitated an abrupt shift (following the Soviet Communist Party's decision to portray the Second World War as an 'imperialist war') towards advocating heightened class struggle. The Nazi invasion of the USSR in 1941 triggered another sharp turn, towards building a people's front. For an exposition of these twists and turns see Fine and Davis (1990:36–57).

18 Also, the African peasantry continued to resist the restructuring of the countryside, although these actions were largely unconnected to the wellsprings of resistance politics lodged in the urban areas.

19 Cited in Fine and Davis (1990:47).

20 *Inkululeko*, 18 September 1943, cited in Fine and Davis (1990:95).

21 Cited in Fine and Davis (1990:74).

22 The best study of the Afrikaner nationalism's rise to power remains O'Meara, D., 1983, *Volkskapitalisme: Class, Capital and Ideology in the Development of Afrikaner Nationalism, 1934–1948*. O'Meara, D., 1996, *The Apartheid State and the Politics of the National Party (1948–1994)* is an unrivalled account of its subsequent exercise of power.

23 O'Meara (1983:5).

24 O'Meara, *op. cit.*, p. 149.

25 Its anti-capitalist, anti-monopoly and anti-imperialist postures, for instance, were designed to win over white farmers and workers, and were abandoned soon after the election victory. Surprisingly, serious efforts to organize Afrikaner workers did not occur until the Second World War when the *Arbeidsfront* (Labour Front) and *Blankewerkers se Beskermingsbond* (White Workers' Defence League) were formed, in 1942 and 1943, respectively.

26 ANC intellectual Harold Wolpe would later critique the notion of a tight fit between apartheid and capitalism; the relationship, he argued, was 'historically contingent' and 'Janus-faced, being simultaneously functional and contradictory' (1988:8).

27 The work of Marxist Nicos Poulantzas exerted a strong pull on the thinking of left intellectuals inside South Africa during the 1970s and 1980s, particularly his *State, Power, Socialism* (1978).

28 A drastic reconfiguration of (white) political society would have ensued. Instead, the NP rapidly established itself as an integral element of a reconstituted ruling bloc which would survive until the early 1980s. Recall that white South Africans lived in a (racially exclusive) parliamentary democracy. After its precarious victory in the 1948 election, the NP succeeded in expanding its base. It won subsequent elections by ever-widening margins, an unlikely feat had its exercise of state power proved dysfunctional to the overall needs of the capitalist class.

29 The economic logic of violent racism, even on this 'parochial' scale, was not unique. US historian Ivy Compton Burnett has shown that 68 per cent of lynchings in the American south targeted black businessmen who were competing with white counterparts (cited in IPS news report, 'Black scholar decries U.S. existential crisis', 13 July 1994).

30 The earliest influx control measures actually date back to 1760 and were applied against slaves in the Cape Colony (Davies *et al.,* 1984:171).

31 Davies *et al.* (1985:23). Contrary to its title, the 1955 Regulation of Monopolistic Conditions Act did not curb monopolies.

32 This also served as a stimulus for housing, vehicle and other durable goods markets.

33 This is not to imply that South Africa as easily could have aped South Korea, a country where social polarization was much less severe and which lay closer to expansive markets.

34 Bureau of Economic Research, Organisation and Development report cited by Saul and Gelb (1981:52).

35 The 1950 Witzieshoek rebellion, for instance, when at least 15 people were killed (including two policemen) and more than 100 injured.

36 See Fine and Davis (1990:111) where Fine also accused the CPSA of disingenuousness: '[T]he Central Committee failed to mention that it was the Communist Party itself which for most of the 1940s had allied itself with the old guard of the ANC on a patriotic programme of constitutional reform and the curtailment of illegal forms of direct action, so that one function of the report was to displace all responsibility for this strategy from the shoulders of the Communist Party onto those of African nationalism'.

37 Nineteen workers died in the action and twice as many were injured.

38 The Congress Alliance mirrored the racial categorizations introduced by the NP government and comprised the ANC, the South African Indian Congress, the Coloured People's Congress and the Congress of Democrats (a grouping of progressive whites).

39 The Group Areas Act, the Suppression of Communism Act, the pass laws, the Voters' Representation Act, the Bantu Authorities Act, and the Stock Limitation Policy.

40 See Lodge (1983:44). It was in response to the defeat of the campaign and growing state repression that Nelson Mandela devised his 'M-Plan', designed to enable the ANC to operate under conditions of illegality.

41 For instance, in academic Tom Lodge's assessment, 'popular demands were canvassed but the ultimate form of the document was decided by a small committee and there were no subsequent attempts to alter it in the light of wider discussion' (1983:72), while Fine has suggested that key elements of the Charter had been decided on beforehand (Fine & Davis 1990:138–45).

42 The overall number of participants was low, though – a mere 6 158 workers participated in the 113 strikes launched in 1957, for instance; see Fine and Davis (1990:159).

43 Part of the problem lay in the many divisions that traversed the working class – racial, ideological and administrative (with or without legal recognition).

44 See Fine and Davis (1990:168–75) for a critical overview.

45 The NP won the election handsomely, while the opposition UP was virtually wiped out at the polls.

46 Stephen Ellis and the pseudonymous Tsepo Sechaba contend that 'the ANC's National Executive Committee in June 1961 debated the issue but took no position on it' (Ellis & Sechaba, 1992:32).

47 For the entire text, see Karis and Gerhardt (1977:716).

48 Govan Mbeki recalls that 'the most important books on guerrilla warfare that were available at the time in South Africa were the writings of Mao Tse-Tung on the Chinese experience and of Che Guevara on the Latin American experience... [which]

emphasised the importance of enlisting the support of the peasantry if a revolutionary war is to succeed' (1992:89).

49 See Wolpe (1980) and Wolpe (1984).

50 Nelson Mandela, 1978, *The Struggle is my Life* speech at the Rivonia Trial, IDAF, London, p. 156.

51 Fine and Davis (1985:41).

52 It is worth noting that the state's crackdown, while severe, was not instantaneous: the new security legislation only took effect in 1963, although detention without trial had been introduced in 1961.

53 For a lucid overview, see Barrel (1991).

54 Barrel, *op. cit.*, p. 69. A great deal of the theoretical impetus towards armed struggle stemmed from the SACP's Colonialism of a Special Type thesis, according to Bundy: 'An analysis which viewed class as subordinate to the national question looked to guerrilla action not only for its military gains but also for its contribution towards politicising and mobilising the masses' (1989:5).

55 J. Slovo in Davidson *et al.* (1977:186) (emphasis added).

56 Morris (1993b:6).

57 Virilio (1978:55).

58 Davidson *et al.* (1977:193).

59 Leading the force was Chris Hani, later secretary-general of the SACP. According to Ellis and Sechaba, 'the security forces noted with consternation that the guerrillas' performance and training was far superior to anything yet seen in Rhodesia' (1992:49).

60 SACTU was buckled by state repression and, after 1964, shifted its focus to international solidarity work. By 1969 only 13 black unions remained in existence, down from 63 in 1961.

61 In the Cape Province, coloureds lost their qualified vote only in the 1950s, a move that triggered heated disputes even within Afrikaner ranks where the linguistic and cultural bonds with coloureds were recognized and even celebrated. In South Africa's first democratic election in 1994, coloured voters would provide one-third of all votes cast for the NP.

62 Figures cited by Anthony Black, 'Manufacturing Development and the Economic Crisis' in Gelb (1991:157). Other, higher figures are also cited – Merle Holden, in Schrire (1992:315), has pegged average growth for the same period at 7,4 per cent.

63 This view is disputed. Economist Nicoli Nattrass has contended, for example, that profit rates actually declined throughout the post-war period. See her 'Wages, Profits and Apartheid' (unpublished D.Phil, Oxford, 1990); and Moll (1991). Radical economists have countered that Nattrass' critique is focused too much on one variable, the rate of profit.

64 They would often point to the 1980–1 rise in the growth rate as proof that the economy was undergoing short-term cyclical swings. That brief upswing, however, was triggered by a gold price rise in response to the 1979 oil price shock following the Iranian revolution.

65 Hence Stephen Gelb's description 'racial Fordism'. In Western Europe, Fordism had rested on boosted mass consumption (through wage increases, larger social spending) and stabilized labour relations (through collective bargaining agreements). Similar measures were applied in South Africa, but only within the white society.

66 For an instructive summary of these debates, see Bond (1992).

67 Of these four had controlling interests in major mining, manufacturing and financial ventures: Anglo American Corporation, Rembrandt Group, Sanlam and Old Mutual; see Lewis (1991:33).

CHAPTER TWO

Managing the crisis

By the end of the 1970s there had arisen what some analysts have described as an *organic crisis*, linking the economic, social and political dimensions. Pressured by capital, the state would respond with a fitful series of adjustments in the social and economic spheres over the next 15 years, deferring formative reforms in the political dimension until the late 1980s.

The use here of the term 'crisis' requires explanation. The definition employed is not that of orthodox Marxism, of a terminal breakdown of the system which necessarily inaugurates profound social transformation. More appropriate is the definition developed within regulation theory, where a crisis denotes a 'turning point' arrived at because 'the capitalist economy cannot continue to develop in the same form and along the same path as before'. This crisis registers also in the social and political structures which underpin an accumulation strategy but which have become increasingly dysfunctional to it (Gelb, 1991:2). Required is profound restructuring which, crucially, can and often does occur within the capitalist system – with distressing regularity and often without altering the patterns of inequality in a society.

In South Africa's case, severe contradictions were engendered within an accumulation strategy that depended on cheap, expendable African labour, but also rested on an import-substitution (and capital-intensive) industrialization strategy which required an ever-expanding market for its products. Simultaneously, the expulsion of the vast majority of the population from the enclave of (even comparative) privilege generated a variety of social and political responses which ranged from low productivity to forms of resistance that threatened the legitimacy and authority of the capitalist state. The result was a burgeoning, multi-dimensional crisis. In itself this did not augur the collapse of the system, but it did produce intense fission within the ruling bloc, rendering it even less coherent and opening new possibilities for advance by resistance organizations. Indeed, Harry Oppenheimer, chair of the country's largest corporation, Anglo American, already had noticed in 1971 that:

... we are approaching the stage where the full potential of the economy, as it is at present organized, will have been realized, so that if structural changes are not made, we will have to content ourselves with a much lower rate of growth ... Prospects for economic growth will not be attained so long as a large majority of the population is prevented by lack of education and technical training or by positive prohibition from playing the full part of which it is capable in the national development.[1]

Resurgence of resistance

In 1972 the first signs emerged that a crucial underpinning of the post-war accumulation strategy – the disciplinary regime in the workplace, which helped enforce a stable, low-wage labour force – was disintegrating. Despite the formidable battery of measures aimed at preventing African workers from organizing independently,[2] industrial workers explicitly challenged the labour relations system by staging the first strike wave in decades. It began with the October 1971 protests for higher wages by 4 000 dockworkers in Durban and Cape Town. Months later the strikes spread to textile factories and transport companies, followed by actions in East London and Johannesburg and on some mines.

The strikes were triggered by extremely low wages and the rising prices of basic consumer items[3] but gradually spurred demands for the legal right to organize. If anything, they announced the end of apartheid's 'golden age' – with class struggle, for the first time in almost 25 years, reaching an organized pitch that could unsettle the rhythms of capital accumulation. A clutch of new black unions was formed, including the Metal and Allied Workers' Union (MAWU), the National Union of Textile Workers (NUTW), the Chemical Workers' Industrial Union (CWIU) and the Transport and General Workers' Union (TGWU), many of them centred around Durban. Unions also mushroomed in the Western Cape and the Witwatersrand regions where training and other support structures were set up. Active in these organizing efforts were former SACTU and ANC activists who had been in hiatus for most of the 1960s, as well as a new generation of radical white students and intellectuals. Mindful of SACTU's experience of state repression, most of the new unions eschewed the 'political unionism' approach and concentrated on shopfloor issues.

Having reached their peak in 1973–4, the strikes continued until 1976.[4] Most, however, were crushed by police and management. On the whole, workers' demands were not met and membership of the new unions declined swiftly. A painstaking process commenced to build sturdy worker organizations capable of weathering the setbacks of strike defeats. But more than two decades after the defeats of the late 1940s and the subsequent rise of African nationalism, working class resistance had re-emerged in its own right. Meanwhile, the country would be rocked by the Soweto uprising, triggered by students protesting a decree that half the subjects in African schools be taught in the *Afrikaans* medium.

Unexpectedly, both capital and the apartheid state were tumbled into damage-control mode, albeit with the odds still stacked dramatically in their favour as they sought to suppress and defuse rising opposition.

The resurgence of popular resistance in the 1970s was propelled by four developments. The first related directly to the economic crisis. Unemployment levels had risen more sharply than in the 1960s and inflation climbed steeply, imposing severe hardship even on employed African workers, who reacted with the post-1972 strikes. The second development was the advance of national liberation struggles in southern Africa where both Mozambique and Angola won independence in 1975. These victories reverberated in South Africa, deepening a growing sense of siege among whites and immeasurably boosting courage and resolve among blacks. Logistically, the makeshift armed struggle benefited also as the infiltration of guerrillas and the exodus of new recruits into exile became easier, and communication channels could be revived with underground cells operating inside South Africa. For the first time since being banned, the ANC was able to narrow (to some extent) the distance between itself and the realities unfolding inside South Africa.

Thirdly, drawing on the writings of African radicals and US black nationalists, an ideological rejuvenation occurred in the form of Black Consciousness (BC). A new emphasis on self-reliance and non-violent militancy emerged from the Black Consciousness Movement's (BCM) propagation of 'psychologism' – the conviction that the key to black liberation lay in psychological liberation – which was expressed explosively in 1976, when the Soweto uprising erupted.[5] BC was perhaps the last independent ideological current to filter into the discourse of the liberation movement.[6] By the late 1970s, however, it had dissipated. State crackdowns had deprived BC of its leadership (through murder, as in the case of Steve Biko, or imprisonment). After the Soweto uprising, thousands of younger adherents fled the country, determined to return with guns in their hands. In exile, however, they discovered they could survive only by joining either the ANC or the PAC – and were thus absorbed into the mainstream liberation traditions.[7] BC turned out to be a godsend for the ANC, which drew into its ranks a new generation of committed and astute young leaders.

The fourth development was the growing tendency within the broad opposition to attribute all forms of deprivation, oppression and discrimination (in short, the multiple travails and contradictions experienced in lived reality) to the apartheid system, thereby enabling a heightened and more widespread politicization of the oppressed. A fresh resolve became evident in popular organizations which multiplied in numbers, drawing ever younger cohorts and cadres into resistance activities. The desolate 1960s were over. From here onwards, the state and capital would have to contend with a steady wave of resistance as they sought antidotes to dilemmas that were beginning to extend into all spheres of society.

The lights dim

In the economic sphere, the apartheid growth model had begun to decay, while in the political, ideological and social spheres, the 'conditions which had hitherto sustained a form of capital accumulation based predominantly on cheap, unskilled black (African) labour' began to function in contradiction to that form of accumulation (Davies *et al.*, 1985:37). Drawing on Antonio Gramsci's writings, Saul and Gelb, in an influential intervention,[8] declared the crisis to be 'organic':

> A crisis occurs, sometimes lasting for decades. This exceptional duration means that incurable structural contradictions have revealed themselves … and that, despite this, the political forces which are struggling to conserve and defend the existing structure itself are making efforts to cure them within certain limits, and to overcome them. These incessant and persistent efforts … form the terrain of the conjunctural and it is upon this terrain that the forces of opposition organize.[9]

The authors tried to avoid a shallow contradistinction between 'reform' and 'revolution', reminding that 'while "reform" is not genuine transformation … it is not meaningless or irrelevant either, for it can affect the shape of the field of battle'.[10] Discourse within the resistance movement, however, had come to orbit around a facile schema that saw reform and revolution in mutually exclusive terms. Centred on the dictum that 'apartheid cannot be reformed', reforms were disparaged as mere attempts to undermine the revolutionary momentum and which, therefore, demanded outright rejection.

This conception was integrally linked to the paradigm shifts introduced by the turn to armed struggle, and was later reinforced by the victories of the MPLA and Frelimo in Angola and Mozambique, respectively. The crucial thrust of Gramsci's analysis – that a 'war of position' had to supplant the 'war of manoeuvre' – would hardly feature in the ANC and SACP's strategic debates, although it earned greater favour within the intellectual strata of the new trade union movements. The exiled organizations' strategies were geared to mobilizing resistance forces for an outright conflict aimed at a cataclysmic outcome: the overthrow of the apartheid state. Generalizing, Morris would later characterize this approach as follows:

> Radical participation in state structures to take advantage of spaces and gaps created by the regime, to create cracks and exacerbate crises, is mostly dismissed as collaborationist, granting legitimacy, confusing the masses, and reactionary. Often those advocating such courses are regarded as more

dangerous than the regime. The discourse of opposition becomes concerned with a fear of cooptation, preservation of the real principles of the struggle, and the correct strategies to create islands of alternative power to that of the regime. (1993a:99)

As well as imposing strategic limitations, this thinking would consolidate within the resistance movement a dominant culture based on a mix of coercion and loyalty, a matter explored in more detail below.

From the mid-1970s onwards, the ruling bloc's efforts to establish a new configuration of social, economic and political relations would open a myriad of spaces and gaps through processes of 'reform from above'. With the eventual (though partial) exception of the trade union movement, popular forces would not take an effective hand in shaping these reforms.

There was no conspiratorial game plan guiding the state reforms. The complex of difficulties arising in the 1970s amplified tensions within, as well as between, the state and capital. Simultaneously, popular organizations exerted fresh pressures, while changes in the regional and international contexts also influenced the search for solutions. Each set of reforms, then, was shaped as much by 'objective need' as it was by a shifting balance of forces within and between the state, capital and the popular forces. Yet, these reforms should not be read as the mere products of panic. Challenges were certainly mounting, but they would not (until the mid-1980s and then only temporarily) force the state and capital into a defensive mode.

Without pretending that the state or leading capitalist organizations viewed matters in such enveloping terms, resolving the accumulating difficulties required innovations on two fronts. A new basis for national consent had to be constructed which, ultimately, implied adjusting (and, eventually, overturning) the political and ideological bases of apartheid rule (Morris & Padayachee, 1989). Secondly, the post-war accumulation strategy had to be restructured, which necessitated adjustments not only in economic policies but also in the extra-economic underpinnings of that strategy – social relations, state structures, political formations and the webs of interaction between the state, capital and popular organizations.

From the mid-1970s onwards, the fitful array of reform initiatives introduced at both the macro and micro levels touched on some of those elements, sometimes stimulating and sometimes retreating before revived bouts of resistance. At their most basic level, they were aimed at shoring up the two fundamental foundations of state power in capitalist society – coercion and consent – and at reshaping the spheres of production, distribution and consumption in order to resuscitate faltering economic growth. As summarized by Stadler, this involved attempts 'to remodel political institutions, increase economic and educational opportunities for blacks, and institutionalize relations between capital and labour, in order to generate some legitimacy for the social order' (1987:160).

Hindsight allows us to compartmentalize these reforms into three phases (Morris & Padayachee, 1989), without suggesting they were conceived or pursued with such coherence. Nor should it hide the fact that they crystallized out of intense differences and debate within and between the state and capital about appropriate courses of action, and that their forms and implementation were often shaped by intensifying popular pressures, heightened class struggle and shifting social dynamics.

The first phase of reforms: 1977–82

This phase was marked primarily by bids to restructure two important aspects of the social relations underpinning the accumulation strategy – the labour regime and urbanization policies. Some political adjustments did occur, but mainly inside the state itself. The overarching political crisis continued to be regarded as a security problem. A 'total strategy' was unveiled to defend the system against the 'total onslaught' mounted by the liberation forces and their allies. It called for the large-scale militarization of white society, closer co-operation between the state and capital, and new initiatives geared at taking 'into account the aspirations of our different population groups' in order to 'gain and keep their trust'.[11]

At the level of macro policies, several commissions were appointed to investigate possible adjustments – reflecting a marked shift towards technicist approaches and a greater emphasis on 'neutral', scientific solutions. To help achieve this, the state-funded Human Sciences Research Council (HSRC) was substantially reorganized and expanded; it would commission and conduct a wide range of surveys and policy research. In 1977, capital's disquiet over the lack of formative government reaction to the Soweto uprising prompted the Anglo American Corporation and the Rembrandt Group to set up a new research body, the Urban Foundation, which would focus on urbanization strategies and housing policies.[12]

Two commissions were specifically tasked with adapting the social relations underpinning the accumulation strategy – urbanization (Riekert) and industrial relations (Wiehahn) – in order to satisfy demands from monopoly capital for an enlarged, stable source of African semi-skilled and skilled labour. In the broadest sense, the key thrust of the resultant reforms was to 'ensure that as many people as possible share in prosperity and find their interests best served by an alliance with capitalism',[13] as part of a wider bid to preempt the overthrow of the system. Viewed more closely, their effect was to accelerate the process of class and intra-class differentiation within African communities.

Reshaping the divide

The 1979 Riekert Report sought 'to underpin, on a new basis, territorial segregation by legislatively strengthening the division between urban and rural Africans' (Morris & Padayachee, 1989:75). Thus, it proposed that Africans be divided into two categories: 'qualified' urban dwellers and the 'disqualified' rest, who would be banished to the homelands.

The aim of dividing South Africa between capitalist and pre-capitalist sectors persisted (Morris, 1991:45). The Two Nation model of society was to be hardened, with the terms of the division redrawn to admit a small layer of urban Africans into the enclave of 'insiders'. In Saul and Gelb's view the effect would be 'to tighten, not relax, the mechanisms of influx control' (1981:49). The new rights and concessions envisioned for the layers of 'officially urbanized' Africans would increasingly differentiate them from their 'insurgent' compatriots. After forcefully compressing classes within African townships, the apartheid state was now relaxing that pressure. This shift stemmed from industries' need for a more settled and sophisticated semi-skilled African labour force, and the political hope that a layer of comparatively privileged urban Africans would emerge to douse the ardour of the masses, as an article in the *Financial Mail* made clear:

> [T]he small group of privileged urban blacks whose quality of life will undoubtedly improve 'may well become less urgent in their demands for political power and serve as the lid on the kettle of revolution for some years to come'.[14]

This dream of a buffer of African moderates was reflected in the Commission's proposal that control and revenue generation in townships be decentralized with local township councils elected and tasked with duties hitherto performed by white apartheid officials. A kind of privatization within an authoritarian framework was attempted,[15] with the central state appearing to retreat from the day-to-day management of Africans' lived realities. In part this was aimed at defusing township discontent. But the attempts to 'depoliticize collective consumption in the townships produced its direct opposite – the massive politicization of struggles', as Morris observed (1991:46). Residents rebelled against huge increases in rent and service fees and targeted the new councils as 'puppets of apartheid'.

Among the other consequences of these adjustments was the intensification of competition for jobs and resources between the settled or permanent sections of the African urban working class and migrant workers. This would fuel animosities between these layers and lead to open, violent conflict in the years ahead,[16] as well as provide a bridgehead for the Zulu Inkatha movement in the industrial heartland around Johannesburg.

Reshaping the labour regime

The Wiehahn Commission on black trade unions was enlisted to restructure labour relations, with two broad aims. It had to revise the control of black workers in the workplace and design measures to increase the productivity and spending power of a well-trained, skilled African urban workforce. The Commission was explicit about its aims: 'The unions' potential strength meant that they must be controlled – their present weakness – meant that this should be done soon'.[17] It warned that reliance on outright repression 'would undoubtedly have the effect of driving black trade unionism underground and uniting black workers – against the system of free enterprise' (Saul and Gelb, 1981:72). Instead repression was to be replaced by a network of mechanisms which could lock black trade unions into the disciplinary and controlling workings of the labour relations system.

The 1981 Labour Relations Amendment Act accorded black trade unions the right to register and negotiate as well as participate in the Industrial Council system, a mediating apparatus designed to deflect worker issues from the shopfloor into a highly legalistic and bureaucrat process. Statutory job reservation for whites was also abolished. A select urban layer was to benefit from reforms – in keeping with the aim of re-fashioning and entrenching the insider/outsider dichotomy along less rigidly racist lines, as Morris and Padayachee recognized:

> The purpose of this new 'reform policy' was to ensure maximum division and differentiation of the popular classes: divide the black petty bourgeoisie from the working class by satisfying some of the former's socio-economic aspirations; pacify the working class by granting trade union reform; divide the general black population by driving a wedge between 'insiders' (with access to urban residential rights) and 'outsiders' (with no urban residential right) (1989:74).

The resultant legislation, however, departed from the Commission's recommendations in important respects. Most significant was the state's decision to forsake the proposal that unions seeking registration could only comprise African workers deemed permanent urban residents; migrant workers would not be allowed to join the unions. But protests from black unions pressured the state into removing those elements from the eventual enabling legislation.[18]

Unions were divided over whether to enter the new system. Some argued that registration subjected them to a debilitating set of controls while others believed that, despite the restrictions, registration offered new opportunities that could be exploited creatively. The Western Province General Workers' Unions, for instance, rejected registration, while the Federation of SA Trade Unions (FOSATU) supported it on condition that non-racial unions would be able to register. FOSATU's approach was controversial in another respect. It opted not to engage with community and political issues that did not bear directly on labour, thus departing from the tradition of 'political unionism' spearheaded by SACTU during the 1950s. Importantly, it also developed a strong commitment to building shopfloor democracy.

Seizing spaces

The fate of the reforms needs to be couched within broader contexts, as well. Economic policy took a sharp turn to the right towards the end of the 1970s, leading to a host of 'free market' adjustments (exchange controls for non-residents were lifted, key surcharges were dropped and monetary policy was tightened). This occurred against the background of a deepening global recession. As a result, 'the liberalization of South Africa's economic links allowed for the easy transmission of the worsening international economic situation into [the] South African economy' (Morris & Padayachee, 1989:76). This led to rising inflation, increased job losses and the removal of state subsidies on basic consumer items. The black working class responded by using the new spaces accorded by the restructured labour relations system to rebuild its organizations and launch a fresh wave of strikes. In the process, the unions also became vehicles for political protest.

The Riekert strategy also backfired. The attempt to redraw and entrench the division between the capitalist and pre-capitalist sectors of African society failed to take into account some far-reaching structural changes. The division between homeland residents and 'settled' urban residents was not as watertight as Riekert and other apartheid planners imagined. Homeland residents were increasingly, though precariously, integrated into 'modern' South Africa – through the migrant labour system, their dependency on wages earned in industrial centres, transport systems and their geographic proximity to urban areas – although their access to its benefits was minimal. The urban/rural divide could no longer be formalized in spatial and geographic terms:[19]

> The classic patterns of labour supply and reproduction based on the migrant/settled rural/urban dichotomies were being superseded by the restructured urban regional economies around the industrial metropolitan areas (Morris & Padayachee, 1989:76).

Attempts by the central state to lessen its fiscal burden by offloading the provision of township services also failed. In order to fulfil their financing and regulatory role, the new township councils were forced to pass on the costs to residents (higher rents, rates and service charges) which generated a surge of opposition.

Instead of consolidating control over the urban proletariat, the reforms became the basis for renewed and reinvigorated protests as the beneficiaries pushed the reforms beyond the limits imposed by the state. By 1982, this set of reforms was frayed and bedraggled.

Several other developments had meanwhile conspired to stir up fresh tensions in the NP which undermined the quest for some strategic coherence in the ruling bloc. They included the revival of resistance activities (the Soweto uprising, the strikes of 1980–1, school and other boycotts during the same period), a large outflow of capital and the onset of a recession in the late 1970s. Intense power struggles within the NP and the government erupted publicly in the form of a government scandal (Muldergate) which was used by a rising band of reformist challengers (grouped around defence minister P. W. Botha) to unseat the incumbent leadership (gathered around prime minister B. J. Vorster). 'Modernizing' fractions of Afrikaner capital became dominant within the party (thanks also to wider support from other capital-ist organizations outside the party), confirming a dramatic shift in the class alliance on which the NP had been built. The traditional core of the NP (white workers, Afrikaner *petite bourgeoisie* and small farmers) – the rightwing of the party – became marginalized[20] and the party came to pivot on the organizations of a maturing Afrikaner capital. Both the ideology and class basis of Afrikaner nationalism were being transformed – prerequisites for further, more far-reaching reformist adjustments.

The second phase of reforms: 1982–7

These reforms were bolder, having been preceded by a change of leadership within the ruling NP, a decisive shift in the class alliance that constituted the party's social base, the rapid spread in the scope and sophistication of black worker organizations, the revival of organized community and political protest, and heightened international hostility. State policies (and the *insti-tutional form* of the state) increasingly became shaped by shifting relations between the contending classes – hence the dizzy and desultory character (and implementation) of many of the ensuing reforms.

The interplay of conflicting demands and initiatives would also generate other social dynamics. Class differentiation in African townships sharp-ened, though it could not be ascribed only to state reforms. Worker strug-gles had won increased social benefits, covert entrepreneurship (including organized crime) had increased, informal trading boomed and even the influx of homeland refugees in many cases became a source of accumulation for shacklords and home owners (who rented and sold living space and other services to newcomers). The state was caught in the slipstream of dynamic social developments to which it would respond with reforms aimed at directing a process of change that, in fact, had acquired consider-able momentum of its own.

The reforms, therefore, were a mix of proactive and reactive measures – tactical adjustments – which tended not to attain strategic harmony. One reason was the increasing incoherence within the state, which had several causes. At one level, different government departments vied to shape and control reforms. The tensions were both ideological and practical: as resistance intensified, security departments demanded (and won) greater authority as they were relied on to contain the opposition. This meant that traditional bureaucratic procedures often were either truncated or circumvented. (This problem was partly overcome when a parallel system emerged in the form of the National Security Management System (NSMS), which vested massive administrative powers in the hands of the security forces.) The 'political distance' between the state and capital further undermined the achievement of a strategic programme of change, despite efforts in the 1970s to shape new policies via consultative committees that actively involved business organizations. Capital continued to engage the state not through corporatist channels but in fragmented fashion through discreet lobbying processes. Often different business organizations represented the same industries, adding to the confusion. Meanwhile, different branches of capital desired different forms of adjustment.[21] Crucially, the state's reforms ran up against the political enclosures erected by the apartheid paradigm. As long as the state tried to 'solve' the national question through attempts to retain the literal division of South Africa along racial and ethnic lines, its reforms would be hobbled by their built-in obsolescence, as the opposition capitalized on the failure to address the central political crisis and exploited the liberalizing openings.

Recasting the terrain

Despite the constraints, the reforms of the second phase went much further than the earlier adjustments and exhibited five, main features.

Most dramatic was the official end to influx control in 1986, when the abolishment of pass laws allowed Africans to enter and work in urban areas without official state permission. This announced a major shift in the apartheid accumulation strategy and was based on a new acceptance of the 'interdependent and interconnected nature of the South African political economy' (Morris, 1991:51). The urban African population was accepted as a given but would be regulated through other means (principally, access to housing). Labour would henceforth be reproduced 'wholly within the confines of capitalist society' through a revised process of regulated urbanization (Morris & Padayachee, 1989:80).

Dovetailing with the new urbanization strategy were a host of initiatives geared at redistributing resources and accelerating class differentiation among urban Africans (through measures like the 99-year leasehold of homes granted to a select layer of residents). These schemes were not plucked from thin air. Key was the Urban Foundation's attempts to devise new urbanization and housing strategies. Diligent, sophisticated and proactive, the Foundation exerted a definitive influence on government housing and urbanization policies,[22] although earlier statements had declared the overall motive with candour:

> [O]nly by having this most responsible section of the urban black population on our side can the whites of South Africa be assured of containing on a long term basis the irresponsible economic and political ambitions of those blacks

who are influenced against their own real interests from within and without our borders.[23]

The redistribution of resources was selective. Targeted for upgrading were those townships deemed to pose potential security problems, resulting in a process of so-called 'oil spot' development. The state pumped more resources into black education and supported improvements in township infrastructure (such as electrification schemes in Soweto). The intention was to undermine political mobilization by removing some of the most distressing material sources of discontent. Again, one of the consequences was to redefine and deepen the divisions between insiders and outsiders, divisions which exploded violently in the late 1980s – albeit in forms unanticipated by the anti-apartheid opposition.[24] In cases like the Crossroads settlement near Cape Town, ominous divisions were prised wide even *within* the most marginalized sections of the African working class.[25]

The state continued to scale back on its fiscal commitments, a move that corresponded to international trends but was also inspired by domestic realities. The economic recession had imposed budgetary constraints which made it necessary to cut back on state spending (where possible) and increase state revenue. At the same time, the integration of the African urban population into 'modern South Africa' threatened to impose a massive new spending burden on the state. In order to sidestep this, the state tried to decrease its social welfare functions. Housing provisions in townships now befell private developers. The state slashed its support to social welfare services and continued to withdraw subsidies on basic consumer items. The effect was to push the marginalized further into destitution while forcing the comparatively 'privileged' sections to rely on privatized social services. Some African business entrepreneurship was boosted through the deregulation of the transport system (giving rise to the taxi industry) and by allowing informal trading. Towards the end of the decade, in a bid to raise additional revenue, the state also privatized several state assets.

Aspects of social life were also deracialized. Non-racial trade unions were allowed to register, thus opening space for the emergence of the trade union federation COSATU (Congress of South African Trade Unions) in 1985. 'Petty apartheid' measures were dropped, although the class undertones of this relaxation were obvious since access to deracialized consumptive and recreational activities was determined by income. Laws prohibiting interracial sexual intercourse and marriage were also abolished. The most telling effect of these reforms lay in their ideological impact: the 'relaxation' of apartheid contradicted the stern dogmatism of the post-war hegemonic project, further alienating the former hardcore social base of the NP and opening the way for further pragmatic shifts in the future. The reforms were accompanied, however, by other attempts to re-racialize political life – for instance, the establishment of the tricameral parliament (with its racially exclusive white, coloured and Indian chambers) and racially segregated affairs government departments.

Often overlooked was the limited democratization that occurred at the beginning of this reform phase. One example was the limited extension of voting rights to coloureds and Indians, who could vote in racial elections for their 'own' representatives, despatching them to the new racially-segregated tricameral parliament. Still, the state proved unable even nominally to address the national question by, for instance, incorporating Africans into such a manoeuvre. Thus, the long-mooted 'fourth' (African) chamber in parliament never materialized. As a result, the limited liberalization became the basis for a new wave of protest and the first campaign of the United Democratic Front (UDF) would be to oppose the tricameral system.

The restricted democratization was intended to let the opposition 'blow off steam' in more regulated and less tumultuous fashion. Instead the openings were used to revive old popular organizations, build new ones and strike fresh alliances around an increasingly unequivocal opposition against the apartheid system. New organizations mushroomed, ranging from high-school students (mobilizing through students' councils) to township residents (who set up civic bodies and mobilized around advice offices), women (grouped in several women's organizations), professionals (who set up progressive lawyers and doctors' structures) and teachers. This inter-sectoral, cross-class mobilization in 1983 merged around the UDF and was directed at challenging the state's reform measures.

As resistance activities mounted, the reforms became more inchoate. The partial relaxations in the political and ideological spheres were reversed in 1986, after the imposition of a state of emergency. But this did not signal a sheer regression back to the 'old days'. The 'democratizing' reforms were withdrawn and a series of repressive measures were introduced to restore the stability required for the other, redistributive reforms to proceed. Indeed, 'the slogan of the early 1980s – "there can be no security without reform" – [was] turned on its head', according to Swilling and Phillips (1989b:147). Thus the state stayed its course in the other areas – particularly the restructured urbanization process and the selective redistribution of resources. In a sense, the state had crossed at least a tributary of the Rubicon.

From resistance to 'revolution'

The first two phases of reforms coincided with the emergence of widespread organizing and mobilizing by the popular forces, particularly among the black working class.

The reactivation of union organizing after the 1973–4 strikes was of a scale that exceeded all previous revivals – affirming a dramatic change in the potential strength of the black working class. The number of workers involved in strike action did decline between 1974 and 1980 but this was a poor indicator of the organizing momentum that had taken hold. Among the several factors fuelling the resurgence, three stood out: the manufacturing sector had become dominated by black workers (many of them occupying skilled and semi-skilled jobs), the effects of the economic recession were disproportionately deflected onto the black working class and the legalization of black trade unions had opened new organizing opportunities. Rather than embark on 'do-or-die' actions, most of the new unions focused on the painstaking process of building their organizations and seeking recognition from employers.

Working class organization and action proceeded by leaps and bounds after 1979. The legalization of black trade unions (recommended by the Wiehahn Report) boosted their total membership to 1,4 million by 1984,[26] while the number of strikes increased from 101 in 1979 to 342 in 1981. The importance of the union movement was not restricted to its own capacity for combative action (which also catalysed township resistance through complimentary tactics such as consumer boycotts). Civics and other popular bodies often drew their leadership from union ranks, a trend which introduced 'a greater degree of leadership accountability, democratic participation, and organizational structure'.[27] Moreover, for the first time since the 1940s, strong components of the resurgent black opposition were self-consciously animated by their working class identities.

Two distinct trends were discernible in the union revival. The twelve unions which joined to form FOSATU in 1979 were openly reluctant to become embroiled in wider political struggles. Their focus was on 'strong factory organization as the expression of a truly independent working-class consciousness' (Lodge & Nasson, 1991:28). Contesting that approach were a variety of 'community unions' which deemed 'it impossible to separate workers' factory demands from their township problems' and which openly identified with the liberation movement. In essence, this was a continuation of the 'political unionism' practised in the 1950s by the ANC's union wing, SACTU.[28] Inscribed into the revitalized workers' struggles of the 1980s, therefore, was the enduring tension between nationalist and class consciousness, which gave rise to fierce, even violent, conflict between so-called 'workerists' and 'populists'. The 'workerist' label, though, rested on a profound misrepresentation of class politics. 'Workerists' were accused of treating 'other issues beyond the point of production ... as secondary matters' and of downplaying 'the very important struggle for state power'.[29] Consequently, 'attempts to revive socialism in the South African struggle', as Dave Lewis pointed out, were equated with 'a narrow workerism' despite the fact that 'the struggle to build socialism is the struggle to unite under the leadership of the working class the disparate groups and classes that are oppressed and exploited under capitalism'.[30]

Nevertheless, the tensions would persist within and beyond the ranks of COSATU, which was formed when FOSATU and the 'community unions' joined forces.[31] The Charterist tradition's emphasis on national oppression would win the day, although some COSATU affiliates continued to manifest a strong socialist bias.

The emergence of this formidable array of popular organizations occurred in a context shaped by two key factors: state reforms and the economic recession. A brief economic upswing in 1980–1 was followed by a steep drop in the gold price and a ballooning imports bill (caused by large-scale capital equipment purchases). The result was a balance of payments crisis. The government reacted by heeding IMF loan conditions which demanded swift measures to offset the difficulties. The burden of these adjustments was deflected onto the black working class. Subsidies on essential consumer items were withdrawn and sales tax was raised (hoisting the inflation rate to almost 17 per cent by 1985), while rents, rates and service payments were hiked in black townships.[32]

The recession also caused a sharp rise in unemployment. Job creation slowed to a crawl, while many industries applied large-scale retrenchments; in the metal industry alone, 84 000 jobs were shed between 1982 and 1984. In agriculture, rising production costs and a sustained drought led to massive retrenchments, triggering a concentrated influx of African workers into cities and towns.

The main spur to action lay with these intensifying material hardships, which led to the setting up of local township organizations. While their organizational forms differed, they all focused on so-called 'bread and butter issues' such as housing, services, transportation, rents and township infrastructure. Activists set up civics in Johannesburg (notably Soweto and Alexandra) and the Eastern Cape (where the Port Elizabeth Black Civic Organization led the way), while a network of 'advice offices' was established in townships in the Cape Peninsula (where they collaborated with feisty grassroots media projects). Their focus was on local community issues, which often included boycott and other activities in support of worker demands. Many of these organizations exhibited a strong class consciousness.[33] Along with the trade unions, student and youth organizations were at the forefront of resistance by the early 1980s.[34]

The national schools and campus boycotts organized by COSAS and AZASCO in 1980–1 also confirmed the generational tensions between youth and parents which had exploded into prominence during the Soweto uprising.[35] Although both organizations thereafter sought to close that gap through greater involvement in broader community issues, generational schisms persisted. As Lodge noted, the members of the youth congresses and other bodies that sprang up:

... were the children of the strongest and most sophisticated urban working class in Africa. Their instincts were shaped by a community that had undergone one of the most rapid industrial revolutions in recent history. A large proportion of them were considerably better educated than their elders. Of all generations, the 'children of Soweto' were the least inclined to accept the limits and restrictions of the apartheid system (Lodge & Nasson, 1991:38).

The ferment of organizing extended broadly. The women's movement was rekindled, with the revival in the Transvaal of the Federation of South African Women (FEDSAW), which had been dormant since the 1960s, and the formation of the United Women's Organization (UWO) in the Cape Province. Black professionals joined as lawyers, doctors and teachers in progressive groupings. Activist religious organizations were formed or revived, with some (like the Young Christian Students) providing formative leadership training for young activists.

It was this multiplicity of organizations that the UDF sought to unite. Launched in August 1983, it targeted the elections for new black local authorities and the new constitution, specifically its introduction of a tri-cameral parliament intended to draw coloured and Indians into the political system. Misnamed, the UDF was in fact a broad popular front whose affiliates grew from an initial 85 to 565 when it was officially launched. Its links with the workers' movement were weak, however, with trade unions comprising only 18 of the UDF's affiliates in 1984. Preponderant were youth, student and civic organizations – among whom the symbols, traditions and rhetoric of the ANC proved especially resonant. The UDF successfully projected itself as the standard bearer of the nationalist movement, but it did not become an organized national movement. Its influence was spread unevenly across the country and was formidable in the Eastern Cape and parts of the Transvaal but relatively weak in Natal and the Western Cape. Depending on the township, its affiliates were either a handful of activists or well-organized, 'representative' grassroots groups (Friedman, 1987).

The Front's leadership was structured at three levels: national (dominated by veteran ANC activists; only two officeholders had a labour background), regional and local. On the whole, the UDF's national and regional leaderships tended to be drawn from radical, middle-class intellectuals and professionals – although the Eastern Cape represented an important exception to that pattern.

Lodge and Nasson (1991) have divided the UDF's development into five phases, each emerging from a mix of proaction and reaction. The first, lasting until mid-1984, was marked by blustering, national campaigning akin to the ANC's populist campaigns of the 1950s 'in which large and excited gatherings, powerful oratory, and strong, attractive leaders substituted for systematically structured organizations, carefully elaborated ideologies and well-coordinated programs' (1991:62–3). A dramatic shift then occurred. The second phase (coinciding with the Vaal uprising of September 1984) saw the UDF lose the initiative to militant, local resistance activities dominated by township youth and schoolchildren. Partly in a bid to catch up with local dynamics, the UDF in early 1985 adopted a controversial line which held grave implications for the democratic movement: it endorsed the ANC's January 1985 call for South Africa to be 'rendered ungovernable' and was caught up in the insurrectionary reveries that swept through the movement.

The third phase followed the declaration of a state of emergency in July 1985, with the UDF reacting often creatively to the effects of increased state repression but having lost the strategic initiative. The withering impact of the June 1986 state of emergency marked a fourth phase, with the UDF pushed into retreat and resistance activities becoming much less coherent and disciplined, culminating in the UDF's banning in early 1988. From this period of decline emerged a fifth phase, in late 1988, when the popular forces regrouped as the Mass Democratic Movement (MDM) around the leadership of church and union organizations, and launched a campaign of mass disobedience.

The UDF resembled the kind of broad popular front outlined by the ANC's Politico-Military Strategy Commission in 1979, a front that 'should express the broadest possible working together of all organizations, groups and individuals genuinely opposed to racist autocracy'.[36] The Commission had been set up as part of the ANC's 1978–9 strategic review conference where unusually strong criticism of the ANC's performance was vented. Its report (summarized in a document known as the 'Green Book') accused the organization of having 'for too long acted as if the repressive conditions made mass legal and semi-legal work impossible' and warned that its 'efforts would reach a dead-end unless they had a broader political base'.[37] Some of the campaigns of the early 1980s took after recommendations by the Commission. The Freedom Charter was to be re-inserted into resistance discourse (utilizing its thirtieth anniversary). Significantly, the Commission urged campaigns against township authorities aimed at their 'permanent destruction' in order to thwart 'their effective functioning and [reduce] the capacity of the enemy to govern out people' (Barrel, 1991:88). The report reflected a revival and elaboration – not a revision – of ANC strategy. Long neglected, mass political mobilization inside South Africa had to be shored up. Political and military struggle became hitched together in a perspective which held that:

> Preparation for the people's armed struggle and its victorious conclusion is not solely a military question. This means that the armed struggle must be based on, and grow out of, mass political support and it must eventually involve our whole people. All military activities must, at every stage, be

guided and determined by the need to generate political mobilisation, organisation and resistance, with the aim of progressively weakening the grip on
the reins of political, economic, social and military action.[38]

A tactical, not a strategic shift had occurred. The instrumentality of political
mobilization and organization within an overall strategy that pivoted on an
armed seizure of power remained clear, as Barrel noted:

> The perspective developed by the 1978–79 strategic review still turned on the
> popular armed struggle for the seizure of state power ... The strategic vision
> remained one in which political organization was ultimately seen as subject
> to military imperatives (1991:89).

During the early 1980s, the ANC moved more to the fore and began occupying the symbolic centre of resistance and narrowing the distance between
itself and the action. Covertly, it more effectively than before 'caught up'
with the masses, setting up activist cells and underground networks. Its
statements and propaganda, issued from Lusaka, reached local activists and
came to function as increasingly authoritative reference points. ANC figures
like Govan Mbeki have contended that the internal organizations 'were not
random developments but the result of a deliberate strategy to form all
kinds of mass-based organizations', claiming further that 'there is no doubt
that a majority of them were led by people who belonged to the ANC
underground or were sympathetic to the ANC' (1996:46). But political
affinities did not necessarily produce situations where the ANC furnished
the organizational impetus of those structures, nor does it warrant the claim
that the organizations arose as sheer internal expressions of ANC strategy
(Barrel, 1991:91). A much more complex process had occurred. The flowering of organizations inside South Africa and the radicalizing impact of the
influx of Soweto uprising activists into the ANC confirmed to the organization's leadership not only the need but also revealed the conditions for re-
asserting its hegemony over internal resistance activities.

The formation of the UDF had occurred largely on the basis of internal
dynamics that were organizationally independent of the ANC. Nor is it
accurate to claim that the ANC was able to direct resistance tactics (even via
the UDF, whose capacity to provide strategic leadership had weakened
demonstrably by the mid-1980s). But its growing authority at the ideological and symbolic levels did enable it to strongly influence the overall terms
in which resistance actions were couched – hence the formidable resonance
of its calls for 'ungovernability' and a 'people's war'. By the late 1980s, the
ANC was clearly the main political beneficiary of the UDF's campaigns.
These were not unmitigated advances, however. In some cases, activists
used the symbols and rhetoric of the ANC to discourage or prevent independent organizing initiatives and suppress ideological heterogeneity,
prompting Friedman to observe that 'the symbolic strength of the exile

movement has often weakened attempts to build grassroots power within the country' (1991:61).

The third phase of reforms: 1987–9

In 1987 the state suspended the 'democratization' aspects of its reforms in a bid to restore stability. But the broad trajectory of the reform process would be maintained albeit in a strikingly different manner. Redistribution would become co-ordinated and carried out within a security framework, the National Security Management System (NSMS).

The NSMS had been set up in 1979, as part of the 'total strategy', although, in the early 1980s, according to one former state functionary, NSMS officials 'were just keeping the seats warm'.[39] By 1987 it had been fully activated and became 'a parallel system of state power' which vested massive repressive and administrative powers in the hands of the military and police.[40] The NSMS spanned a national network of several hundred committees, each of which comprised local security officials, administrators and businesspeople – forming a 'shadow bureaucracy running alongside the official government bureaucracy'.[41] Its nerve centre lay in these committees which had the task of surveying, monitoring and recommending appropriate actions (by the state and its civil society allies) in 'trouble spots'. Each had to identify potential 'security problems' in its area (for example, a shortage of medical facilities or transport or schools) and design measures to defuse the risk. Implementation agencies would then be assigned to carry out the required upgrading in a speeded up process which, if necessary, would by-pass the sluggish procedures of the state bureaucracy.

The distribution of state power had already shifted somewhat by the early 1980s, after executive powers had been vested in the previously cere-monial office of the state president. But the power of the executive was still counter-balanced by the cabinet, parliament and the state bureaucracy. With the full-scale activation of the NSMS the balance of forces within the state shifted profoundly, with power increasing anchored with the state president, the security forces and the law and order ministry. In some circles these developments were likened to a 'palace coup' which allegedly trans-ferred state power to the security establishment. Lost in such a dramatic reading of the NSMS was the continuity of reformist restructuring that the network serviced. The NSMS did not substitute itself for the state; it func-tioned parallel to it. While the overt political dimension of reforms were put on the backburner from 1986 onwards, the short-term aim of the state was to restore stability and defuse the threats posed by the democratic opposi-tion. But the redistributive (and class restructuring) thrust of reforms con-tinued. Much of the selective redistribution was now applied not through the traditional channels of the government bureaucracy, but through the NSMS's shadow apparatus, with the commandist approach specifically designed to ensure speedy and efficient delivery. Thirty-four of the most volatile townships (the so-called 'oil-spots') were targeted for rapid upgrading, while a further 1 800 urban renewal projects were launched in 200 other townships (Swilling & Phillips, 1989a). The thinking behind these initiatives was that:

> ... [t]he lack of a classroom is not a security matter, but a lack of proper facilities or sufficient facilities can become a security problem ... Nobody can tell a [government] department they must build a new school. But from the security point of view you can tell them that if they don't there is going to be a problem. It is now your problem to build the school; if you don't it will become my problem and the [security] system's problem. And prevention is better than cure.[42]

The NSMS therefore made it possible to expedite the implementation of reform measures, as Swilling and Phillips noted: 'Some of these reforms were articulated by the political reformists before 1986, but they have since been appropriated and recast by the "counter-revolutionary warfare" strategists' (1989b:145). State tactics had not regressed into the sheer reactive repression commonly highlighted. If security measures could keep a lid on the revolt, the commandist delivery programme co-ordinated within the NSMS could, it was hoped, provide the kinds of social services that would stabilize the most rebellious townships. This foray represented the most sophisticated attempt yet by the ruling bloc to combine reforms and repression in ways that could alter the balance of forces. Still eluding the state, however, was a strategy to succeed the temporary containment of resistance.

The vagaries of insurrectionism

Two signal developments had impacted on the democratic movement, each reinforcing the other: the ANC's success at achieving hegemony (though not organizational control) within the movement, and its push for a 'people's war'. The all-or-nothing paradigm heralded by the turn to armed struggle became predominant in internal resistance discourse which, increasingly, looked to a headlong onslaught against the apartheid state.

Between 1981 and 1985 debates had raged in the SACP's *African Communist* journal between activists advocating the 'arming of the people'[43] and critics who argued against 'too narrow and military-technical a view of arming the people'.[44] The SACP and ANC leaderships, however, officially still opposed the insurrectionist strategies. Soon, this changed. At the ANC's Kabwe Consultative Conference in 1985, the national executive again spoke of preparing for a 'people's war'.[45] In July 1986, Joe Slovo came out supporting the insurrectionist line which, while not precluding 'a protracted conflict', meant that liberation movement's supporters 'had also to prepare and be ready to adjust to a much swifter transformation which would involve insurrectionary ingredients'.[46] By 1987, one of the chief theorists in the ANC and SACP – Mzala – was writing confidently that an insurrection was on the cards.[47] A year later, SACP analyst Harold Wolpe declared that 'the mass insurrectionary political movement is the principal agent of the struggle for national liberation'[48] – a considerable shift away from perspectives centred on a lengthy guerrilla war as the ideal form of armed struggle.

The insurrectionary approach presumed that a revolutionary situation was developing, a corrupt reading of the dynamics at play.[49] The ideological dominance of the ruling bloc was at its lowest ebb and was being challenged by crystallizing visions of an alternative order. But even in 1987, with state repression at its most intense, the continuance of socio-economic reforms (causing ideological and organizational disruption among the popular masses) prevented its complete collapse. Severe tensions had surfaced, as shown by the 1982 split in the NP, struggles between state departments (especially after the activation of the NSMS) and the defection of some ruling class intellectuals. But these were mitigated by other developments: the centralization of power in the NP and the government, the failure of capitalist organizations to produce coherent alternative strategies challenging those pursued by the state, and the government's success at marshalling support from the capitalist class for its repressive interventions. In Bundy's judgment, 'the cohesion and capacities of the state remained largely intact' (1989:16). By mid-1986, the prevarications of liberal sections of capital had grown faint and the state was entrusted with the restoration of 'order'.

The security apparatuses remained relatively cohesive, unthreatened at the military level and insulated at the ideological level against the swell of resistance. They were able to contain and invert militant energies within townships, by spatially isolating certain townships and concentrating repressive force on them and by introducing or supporting vigilante groups. This turned the 'revolutionary' violence inwards, catalysing a frenzy of internecine bloodletting that assisted state control. In addition, the core elements of these apparatuses were white and, despite the efforts of the End Conscription Campaign (ECC), stayed for the most part unmoved by calls on their consciences.[50] There was not the dimmest prospect of meeting a central precondition for revolution – the breakdown of the armed forces.[51] The state's security capacities were at no point stretched to the full, indicating that the state could still contain any feasible attempt to overthrow it by force.

Whether or not 'dual power' situations arose is moot. In some townships, certain state functions were arrogated. These instances, though, were sporadic and localized with little if any spillover effect on the broader functioning of state administration. Thus, the state could seal of these initiatives within particular communities, and attack them through a combination of repressive force and developmental interventions – often successfully.[52] In most cases, these organs were ephemeral and quickly escaped the bounds of disciplined co-ordination; only in exceptional, shortlived cases were they 'controlled by, and accountable to, the masses of people in each area'[53]. As Friedman noted at the time:

> ... while some street committees appear to have enjoyed the support of residents, others seemed to have been imposed on them. While some 'people's courts' seemed to enjoy a high degree of legitimacy, others were allegedly used to impose the will of small groups of unelected activists (1987:62).

Even in the most militant townships the 'dual power' situations detected by insurrectionists could be more accurately described as 'ungovernability', reflecting not the usurping of power but its dispersal. They were marked by the absence of effective control by either the state or its challengers. As long as those zones were isolated by the police and army they posed no wider threat to the functioning of the state. At no point were 'liberated zones', in any meaningful sense of the term, established where popular forces could organize and defend elements of a 'proto-state'.[54]

If anything it was the explosion of political activism in a wide assortment of forms that emboldened the insurrectionists. Great potential was vested in these developments. Yet, closer scrutiny might have tempered expectations. Firstly, there was the mistaken notion that the country's townships were simultaneously attaining a critical pitch of militant resistance. In reality, the geographical focus shifted constantly as the state concentrated its repression on the 'hot spots'. As Steve Friedman noted, the 1986 state of emergency was remarkably successful at narrowing the options for mass mobilization:

> Short-term mobilization is likely to pose an enduring threat to white rule only if it creates a space in which long-term organization can emerge. Boycotts, stayaways and similar actions are often the products of organization, but many have been imposed by small groups of activists without thoroughly consulting their constituents (1987:61).

The spectacle of mass campaigns and the seemingly inexorable succession of militant actions hid from the casual gaze the UDF's failure to build and consolidate an organized national power base. Despite constant efforts the Front failed to overcome the poor communication with its grassroots components and, hence, a weak capacity to direct and discipline their activities. In Friedman's assessment:

> ... its national leadership is often not in control of events on the ground. Despite gains over the past three years, it is a long way from becoming a disciplined and organized national movement which could pose a direct threat to white rule (1987:63).

Moreover, its 'reliance on mobilization and protest often conflict[ed] with organizational requirements, and resources which could [have been] devoted to organization [were] dissipated in attempts to mobilize dramatic local and regional campaigns'.[55] Throughout, the UDF launched attempts to overcome these shortcomings.[56] The formation of the South African Youth Congress (SAYCO) in April 1987, for instance, was intended to draw the youth back into line, but its fierce rhetoric instead seemed to spur activist youth along paths of action that had become unnervingly morbid. Many real or potential supporters were alienated by a situation where 'the children called the tune and our only role was to sit and listen, in angry silence'.[57] It was not surprising, in such a context, that more and more vigilante groups (usually composed of older African men) sprung into action, with the support of the security forces; or that the victims of so-called 'black-on-black violence' seemed to outnumber those killed directly by the security forces. The resort to violence in the townships had paradoxically strengthened the state's ability to hold at bay the challenge from the democratic movement.

State repression induced and compounded many of these weaknesses – by 'decapitating' popular organizations',[58] fomenting internecine violence, banning organizations, and (especially from late-1986 onwards) severely narrowing the political space opened earlier in the decade. At first, the state did not wield its repressive force with complete abandon; until late-1986 the 'liberalization' of political space had not been entirely reversed. Indeed, the security police chief, General Johan Coetzee, was said to believe that the threats posed by the UDF and other organizations 'could be countered most effectively through propaganda, highly selective restrictions, and the "defusing" of conflict by allowing outlets for political expression'.[59] Towards the end of 1986 that thinking was abandoned and political space became choked. By late 1987, most of the UDF leadership was either in prison (70 per cent of detainees were alleged members of UDF affiliates), in hiding or dead.

Ideologically the UDF functioned as an interlocutor for the ANC/SACP alliance but it failed to apply a coherent strategy to guide an escalation of resistance. By its own account, it was forced to react to the 'spontaneity of actions in the townships', and was 'trail[ing] behind the masses, thus making it more difficult for a disciplined mass action to take place'.[60] In Friedman's view, the UDF failed to become 'a disciplined and organized national movement' (1987:63). Meanwhile, the ANC by late 1986 had not yet extensively set up underground structures and built links between trained cadres and 'mass combat groups' – as it acknowledged in a NEC and Politico-Military Council document.[61] Its ideological predominance amongst the popular masses did not substitute for these shortcomings.

Viewed in this light, the insurrectionists seemed animated by a kind of chaos theory of revolution, whereby often uncoordinated and poorly strategized activities would, through an undefined alchemical process, achieve a critical mass and sweep away the apartheid state.

In the short term, the strategy of insurrectionism combined with the brutal weight of state repression to push the resistance campaigns of the 1980s off the rails. Coercive tactics and 'revolutionary violence' had by 1986 become acceptable methods of struggle among many of the youth who occupied the frontlines. While it is true that the UDF never openly endorsed these practices, its leaders were slow to denounce them. It was only after Winnie Mandela's infamous statement in April 1986 ('With necklaces and our little boxes of matches we shall liberate this country') that the UDF unequivocally condemned these methods. The UDF and its key affiliates did try to regain the initiative by mounting new, co-ordinated campaigns. but the driving impetus of resistance at the local level lay with youths whose millenarian determination placed them beyond the reach of coherent, strategized initiatives that could consolidate and extend gains. Such initiatives had to include tactical entry into the spaces opened by state reforms – a point confirmed by the labour movement's success at exploiting the restructuring of labour relations. Dominant among other popular organizations was a struggle ideology that mirrored the very exclusionism of the system that was being opposed: any engagement with the enemy other than outright confrontation was deemed to carry the risk of contamination and betrayal. Instead of separating 'those elements of reform, such as "democratization" and "deracialization", that were integral to their own struggles and required defending, all reforms were denounced as mere window-dressing'.[62] This tunnel vision was by no means unique to South Africa, as Morris has pointed out:

> Ideologically exclusionary regimes of a totalitarian nature, when viewed from the perspective of those who are excluded, create conditions which often make it extremely difficult for the excluded to comprehend the possibilities, and hence take advantage of, incremental reformist measures in order to stretch these to the maximum and create internal regime crises ... Principles and strategies are conflated and ... slogans such as boycottism, non-collaboration, non-participation predominate (1993a:98–9).

The success at resisting and scuttling reforms became confused with the ability to selectively reject some reforms and extend the parameters of others within an alternative strategic programme. Several ironies were at work here. The absolutism took hold during a period when, for the first time since 1948, the state's fitful restructuring efforts were creating highly favourable conditions for a 'war of position'. The democratic movement eschewed that route at a point when, for the first time since the 1950s, it was strong enough to exploit those openings. And rejectionism had by no means been an intrinsic feature of the Congress tradition, with which the democratic movement had clearly identified itself. Why then did it take hold? Firstly, the turn to armed struggle had marked an important shift in that tradition, by introducing a confrontationist/militarist paradigm. Secondly, the ANC had since the late-1970s taken on board the rejectionist approaches of the BCM (themselves inherited from the old Non-European Unity Movement) when large numbers of BC activists joined the organization. But it would also be wrong to allege that the insurrectionist line was merely imposed by the exiled ANC and SACP leadership or that is purchase among militant youth was an inevitable outgrowth of the militarism induced by the armed struggle paradigm. Important as those factors were, the prospect of a cataclysmic confrontation with the apartheid state resonated loudly with township youth. The ANC's call for ungovernability must, therefore, be seen in a wider context. While it fitted with the militarism of an armed struggle strategy, it was also an opportunistic attempt to slipstream behind the militancy erupting in townships. The alternative (to advise a more cautious and incremental strategy) would likely have diminished the ANC's stature among the leading militant currents inside the country. Having finally arrived on the brink of achieving hegemony over the internal resistance forces, the ANC would have been disinclined to urge a more circumspect and restrained approach.

The sum of these developments was an upsurge in resistance which came to rest on flimsy organizational and misconceived strategic buttresses.

Moments of truth

The insurrectionary challenge was defeated. The same could not be said of the democratic movement in general, however. Although the union movement had been bruised both by the ongoing effects of the recession (which reached its deepest ebb by 1988–9) and by some of the massive strikes and stayaways, it had confirmed its status as the most powerful component of the democratic movement. More than any other organized force, it retained the capacity to challenge the ruling bloc through tactical engagements that included but were not restricted to mass protests. With the UDF battered onto the sidelines, popular organizations regrouped around the union movement and progressive church bodies, which assumed the mantle of political leadership of the MDM. But the defiance campaigns that ensued in 1989 could not be slotted into a linear narrative of cumulative challenges pushing the ruling bloc into a corner. They represented the beginnings of an arduous process of rebuilding the democratic movement.

The imminent defeat of the system was not on the cards. But the interventions fashioned by technocrats and security strategists (and implemented under an exclusionary, repressive administration) merely bought time. They amounted to a set of tactics; the content of a more encompassing strategic response awaited the resolution of profound divisions that had emerged within the ruling bloc.

After 1987, capital had temporarily grouped around the state's turn to outright repression. But severe differences had surfaced within the ranks of capital, the state and the NP government over how to defend the capitalist system in the medium- to long-term. Internally the state was beset by continuing interdepartmental feuds and growing ideological rifts as conservatives reacted against the meandering adjustments advocated by the leadership. The economic crisis persisted and was being exacerbated by increased international isolation. It registered in increasingly grim terms: formal sector unemployment hovered around 30 per cent, services in most townships had collapsed, violent crime boomed, balance of payments problems worsened, the far-right (exploiting the economic and physical insecurities of rural and working class whites) was maturing into a potential political threat, and the anti-apartheid opposition was slowly regrouping around the MDM.

This was the signal achievement of the challenges mounted by the democratic movement during the 1980s: deepening and extending the complex of difficulties encountered by the ruling bloc and forcing it to try and fashion a response that would transcend the exclusionary political framework.

The wilting of civil society

The democratic movement came into its own during the 1980s. But the upsurge of resistance did not represent an irrepressible juggernaut as much as it did an aggregation of widespread but uneven organizing and mobilizing initiatives which, while occasionally pushing the state onto its heels, never threatened the overthrow of the system.

The decade represented perhaps the heyday of South African civil society. For a while, the variety and sweep of initiatives, broadly gathered under the canopy of the anti-apartheid struggle, offered hints of Gilles Deleuzes's concept of rhizomatic phenomena: a flowering of autonomous activities, linked laterally and not subjugated to hierarchical ideological and strategic conformity. Internal resistance had adopted innovative forms in a process suggestive of the 'deterritorialization' championed by Deleuze – the replacement of orthodoxy with flux and experimentation. Fine would describe this as the search for 'third way'. But by 1985, a process of 'reterritorialization' had occurred, as the codes of post-Bandung era liberation movements were reimposed, principally by the ANC and SACP.

The paths navigated by the popular forces became staked out by two key factors: state repression (which influenced their margin of manoeuvre) and the paradigmatic constraints imposed by the dogma that apartheid could not be reformed but could be overthrown. A few short years before negotiations would start, activists were widely invoking the examples of the Bolshevik and Iranian revolutions as 'suggestive alternative precedents for a South African insurrectionary change of regime' (Lodge, 1989:45). Morris has aptly summarized the thinking that propped up such misconceptions:

The mass of the population had recently embarked on the process of spontaneously gaining an angry consciousness of their potential power. The insurrectionist strategy mistook this for a period when a disorganized state and capitalist class, unable to rule, were confronted with a nationally consolidating real organs of alternative and countervailing popular power (1991:49).

There is no point casting the resistance upsurge in unambiguously romantic terms. The fortitude, determination and perseverance demonstrated by millions of South Africans carried traumatic costs. Thousands had died and countless more bore the physical and psychological scars of conflict. Thousands of protestors and activists were killed – in police attacks on protests and marches, by police death squads and a distressing number in internecine battles between political factions and organizations. Fighting escalated between rival factions (sometimes even within organizations) as resistance became increasingly violent, disorganized and alienated. The 'comtsotsi' phenomenon (lumpen township elements combining politics with crime), the use of young gangsters as political shock troops, the remorseless and sometimes violent intolerance shown towards dissent and heterodoxy within the popular movement combined with the brutal methods used by the security apparatus to exploit these dynamics and sap resistance of direction and discipline.

The suppression of dissent was manifest also in exile, where it led to tragic episodes in the ANC's Angolan camps.[63] Even a prominent intellectual like Pallo Jordan did not escape the Stalinist culture imposed in exile; he was detained by the ANC's security apparatus, Mbokodo, for criticizing the security system. According to the Motsuenyane Commission, later appointed by Nelson Mandela to investigate abuses committed in the camps, detention centres like the notorious Quadro 'developed a widespread reputation as a hell-hole where persons were sent to rot'.[64] In many cases, the distinctions between seditious activity, the expression of genuine grievances and sincere dissent, or sheer ill-discipline was made to disappear.[65]

A culture developed whereby any means were justified in the struggle against the apartheid state – bequeathing to the popular movement a variety of morbid tendencies which were more commonly associated with the apartheid regime and its allies. These tendencies existed alongside and sometimes eclipsed the publicly hallowed traditions of pluralism, debate and tolerance. They were displayed across the country, perhaps most horrifyingly in the 'Natal war', between supporters of the UDF and the conservative Zulu Inkatha movement led by homeland leader Mangosuthu Buthelezi.

Stalemate

The end of the decade became something of a respite. Battered popular forces were slowly regrouping around tactics reminiscent of the 1950s. The armed struggle had been eliminated from the ANC's arsenal by the USSR's decisions to push for a settlement and the shutting down of ANC bases in the region. On the security front, the state held the upper hand but was riven with internal conflict. In the background, a proto-negotiations process was gathering steam. A point had been reached where all sides could – indeed, had to – raise their heads above the parapets, scan the terrain and weigh their options.

More than a decade of chopping and changing the system had profoundly restructured the social and ideological undercarriage of the postwar accumulation strategy, and fitfully adjusted the economic realm. But because the reforms had steered a wide berth around fundamental political change, South Africa was not turned away from what appeared to be a slide towards chronic instability, tempered only by crisis management. No matter the alarmist rhetoric of the state, it was not so much the prospect of a revolution that had jolted the apartheid managers: it was the likelihood that the state and opposition would become entangled in a death embrace that could destroy South Africa's integrity as a nation-state and a viable zone for capital accumulation – and with it white privilege. Security measures and socio-economic reforms had not improved the outlook.

A stalemate had been reached. One option was to resort to an indefinite period of unmitigated totalitarian management of society – essentially a tactical response awaiting the emergence of an alternative strategy. Another was a further phase of political liberalization which was likely to accelerate the recovery of resistance organizations and generate another security crisis. The other option was to dramatically restructure the political basis of the system – a response which could proceed on the basis of the restructurings achieved since the 1970s in the social and economic spheres.

State analysts had viewed the political crisis in two, often complementary ways: as a security issue and, at a deeper level, as a symptom of socio-economic 'dysfunction'. The political was seen as contingent on more elemental material contradictions (mimicking Marxist accounts of societal crisis). Each of the three reform phases had circumvented the political aspects of the crisis, although the third phase (1987–9) had the hallmarks of a 'preparatory' intervention aimed at undermining the organizational capabilities and political appeal of the opposition, in order to tilt the balance of forces more in the state's favour. The influence of US counter-revolutionary theory (practised in countries like El Salvador during the same period) is discernible in the groundwork laid during the 1980s for a strategic shift towards a tightly managed transition of the type the SACP's Jeremy Cronin described as 'low-intensity democracy'.[66]

What the regime's strategists underestimated was the extent to which poverty, dispossession, landlessness and social disintegration had become politicized by the democratic movement. Every conceivable ill had been made attributable to apartheid.[67] The 1980s had confirmed that the state could not engage the popular forces within a reformist project based strictly on adjustments in the socio-economic realm. Early in the 1980s, former president P. W. Botha had warned that whites had to 'adapt or die'; by the late 1980s it was clear that adaptation within the paradigm of apartheid offered no escape. The political and social stability needed to restore and consolidate a new cycle of accumulation required a new political model which had to incorporate the basic demands of the political opposition: a non-racial democracy based on universal suffrage in a unified nation-state. As early as March 1986, NP ministers had already grasped this point; bedeviling them was how to proceed. This excerpt from notes of a special cabinet meeting on 1 March 1986 conveys the rudderless mood of the time:

> Internal violence and foreign pressure was on the increase, and (President PW Botha) wanted to know whether the NP should implement more dramatic things in the country, in place of the programme of gradual adaptations which apparently was not taken to heart by anybody. Mr Heunis [Minister of Constitutional Planning and Development] responded by saying (a) the NP did not know where it was going, and (b) the government was not in a position to deal with the circumstances in the country. Mr De Klerk was of the opinion that (a) negotiations with people who counted were on the rocks, (b) he was almost powerless because qualifications which accompanied change were often allowed to lapse, (c) there were fundamental differences between ministers over the question of where the NP and the country was heading, and (d) measures of the present did not meet the demands of the time.[68]

The need for a leap had been recognized. Yet, the strategic coherence required to make it seemed not to exist. The blame could not be laid solely at the door of the apartheid state. It stemmed also from the 'political incoherence' of capital (Morris & Padayachee, 1989) – a common feature of capitalist society, which tends to be overcome only during extraordinary periods. Capital traditionally engaged the South African state through discreet channels, mostly through engagements performed by business organizations grouped according to sector and even language. Its input into political and social policy tended, therefore, to be hide-bound and parochial. Concentrated pressure and coherent macro-reform proposals did not materialize (the notable exception being around urban planning, where the corporate-sponsored Urban Foundation made telling interventions). Instead capitalist organizations generally preferred to slipstream behind state policies, intervening when specific interests were at stake. The result was a political distance between state and capital, despite the state's attempts during the 1980s to rationalize the political input of capital by organizing consultative conferences and channels. This political incoherence had several origins:

- The economic crisis differentially affected different sectors of capital. Attempts to stabilize the balance of payments in the late 1970s benefited mining (the main export earner) at the expense of manufacturing, which was hit hard by rising wages and expensive working capital (caused by rising interest rates). The weakened currency favoured exporting sectors but made imports more expensive. As a result, bankruptcies in the manufacturing and commercial sectors grew, while the mining and finance sectors boomed. Finance capital went on merger and acquisition sprees as the casualties of the crisis were bought or bailed out, leading to even greater concentration of ownership in the economy. The crisis, therefore, registered distinctly within different sectors of capital.
- Cultural and linguistic schisms continued to divide South African capital, with so-called English and Afrikaner capital (despite increasing functional enmeshing since the 1970s) organized in separate business organizations. The ideological aspects of the system retained some (though diminishing) currency within Afrikaner business organizations like the *Afrikaner Handels Instituut*. These cultural tensions also hampered relations between English capital and the state. Common circuits for élite engagements had not evolved until the 1980s and were unenthusiastically urilized.

A consistent institutional intimacy did not exist between the state and capital. Even by the late 1980s, no common vision was evident amongst state and capital about routes out of the political crisis. Sections of capital had long sponsored a succession of gadfly opposition political parties opposed to the naked racism of the apartheid system. As late as 1983, with the crisis in full view, these sections loudly opposed the introduction of a tri-cameral parliament. In 1986, with the uprising in full swing, capital fell in line behind state repression – but without offering a congruous strategy as to what might follow once the uprising had been crushed. However, by the mid-1980s, sections had also begun actively entertaining the possibility of a negotiated settlement. These tendencies were not hegemonic within capital. It would be up to a cluster of 'visionary' fractions of capital and a band of reformist adventurers within the NP and the state (including top security officials) – alert to the fact that racial political domination was not inevitably and perennially functional to South African capitalism – to devise an exit.

Meanwhile, two developments had combined to establish a favourable balance of forces within the NP and the government. The weight of the white working class and *petite bourgeoisie* had been supplanted by the white middle classes and the capitalist class as the core social base of the NP, and power had been centralized within the NP and the government.

The crushing of the mid-1980s uprisings saw the reformists take heart: by 1990, a five-member committee headed by Coetzee and National Intelligence Service chief (NIS) Niel Barnard had met with Nelson Mandela 47 times.[69] The 'facilitation' provided by social-democratic institutes like Idasa – and funded by Western governments and development agencies – was instrumental in establishing the climate and forging the relations that would lead to formal political negotiations. In February 1990, the ANC, PAC and other anti-apartheid organizations were unbanned, and Nelson Mandela and other political leaders released from prison. A new pack of cards had been dealt, but the ruling bloc still held a strong hand.

A new conjuncture

The multitude of factors that combined to create this conjuncture have been discussed in detail elsewhere,[70] but they bear repetition. Many resonated simultaneously (but distinctly) in the ANC and the NP party and government camps, tilting the balance of forces within them towards the proponents of negotiations. Others helped to established an objective context that could be interpreted to favour that route. The precise internal dynamics within the two camps remain obscured by a lack of information. Official accounts and even personal memoirs that have emerged offer little insight into the debates and struggles that raged within the ANC, NP and government leadership circles. Nevertheless, those debates occurred on the basis of these (and possibly other) factors that conspired to produce this unique conjuncture. An ensemble of factors weighed on the minds of the NP and the government:

- Efforts to slow the slide of the economy were being hampered by international sanctions – although just how severely remains a point of debate. Certainly, the government's options in dealing with internal resistance were influenced by the chances of increased sanctions. At the same time, South African exports experienced an upturn from 1987 onwards, despite sanctions. The main value of sanctions appeared to lie in their negative effect on foreign investment flows and on the government's ability to secure financial assistance to offset balance of payments difficulties. Those pressures would not be relieved substantially until a political settlement was reached.

- The absurd duplication of state institutions (three chambers of parliament, multiple government departments performing the same tasks for racially defined sections of the population, expensive homeland administrations), as well as the cost of the Namibian occupation and the war in Angola, increased fiscal strains at a point when the economy was slumping into its worst recession since the 1930s.

- Maturing within ruling circles was an understanding that economic recovery was impossible without social and political stability. The failure of the reforms introduced since the late 1970s to defuse political resistance confirmed that medium-term stability could not be achieved without addressing the political demands of the majority. Shifting to the outright totalitarian management of society appeared unattractive since it would postpone rather than resolve the political question, leading to ongoing instability. The economic costs would be destructive since capital inflows needed to avert balance of payments crises would not materialize, triggering a sequence of predictable effects. Sanctions would make it difficult and hugely expensive to secure foreign loans and other forms of finance; foreign debt repayment obligations would tighten, forcing the government to introduce economic austerity measures that would spur further waves of resistance, producing a constricting cycle of deepening economic decline and political instability. In other words, rescuing the economic made it essential to restructure the political framework of the accumulation strategy.

- The internal popular forces had regrouped within the MDM and were still capable of mounting resistance campaigns which, although they did not pose immediate threats to the state, could escalate into more formidable forms in the future, thereby further raising the costs of avoiding a political settlement.
- Negotiations required the existence of a coherent political force with sufficient legitimacy and authority among the popular masses to make a deal stick – the ANC had clearly emerged as that force. At the same time, the sweep of its authority and power could conceivably be limited by destabilization campaigns (of the sort launched with the Inkatha Freedom Party – IFP – in KwaZulu-Natal since the mid-1980s).
- A dramatic process of class restructuring had been unleashed within African communities – further undermining efforts to achieve unequivocal unity among the oppressed and yielding a small but distinct black élite, especially in the homelands where this stratum was also invested with political and administrative power. The rise of the IFP in particular – and with it organized, politicized ethnicity – raised hopes that the hegemony of the liberation organizations could be reduced during and after a negotiations process.
- The latter developments fuelled exaggerated expectations within the NP that a 'non-racial' centre-right political alliance could be mustered to challenge or hold in check the ANC.
- Militarist hardliners were pushed onto the defensive within the state by the military defeat suffered by the South African Defence Force (SADF) at Cuito Cuanavale in Angola, Namibia's almost anti-climactic achievement of independence, and progress in Angola towards a peaceful settlement.
- The NP had weaned itself from its old multi-class social base, enabling it to free its policies from the ideological straitjacket of apartheid, and

transform itself into a party championing the interests of the white middle classes and bourgeoisie.[71]

■ A power struggle within the ruling NP was resolved with the election of F. W. de Klerk as leader, with the party's 'young turks' grouping around him.

■ Pressure from Western governments, principally the US, and their touting of the reassuring examples of 'managed transitions' to democracy in the Philippines and Namibia diminished the reluctance to opt for negotiations.

The options appearing before the ANC, in particular, and the democratic movement, in general, were influenced by the following factors:

■ The dream of overthrowing the apartheid state had been dashed by withering state repression, as well as by organizational and strategic dysfunction within the democratic movement. A lengthy period of rebuilding the internal popular forces lay ahead. This weakened the power of ANC elements that favoured an unremitting confrontational engagement with the state.

■ The armed struggle never matured to the point where it posed a military threat to white rule. By the late 1980s its potency had faded to the point where the ANC would later admit that 'there was no visible intensification'.[72] The radical social transformation projects attempted in Mozambique and Angola had been destroyed, in large part through a massive destabilization campaign by the apartheid state, reinforcing South African hegemony throughout the subcontinent.[73]

■ After the Namibian settlement, the ANC lost its military bases in Angola and was forced to transplant them as far afield as East Africa. There was no foreseeable prospect of re-establishing them in the region.

■ The collapse of Eastern Europe and the USSR's shift towards demilitarizing its relations with the West (and dramatically lessening its support for revolutionary projects in the South) deprived the ANC of its main backers and effectively curtailed its armed struggle,[74] and accelerated an endemic retreat by radical forces world-wide.[75]

■ During the 1980s, the ANC had achieved substantial ideological hegemony among the popular masses and their main forces, bolstering its claim to be the government-in-waiting.

■ Overall, the balance of power within the ANC tilted towards a well-organized pro-negotiations faction which got the upperhand over hardliners embarrassed by the collapse of their insurrectionary strategy and alarmed by the disappearance of long-term support traditionally drawn from the Soviet bloc.

Internationally, the main Western imperialist powers had since the early 1980s successfully pushed for and facilitated a series of 'peaceful' transitions to democracy on terms that prevented or set back efforts by the popular forces to achieve deep social transformation in their respective countries.[76] Pressure was exerted on the South African government by its counterparts in Washington, London and Bonn to follow suit. They argued that their support (although at times ambivalent) had presented Pretoria with the strategic room to bring about a negotiated settlement, and probably warned it that shirking this historic opportunity would end their policies of 'constructive engagement'. At the same time, the ANC was almost certainly notified that it, too, had to seize the opportunity if an ANC government was to qualify for substantial 'rewards' from the West (in the form of development aid, new investment, favourable trading terms, and political support in international fora). The collapse of the Soviet bloc and the USSR's abandonment of its commitments to radical states of the South (even given the wavering and mercenary nature of that support) meant that post-apartheid South Africa would be knotted into a world economic system dominated by the Western powers, principally the US, Western Europe and Japan.

None of this should be taken to imply that South Africa had attained much more than peripheral importance for the West, whatever the inflated sense of importance harboured by South Africans of all political stripes. What significance it did have derived primarily from the activities of anti-apartheid solidarity movements and from the Cold War context into which South Africa, like other contested Third World countries, had been slotted. Once the Cold War ended, South Africa's 'strategic significance' – already putative and exaggerated – ebbed markedly. It is highly questionable whether a negotiated settlement was viewed by, for instance, Washington as a priority by the late 1980s – although a failure to settle the conflict probably carried sufficient 'nuisance value' to warrant words of encouragement from Washington. At the same time, the potential utility of a democratic South Africa to expanded spheres of US influence in southern, central and east Africa would not have passed unnoticed in the State Department.

While neither side could claim to have triumphed, the balance of forces still favoured the incumbents, who remained firmly in control of the economy, the state (and its repressive apparatus) and the media. The ruling bloc had won space to manoeuvre in. Although confronted by a crisis, it was not acting in panic-stricken mode.

The apartheid state had emerged from turbulent uncertainties with the support of most Western governments and South African capital intact, though provisional. The retreat of radical projects internationally before homespun failures, imperialist intervention and strategic and theoretical disorientation enabled the consolidation of centrist political alternatives (viz. the growing number of 'transitions to democracy' in the Third World). The claims of the liberation movement to represent the undifferentiated 'oppressed masses' were in doubt. Accelerated class differentiation and the growing prominence of other contradictions in African communities emboldened those who believed the NP could traverse and survive the gauntlet of negotiations.

The leap into the unknown

The launch of formal negotiations in 1990 confirmed the realization that an enduring resolution of the crisis first required addressing its political dimensions by fundamentally restructuring the political and ideological basis of the post-war accumulation strategy. But NP politicians embarked on this path without a strategic master plan. Clarity existed on the need to incorporate the democratic opposition into the political system and restructure the system in order to achieve this. Less clear were the terms on which incorporation could occur, short of the fact that these had to constrain the ANC's ability to wield political power in the service of a radical agenda of socio-economic transformation. As a result, the NP throughout the negotiations process would experiment with a bewildering assortment of proposals,[77] causing ANC negotiators to complain throughout that their NP counterparts were 'constantly cutting and changing their positions'.[78] Doubtless, there were nervous recollections of the insurrectionary course taken by popular forces when much narrower political openings had appeared during the early 1980s. It was not as if the floodgates of possibility had suddenly been opened, but the outcome of such forthright political restructuring was by no means certain.

Understandably, the ANC and its allies claimed a historic victory. Alongside the insurrectionary headiness of the mid-1980s were pronouncements by the ANC leadership that seemed to illuminate a path that might end in negotiations. In 1985, at the height of insurrectionary fervour, the Lusaka leadership had issued preconditions for negotiations – the same year in which its customary 8 January statement had called on supporters to prepare for a 'people's war'. Throughout the subsequent period, the organization issued starkly contradictory statements – some conciliatory, others patently martial. In part these were directed at specific audiences: moderate postures were designed to shore up the ANC's impressive knack at winning support on the international front, while the injunctions issued to its supporters glossed over any talk of compromise and negotiations with 'the enemy'. By the end of 1987 (after Mandela had commenced his talks with the government, and with the internal movement on the retreat), the organization appeared more inclined towards a negotiations route. It refined its preconditions, and two years later formalized them in the Harare Declaration which made it public knowledge that the door was open for negotiations.

Yet, the swiftness with which De Klerk moved through that portal and began meeting the preconditions caught by surprise the base of the ANC and the popular movement – and, indeed, even key ANC theorists, if

Mzala's observations shortly before Mandela's release in February 1990 (though published later) were earnest:

> There is no prospect of the apartheid regime under De Klerk agreeing to the most elementary demands of the ANC such as the establishment of a one-person, one-vote political system (1990:571).

That incredulity was anchored partly in the tenet that 'apartheid cannot be reformed' – change would be achieved by sweeping away the old order, not by enabling it to help decide its fate through negotiations. Linked was the cliché that the NP government could not meet the basic preconditions for negotiations set by the ANC, because doing so would be akin to signing its own death warrant.

By early 1990, the regime was meeting, steadily though stealthily, many of the preconditions set by the ANC for 'genuine negotiations'. What surprised the base of the ANC and its allies was that the government opted to approach the negotiations table in circumstances that were far from 'insurrectionary'. In contrast to the ruling bloc (which had sought to avoid far-reaching adjustments in the political sphere), the popular movement and the ANC in particular were guilty of over-privileging the political – reducing not only the oppression experienced by the majority but the entire system of exploitation to the political and ideological form of the apartheid state. In such reasoning, the ordering of economic and social relations pivoted on the state – once it changed, everything else would follow. Therefore, it was argued, the apartheid regime would – and could – not initiate the kinds of reforms demanded by the ANC, since they would amount to the regime wilfully engineering the collapse of the entire system of white privilege. Alas, such political reductionism did not prepare the movement for the ruling bloc's gamble that the defence of capitalism required abandoning the exclusionary political and ideological framework of the post-war growth path – and that a conjuncture had arrived when, perhaps for the last time, the balance of forces still favoured that bloc strongly enough to enable it to make the formative moves in that direction.

The confusion gripping the internal popular movement had important ramifications for the negotiations process and the settlement it produced. Still smarting from its setbacks in the late-1980s, the movement was only beginning to regroup when its organizational disarray was compounded by the profound strategic disorientation caused by the advent of negotiations. A mere five years earlier, the ANC had been labouring to catch up with dynamic internal developments; now the woozy state of the internal movement rendered it more prone to the organizational and strategic discipline of the ANC. The UDF was disbanded on 4 March 1991, with UDF leader Patrick Lekota justifying the decision with the claim that 'the purpose for which we were set up has been achieved' – apparently endorsing the mistaken view that the UDF (and, by implication, the bulk of the popular movement) was a mere stand-in for the ANC-in-exile. The move evoked widespread but impotent disgruntlement at rank-and-file level. Shortly afterwards, Lodge warned with prescience that:

> ... rendering the UDF's lively and heterodox following into neat bureaucratic units that can be incorporated into the organizational forms of a disciplined political party represents a task which will be not only difficult but also dangerous; the process of imposing bureaucratic uniformity on a popular movement may take away is spirit and vitality (Lodge & Nasson, 1991:204).

Within a short space of time SAYCO and several women's organizations opted to become conflated into their counterpart structures within the ANC. SACP deputy general secretary Jeremy Cronin has termed this the 'B-team mentality':

> People abandoned their organizations and joined the main political organization. The real experience and worth of the popular movements was not understood; they were seen as a kind of 'B-team', a substitute until the 'A-team' [the ANC] could enter the playing field.[79]

The ANC's ideological pre-eminence was now supplemented by organizational supremacy – with the partial exception of COSATU, which, despite its political allegiance to the ANC, retained an independent base and massed organizational strength. In slightly more than a decade, the ANC had returned from the wilderness and assumed the now incontestable mantle of a government-in-waiting.

A few secrets of success

As an assembly of different classes, traditions and cultures, the ANC's ideological character and strategic direction has been contested throughout most of its history. One of its several achievements has been its success at preventing this heterogeneity from generating the sorts of internal turmoil that have plagued many other liberation movements (including the ANC's offshoot, the PAC).[80] Whilst dominant strategic and tactical positions were intermittently fought for and established, they did not achieve invulnerability. The fierce discourse angled towards the overthrow of the apartheid state was shadowed by another, more moderate one which seemed inclined towards a negotiated settlement. The latter was more consistent with perspectives that predominated during the ANC's first five decades of existence and which endured among older exiles and Robben Island prisoners.[81] Both strategic visions incorporated other pressures that included economic sanctions and boycotts, international isolation of the apartheid state, mass action by the popular organizations (strikes, protests, marches, boycotts, armed action, etc.), and armed struggle. The relative importance of these ingredients was disputed – except in the case of armed struggle which had remained paramount.[82] Indeed, it was the patent failure of a strategy cen- tred on an insurrectionary variant of armed struggle that probably tilted the ANC onto the negotiations path reconnoitred by Nelson Mandela since 1986.[83]

One might expect an organization which opts for negotiations during a period which, in its estimation, bristles with radical fervour to be inviting turbulent internal disputes and perhaps even open rebellion. Yet, there is little to suggest this happened inside the ANC. One reason is that the orga- nization traditionally kept a tight reign on heterodoxy and dissent within its ranks. As important is the fact that the co-existence of radical and moderate postures in the leadership and historical discourse of the ANC equipped it with an ambiguity that could cushion sharp policy turns. Entering into negotiations therefore could not be portrayed as an about-turn or a betrayal of organizational principles. Likewise, the basically social-democratic con- stitutional principles issued by the ANC in mid-1989 could earnestly be pre- sented as a distillation of its historical vision of change.

That vision, of course, resided in the Freedom Charter – which formed an ideological bedrock and key hegemonic instrument for the ANC. Idealistic and emotively phrased, it bore close resemblance to the French Declaration of the Rights of Man or the Declaration of Independence of the North American colonies.[84] It was not a policy document and its specific points steadily became detached from concrete moorings as time passed. From its adoption, the Charter had been hoisted above debate and dispute; it came to hover in a sacred zone of popular consciousness in the ANC. In order to marshal as broad and large a constituency as possible behind the banner of African nationalism, the ANC had pointedly refrained from elaborating and imposing a precise ideological 'line' derived from the Charter. In exile, the organization generally avoided substantive (and potentially divisive) elaborations. Discussion of alleged contradictions and ambiguities in the Charter was either actively suppressed or smoothed over with platitudes. Its formulation of post-apartheid policy was unexplicit, functioning not as road signs for transformation but as flagstones for mobilization and organi- zation. Thus the promotion of the Freedom Charter ('The Year of the Freedom Charter' campaign in 1985), in a period when the country was deemed to be poised on the brink of liberation, was not used to refine and develop the document as a rough draft of some post-apartheid policies. Instead it was sanctified and deployed as a set of symbolic reference points geared at asserting the pre-eminence of the ANC in the liberation struggle.[85] The outcome was that the ANC retained considerable ideological manoeu- vrability.

Indeed, the ANC's rise to pre-eminence stemmed less from its officially exulted 'successes' – mass mobilization and the armed struggle – than from its mastery in two other arenas: international diplomacy and symbolic struggle. Its achievements in those realms also reflected the absence of viable alternative political forces.[86] The only possible challenger, the PAC, was racked by interminable organizational dysfunction, internal rivalries and corruption scandals; it was not until the late 1980s that it recovered a semblance of international respect, thanks mainly to pressure from the governments of Nigeria and Zimbabwe.

In the diplomatic field the ANC achieved dazzling victories. By stressing the non-racial and moderate aspects of its programme it built a huge network of international representatives (far outnumbering the embassies of the apartheid state) and a powerful network of backstage and public solidarity groups and sympathizers. Internationally, the bulk of the publicity, mobilizing and campaigning work was carried out by the latter. The ANC's inclusive rhetoric – counterpoised by the increasing visual representations of apartheid violence in international media – drew waves of international solidarity that vexed other liberation organizations. In continental (the Organization of African Unity) and international fora (United Nations, sports and cultural bodies) the ANC established for itself the status of a 'government-in-waiting'. This enabled it to spearhead a formidable array of international boycotts and sanctions aimed against the apartheid system. Meanwhile, the SACP cultivated strong material, logistical and training links with socialist bloc countries. By the mid-1980s South Africa had become a domestic issue in most Western countries and the ANC was able to position itself centre-stage in these solidarity initiatives as the 'authentic voice' of the oppressed majority.

These accomplishments also enabled the ANC to capitalize on the exodus of youth into exile after 1976, at a point when the political stage belonged to the BCM. Awaiting them beyond South Africa's borders, thanks to the web of relations established internationally, were two choices: join the ANC or the PAC.[87] The former was much better organized and positioned for the intake, which infused the ANC with a new generations of radicalized recruits often with links to internal popular organizations.[88]

In important respects the ANC's success stemmed from its ability to dominate the symbolic aspects of struggle through a variety of adroit interventions, particularly in the 1980s.[89] At the (organizational and tactical) helm of the internal cycle of resistance of the 1980s were, first, unionists and student leaders and later township youth. However, the ANC made up lost ground through (among other methods) acting as international spokesperson for the uprising and by pushing key symbols to the fore. One such coup was the Free Nelson Mandela campaign (started in the early 1980s). The ANC in particular and the liberation struggle in general was personalized, condensed within the persona of Mandela: a link was thus established between Mandela, the legality of the ANC and the legitimacy of the struggle for national liberation. Likewise, the campaign celebrating the thirtieth anniversary of the Freedom Charter in 1985 served to place the uprising within the historical tradition of the ANC and provided it with a rough but embracing manifesto that resonated across ideological lines. The armed struggle, too, was more effective as a galvanizing, morale-boosting symbol of resistance than as a military strategy. Though armed attacks had multiplied in the 1980s,[90] they never posed a military threat to the state which developed a disarming success rate at pre-empting attacks. The import of attacks on the Sasol refinery or Air Force Headquarters lay in their symbolic demonstration that the system could be struck at its 'heart' and in the resulting cathartic, vicarious thrill this imparted. Later, armed action was also linked to community and union resistance. While this often had practical impact, again its prime effect was to stiffen the activists' resolve (as opposed to militarily threaten the apartheid state or effectively defend activists against repression) and confirm the pre-eminence of the ANC in the liberation struggle. In Lodge's view, 'Umkhonto's most significant contribution to the liberation struggle was helping the ANC exercise political leadership over constituencies it was unable to organize directly' (Lodge & Nasson, 1991:183).

For all these successes, the ANC's conceptions of a post-apartheid society remained rudimentary and impressionistic – a shortcoming that would become telling during negotiations and beyond. Roughly hewn, they had, until the mid-1980s, drawn heavily on the Soviet model and 'Third World' visions of the Bandung era. In most policy areas, the sweeping injunctions of the Freedom Charter ('There shall be houses, security and comfort! ... The people shall share in the country's wealth! ... The land shall be shared among those who work it!')[91] had been barely elaborated in the preceding 35 years.

Shortly before 1990, the ANC hurriedly set up embryonic policy structures to explore economic and land policies. The failure of the SACP – prominent in most other aspects of the organization – to take a profound role in policy debates was remarkable. ANC policies, according to Tito Mboweni (current labour minister and former deputy head of the ANC's economic planning department), would after 1990 emerge from an interplay of inputs from the ANC's:

> ... organizational structures; the policy departments; the positions of allies of the ANC (in particular Cosatu); the experiences of developing countries; the lobbying efforts of capital, the media, western governments, and independent commentators; and the policy research work of the IMF and World Bank (1994:69).

Less than five years had passed since a writer in the ANC's journal *Sechaba* had exhorted supporters with words that seemed to resonate loudly:

[T]he enemy has no role in the solution of our problems ... There can be no going back to the practice of frittering away our energy in activities calculated to prise the case-hardened conscience of white oppressors to invite us to negotiations to bring about a dispensation acceptable to them and us.[92]

At roughly the same time, Nelson Mandela was initiating dialogue with the apartheid regime – at first without the explicit consent of the ANC leadership in Lusaka. A propensity for negotiating an end to the conflict had emerged also within a ruling bloc aware that the formidable array of political, social and economic barriers could no longer be surmounted within the apartheid framework. The need for dramatic political restructuring had become manifest and the courage to proceed had been mustered.[93] Implicit was the recognition that:

> ... [w]hen the problem-solving capacities of the rulers begin to fail, the hegemony enters a crisis; control will keep these social and political forces in power for a certain period, but they are already doomed.[94]

The political basis of the South African system had to be revised – a project which had to include (and, most likely, pivot) on the ANC. The gamble taken by the state – and supported in rough outline by capital – was to suspend the desultory attempts to achieve stability via socio-economic reform packages and to try to resolve, instead, the political dimension of the multifold crises gripping South Africa. This could provide a relatively stable basis for restructurings in the economic and social spheres. The eventual settlement would constitute the most sophisticated and successful attempt yet to achieve this – essentially through 'élite-pacting', a political reformist path which, as summarized by Cronin, demands that 'élites, capable of "delivering" major constituencies, jointly manage the transition to a new constitutional dispensation'. In doing so, he continued, 'a new centrist (ruling) bloc is consolidated and right and left forces are marginalized'.[95] The survival of such a breakthrough, though, required that the consensus be extended across the political and social terrain.

The next four years would determine whether a sturdy enough envelope of restraint could be fashioned to ensure that the ANC and its popular allies did not transgress the boundaries of permissible change desired by the ruling bloc.

Notes

1 Cited in Gelb (1991:19–20).
2 These included outright repressive measures (banning unionists, violently crushing strikes) and a system of parallel unions whereby African workers' interests had to be presented to management and the state via white-controlled union bodies like the Trade Union Council of South Africa (TUCSA).
3 African workers in Durban were earning an average weekly wage of R13 at the time (Baskin, 1991:17).

4 In 1972, black workers staged 71 strikes. In the next years, the figures rocketed –
   370 strikes (1973), 384 (1974), 275 (1975), 245 (1976). Severe repression saw the
   figure drop to 90 strikes in 1977 (Davies *et al.*, 1985:34).

5 The precise organizational lineage of the uprising has proved difficult to discern. The
   South African Students' Movement (SASM) was a prominent force. Equally important was the fact that in the early 1970s a new generation of African students had
   begun teaching in township schools. Influenced by the BCM, they conveyed BC
   thinking to their students. The ANC's role in the uprising is unclear. There is little evidence of an active hand, although some researchers have claimed that the ANC managed to establish underground cells in Soweto via SASM; see Marks and Trapido
   (1991:4–5).

6 For a valuable review of BC, see Pityana *et al.* (1991).

7 Politically, BC underwent traumatic detours, with the Azanian People's Organization
   (AZAPO) eventually emerging as the standard bearer of the tradition. It soon drifted
   to the far-left and entangled itself in rejectionist postures that saw it boycott even the
   April 1994 election.

8 Saul and Celb (1981).

9 Gramsci, A., *Prison Notebooks*, p. 178, cited in Saul and Gelb (1981:3).

10 Saul and Celb (1981).

11 Army Chief of Staff (later defence minister) General Magnus Malan, cited in
   O'Meara (1983:253).

12 For a summary of the Urban Foundation's origins and brief, see Davies *et al.*
   (1984:122–5).

13 The editorial view of the *Financial Mail*, the country's flagship business weekly, cited
   in Davies *et al.* (1984:39).

14 *Financial Mail*, 25 January 1980, quoting liberal critic Sheena Duncan; cited in Saul
   and Gelb (1981:49).

15 In the Riekert Commission's phrasing, 'black communities [should] bear to an
   increasing extent a greater part of the total burden in connection with the provision
   of services in their own community'.

16 These antagonisms were not new. In the 1950s, Soweto was rocked by violent riots
   when migrant hostel dwellers attacked 'permanent' township residents (Stadler,
   1987:175). By the early 1970s, however, these tensions appeared to have abated.
   Migrant workers strongly supported the new trade unions that emerged earlier in the
   decade. Indeed, researcher Ari Sitas found that, until the late 1970s, 'the distinction
   between urban and migrant workers was apparently dissolving as was the relationship between migrant trade unions and the community' (cited in Marks & Trapido,
   1991:14).

17 Paraphrased in Baskin (1991:26).

18 See Baskin (1991:26–8).

19 This is not to suggest, as ANC ideologues argued, that the romanticized 'unity of the
   oppressed' was taking shape – the contrary was in fact happening, as class and other
   forms of social differentiation became more pronounced in African communities.

20 In 1982 the NP split, and the far-right Conservative Party (CP) adopted these former
   core constituencies, equating their interests with the defence of 'classic' apartheid ideology. Violent racism and bigotry, and the promotion of hermetic and nostalgic versions of Afrikaner culture became the preserve of the far-right. This freed the NP, as a
   party, to spearhead further reforms that departed from 'classic' apartheid. But it also
   raised the spectre of a challenge to its authority within the white electorate emerging
   from the far-right.

21 Poulantzians has defined these fractions in terms of sectors – branches of production
   (mining, manufacturing), 'ethnicity' (English, *Afrikaans*), domicile (local, foreign)

and types of accumulation (financial, industrial, commercial). The conglomerizing tendency in the economy saw major corporations straddle many of the divides.

22 See, for instance, Cole's account of its role in squatter crises around Cape Town (1987).

23 Urban Foundation statement, cited in Davies *et al.* (1984:122).

24 These upgrading schemes, for instance, bypassed migrant worker hostels whose residents were becoming marginalized and alienated from wider society. It was on the basis of such material and social tensions that Inkatha later intervened politically, establishing footholds in hostels, while tensions between residents living in formal townships and those living precariously in squatter camps or hostels would later explode violently. See Cole (1987), Segal (1991), Everatt (1992), Marais (1992a), Hindson and Morris (1992).

25 Importantly, Cole reminded that 'reducing (these divisions) to state strategies alone merely mystifies the reality on the ground' (1987:163). Other contributing factors included economic recessions (forcing reliance on state and other forms of patronage), the disorientation caused by social systems transplanted into new settings, and communities' own differentiated histories.

26 *A Survey of Race Relations in South Africa*, South African Institute for Race Relations, 1985, Johannesburg.

27 Lodge and Nasson (1991:39). However, this 'democratic culture' within the ranks of the opposition would later become offset by coercive and authoritarian forms of mobilization and action.

28 Baskin (1991:28); Lodge and Nasson (1991:28). Borrowing another tactic of the 1950s, the unions buttressed their factory actions by enlisting community support for consumer boycotts against employers.

29 'Izizwe', 1987, 'Errors of Workerism' in *SA Labour Bulletin*, Vol. 12, No. 3, cited in Fine and Davis (1990:278).

30 Dave Lewis, 1986, 'Capital, the Trade Unions and the National Liberation Struggle', *Monthly Review*, No. 37, cited in Fine and Davis (1990:278).

31 In October 1985, COSATU federated the four largest trade union bodies, triggering a massive strike wave that coincided with the 1985–6 uprising.

32 The new councillors exemplified the process of class differentiation in African townships: 'Councillors were often members of a growing commercial and entrepreneurial middle class ... [who] had benefited from the government reforms.' Their duties of fiscal administration in the townships 'greatly expanded the opportunities for venality ... and made them the target of widespread discontent generated by the economic recession' (Lodge and Nasson, 1991:31).

33 The Uitenhage Black Civics Organization, for instance, was formed by shopstewards from the Volkswagen factory in Port Elizabeth.

34 Lodge and Nasson (1991:51).

35 COSAS aligned itself with the 'charterist' tradition of the ANC while AZASCO at first adopted a BC outlook but soon embraced the non-racial approach of COSAS.

36 Barrel (1991:85–6).

37 Paraphrasing of the report by ANC officials interviewed by Barrel, *op. cit.*

38 'Green Book', ANC Files, p. 5, cited by Mbeki (1996:43).

39 Swilling and Phillips (1989a:76).

40 Morris and Padayachee (1989:87–95). For more a detailed overview of the NSMS, see Swilling and Phillips (1989a:75–89).

41 Morris and Padayachee (1989:88).

42 Senior NSMS official, quoted in *Weekly Mail*, 3 October 1986, cited in Morris and Padayachee (1989:89).

43 See, for instance, Mzala (1981) and (1987).
44 Trevor (1984).
45 The phrase was not new. It had featured in the Operation Mayibuye planning document, drawn up in 1963 by the high command of MK – but with starkly different meaning, functioning in the context of a rural-based guerrilla war.
46 Slovo, 1986, 'SACP: One of the Great Pillars of our Revolution', *African Communist*, No. 107 (Second Quarter); paraphrased by Bundy (1989:8). Supporters wrote enthusiastically of the factors required for a transfer of power: '[T]he South African state and its military power must be destroyed; the country must he conquered; the will of the enemy must be subdued'; see Cabesa (1986).
47 Mzala (1987).
48 Wolpe (1988), cited in Bundy (1989:9).
49 This section draws on Bundy (1989:14–18).
50 For a survey of attempts to undermine the military system from within, see Cawthra *et al.* (1994).
51 'No government has ever fallen before revolutionises until is has lost control over its armed forces or lost the ability to use them effectively' – C. Brinton, *The Anatomy of Revolution*, cited in Bundy (1989:1).
52 The mere existence of civics and youth groups did not, of themselves, constitute such organs of popular power – they were the potential basis for constructing such organs, a point often lost on celebrants of those initiatives.
53 As claimed, for instance, by Zwelakhe Sisulu in his keynote address to a National Education Crisis Committee (NECC) conference in Durban, 29 March 1986. Only in the small, compact towns of the Eastern Cape (especially the Karoo) did such claims contain even a measure of accuracy, and then only for short periods.
54 Along the lines of, for instance, El Salvador during the same period when the Popular Liberation Forces (FPL) and People's Revolutionary Army (ERP) respectively controlled large areas of Chalatenango, San Vicente and Morazan regions. In South Africa, earnest debates over 'dual power' would persist into 1990, when the popular forces were licking their wounds – see Niddrie (1990).
55 *Op. cit.*
56 Among them the 'Black Christmas' campaign of 1986; the 'People's Education' campaign of the NECC which, however made only marginal inroads against the 'No Education Until Liberation' rhetoric popular among many students; and worker stayaways.
57 Journalist Nomavenda Mathiane's account of a 1986 meeting called by students (cited in Lodge & Nasson, 1991:97). Her description applied also generally to adult township residents' reactions to the careening militancy of activist youth.
58 By mid-1986, 50 national and regional UDF leaders had been removed from active politics through arrests. Within another year, almost 30 000 activists (70 per cent of them members of UDF affiliates) had been arrested or detained, and more than 3 000 blacks had been killed (either by the police or in internecine violence).
59 As paraphrased by Lodge and Nasson (1991:89).
60 Report to UDF national congress, 5 April 1985.
61 See Bundy (1989:16).
62 Morris and Padayachee (1989:84). There were exceptions to this trend, notably in small Eastern Cape towns like Port Alfred. In 1985, through boycotts and other campaigns, telling divisions were fomented within the business community and local state structures. Rather than press ahead blindly, local activists exploited the disarray of their opponents by negotiating – and winning – specific local reforms.
63 See Marais (1992b:14–17).
64 *Motsuenyane Commission Report*, 1993, 'Executive Summary', Johannesburg, p. iii.

65 For an elliptical but instructive account of those trends, see *Appendices to the African National Congress Policy Statement to the Truth & Reconciliation Commission*, August 1996, Johannesburg; see also Marais (1992b).

66 See Cronin (1994a:3–6).

67 An eminently practical basis for mobilization, enabling activists to 'make visible' the underpinnings of oppression and suffering, and to focus protests more acutely. But it also fed the notion that the removal of apartheid would unlock a cornucopia of opportunity and power.

68 Excerpts from an expurgated political biography of former President P. W. Botha, *Sunday Times*, 28 August 1994.

69 See Sparks (1994).

70 See, for example, essays collected in Moss and Obery (1991); Saul (1993).

71 Shadowing this was a measure of uncertainty about the NP's political fate. In the September 1989 election, the party lost support to both the right (CP) and the 'left' (Democratic Party). Also, leading figures had abandoned the party. Reformists within the party were almost certainly alert to the fact that staying the course of political vacillation would have exacerbated these trends.

72 ANC National Executive Committee, 'Negotiations: A strategic perspective' (November 1992), discussion paper, Johannesburg.

73 For a survey of that campaign, see Hanlon (1986a).

74 This development also removed the ruling bloc's fear of strong Soviet influence in the policies of an ANC-led post-apartheid government.

75 Particularly in Latin America, where radical forces had failed to seize state power (El Salvador), were besieged (Nicaragua) or were repositioning themselves to enter existing political systems on highly compromised terms (Brazil, Chile, Colombia).

76 The textbook example was the Philippines, though it would soon be joined by Namibia, El Salvador and South Africa.

77 The confusion was worsened by the fact that the NP's negotiating postures had two objectives: shaping the constitutional settlement and addressing the concerns of its constituency. Thus its insistence (as late as 1991) that a non-racial democracy in a unitary South Africa was not on the cards was not a bargaining principle but rather a sop to restive whites.

78 Author's interview with ANC negotiator Mohammed Valli Moosa, November 1992.

79 Presentation to the 'Prospects and Constraints for Transformation' workshop, December 1994, Johannesburg.

80 Although there were periodic, small-scale breakaways and departures by individuals.

81 The dynamics of this dramatic reversal from insurrectionist postures to negotiations overtures remain obscured in renditions of this period in ANG history. Most suggestive perhaps was Lodge's reference to the 'strong respect for tradition and continuity' in the ANC's 'historical consciousness' (1989:53).

82 Whether in the guise of a protracted guerrilla war (as it was originally conceived) or an urban insurrection (the strategy from 1985 onwards). Belatedly, thinkers within the ANC alliance are now acknowledging the negative effects of this fixation – for tentative criticism, see Cronin (1994a:15) and Barrel (1990); for stronger dissent, see Fine and Davis (1990:251–5).

83 The fact that Mandela opened a channel of communication with the regime – while his Lusaka colleagues were detecting the emergence of a 'pre-revolutionary' climate in South Africa – suggests an acute awareness on his part of the foolhardiness of that strategy.

84 This section draws on insights provided by Bill Freund.

85 As illustrated by Raymond Suttner and Jeremy Cronin (1986).

86 This, of course, is not a rare phenomenon in oppositional struggles. The socialist parties in Portugal and Spain, for instance, adroitly capitalized on the organizational deficiencies of the respective communist parties and popular forces – which were manifested in acute forms on the eve of these countries' transitions to democracy in the mid-1970s. For a detailed analysis, see Poulantzas (1976:134–62).

87 Exiles could not remain in several African countries without the blessing of the ANC or PAC; the BC movement had no external presence to speak of.

88 Along with other factors (notably sectarianism) also accelerated the decline of the BC tradition, an independent current of resistance ideology which stood outside the charterist tradition.

89 The apartheid state inadvertently help: its frantic efforts to demonize the ANC had the opposite effect – and added to the organization's stature.

90 Up from about 23 in 1977 to 228 in 1986 by Tom Lodge's count (Lodge & Nasson, 1991:178). See also Lodge (1987).

91 From the Freedom Charter, adopted by the Congress of the People on 26 June 1955.

92 Cassius Mandla, 1935, 'Let us move to all-out war', *Seckaba* (November), p. 25, cited by Lodge (1989:46).

93 According to journalist Allister Sparks, for De Klerk (and the NP élite) 'it was not a question of morality ... but of practical politics – it was part of a gradual realization within the National Party that apartheid was unworkable and had to be changed' (1994:91).

94 Gruppi, L., 1969, *Democrazia e socialismo*, Edizioni del Calendario, Milan, cited by Pellicani (1981:32–3).

95 Cronin (1994a:7). It must be noted that Cronin does not necessarily share the view that this description applies neatly to the South African transition.

CHAPTER THREE

The shape of the transition

South Africa entered the twilight zone of the interregnum in February 1990 with the coherence presented until then by a repressive state replaced by the flux of process. A fitful, convoluted and often impenetrable process of 'talks about talks', 'protocol meetings' and, finally, negotiations was unleashed. This occurred against the background of the convulsive violence that raged across the country – signalling a 'centrifugal pull towards anarchy in South African society' (Saul, 1993:104). To a considerable extent, the violence was promoted through the action and inaction of the apartheid state, as subsequent revelations would confirm. The effect was to embolden attempts by the leadership of the democratic movement to reach a negotiated settlement:

> South Africa is on fire from end to end. The horrifying catalogue of assaults and killings must be brought to an end if we are not to sink into a state of self-perpetuating violence in which all our hopes of reform and social progress will be destroyed.[1]

The intrigues and manoeuvres of the public meetings, secret consultations, consultative seminars and talk-shops, the two main multiparty negotiating forums, breakdowns and worse are documented in reporting, analysis and punditry which, if stacked, would probably rise hundreds of metres into the sky.[2] Fascinating as some of those chronicles are, this chapter is concerned not with the minutiae of negotiations but the underlying agendas, trends and shifts which laid the basis for the settlement and established the parameters of the transition.

The stakes are stacked

Notwithstanding the ensemble of specific factors that inaugurated negotiations, in broad outline this phase was the outcome of the apartheid state's failure to resolve the political dimensions of a multifold crisis. By 1990, important sections of the state and capital were scanning the future through the prism of politics. As Mike Morris noted:

> [Capital sees] a specific political role for redistributive policies: economic growth will not occur without a political settlement, and long-term peace and stability demands policies that can restore political and social conditions for economic growth (1993c:9).

South African capitalists would differ about the policies most likely to restore profit-making to the heights last relished in the early 1970s, producing desiderata that contained a mix of neo-liberal and crypto-Keynesian features. Nonetheless, the central concerns of capital were transparent and aggressively expressed: the need for a market economy, for social and political stability, for continuity in state institutions and for restraint from radical redistributive programmes. Unanimity was also absent among the democratic forces. Officially, the ANC supported a mixed economy. Its constitutional proposals, political analyst Tom Lodge noted, fell 'well short of a socialist reconstruction of South Africa'. Indeed:

> ... the political provisions of the guidelines suggest a more radical degree of restructuring than do the prescriptions for the economy (1989:49).

But within the ANC, and among its allies, debates raged on how robust a role should be reserved for the state. Even within the ANC, the Jacobin call for 'a dispensation that excludes the enemy as a factor in its making' retained some currency.[3] Though disoriented by the collapse of 'existing socialism' in the Soviet bloc, many SACP members harboured a residual commitment to a commandist state. Others rejected a commandist approach and, like former unionist Alec Erwin, argued for a 'planned socialist alternative' based on a 'democratically controlled economy which goes beyond simplistic notions of nationalisation'.[4] Overshadowing such specific differences, though, was the shared desire to fashion a development path that could redress the legacies of apartheid.

Required by South African capital was 'the reorganisation of hegemony through various kinds of passive revolution ... while providing for the continued development of the forces of production'.[5] Whilst eminently *political,* the required changes would not constitute an end in themselves. A resolution to the crisis had to rest on two key pillars.[6] It required, firstly, a political settlement which could enable the reconfiguration of the ruling bloc around a political axis capable of constructing and managing a new national consensus. Secondly, a new development path capable of guiding South Africa out of its economic and social crisis had to be devised and implemented. Both between and *within* the democratic forces and capitalist organizations there was considerable disagreement about the details of such a path.[7]

In Gramscian terms, the first element required that the hegemony of the ruling bloc be refurbished along dramatically new lines and become based on inclusive principles.[8] This implied a major risk: that the main political force in the democratic movement (the ANC) could be saddled with the task of salvaging South African capitalism by accepting and then managing a historic class compromise. As indicated, the ANC's history had not equipped it with an intrinsic aversion to such a role. As a liberation movement its struggle orbited around the ideals of democracy and civil rights. Its remarkable political unity had been cemented partially by consigning the class dimension to the margins of its analyses, which located the core fount of oppression and inequality in the apartheid state. The key to liberation, therefore, lay in a process of political transformation which centred on the winning of state power, which would serve as a *deus ex machina,* enabling it to gradually vanquish social and economic inequalities.

The negotiations process rested, therefore, on the fact that similar *methodological* predispositions had emerged in the ANC, and in the apartheid state and capital. In short, a convergence had occurred around the need to recast the *political* and *ideological* bases of state power. The major differences revolved around the extent to which the terms of this process would break and/or maintain continuities with the past. The ANC's historical privileging of the *political* over the economic[9] allowed for the possibility of a settlement based on significant restructuring of the political sphere, and broad continuity in the economic sphere. For obvious reasons, the restructuring could not be imposed unilaterally by the incumbent state but had to be negotiated with the political opposition – a perilous venture, nonetheless.

The NP maintained crucial advantages. It still controlled the state apparatus (not the least its repressive machinery which had been augmented by an assortment of covert and allied forces which became euphemized as the 'Third Force'), and retained the generalized support of the capitalist class. But negotiations launched the country into treacherous waters. The NP government could (be forced to) abandon the process and retreat into the defensive *laager* of the repressive state if the terms of the likely settlement seemed unacceptable. Likewise, the democratic movement could rekindle the insurrectionist fires of the mid-1980s and exploit the new space to try and topple the NP government and seize control of the state.[10] Active on the fringes, meanwhile, were increasingly militant white, ultra-right groupings, skittish homeland administrations, and, most ominously, an IFP institutionally ensconced in the KwaZulu homeland and militarily supported by security apparatuses.

The old and the new

'[T]his was a war without absolute winners ... the two major political forces in South Africa had fought to a draw,' the ANC's Govan Mbeki later wrote, 'And so it happened that the oppressor and the oppressed came together to chart the road to a democratic South Africa.'[11]

At hand was not the replacement of the old by the new, but their assimilation, according to terms that had yet to be established. In Morris' view:

> The negotiations process is not about a government negotiating its surrender because it was defeated by a superior force. It is not about an already cemented nation poised on the brink of decolonisation or the seizure of power. It is about a political struggle to forge a new nation and new alliances that can ensure the broadest basis of social consent. The opposition is not sweeping aside the old institutions of state power. It has to try and shape the terms on which it is incorporated into the state as a new ruling group (1993c:8).

An ensemble of factors seemed to indicate the boundaries of possible change – some of which were quite candidly itemized in a November 1992 paper by the ANC's National Executive Committee (NEC).[12] It noted that the government appeared highly divided but still commanded 'vast state and other military resources' and 'enjoyed the support of powerful economic forces'. The liberation movement, whilst having attained 'a very high level of mass mobilisation and mass defiance', was hamstrung by 'many organisational weaknesses' and a paucity of financial and military resources. These rendered it 'unable to militarily defeat the counter-revolutionary movement or adequately defend the people'. Meanwhile, the radically redrawn international context had increased pressures for a peaceful settlement that fell 'in line with the emerging international "culture" of multi-party democracy'.[13]

The NEC's conclusion was that this stalemate could best be surmounted through:

> ... a negotiations process combined with mass action and international pressure which takes into account the need to combat counter-revolutionary forces and at the same time uses phases in the transition to qualitatively change the balance of forces in order to secure a thorough-going democratic transition.[14]

It stressed that the balance of forces is 'not static'. But weighing heavily on the minds of the ANC leadership was the fear that South Africa could implode and fragment along the lines of the former Yugoslavia. Euphemizing this concern, the NEC declared that 'the new democratic government would need to adopt a wide range of measures in order to minimize the potential threat to the new democracy', some of which 'may have to be part and parcel of a negotiated settlement'.[15]

Evident here was the view that the ANC's moral and political weight would, during negotiations, be heavily mitigated by the perceived need to bring its main antagonists 'on board' through compromises which might rile many of its supporters. Yet, it had to reduce the risk of unleashing a sequence of events that could lead to civil war. Shadowing the ANC's negotiating positions would be the need to preserve the South African nation-state. According to SACP deputy general secretary (and ANC NEC member) Jeremy Cronin, so alarmed was the ANC by the perceived counter-revolutionary threat that:

> ... most of its energy went into trying to engage those forces ... We may have exaggerated the threat (our sources were often the government intelligence forces), but we shouldn't be complacent about the threat we were facing.[16]

For Cronin, the main political compromise eventually negotiated – the Government of National Unity (GNU) – has to be understood 'as an attempt to hold it all together and avoid a Bosnia'.

By late 1992, the ANC had geared itself to forging a political consensus through 'certain retreats from previously held positions which would create the possibility of a major positive breakthrough in the negotiating process without permanently hampering real democratic advance'.[17] Prominent among them was a 'sunset clause' providing for a period of compulsory power-sharing in the form the GNU, an offer not to purge the security forces and civil service of 'counter-revolutionary' elements, and the willingness to establish (during negotiations) a set of Constitutional Principles that could not be violated by the final Constitution.

This caused considerable consternation throughout the democratic movement. NEC member Pallo Jordan accused his colleagues of elevating negotiations to the level of strategy and warned that they risked giving 'away what we have won on [other] fronts' (1992a:15). SACP Central Committee member Blade Nzimande accused Slovo of developing a scenario in which 'the masses are absent and, instead, the issue becomes primarily that of trade-offs between negotiators, constrained by the logic of the negotiations process' (1992:20). Troubling both were signs that negotiations would replace the other traditional prongs of the ANC's struggle and produce a corporatist outcome cemented by an élite consensus. Many activists concurred. However, as writer Anthony Marx observed, the ANC's arsenal had been depleted:

> The ANC's suspension of its armed struggle and reorganisation of underground structures into legal entities, together with international pressure to end sanctions, had by early 1991 weakened three of the congress's 'four pillars of struggle', leaving mass mobilisation as its only remaining form of pressure on the state (1992:264).

Traumatic levels of violence provided the backdrop to these strategic debates. Fighting continued to rage in KwaZulu-Natal – ostensibly between ANC and IFP supporters. Transformed from a moribund cultural organization in 1975, Inkatha (the IFP), with a politically adroit Mangosuthu Buthelezi (a former ANC member) at the helm, achieved a 'political mobilization of ethnicity to compete for power and privilege'.[18] By manipulating Zulu history and identity, Buthelezi positioned Inkatha as the vehicle for rescuing what he portrayed as a proud but denigrated people and culture.[19] Controlling access to resources in the KwaZulu homeland (via a system of patronage deployed through the homeland administration and networks of appointed chiefs), Inkatha expanded its support in rural areas and extended it into some urban pockets. The strategy was assisted by Inkatha's control of the KwaZulu police and by the often overt support of the apartheid security forces.[20] When the UDF tried to unseat Inkatha-supporting chiefs in rural areas, a *de facto* civil war erupted – pitting the pan-ethnic, nationalist traditions of the ANC against the Zulu chauvinism advanced by Inkatha. This conflict continues today, overlapping and blending with other conflicts – although the tendency within the democratic movement has been to collapse this web of conflict for political, social and economic advantage into the rubric of the *political*.[21]

By the end of 1990, the death toll in political violence had risen 163 per cent over the already high 1989 figures. This was attributable largely to the IFP's attempts to expand its base into townships around Johannesburg. Massacres (such as the attacks on funeral vigils in Sebokeng, Alexandra and Soweto) became commonplace, as did terror attacks on train commuters. Many of the incidents showed evidence or indications of state complicity in the violence – prompting international human rights organizations to accuse the security forces of going about 'business as usual'.[22] Subsequent evidence[23] suggests that the strategy of low-intensity conflict, employed in neighbouring countries to devastating effect, was applied also inside South Africa through covert units such as the cynically named Civil Cooperation Bureau (CCB) and structures of Military Intelligence. These units exploited and exacerbated the multifold lines of tensions coursing through many African townships. Inkatha shock troops were trained in SADF bases and provided with arms, intelligence and logistical support. Reports abounded of police allowing marauding Inkatha gangs access to township areas, not intervening in the attacks or arresting the attackers. Apparently motiveless attacks on train commuters and taxis, combined with the violence of vigilante groups and warlords to severely destabilize African townships, creating a pervasive sense of insecurity, demoralization and disorganization. Attempts by residents and the ANC structures to marshall community defence units turned many townships on the East Rand and in KwaZulu-Natal into virtual war zones. Overlapping were other dynamics – competition for scarce resources, feuding between warlords and criminal gangs, disputes over the control of taxi routes, tensions between settled residents, squatters and hostel dwellers, political conflicts, and more. As Canadian analyst Pierre Beaudet noted, the enduring social and economic crisis thrust some social segments (notably among the youth) 'towards violence and greater marginalisation', making them 'the social base for the emergence of urban gangsterism and political warlordism' (1994:217). For millions of South Africans the constant threat and reality of violence became common-place.

The view that the NP government was following a 'twin-track strategy' – negotiating with the opposition while simultaneously attempting to destabi-lize it – became axiomatic within the ANC. The June 1992 Boipatong mas-sacre, in which 48 residents were slaughtered, eventually prompted the ANC to walk out of the Codesa negotiations. It launched a campaign of 'rolling mass action' which unofficially culminated in early September when Ciskei homeland troops mowed down ANC protestors outside Bisho. A mood of panic was palpable in ruling circles. Not only was the patchwork of political allies the NP government had tried to assemble around the nego-tiating table disintegrating,[24] but there was deep concern whether the ANC could 'control' its supporters, and resume negotiations. On the latter score, their fears were unfounded. The mass action campaign was halted when the NP signed a Record of Understanding with the ANC in late September, 1992. This not only salvaged but reconfigured the negotiations process to orbit primarily around the NP and ANC.[25] Consensus-building became the name of the game, directly giving rise to the strategic debates outlined here, with Joe Slovo's 'strategic perspectives' view holding sway to define the con-tours of the negotiated settlement. Meanwhile, Mandela had made his views of rank-and-file anger known:

> We are sitting on a time-bomb. The youths in the townships have had over the decades a visible enemy, the government. Now that enemy is no longer visible, because of the transformation taking place. Their enemy now is you and me, people who drive a car and have a house. It's order, anything that relates to order, and it is a very grave situation.[26]

The upshot was a strategic perspective that saddled the ANC with the responsibility of establishing a new political and social consensus – a mis-sion that would become elaborated into the ANC government's nation-building endeavours. At the micro-level, this produced specific political compromises which could later restrict the scope of changes desired by an ANC government.

Another consequence was more encompassing, however. A kind of short-term 'two-stage theory' emerged. Defining the ANC's negotiating strategy was the need to nurture compromises that could yield a settlement. This meant that the ANC – only temporarily, it believed – retreated from posi-tions necessary to establish and safeguard an institutional bedrock for a socio-economic programme that could weaken the structural foundations of the 'two-nation' society. The political/ideological project of nation-build-ing became paramount and supplanted – or at least overshadowed – the socio-economic features of the crisis. 'The tendencies propelling us towards a new 50 per cent solution,' Morris warned at the time, 'lie … in the down-playing of the social and economic fault lines in our society' – a tendency he detected throughout much of the democratic opposition's history (1993c:8). Societal crisis tended to be cast in political and not economic terms, spawning the assumption that once the political and constitutional issues were resolved, 'the dozing South African "economic giant" would lumber to its feet and cart us off to the land of promise' (Morris, 1993c:9). Nzimande was among the few alliance figures to draw public attention to this legacy. Quoting Mexican sociologist Carlos Vilas, he reminded that:

> … most important about 'transitions' [initiated by previously repressive regimes] is that 'they do not project into the economic sphere, nor do they provide a framework for any substantial changes in the level of access of sub-ordinate groups to socio-economic resources – by income redistribution, creating employment, improving living conditions, etc.'.[27]

Outlines of the settlement

Interrupted periodically by deadlocks and brinkmanship, three years of formal negotiations ended in late 1993 with a political settlement that detoured significantly from the positions held by both the NP and ANC at the beginning of the process.

The political basis of post-apartheid South Africa would be a liberal-democratic system, as defined in an interim Constitution agreed to in late 1993. Completed and adopted in 1996, the final Constitution replicates much of the 1993 version – with the exception of refinements and nuanced changes introduced in some areas, notably on property rights, access to information, minority rights and the delegation of powers to provincial governments.

The new system is based on universal suffrage in a unitary South Africa; the separation of legislative, executive and judicial powers; multiparty elections every five years; gradual (and circumscribed) delegation of power from central to local levels of government; and the enshrinement of individual and collective rights in a Bill of Rights that ranks among the most progressive in the world.

A Constitutional Court adjudicates disputes arising from the constitution. Parliament comprises two houses: a National Assembly (400 members) and a National Council of Provinces (10 members from each of the nine new provinces). Several parastatal bodies would be created to monitor and advance implementation of the Constitution. These include a Public Protector's Office (to ensure democratic and ethical practices in the public service), a Human Rights Commission, a Commission on Gender Equality, an Electoral Commission (to help organize democratic elections), an

Independent Broadcasting Authority (to regulate the electronic media), an Auditor-General, and a Cultural Commission (to protect minority cultural rights).

The final Constitution had to comply with a set of 33 binding Constitutional Principles[28] which crystallized important compromises agreed to in the final stages of negotiations. Altering these principles requires a two-thirds majority in a constitutional assembly (Parliament). They demand, for instance, that:

- the 'diversity of language and culture' be protected;
- 'collective rights of self-determination in forming, joining and maintaining organs of civil society' be recognized and protected;
- 'the institution, status and role of traditional leadership' be recognized (possibly undermining the commitment to democratic representation at all levels of government);
- exclusive and concurrent powers and functions be delegated to provincial governments;
- national government be prevented from exercising its powers in ways that 'encroach upon the geographical, functional or institutional integrity of the provinces';
- minority parties be enabled to participate in the legislative process; and
- the 'independence and impartiality' of the Reserve Bank be protected.[29]

The Bill of Rights outlaws discrimination on the grounds of 'race, gender, sex, pregnancy, marital status, ethnic or social origin, colour, sexual orientation, age, disability, religion, conscience, belief, culture, language or birth'. It also allows for the declaration of states of emergency under certain circumstances.

Most dramatic was the postponement of majority rule to 1999. Until then, the country would be governed by the GNU, with executive power shared between political parties that won more than five per cent of the popular vote (the ANC, NP and IFP, as it turned out). Consensus-making was thus formalized within the executive in the hope of establishing political stability.

The system contains significant federal elements, reflecting the ANC's belated conversion to the belief that the country requires 'strong national government for national tasks, strong regional government for regional tasks, strong local government for local tasks', in the words of the ANC's Albie Sachs. At the insistence of the NP, IFP and Democratic Party (DP), key powers will be exercised exclusively or concurrently by provincial governments (for instance, provincial governments are forbidden to budget for a deficit but can decide on the allocation of monies within certain parameters). Critics felt this threatened the authority of the central government. But it represented a coup for the NP and IFP, providing each the chance to secure a solid institutional and administrative base in the 1994 election, when the NP triumphed in the Western Cape and the IFP in KwaZulu-Natal. Still, this did not meet the confederate demands of the IFP, which responded by boycotting the final Constitution drafting process.

The terms of the settlement also reflected the influence of forces outside the multiparty negotiations, specifically the IFP and the white far-right. In both cases the destabilizing pressures they exerted were welcomed (if not encouraged) and deflected by the NP onto the ANC. As a result, the ANC made some surprising concessions in the final stages of negotiations.

As part of its attempts to defuse right-wing reaction, it allowed a racist guarantee which reserved 30 per cent of the seats in some local government structures for minorities.[30] According to some interpretations it also afforded minority representatives in municipal councils a 'formal veto over redistributive budgets'.[31] The ANC agreed to support the investigation of the feasibility of an Afrikaner homeland ('volkstaat') by the far-right. Fearful of disloyalty in the security forces, the party also agreed to an amnesty which allows human rights violators to evade criminal and civil action court cases – on the condition that amnesty seekers fully disclose their crimes. Drawing on recent Latin American experiments, a Truth and Reconciliation Commission (TRC) was chosen as a potentially less destabilizing method to pursue human rights abuses (the TRC began functioning in April 1996). The powers of the Zulu monarchy and, less publicly, other traditional leaders through the country were protected, lending politicized ethnicity a menacing lease of life while also threatening to diminish and delay democratization in rural areas. The NP had demanded an 'education clause', allowing parents and students to choose the language of instruction in state or state-assisted schools; eventually, the ANC agreed to a compromise clause guaranteeing that right where it could 'reasonably be provided'. Finally, the ANC agreed to refrain from purging the civil service, thus leaving intact much of the institutional culture and personnel of the old order.[32]

Capital succeeded in fashioning, among others, a crucial detail of the settlement: the Bill of Rights sports a clause protecting property rights. Although diluted in the final Constitution, this limits the circumstances in which the state can expropriate privately-owned property, narrows the scope of a land reform programme[33] and reduces the redistributive options of an ANC government.

The settlement favours capital in another, less obvious respect. The justiciable Bill of Rights provides for constitutional litigation as a pathway towards sabotaging or holding up attempts to push ahead with socio-economic reforms that transcend the boundaries patrolled by capital.[34] Furthermore, the 'independence' of the Reserve Bank (historically intimately attuned and subservient to the needs of capital) now enjoys constitutional protection.[35]

Despite these limitations, the settlement represented a political milestone which, justifiably, earned the admiration and envy of citizens and governments internationally. A seemingly intractable and potentially catastrophic conflict had been resolved, yielding a constitution that ranked among the most liberal in the world. It included guarantees of the right to collective bargaining, to strike (although limited to collective bargaining issues and counterposed by employers' right to lock-out striking workers), to freedom of expression, speech and assembly, to privacy, equality before the law, access to information and to sexual orientation, opening new pathways towards freedom and equality. 'I think we've reached an effective instrument for governing the country, one that does not in any way constitute an obstacle to the process of completely transforming the country into a democratic state,' was ANC and SACP leader Joe Slovo's understandably blithe verdict in early 1994.[36]

The settlement paved the way for the historic 1994 elections which, despite far-right bombing campaigns during the run-up, were not marred by the anticipated bloodshed. The ANC won a landslide victory. Its 62,7 per cent of the vote earned it 252 of the 400 National Assembly seats, putting it well clear of the NP (20,4 per cent of the vote) and the IFP (10,5 per cent).[37] In some provinces, the ANC's share of ballots rose as high as 90 per cent.

Less joyous results awaited the ANC in KwaZulu-Natal and the Western Cape, however. The NP's appeal to coloured and white voters in the Western Cape handed it control of that provincial government in post-apartheid South Africa. The outcome in KwaZulu-Natal was more controversial. Weathering complaints of chaotic logistics and widespread fraud, the Independent Electoral Commission adjusted the results to reflect an allegedly projected outcome. The IFP won the province, its 50 per cent share of votes outstripping the ANC's 32 per cent. To prevent widespread violence in the province, the ANC's national leadership suppressed furious demands by its provincial colleagues that the result be challenged in court.

The results confirmed the ANC's status as by far the most popular and the only national party in South Africa. Even where vanquished, it won a third of the votes, a feat no other party could match. Political and symbolically the threshold of a new South Africa had been crossed.

Hidden contours of the transition

The task assumed by the ANC was to construct and administer a hegemonic project that would be based on a radical break with the exclusionary paradigms enforced under apartheid. The principles of conciliation and concession replaced conflict and triumph as the key catalysts for societal change. Abandoned were visions of change that centred on momentary historical ruptures, the seizure of power, the destruction of the old, and the construction, *ab initio*, of the new. The exclusionary basis of South African society would be replaced with an inclusionary one. The partitioning of South Africa into confederal units was abandoned, likewise the deprival of citizenship and the franchise to the African majority. A century-old ideological model was discarded. This notwithstanding the attempts of the IFP and right-wing Afrikaner organizations to establish federal units – respectively, KwaZulu-Natal and an unspecified 'Afrikaner homeland'.

One cannot underestimate the profundity of these conceptual sea-changes, as Mike Morris has noted:

> All the secure landmarks of the past, the defining features and political geography of the apartheid regime and its counterpart in the liberation movement ... started to crumble. Instead of revolution, negotiation; instead of uncompromising transformation, compromising concession; instead of a violent struggle for the seizure of power, negotiation over the distribution of power; instead of sweeping aside the old order and all who had implemented it, dismantling the old order jointly with its old architects; instead of radical exclusion of the old to the benefit of the new, inclusion of both old and new in a newly created social framework (1993a:11).

The dominant discourse came to orbit around postulated common interests and destinies – rather than difference, contradiction and antagonism – as the fundamental dynamics at work in society. Commonalities (whether authentic or invented) are emphasized and amplified in service of a hegemonic project which, for the first time in South Africa's history, seeks to organize society on the basis of inclusion.

The settlement and the launch of the transition depended on an activated awareness of 'common interests' between the old order and the popular movement – on an acknowledgment that friend and foe have to pass through a gateway of concessions and compromises in order to avert disaster for their respective agendas. This principle of inclusion became the central ideological tenet of the new South Africa. Not only were all South Africans deemed equal in one nation-state, but the reconstruction and development of society would become presented as a common endeavour, hence the intense pressure on the popular sector to 'exercise restraint' in its demands and pursuit of change. The transition proceeded on the basis of mechanisms and structures that attempt to 'reconcile' – even *transform* – conflicting interests into inclusive policies, projects and programmes.

Essentially, this amounted to an attempt to forge a new basis for social consent – an essential ingredient of any sustainable bid to restructure South African society, whether along unequal or more egalitarian lines. The impulse of some leftists to detect in the very principles of inclusion, assimilation and conciliation the seeds of a betrayal and sell-out was wrong.[38] In themselves these principles did not scuttle attempts to marshall a popular transformation project. What mattered were the terms on which inclusion and assimilation occurred – specifically, which social classes' interests would become privileged in the resultant hegemonic project. In the South Africa of 1994, the class content of that project was still undefined. However, as we shall see, several telling clues had emerged.

Evident soon after the 1994 election was a conviction that – in a capitalist country in the post-1989 world – the appeasement of domestic and, crucially, international capital had become unavoidable. Nelson Mandela soon assured investors that 'not a single reference to things like nationalisation' remained in ANC economic policies and that these had been cleansed of anything 'that will connect us with any Marxist ideology'.[39]

Months later Mandela lambasted striking workers in the auto and service sectors for causing instability and putting their interests above those of their compatriots. The auto strike was abruptly called off when the trade and industry minister, with cunning timing, announced the pruning of protective tariffs in that sector. These and other developments (like the property rights clause, the earlier signing of an IMF Letter of Intent, and increasingly strident commitments to macro-economic 'stability') prompted the SACP's Jeremy Cronin to acknowledge that 'real inroads have been made by capital into the ANC ... their arguments are more attractive and more persuasive to a wide range of ANC leadership than the counter-arguments that are less confident, less coherent'.[40]

Not only the counter-arguments were at fault. The ANC negotiated the settlement without a vivid programme geared at dismantling the structural foundations of the 'Two Nation' society.[41] Indeed it was in recognition of this lacuna that trade unionists devised the Reconstruction and Development Programme (RDP), which became touted as the hub of a strategic programme and was adopted by the ANC shortly before the 1994 election. However, the transformative thrust of the RDP was soon dispersed as the ANC sheared its potentially conflictual elements and refashioned it along ostensibly consensual lines.[42]

What the ANC did bring into office was its adeptness at nurturing and consolidating hegemony, which, in the post-1994 context, would be extended to include a much wider range of class forces. As Cronin observed:

> It might be historically equipped to tackle that project, but the problem is whether it is now equipped to be the central vehicle to take forward this transformation project, to deepen the democratic revolution or achieve social-economic transformation.[43]

Once it became the programme of government, the RDP did not represent a coherent strategic programme for popular transformation. Indeed, though for different reasons, it is questionable whether even the vaunted Base

Document did. Neither would the state be re-oriented around a definable social base. The ANC has been *assimilated* into a web of institutional relations, systems and practices tailored to service the interests of (in the first instance) white privilege and (in the final instance) the capitalist class. Compared with its predecessor, the relative autonomy of the democratic state has perhaps *diminished*, further curtailing the ANC's ability to redistribute opportunity, infrastructural resources, access to productive activity and institutional power in favour of the popular classes.

The settlement and the 1994 elections in some respects created and in others *punctuated* marked shifts in South African society. The salient achievement was to resolve the political dimension of South Africa's crisis – an outcome desired by both the democratic opposition and the capitalist class. But an organic solution to the crisis required more than revising the political basis for hegemonic consent. It also demanded co-ordinated social and economic restructurings – a new development path.

Left unanswered by the settlement was the fundamental question: Which social and economic interests would be privileged by that path? In Morris' words:

> Will the new society perpetuate the highly divisive social elitism of the past, but on a more non-racial basis? Or will it tend towards a more egalitarian system that strives to muffle inherited frictions by redistributing resources and institutional power? (1993c:8)

Broadly sketched, the answer would launch the country in one of two possible directions. The first would see the gradual dismantlement of the country's 'Two Nation' character through the redistribution of resources, power and security in favour of the 'outsiders'. It is on the basis of such strategies that a new, expansive hegemony could be achieved. The other option would entrench the 'Two Nation' society in which a small, increasingly multiracial enclave of privilege and a massive, impoverished majority co-exist precariously. Social and economic restructuring would benefit narrow layers of society, whilst the costs of that restructuring would be deflected onto the rest of society. Building and maintaining political hegemony is a prerequisite for the success of such a venture and becomes paramount – and would be expressed mainly in the forms of nation-building initiatives. But the basis of that hegemony would gradually become whittled down to the mobilized support of the main beneficiaries of the new growth path, eventually introducing the need to resort to overt coercion.

The convivial ideology underpinning the settlement did not settle or suspend the intense contest to determine which of those outcomes would materialize. That contest continued but on reshaped terrain, in new ways and on new terms. These factors were manifold: the political breakthroughs of the settlement, the opening of new political and social spaces for activity, the assimilation of the new into the old, the ostensible shift from conflict to conciliation, the restructuring of state-civil society relations, the realignment of affinities along class and other lines (even among customary allies in the democratic movement), weakened ideological cohesion and confidence among the democratic forces, South Africa's weak standing in the global economic system, and more. Together they would radically affect the struggles to determine the course and scale of change.

Understood in this manner, the settlement constituted (and inaugurated) not a rupture but a highly ambivalent (and nonetheless dramatic) series of reconfigurations that also extended far beyond the formal political agreements. In some respects these shifts favoured the popular forces; in others they introduced new, or magnified existing difficulties and challenges.

If negotiations started because, as Govan Mbeki noted, 'this was a war without absolute winners'[44] then they also ended without producing a clear victor. This was so not only because of the compromises that produced the settlement. Most importantly, the settlement reshaped the political and ideological bases and affinities on which would proceed the ongoing struggles to determine the nature of a new development path. In short, 1994 marked a sea-change – but in ways and to degrees that far exceeded conventional assumptions.

Notes

1 Anon (1990:10).
2 See, In particular, Friedman (1993b), Sparks (1994), Mandela (1994).
3 Cassius Mandla, *Sechaba* (November, 1985), cited by Lodge (1989:46).
4 Erwin (1989:47). Having apparently abandoned such prescriptions, Erwin was appointed minister of trade and industry in March 1996.
5 Bottomore (1983:195), paraphrasing Gramsci.
6 See Morris and Padayachee (1989); Morris (1993c).
7 See Chapter 5 of this volume.
8 *A hegemonic project* could be defined as 'societally projected policies aimed at concretely resolving particular conflicting (primarily class) interests by defining a socially acceptable national general interest' (Morris & Padayachee, 1989:67).
9 To the extent that, until 1990, it had no economic policy worthy of the description – see below.
10 Memories remained fresh of the events that followed the marginal opening of political space during the early 1980s. Those fears were amplified by the discovery, in 1990, of the ANC-run Operation Vula – essentially a bid to enable the swift resort to underground activities if the negotiations process were abandoned.
11 Mbeki (1996:119). Note Mbeki's retroactive application of the inclusionary rhetoric that would become elaborated in the ANC's nation-building efforts.
12 ANC NEC (1992:48–53).
13 *Op. cit.*
14 *Ibid.*, p. 50.
15 *Ibid.*, p. 53.
16 Comments made to the 'Prospects and Constraints for Transformation' seminar in Johannesburg, November 1994.

17 Slovo (1992:37). Initially Slovo's 'own individual contribution' to debates in the ANC alliance, this perspective was soon adopted by the ANC leadership. See, for instance, the October 1992 'Strategic Perspectives' document drafted by the ANC Negotiations Commission.

18 Mare (1992:3). See also Mare and Hamilton (1987) and Forsythe and Mare (1992).

19 A comprehensive account of the many factors that propelled Inkatha's transformation remains to be written. Hopefully, it will include an examination of the ANC's treatment of ethnic identity and a recognition of Inkatha's historical origins in the racist repression of the Zulu *petit bourgeoisie* early in the century. On the latter score, see Cope (1990).

20 Buthelezi in 1985 – two years before the conflict erupted – approached security force leaders for military assistance. In response, the R3,5-million Operation Marion was launched, following a meeting of the State Security Council. A group of 200 Inkatha members received military training at Hippo Camp in the Caprivi Strip and were sent into action against UDF and COSATU supporters in KwaZulu-Natal, with ongoing support from the police and army. These events formed the basis of the trial of 13 top security officials in 1996.

21 See the Human Rights' Commission's 1991 booklet *A New Total Strategy* for a good example of this tendency. For an alternative perspective, see Hindson and Morris (1992:43–59).

22 The violence has been extensively researched and analysed. For examples, see Africa Watch (1991); Human Rights Commission (1991); Everatt (1992); Morris and Hindson (1992). For an overview of the debates, see Marais (1992a).

23 Emerging from the TRC's hearings since April 1996.

24 Its alliance with the IFP ended after the suspension of negotiations.

25 The first Codesa session saw the absurd spectacle of minuscule political parties (dubbed 'one-phone-and-a-fax' parties by observers) accorded nominally equal negotiating weight to the major parties.

26 *The Star*, 15 September 1992, cited by Bond *et al.* (1996:37).

27 Nzimande (1992:17). The quote was drawn from Vilas (1989).

28 The Constitutional Court in September 1996 refused to uphold the final Constitution agreed to four months earlier because it violated some of those principles. Altered accordingly, the Constitution came into effect in December 1996.

29 See 'Schedule 4: Constitutional Principles' of the 1993 *Interim Constitution*, pp. 244–9.

30 Ironically, this recalled the 'group rights' guarantees initially demanded by the NP.

31 See Bond *et al.* (1996:38).

32 Whether this concession was in fact made remains a point of debate. ANC MP Philip Dexter, for instance, has argued that 'nowhere [in the Interim Constitution] is there anv guarantee of jobs'. Instead, 'the continuity of public *service*' was guaranteed. See Dexter (1995a:55–7).

33 See Marais (1994b).

34 Of course, it is also available for the defence and advance of popular agendas – an exaggerated potential, however, as the flirtations of popular movements in industrialized countries with constitutionalism have reminded.

35 For a survey of this debate, see Bowles and White (1993).

36 Interview, 'Don't worry, be happy', *Work in Progress*, No. 95 (Feb/March 1994), p. 17.

37 The PAC collapsed in the contest, garnering a mere 1,3 per cent of the vote – less than the urban and largely white DP's 1,7 per cent and the right-wing Freedom Front's 2,2 per cent.

38 See, for instance, Bond *et al.* (1996).

39 Interview published on May Day, 1994, in the *Sunday Times*.
40 Interview with author, October 1994.
41 The ANC's Albie Sachs (now a Constitutional Court judge) admitted as much in late 1993, saying that the ANC had 'no analytical framework at all' and had been reduced to 'merely improvising'. See 'Preparing Ourselves for Power' (interview with Sachs), *Southern Africa Report*, Vol. 9, No. 2 (November 1993), p. 15.
42 The RDP draft the ANC carried into office was an outline for such a programme. Its eventual fate would reflect, at least provisionally, the outcome of the struggle to determine the class bias of an ANC-managed hegemonic project.
43 Jeremy Cronin, interview with author, October 1994.
44 Mbeki (1996:119).

CHAPTER FOUR

The battleground of the economy

South Africa entered the transition with an economy buckled by almost two decades of steadily worsening difficulties that manifested in earnest after the 1973 oil shock. Mainstream economists sought solace in ephemeral cyclical upswings (notably the gold-led boom of 1979–80 and the fleeting consumption-led upturn of 1983–4). But key indicators betrayed the onset of a structural crisis, which Stephen Gelb (1991:6; 1994:3–4) detected in:

- The feeble GDP growth rate, which descended from its 5,5 per cent average during the 1960s to 1,8 per cent in the 1980s, eventually plunging into the negative range (–1,1 per cent) in the early 1990s.[1]
- Declining rates of gross fixed investment (which plunged as low as –18,6 per cent in 1986, and stayed negative from 1990 to 1993) and high rates of capital flight.
- Low rates of private investment, which led to under-utilization of manufacturing plant capacity (dropping from 90 per cent in 1981 to 78 per cent in 1993) and declining competitiveness.
- Plummeting levels of personal savings, which, as a proportion of disposable income, dropped from 11 per cent in 1975 to 3 per cent in 1987.
- Very high unemployment and the economy's inability to create enough new jobs to absorb even a fraction of new entrants into the labour market,[2] a trend exacerbated by under-investment in labour-intensive sectors.
- Chronic balance of payments difficulties.

In broad terms, the crisis reflected the breakdown of the post-war accumulation strategy based on primary product exports and inward industrialization (including import-substitution) based on a violently regimented labour supply. The latter feature fuelled increasingly powerful cycles of resistance that ultimately required the profound restructuring of the social, political and ideological basis of this strategy. It also imposed structural limits on the growth of domestic demand, inhibited productivity and led to a severe shortage of skilled labour.

Export earnings remained largely dependent on raw materials (mainly minerals) and were vulnerable to exchange rate fluctuations and fluctuating commodity prices, particularly the gold price that began dropping sharply in 1982.[3] South Africa did not evade the trend, evident in other industrial-izing countries, whereby even short periods of sustained economic growth deepened reliance on imported capital goods, leading to balance of payment problems. As Kaplan noted, the country's capital goods sector performed relatively well until the early 1970s when its expansion slowed profoundly – with 'adverse repercussions on the balance of payments, on the development of skills, and the generation and diffusion of more pro-ductive technologies through the wider economy' (1991:176).

In the throes of a balance of payments crisis, the NP government in 1982 sought an International Monetary Fund (IMF) standby loan of R1,24 bil-lion.[4] Shortly afterwards, exchange controls were lifted for non-residents, triggering a large outflow of capital, which swelled further during the 1984–7 uprisings. Compounding this were the financial sanctions of the late 1980s that saw international creditors refusing to roll-over loans or issue new ones. Fiscal spending soared and the budget deficit increased as the state sought to meet its external 'defence' and internal 'law and order' needs and bankrolled its reform initiatives. Against this backdrop, fixed investment levels crumpled from 26,5 per cent of GDP in 1983 to well below 20 per cent in the late 1980s (eventually dropping to 15,7 per cent in 1993).[5] By 1990, net investment was hovering near the zero mark (Gelb, 1994:2).

The economy was bedridden. Partially in compliance with the IMF's prescriptions, the apartheid state responded by applying severe deflationary measures. It tightened monetary policies, hoisted interest rates to encour-age savings (with scant success), froze consumer subsidies and off-loaded the fiscal burden onto the poor by increasing indirect taxation. The overall effect was to lower living standards – one of the often overlooked dynamics that fuelled the 1984–7 uprisings.[6] The government also introduced a dual exchange rate mechanism in a bid to stem capital outflows.

The adjustments, however, failed to address the structural factors hobbling the economy:

- Low investment rates, linked with the tendency of the private sector to direct its funds abroad.
- A shortage of skilled and a surplus of unskilled, poorly educated and low-productivity labour – the cumulative result of business treating 'black workers as a replaceable factor of production rather than as a human resource'.[7]
- Poor, conflict-ridden industrial relations.
- The state's failure to reverse the latter trend by encouraging or com-pelling productive investment by business, which 'has led to an orgy of

speculative investment and the shrinking of the manufacturing sector in the past 20 years'.[8]

- Industrial decay, which was reflected in ageing capital stock, limited capital goods production and the failure to develop exports by beneficiating raw materials and expanding the scope of the manufacturing sector. This compounded the poor export performance in manufactures, compared to other middle-income countries. Matters improved slightly during the early 1990s, but without reflecting a 'fundamental shift in underlying conditions', according to the Macro-Economic Research Group (MERG) (1993:212).
- Low investment in research and development, with most technological development occurring in the armaments and telecommunications industries.
- A heavy bias against the small and medium-sized business sector.
- Maldistribution of social infrastructure (such as housing, education facilities, health care and transport), which restricted labour productivity.
- Rampant poverty, entrenched by a very high unemployment rate, which stifled productive potential and domestic demand for manufactured goods, the latter having been depressed by deflationary policies.

The effects of these inherited weaknesses worsened during the negotiations period. Between early 1989 and late 1993, the economy sank into its longest-ever recession, registering negative real economic growth until 1993, when a strong upturn in agricultural production (after the acute 1991–2 drought) brought some respite. The mood among economic élites was unreservedly downcast, with Reserve Bank governor Chris Stals warning that the country would plunge into ungovernability by 1996 if the annual growth rate remained at around 1 per cent while the population grew by 2,5 per cent.[9]

Other macro-economic indicators confirmed the gravity of the situation. Ominously, real fixed investment growth remained negative (improving slightly from −7,4 per cent in 1991 to −3,1 per cent in 1993). Private (non-housing) investment amounted to 10 per cent of GDP, well below the 16 per cent deemed necessary to sustain positive economic growth. Domestic savings stood at 16,5 per cent of GDP in mid-1994, down from the 24 per cent mark (achieved in the 1980s) the Reserve Bank calculated was needed for an annual economic growth rate of 3,5 per cent. Per capita disposable income continued to decline (by −11 per cent in real terms between 1980 and 1993).[10]

The impact of these trends was graphically visible in the performances of each economic sector, with disastrous effects on employment levels. The precise unemployment rate is controversial, though. The Ministry of Finance in the early 1990s pegged it at 19,3 per cent; a South African Labour and Development Research Unit (SALDRU) survey put it at about 30 per cent in 1993, the 1994 October Household Survey found it to be 32,6 per cent, while some analysts believe it is closer to 50 per cent. The ILO, using a 'strict' definition, believes it is below 20 per cent, 'still a very high figure [which] should not be belittled'.[11] More than 400 000 formal sector jobs were lost (excluding agriculture) between 1989 and 1993;[12] almost 8 in every 100 positions became redundant.[13] The trend was long term: the labour absorption capacity of the economy declined from 97 per cent in the 1960s, to 22 per cent in the 1980s, to 7 per cent between 1985 and 1990.[14]

The manufacturing sector was in the doldrums. Local demand remained sluggish and the sector failed to penetrate export markets – indeed, between 1960 and 1988, manufactured products' share of total exports slumped from 31 per cent to 12 per cent, while growth in manufacturing output in the same period dropped from 9,9 per cent to –1,2 per cent.[15] One result was massive labour attrition from the early 1980s onwards leading to the loss of 200 000 jobs in the metal and related sectors alone since 1982.[16]

The mining sector, responsible for 65,6 per cent of export earnings in 1991, shed 30 per cent of its workforce between 1987 and 1995, with employment levels tumbling from 752 460 to 512 722. Responding to low commodity prices on the world market, companies shut or scaled down mines they viewed as marginal and unprofitable. Employment levels in the two largest sectors (gold and coal) shrank by 35 per cent and 47 per cent, respectively. The platinum sector showed a 7 per cent increase.[17] Analysts expected mining employment to continue dropping, largely due to the sector's vulnerability to 'international economic fluctuations and competition', the lack of major gold fields discoveries and the fact that 'marginal mines become viable or not by virtue of small changes in the gold price' (ILO, 1996:279).

Agriculture's contribution to GDP dropped steadily, from 9 per cent (1965) to 6 per cent (1988), causing an estimated 30 per cent drop in employment over the same period (SAIRR, 1992:396). In the 1990s, farmers sacked hundreds of thousands more, in anticipation of new legislation aimed at bolstering the rights of rural workers and labour tenants. The sector remained hampered by periodic droughts, low levels of return on investment, low levels of liquidity and a steady build-up of debt.

The negligible welfare provisions for unemployed Africans resulted in income-earners supporting more jobless family members and friends, forcing them to make more stern demands for higher-than-inflation wage increases.[18] Nominal wages increased, but fell in the early 1990s (from 18,3 per cent in 1989 to 11,1 per cent in 1993) and put extra strain on such cross-subsidization as a makeshift safety net.

Meanwhile, the decline of the formal economy was accompanied by the exponential rise of an underground economy, commonly referred to as crime. A 1996 Nedcor survey claimed that crime cost the country R31,3 billion, ignoring the fact that the bulk of this money continued to circulate in the economy in ways that ranged from basic consumption to real estate and productive investment (shopping complexes in rural towns, transport firms, small- and medium-scale enterprises, retail outlets, etc.).

One potentially positive factor was the country's relatively low *external* debt to GDP ratio. In 1990, this stood at 27,3 per cent – 'lower than for any Latin American country in that year, with the exception of Chile, [and] lower than for all ASEAN countries' (ILO, 1996:31). By 1994, it had dropped to 22,9 per cent. The country, therefore, had not yet stepped into a 'debt trap' – leaving the new government some latitude in devising an alternative economic strategy.

Balance of payments problems persisted, as the lifting of sanctions and expectations of an economic upturn precipitated an increase in imports (largely luxury items and new machinery and technology). Great faith was staked on a sharp rise in foreign capital inflows off-setting these difficulties. That hope stemmed partially from a belief that the disinvestment of the 1980s had been strictly politically motivated. Less uplifting were the reminders from Blumenfeld, among others, that the reasons lay elsewhere. South Africa had become an unprofitable zone for investment, as:

> ...rand-denominated profits had been significantly reduced by the long-running recession, and, via the falling external value of the rand, there had been further serious reductions in attributable foreign currency value of these profits. In short, the fundamental problem of the relationship between political risk and financial rate of return ... had finally reasserted itself with a vengeance.[19]

In response, South Africa's caretaker government (the Transitional Executive Council, which included the ANC) in late 1993 approached the IMF for a $850 million five-year loan in terms of a special facility for countries suffering balance of payment problems. Surprising many observers, the government signed a controversial letter of intent, which, as Padayachee recorded, 'was at pains to point to the dangers of increases in real wages in the private and public sector [and] stressed the need to control inflation, promised monetary targeting, trade and industrial liberalization, and repeatedly espoused the virtues of "market forces" over "regulatory interventions" '.[20] Several economists argued that the IMF would have accepted a less conservative letter of intent.

Clearly visible in that letter were the parameters of the dominant discourse around 'realistic' options for economic restructuring. The NP government and important sections of big business had since the late 1980s already begun implementing elements of a neoliberal accumulation strategy. This attempted to restrict the state's involvement in the economy by withdrawing it from the provision of goods and services (through privatization programmes, deregulation and fiscal stringency) and by limiting its role to establishing the broad economic parameters that could optimize the operation of market forces (Gelb, 1991:29–30). The continuation of that strategy, though, was by no means guaranteed.

A flood of economic scenarios and policy frameworks was generated while political negotiations proceeded. Business organizations spearheaded this flurry of interventions, aided by the dominance of neoliberal ideology, as they sought to forestall the possible adoption of a new economic strategy that might be predicated on increased controls over capital. These intercessions meshed neatly with a political strategy that could meet the demands for majority rule – but, as Morris foresaw, with minimal concessions to demands for restructuring the economic and social spheres in favour of the black majority:

> The thrust of this strategy would be to establish hegemonic consent by politically appealing to the material interests of those classes of the black population who are to become the greatest beneficiaries of a '50 percent solution'. Those on the other side of the divide would be symbolically accommodated but their material needs would not be systematically catered for (1991:57).

Some redistribution would occur, but 'on a differential basis, and over a relatively long time-scale', Morris predicted with great prescience.[21]

South Africa in the world system

Essentially, South Africa's economy combines three chief features, two of which are endemic to middle-income developing countries. It is heavily reliant on commodity exports for foreign exchange, and it has an industrial sector that is arrested in the semi-industrialized phase (marked by the standard ensemble of attendant factors such as low productivity, limited skills base, ageing plants and, hence, large surplus capacity, a preponderant dependency on capital goods imports, etc.). The other feature – developed information, communications and transport systems – sets it apart from most other developing countries and is commonly likened, in sophistication (though not necessarily efficiency), to those associated with First World countries. But the claim seems somewhat hyperbolic. On those fronts, South Africa can more accurately be categorized somewhere between countries such as South Korea or Taiwan, and Brazil.

Prevalent, too, is the nostalgic belief that the country at one stage was situated in the mainstream of the global economic community – a revisionist fantasy that lacks supportive evidence – and the sibling contention that from the 1960s onwards it became progressively delinked from the world economy. Required, in that view, was the introduction of a set of 'normalizing' adjustments that would bring the economy in line with 'the global consensus' and launch it towards deeper and more advantageous integration into the world economy.

The claim rang truer for the diplomatic, cultural and sports arenas than for the economic sphere. Despite the hobbling effect of sanctions in trade and investment fields, a great deal of the South African economy remained outward-looking – principally its mineral and agricultural sectors. Its industrial sector failed to stay apace with new technological developments largely because of the structural decline of the economy since the 1970s, which generated chronic balance of payments problems and foreign exchange squeezes. It was only in the mid-1980s that access to new technologies and international loan finance was significantly affected by international sanctions. Meanwhile, its core economic sector – mining – continued to draw large portions of its labour needs from beyond South Africa's borders. In summary, the image of an economy structured along autarchic lines is not corroborated by the facts.

In truth, South Africa had been integrated into the world economy along lines similar to most other semi-industrialized developing countries. In one respect, however, its post-1945 growth path did acquire an inward-looking bias: in the production of luxury, consumer durables. These sections of industry were parochial only insofar as the production and/or assembly of products was concerned; capital goods and a high percentage of components were still imported from abroad. A more accurate description, therefore, would speak of a 'a pedestrian middle income developing country' which 'does not add up to a great deal in global economic league tables'.[22]

South Africa's incorporation into the world economy remained largely unchanged for most of the century, and rested on three, narrow pillars: as a primary product (mainly minerals) exporter, an importer of capital goods and technology, and a net recipient of indirect portfolio investment and direct foreign investment by multinational corporations.[23] Trend swings occurred in each of these aspects, but they reflected the essence of the country's incorporation into the world economy. The major and hugely problematic change was that, following the debt crisis of 1985, South Africa became a net exporter of capital.

The similarities with many Latin American countries were striking. Like them, South Africa followed the model of state-led industrialization and import-substitution propagated by Raul Prebish in the 1950s. On both sides of the Atlantic, this yielded impressive levels of industrialization and rates of economic growth. Import-substitution *per se* was not a misguided route, as Massachusetts Institute for Technology economist Lance Taylor has pointed out: 'Import-substitution is about the only way anybody's ever figured out to industrialise'.[24] One common problem, though, was the associated maze of regulations, subsidies and tax mechanisms that made it 'more interesting for firms to play games with the rules than to go out and produce goods'.[25]

But unlike its Latin American counterparts, South Africa did not try to spend its way out of trouble when these growth phases began ebbing. At 22,9 per cent of GDP in 1994, its *external* debt burden was small for a developing country (ILO, 1996:32). Leaving aside the political and policy implications of such a move, the country had some scope for increasing its debt load – provided this occurred within the framework and in support of a strategic programme rather than haphazardly as the perceived need arose.

In another major departure from the Latin American experiences, South Africa failed to shift its exports to manufactured goods and away from primary products. By 1988, raw materials made up 88 per cent of exports – almost half of that gold, leaving the economy highly vulnerable to fluctuations in the gold price.

This is not to say that the manufacturing sector remained undeveloped. Attempts were made to promote it behind protectionist barriers, enabling it to grow until the late 1960s, after which it 'entered an as yet endless spiral of decline' (Macro-Economic Research Group, 1993:212). The sector remained heavily dependent on imports, which had to be financed through primary exports. Manufactured products' share of total exports declined steadily from 1970 (31 per cent) to 1988 (12 per cent) (Macro-Economic Research Group, 1993:241, Table 7.4), only partially because the gold price pushed the exchange rate up, making manufactured exports less competitive in global markets.[26] Also hampering the sector's development was the high cost of locally produced raw materials to domestic downstream manufacturers, as noted by a 1997 Industrial Development Corporation (IDC) study.[27]

In summary, the economy remained reliant on resource- and energy-based products that were of declining importance in world trade and subject to drastic price fluctuations. According to the United Nations Conference on Trade and Development (UNCTAD), most African countries rely on one or two primary commodities for 90 per cent of their export earnings. In South Africa's case, the figure in the early 1990s was about 65 per cent (Kahn, 1991). Meanwhile, its heavy dependence on capital goods imports and foreign technology left it extremely vulnerable to global pressures. As a result, South Africa was chronically subject to balance of payment difficulties.

Trends in trade

As noted, the country had a relatively extroverted economy, with trade representing about 60 per cent of GDP. Mining was without doubt the most outward-oriented sector (accounting for 62 per cent of exports in 1990, down from 73 per cent in 1980), while the agricultural sector exported grains, wines and deciduous fruits (accounting for 5 per cent of exports in 1990).[28]

South Africa did not escape the fate suffered by the continent generally: increased marginalization in the world economy. It did not share in the more than 30 per cent swell in the volume of world trade that occurred in the 1980s; instead its share of world exports dropped from 1,3 per cent in 1980 to 0,7 per cent in 1989, while Africa's share in the same period fell from 6 per cent to 2,6 per cent.[29]

The particular character of the economy's relative openness is worth noting. Gold continued to dominate exports (accounting for almost half the total value), followed by non-precious metals. In absolute terms, manufactured exports expanded impressively in the 1960s and 1970s, but the economy's share of global manufacturing exports dropped steadily from 1968, while its share of agricultural exports also declined.[30] The sectors that performed best in more open markets were timber and steel. Secondary industry has never been competitive internationally, except in neighbouring countries where South Africa has enjoyed the advantage of lower transport costs, and bilateral and regional trade deals that are weighted in its favour. Overall, manufacturing's share of exports plummeted from 31 per cent in 1960 to 12 per cent in 1988.

On the import side, capital goods (chiefly machinery, transport equipment and information technologies) eclipsed manufactured consumer goods. The sourcing of imports became more concentrated, with its four largest suppliers (the United States, United Kingdom, Germany and Japan) increasing their share of total imports by 1992.[31]

Although still small overall, trade with Africa rose by some 40 per cent from 1990, comprising by the mid-1990s about 10 per cent of exports, with the trade balance skewed in its favour. One-third was in manufactures, a much higher percentage than for exports elsewhere in the world. Most of it occurred with neighbouring and West African countries. In 1990, South Africa provided 80–90 per cent of Botswana, Lesotho and Swaziland's imports, 30 per cent of Malawi's, 21 per cent of Zimbabwe's, 15 per cent of Zambia's and 12 per cent of Mozambique's. Since then, these figures have swelled. In turn, South Africa imported mostly unprocessed primary products from the continent, often through barter deals with countries such as Nigeria (steel for oil), Mauritius and (then) Zaïre. While those deals reduced the strain on foreign currency reserves, they were insulated from the more competitively driven trade dynamics in the 'open market' and tended not to lead to practices and innovations that could be applied to South Africa's benefit in more conventional trade relations.

In sum, in the 1960s South Africa seemed to be developing into a semi-industrialized country with a relatively diversified export base.

By the 1990s, its profile resembled that of most developing countries: as a traditional commodity exporter and importer of capital goods and technologies.

Trends in financial relations

Since its early phases of industrialization, South Africa received large amounts of portfolio investment (mainly from the United Kingdom). During the boom years of the 1960s, it attracted large inflows of foreign direct investment (FDI), mainly from the USA – luring them with low wages, a growing domestic market (mainly due to rising white incomes) and apparent political stability. Much of this capital was invested productively in the manufacturing sector. Syndicated bank loans and bonds raised in the international capital markets made up the bulk of foreign investment after 1976.

Subsequently, economic decline and political instability combined to wreak havoc on its international economic relations and forced the monetary authorities, unilaterally, to declare a debt standstill in August 1985. After that, the country became a net exporter of capital, reversing the positive flows that had prevailed (with minor disruptions) for most of its modern economic history. Massive capital flight occurred in the 1980s – some 40 per cent of transnational firms disinvested[32] and, according to the South African Reserve Bank, capital outflows from 1982 to 1988 amounted to more than $5,5 billion. Some local corporations followed that trend and undertook direct investments abroad, mainly in Europe.

In addition to the net outflows of FDI and portfolio investment, from 1985 to 1988 the country had no access to long-term debt capital, nor were syndicated bank loans extended or private or public bond issues made. In short, most forms of foreign capital inflows dried up altogether. There was one exception. Although no official development assistance was received in the period 1985–92, there were strong inflows of overseas development aid (ODA) to anti-apartheid and humanitarian organizations.

More positively, Pretoria had repaid and discharged all its loan obligations to the World Bank in 1976. An IMF loan received in 1982 was repaid by the end of 1987. As a result, the country's ratio of *foreign* debt to GDP was low by international standards.

Portfolio (equity) capital flows to South Africa increased in the 1990s. The primary causes for this were cyclical: the bottoming out of the recession, the strong coinciding rally in gold markets, and significant progress in political negotiations at the time. Whereas the net outflow of capital from 1985 to 1993 averaged 2,3 per cent of GDP, net inflows from 1994 to 1996 averaged 2,6 per cent of GDP.[33]

Net purchases of equities by foreigners on the Johannesburg Stock Exchange (JSE) increased in the early 1990s. But the renewed access to foreign capital was limited mainly to equity capital and bond issues on the

European capital markets – most of which were effectively short-term credits at relatively high costs. This trend in the flow of equity funds to emerging markets was in line with global developments and represented volatile, short-term investments that were swiftly and easily sold off.

Changing the terms of incorporation

While the world fêted South Africa for its successful transition to democracy, other equally important conundrums remained unresolved. One was how to devise a set of policies that could reconcile the country's insertion into the global division of labour with the commitment to improve the living standards of the majority. New opportunities and new pressures made it possible to alter the manner and terms of South Africa's insertion into the world economy. The new opportunities were patent: the advent of political democracy, a new government, greater international goodwill and the removal of sanctions and trade boycotts.

The 'internationalizing' trend was the paramount pressure, and, politically, was brought to bear mainly by the IMF and World Bank, and to a lesser degree the General Agreement on Tariffs and Trade (GATT). Typically, this would involve 'liberalizing' trade relations by reducing tariffs and removing non-tariff protective barriers for domestic industry, removing financial controls and guaranteeing the free flow of capital, and remedying other features seen as deterring foreign investment.

That far-reaching adjustments were needed in South Africa's case was not in dispute – but that was where the agreement ended. The platitudes that accompanied those debates were often mind-numbing, likening the world economy to 'a picnic', as (former) SACP general secretary Charles Nqakula wryly remarked, where attendance is automatically welcomed if the requisite dress and manners are displayed.[34]

Proposals ranged from standard neoliberal packages of free markets, trade and financial liberalization, to supply-side formulas (such as those devised by the Industrial Strategy Project – ISP), to strategies that envision a creative division of labour between the private sector and the state within the context of innovative, targeted policies (such as the Macro-Economic Research Group recommendations).

The argument generally deployed by business and sections of government casually connected liberalization to increased foreign investment and, consequently, economic growth. The emphasis placed by South African business leaders on foreign investment seemed disingenuous, however, given the low rate of domestic investment by South African capital. So narrow was the debate, though, that Jeremy Cronin was ridiculed in the business press for suggesting that the best advert for foreign investors would be large productive investments by domestic firms. On the contrary, 'this is simply not happening, as millions of rands continue to be disinvested, or used speculatively on the stock exchanges and in shopping mall developments', Cronin noted.[35] Private sector (non-housing) fixed investment constituted a scant 10 per cent of GDP in early 1994.[36] At the same time, capital *outflows* persisted in the early 1990s, causing the economy to lose as much as 2 per cent real GDP growth annually.[37] Indeed, while demanding increased liberalization (ostensibly to sweeten investment opportunities in South Africa), the country's major corporations in the 1990s embarked on a spree of investments *abroad*. Thus, the largest conglomerates invested heavily in Indonesia, Australia, Zambia, Brazil, Ghana, China, New Zealand, Chile, Venezuela, Ecuador and Vietnam – with the Trade and Industry Ministry later defending the trend on the basis that the country needed a corporate presence in countries with which it trades.[38]

Nevertheless, the need to attract substantial amounts of foreign investment was axiomatic. Success, according to Krugman, depended on whether South Africa 'can get any restructuring of property rights behind it; if it can demonstrate that it is more market-oriented than investors now expect; and if it can offer what appears to be a more competitive rand' (Baker *et al.*, 1993:47).

By mid-1996, substantial adjustments had occurred on these fronts. Property rights were ensconced in the constitution (without any significant 'restructuring' having taken place), the government's macro-economic strategy (see Chapter 6) heeded most neoliberal injunctions, and the rand devalued by more than 30 per cent in six months.

The South African debate tended to regard the country as *sui generis* and somehow able to evade the pressures experienced by the rest of Africa – where overall FDI grew by a third from 1980 to 1990 but the continent's share of overall global FDI *dropped* from 6,8 per cent to 2 per cent.[39] Capital outflows, in 1991, equalled 90 per cent of Africa's GDP – more than five times the total investment, 11 times private sector investment and 120 times foreign investment.[40] 'Not only has the region lost ground to the rest of the world as an investment location', noted one assessment, 'but within Africa the pattern of flows is heavily skewed in favour of oil-producing nations which account for two thirds of the total [FDI].'[41] All evidence pointed to South Africa being locked into those trends. Thus Nigeria attracted 45 per cent of FDI to sub-Saharan Africa from 1990 to 1994, while South Africa experienced a net outflow.

Overall, flows of FDI delineate a much more differentiated 'Third World' than that described in the cheery auguries of orthodoxy. David Gordon has shown that 'instead of flowing more and more widely around the globe, capital is on the contrary settling down in a few carefuly chosen locations', of four types. The East Asian NICs receive investment mainly for financial services and production for re-export back to the advanced countries. Latin American NICs represent a second category and receive foreign investment aimed almost exclusively at production for large domestic markets. The third comprises oil-exporting countries whose fortunes 'vacillate with the cob-web cycles of price hikes and oil gluts'. Finally, there are 75–80 developing countries who 'have been shunted off to a side spur, virtually derailed in the drive for access to global resources' (1988:57).

After the 1994 elections, foreign investment in South Africa did revive, but along three lines. Direct investment increased as firms that had divested returned to the country and expanded or upgraded their operations. There was also a surge of mergers and acquisitions. The other trend was towards investment in stocks and bonds.

The net private capital outflows of 1985–93 were reversing slightly by late 1994, with one estimate putting FDI at $2,5 billion in 1994/5.[42] But these were 'largely due, however, to investments through the stock exchange', according to the Department of Trade and Industry's Alan Hirsch, who added that FDI 'defined as more than 50% ownership remains relatively small'.[43] Productive investments targeted the 'traditional middle-class and business market, such as media and infotech investments', hotels and tourism, and the food, appliance and construction industries. But there was an 'almost total lack of investment in outward-oriented manufacturing'.[44] In Hirsch's summary, 'the problem is that most [FDI] is basically buying market share and going into partnership with South African companies, or buying control of South African resources for export'.[45]

What would it take, then, to encourage foreign investment in export-oriented manufacturing industries? The prognosis seemed gloomy, for there 'appears to be little to support the widely held belief that low-cost labour will encourage multinationals to relocate job-intensive operations in parts of Africa', according to Hawkins. Among the reasons were low labour productivity and the 'relative insignificance of labour costs when compared with material, transport and other costs in many manufacturing operations'.[46]

Simply conforming to the commonly touted requirements – whereby, in (former) trade union leader Enoch Godongwana's metaphor, the world economy becomes a 'beauty competition' where you stand to win if you can display the 'slimmest legs' and 'skimpiest costume' – was inappropriate. South Africa could not wish away its geographical location on a continent that barely features in the world economy. Neither could it ignore the need for massive increases in both social and economic investment. Increasingly beguiling policy-makers was the view that the answer lay in a set of liberalizing economic adjustments.

But international experience also showed that foreign investment is more likely to flow to vibrant economies with strong internal demand and that are integrated into economically dynamic regions.[47] Indeed, the dominant belief that low wages and relatively high skills levels are the key determinants of FDI is not borne out by research. A study of FDI flows to 54 developing countries has shown that those elements tend to rank lowest among the criteria affecting FDI (Schneider & Frei, 1985:167–75). Paramount is the size of the domestic market, price/exchange rate stability and political/institutional stability. As Gordon argued, 'in many commodities, labour costs are a relatively small proportion of total costs [while] countries with relatively stable price and trade horizons are much more exceptional than those with relatively low labour costs' (1988:58–9). Adopting neoliberal policies offered 'no guarantee', as Krugman warned, 'that [those] conditions will produce large capital inflows'[48] – let alone the broader, advertised benefits.

Moreover, the emphasis on FDI as a catalyst for growth lets domestic capital off the hook. Two of the most dynamic performers in the South (South Korea and China) succeeded by harnessing local capital investment into virtuous cycles that guaranteed high rates of return but also demanded that large portions of the surplus be reinvested in targeted activities.

Neoliberal orthodoxy could not claim credit for any of the East and South East Asian success stories. Meanwhile, its widely touted success (Chile) offered ample cause for alarm. Along with severely deepened social inequalities, 'whole sectors of industry were wiped out, manufacturing employment fell by half' and growth occurred mainly on the basis of agriculture-based exports.[49] Such evidence, though, barely distracted most economic policy-makers.

The new government's strategy for growth centred on invigorating an export-oriented manufacturing sector, an approach that was in step with the international trend away from trade in primary commodities. The economy's inherited weaknesses, however, made this a daunting task.

The guiding doctrine became that of 'enhanced competitiveness', often glibly conflated into the purported need to get the 'prices right' with trade liberalization typically held out as the best device. This was flanked by an emphasis on boosted productivity that, in business discourse, tended to be reduced to labour productivity, downplaying the importance of capital productivity, social productivity (defined as 'the efficiency with which the population's needs might be satisfied') and managerial productivity.[50]

Both assumptions were problematic. Firstly, as economist Sanjaya Lall cautioned, 'neither theory nor practice supports the case for completely liberal trade policies.' Indeed, he found 'no instance of a developing country mastering complex industrial activities ... without protection or subsidisation to overcome the costs of learning'.[51] Meanwhile, citing a WIDER study and its own research, the ISP found no evidence of an unambiguous link between export expansion and productivity growth (Baker *et al.*, 1993:99). Summarizing the ISP's findings, Bill Freund noted that:

> ... South Africa needs more than a trade policy; it needs an overall indus-
> trial policy aimed at building research and development capacity, develop-
> ing industrial exports through targeting strengths, rewarding both job
> creation and improving productivity, and advancing competition through
> breaking up conglomerates (although they equivocate on this final point)
> (1994b:61).

The government's reformed trade policy became explicitly geared to
fostering export orientation, by making a committed move towards trade
liberalization and applying supply-side measures.[52] The latter included
efforts to improve productivity and work organization, nurturing small and
medium-sized enterprises, helping develop new industries (especially in
biotechnology and information technology), encouraging more investment
in research and development, lowering the corporate tax rate (despite
resistance of the government-appointed Katz Commission) and providing
more tax incentives, and human resource development. However, it did
not add up to a strategic policy of the South Korean or even Malaysian
varieties. Measures were concentrated on the supply side and bereft of an
overt role for the state in targeting and buttressing, for instance, the
development of labour-intensive industries or of coaxing and rewarding
job creation and productivity advances.

On trade liberalization, the government leapt out of the starting blocks.
Common wisdom had detected in South Africa's tariff system a prime
obstacle to competitiveness. The view was both right and wrong. Compared
with 32 LDCs (least developed countries), tariff protection was not high,
except in the case of final consumer goods. Once the actual utilization of
tariffs was considered, South Africa 'appear[ed] to be amongst the least
protected of all of these 32 countries' (Industrial Strategy Project, 1994:98).
On the other hand, the inherited system was fiendishly complex while, in
Lalls's view, '[protected] industries without regard to their competitive
potential, [had] no strategy for promoting new infant industries, and
[failed] to offset the effects of protection by forcing firms to invest in building export markets'.[53] A strong case could be made for restructuring (as
opposed to dismantling) the protective regime. South Africa took a rather
more direct route, however, and signed the 1994 Uruguay Round of GATT.
Weighty obligations were incurred:

- Some 12 800 industrial tariffs would be rationalized into no more
  than 1 000.
- Industrial tariffs would be cut by an average of 33 per cent by 1999 with
  maximum levels for consumer goods set at 30 per cent, for capital goods
  at 15 per cent and for raw materials at 5 per cent.
- Agricultural tariffs would be cut by an average of 36 per cent over
  10 years.

- Textile tariffs would be scaled down over 12 years to a maximum of 25–45 per cent, depending on the product.
- Local content measures would be phased out in the automobile industry.
- The General Export Incentive Scheme (GEIS) export subsidies would end by 1997.

In August 1994, the new Department of Trade and Industry announced deep tariff reductions in clothing and textiles and automobile components that went far beyond those demanded under GATT.[54] At the time, the cuts did not slot into a strategic package, aimed at impelling those industries into new or more competitive directions. It was 'sheer economic Darwinism', as one commentator put it. Simultaneously, the minister responsible (Trevor Manuel) could declare that 'the worst case for this economy is for us to throw our industries ... to the vagaries of international competition rapidly and so destroy investment and jobs'.[55] In 1996, Manuel would preside over a new macro-economic strategy that described 'the central thrust of trade and industrial policy' as 'the pursuit of employment creating international competitiveness' (Department of Finance, 1996:11). Among the measures employed would be the abolition of import sur-charges, phasing out of GEIS by the end of 1997 (Department of Finance, 1996:11–12) and, in the case of telecommunications, lowering tariffs to zero per cent – far below the 20 per cent level required under GATT.

The GEIS was long trouble-ridden, largely benefited conglomerates 'who would have exported anyway',[56] and was plagued by fraudulent double claims. Moreover, GEIS was not structured to specifically encourage the export of finished goods. The World Bank, however, was doubtful whether South Africa could achieve export competitiveness without a scheme such as GEIS. Proposals came from labour and other circles to restructure GEIS to benefit more small and medium-sized, labour-intensive industries. Government, though, opted for the harsher option.

Worst hit by the tariff cuts has been the labour-intensive clothing industry (one of the largest industrial employers of women) and the beleaguered agricultural sector, particularly maize farming. At the same time, if this leads to lower maize prices for consumers (mainly the poor) these effects could be mitigated to some extent.

A further liberalizing adjustment embarked on was the abolition of foreign exchange controls. These had been introduced in 1961, in a bid to stem capital outflows after the Sharpeville massacre. Regulations were modified in subsequent years, including strong liberalization in the early 1980s following the gold price boom. The government's debt standstill – and the uprisings – of 1985 triggered massive capital outflows, prompting the re-introduction of the financial rand mechanism and the tightening of controls. The financial rand, which traded at a lower rate than the commercial rand, was the principal means for moving capital in and out of South Africa, whether in the form of direct or portfolio investments. Capital could only be removed at a discount and was thus encouraged to remain, in theory protecting foreign exchange reserves.

The global trend, however, was running against exchange controls, which were seen as a hindrance to the free flow of capital and a major factor discouraging foreign investment.[57] South Africa's low savings rate and declining investment levels (the investment rate fell from 20,6 per cent of GDP in 1989 to 15,5 per cent in 1993)[58] added succour to that policy stance. As a result, the South African debate was not whether or not to discard these controls, but whether this should be done in one, fell swoop (the 'big bang') or in phases. Financial institutions pushed for the 'shock therapy' option, which the IMF also advocated in late 1994.[59] The new government opted for a phased approach. As a first step, the financial rand was abolished in 1995. According to government policy, 'all remaining exchange controls will be dismantled as soon as circumstances are favourable' (Department of Finance, 1996:11). By 1999, 75 per cent of the controls had disappeared.

The irony was that the gradual approach was accompanied by many of the difficulties associated with the 'big bang' approach. In early 1996, the currency devalued dramatically, losing more than 30 per cent of its 1995 value against the US dollar. A familiar train of events ensued. Import costs soared, causing a slow-down in the retooling and upgrading of plants and, more menacingly, a major shortage of foreign exchange. On the positive side, exports became more price competitive. The devalued rand and mega-projects going into production saw manufactured export volumes rise by 12 per cent in 1996 while its percentage share of overall exports rose from 26 per cent to 29 per cent.[60] In early 1997, however, the rise faltered to 3,4 per cent.[61] But the stunted export capacity of the manufacturing sector prevented it from capitalizing markedly on that boon; the crucial link between an activated new industrial policy and exchange control liberalization was absent. Meanwhile, capital inflows slowed dramatically in 1996 and were down to R3,9 billion from R19,2 billion in 1995, tempting the government to use privatization to boost inflows.

The triumph of orthodoxy

By 1996, the government had nailed its colours to the mast of export-oriented growth. Even some ANC economists, such as Rob Davies, warned that South Africa was seeking to hop aboard the export-led bandwagon at a time when '[a]lmost all semi-peripheral and many peripheral countries are now attempting such a strategy under global conditions that are becoming less and less favourable for all to succeed' (1995:63). The caution went unheeded. Referring to the experiences of the NICs in South East Asia, Lall reminded that '… the experience of the most dynamic industrialisers in the developing world suggests that their [states'] selective interventions determined the nature and success of their industrial development.'[62]

Government policy, however, refrained for the most part from such 'selective interventions'. Whilst not quite hands-off, the approach became one of highly restrained facilitation within an overall context governed by the reactions of market forces.

At the same time, many of the conditions for replicating the policies of the NICs seemed not to exist in South Africa's case. Both South Korea and Taiwan had used their geostrategic significance during the Cold War to great effect, winning preferential access to US markets without having to reciprocate by opening their own markets. Moreover, as Davies (1995) has noted, 'they embarked on export-led growth when most industrialising countries were still pursuing import-substitution programmes'. Instead of an authoritarian regime able to suppress labour, South Africa has a democratic government and a comparatively powerful labour movement. It does not have the 'luxury' of a weak capitalist class, nor a homogenous population or an even relatively favourable income distribution pattern (key elements of Taiwan and South Korea's successes). Its unrestructured rural economy could not function as an employment and income safeguard. Situated in a sub-region and on a continent that enjoys barely a toe-hold in the world economy, it lacks dynamic markets in close proximity. And it starts:

> … from a low, narrow and uneven base marked by an inward-looking economic premised on 75 years of import-substitution policies, minimal domestic competition, a continued dependence on our natural resource base, low labour absorption and an insufficient emphasis on human capital formation, falling rates of gross domestic fixed investment and a capital that has aged.[63]

Such a catalogue suggests that South Africa had no alternative but to buy into the dominant ideology in the economic sphere. Not so, as the next chapters show. South Africa is not, in economic terms, Mauritania or Sri Lanka. It could fashion a growth path that combines carefully inflected orthodox adjustments with more traditional Keynesian measures and more radical innovations. It shunned this, admittedly difficult, route and opted for a path that would leave it prone in a world system in which, as Samir Amin has reminded, 'capital adjusts the weaker zones of the world to the requirements of global accumulation'.[64]

The anticipated pay-off is that this would enable the economy gradually to 'catch up' with the industrialized world. The idea of 'catching up' is not new, of course. In the post-1945 era, decolonized states without exception concentrated their efforts on such a venture. In Latin America,

Africa and the Middle East, this occurred largely via the route of inward industrialization, behind protective barriers, often with the material support of one of the two former superpowers, and without exception fuelled by highly active 'development states'.

What are the prospects of 'catching up' in the current economic and geopolitical order by adjusting themselves to the prevailing framework of free market economics? Amin's answer is both compelling and sobering. The world system is characterized not by a steadily growing circle of 'winners' but by the enforcement of 'a new hierarchy in the distribution of income' and greater, not less inequality, on the world scale (Amin, 1997:14). Fundamentally skewed, the world system is marked by an ensemble of monopolies, he argues, exercised by one or more of what we might call 'the centres' – the US, Western Europe and Japan. Those precincts of dominance include:

- The development and deployment of weapons of mass destruction.
- Domination in (as opposed to *control* of) the world financial markets.
- Monopolized access to the world's natural resources.
- Domination of supra-national institutions tasked with managing or modulating the operation of the market at the global level.
- Predominance in the fields of media and communication.
- The development and deployment of new technologies (hence, the strong emphasis on patent protection and defending intellectual property rights at the World Trade Organization).

Clearly, the notion of 'catching up' loses its purchase in a system organized in such a manner. The feat of successful industrialization no longer implies entry into a centre *that is defined not by levels of development and competitiveness, but by pre-eminence in the zones described.*

The NICs of East Asia and a few Latin American countries constitute what can be termed today's 'Third World'. Integrated quite firmly into the world system, some of them are able sporadically to challenge some of the monopolies commanded at the centre, but in the short- to medium-term none are capable of usurping those monopolies. The rest of the planet makes up the 'Fourth World', marginalized in moderate to extreme degrees and weakly integrated into the world system. Included are those countries:

- That have partially industrialized but remain uncompetitive and require radical restructuring to reverse that state of affairs (for example, South Africa, industrialized Arab countries such as Algeria and Egypt, as well as Russia and Eastern Europe).
- That are still essentially pre-industrial but have achieved comparative prosperity on the basis of agricultural, mineral and oil exports (such as the Gulf states, Gabon and Côte d'Ivoire).

- That are unable to successfully promote even traditional commodity exports and that founder as a result (most of sub-Saharan Africa) (Amin, 1997).

A different paradigm is required to the 'catching up' frame of thought. It has to focus instead on what arrangements offer sufficient leeway and manoeuvring space for the achievement of national developmental priorities that run counter to the global trend of polarization and impoverishment. But before sketching the rudiments of such an approach, it is necessary to examine in more detail the origins and current fate of the post-apartheid growth path.

Notes

1 South African Reserve Bank figures (June 1995), calculated in 1990 constant prices.
2 During the 1960s, with the economy at its peak, 74 per cent of new entrants into the job market found jobs in the enumerated sectors. By the late 1980s, this had dropped to 12,5 per cent, prompting the NP government to admit that the unemployment crisis was structural (Gelb, 1994:3). By the early 1990s, fewer than 7 per cent of new entrants found work in the formal sector. See Dave Lewis in Gelb (1991:244–66) and ILO (1996) for overviews of the unemployment crisis.
3 In 1993, 63,7 per cent of exports were primary or primary processed products.
4 For more, see Vishnu Padayachee's 'The politics of South Africa's international financial relations, 1970–1990' in Gelb (1991).
5 ABSA Bank, 1994, *Quarterly Economic Monitor* (July).
6 Anthony Marx was one of few analysts not guilty of this oversight: 'With no cushion for hard times, South Africa's urban poor have been highly vulnerable to economic shifts reflected most directly in higher prices for corn "mealies" and other food on which they spend much of their income. Their anger over increased hardship has exploded during economic downturns ... the unrest in 1976–1977 and 1984–1987 came in the wake of major recessions' (1992:245).
7 Former COSATU spokesperson Neil Coleman, writing in *Business Times*, 3 July 1994.
8 *Ibid.*
9 *SAIRR, Race Relations Survey 1991/1992*, Johannesburg, pp. 406–7. Whilst reflecting poorly on Stals' political acumen, the prediction underlined the widespread concern over South Africa's economic malaise.
10 Standard Bank, 1994, *Economic Review* (Third Quarter), Johannesburg.
11 For a survey of the controversy, see ILO (1996:65–71, 101–23).
12 Derek Keys (former minister of finance), Budget Speech, June 1994, Cape Town.
13 See *SA Reserve Bank Quarterly Bulletin* (March 1994).
14 See *SA Reserve Bank Quarterly Bulletin* (September 1991).
15 For more, see Kahn, B., 'Exchange rate policy and industrial restructuring' in Moss and Obery (1991) and Black, A., 'Manufacturing development and the economic crisis: A reversion to primary production?' in Gelb (1991).
16 Former NUMSA general secretary Enoch Godongwana quoted in *Business Day*, 7 April 1997.
17 Mineral Bureau figures, cited in ILO (1996:277).

18 According to the 1994 October Household Survey, only 2,4 per cent of unemployed African men and 0,9 per cent of African women received unemployment benefits. See ILO (1996:109).
19 Blumenfeld, J., 'The international dimension' in Schrire (1992:71).
20 Padayachee (1994a:26). He went on to note the 'striking' similarities between these commitments and the NP government's controversial Normative Economic Model (NEM), which had earned the wrath of the ANC in the early 1990s.
21 Cited in Gelb (1991:30).
22 Thomas Scott in Mills *et al.* (1995:200).
23 For parts of this section I am indebted to comments and material provided by Vishnu Padayachee.
24 'Agents of inequality', *Dollars and Sense*, November 1991, p. 15.
25 *Ibid.*
26 These factors by no means exhaust the list of structural handicaps that plagued this sector. For a more extensive account, see ISP, 'Meeting the global challenge: A framework for industrial revival in South Africa' in Baker *et al.* (1993: 91–126).
27 'Exports rise as domestic demand cools', *Business Day*, 13 June 1997.
28 The five largest export markets in 1992 were the USA, Germany, the UK, Japan and Switzerland. Only in the latter instance did the trade balance lie in South Africa's favour.
29 UN, *World Economic Survey*, 1992, cited by Paul Krugman, 'Trends in world trade and foreign direct investment' in Baker *et al.* (1993:24).
30 Freund (1994a:46) has noted that 'South African agricultural capitalism is characterised by a negative international trade balance in most years, heavy debts and low productivity in many spheres'.
31 *Trade Monitor*, August 1993, p. 11.
32 Although, in many cases, they retained an indirect presence through financial and technological arrangements.
33 'Indicators point to progress on growth', *Business Day*, 11 June 1997.
34 'As South Africa is welcomed back into the international economic fold and prepares itself for full participation in the global economy' was a standard cliché in economic circles – in this case it introduced the Standard Bank's journal *Economic Review* in May 1994.
35 See Cronin, J., 'Exploding the myths of the neoliberal agenda', *Business Day*, 9 November 1994.
36 The rise in private sector fixed investment during 1994 (by approximately 13 per cent) was 'mainly limited to a number of major projects, spurred by tax concessions', according to the *SA Reserve Bank Quarterly Bulletin*, No. 197 (September 1995), p. 5.
37 Standard Bank chief economist Nico Czypionka, quoted in the *Argus*, 25 June 1994.
38 *Business Map Update*, 10 February 1997.
39 World Bank, *Global Economic Prospects 1996*.
40 According to the International Finance Corporation (the World Bank's private sector investment arm), cited by Hawkins, T., 'Africa left out in the cold', *Financial Times*, 15 June 1996.
41 *Ibid.*
42 *Business Map Quarterly Review* (January 1996).
43 Hirsch, A., 1995, 'Productive investment trends in South Africa' (workshop paper).
44 *Ibid.*
45 Cited in *Business Map Quarterly Review* (January 1996), p. 12.
46 Hawkins, T., 'Africa left out in the cold', *Financial Times*, 15 June 1996.

47 As even a 1995 Ernst & Young survey noted, 'the primary motivation for entering countries' was 'not low production costs' but the 'potential rate of return and local market demand' – a self-evident point.

48 *Op. cit.* p. 47.

49 See *Trade Monitor*, No. 3 (August 1993), p. 3.

50 See ISP, 'Meeting the global challenge: A framework for industrial revival in South Africa' in Baker *et al.* (1993:93–7).

51 'What will make South Africa competitive?' in Baker *et al.* (1993:56).

52 See *Support Measures for the Enhancement of the International Competitiveness of South Africa's Industrial Sector*, a document by the Department of Trade and Industry, released in 1995. An earlier version prompted one business journalist to ask whether its 'brand of economics' represented 'Keynesian Thatcherism, or the opposite?' (*Business Day*, 14 September 1994).

53 Lall, S. in Baker *et al.* (1993:61–2).

54 The announcement ended a bruising, five-week autoworkers strike within hours. It is suspected that the announcement was timed to end the strike, after the Labour Ministry had refused to intervene in the dispute.

55 Former trade and industry minister Trevor Manuel, quoted in *Business Day*, 1 September 1994.

56 ISP, 'Meeting the global challenge' in Baker *et al.* (1993:98). These conglomerates received 55 per cent of pay-outs in 1992/3.

57 The next chapter traces the origins of this stance to the post-1970 downturn in the advanced capitalist economies.

58 *SA Reserve Bank Quarterly Bulletin* (various issues), Pretoria.

59 'Forex controls "need to go with a big bang"', *Sunday Times*, 18 September 1994.

60 'SA's big export surge', *Mail & Guardian*, 27 March 1997.

61 'Growth forecasts drop as GDP dips', *Business Day*, 3 June 1997.

62 Lall in Baker *et al.* (1993:69).

63 Former trade and industry minister, Trevor Manuel, *Business Day*, 1 September 1994.

64 Samir Amin, interview, Johannesburg, August 1993.

CHAPTER FIVE

The evolution of ANC economic policy: a short walk to orthodoxy

On May Day, 1994, Nelson Mandela declared in South Africa's largest newspaper that: 'In our economic policies ... there is not a single reference to things like nationalisation, and this is not accidental. There is not a single slogan that will connect us with any Marxist ideology.'[1]

The announcement drew relieved praise from business leaders who, despite ample evidence to the contrary, still worried that ANC economic policy might lurch in a radical direction. In their discomfort, they recalled Mandela's assurance four years earlier, upon his release from prison, that: '... the nationalisation of the mines, banks and monopoly industry is the policy of the ANC and a change or modification of our views in this regard is inconceivable'.[2]

Those words had exposed Mandela for the first time to the fickle and fierce dynamics ANC economic policy would become subjected to: within hours JSE traders were, as one observer put it, 'unceremoniously falling out of bed' to launch a selling spree.[3] More than any other aspect of ANC policy, the party's economic thinking was launched on a roller-coaster ride – buffeted by threats, ridicule and cajoling from business organizations, financial institutions, Western governments, activists, trade unions, foreign lending institutions, economists and consultants.

The first target for attack was the ANC's alleged penchant for nationalization,[4] which it soon dropped, to the alarm of many supporters. Nationalization was a red herring, though. Its resonance in popular discourse stemmed less from its literal prescription than from its symbolic power; encoded in that instrument was an overriding commitment to redistribute resources and opportunity in favour of the majority. The retreat from nationalization was read, therefore, as hinting at the likely dilution of that broader avowal.

Mandela's May Day statement reflected the extent to which the terms of the political transition had also been projected into the sphere of economic policy-making. The need to defuse potential hostility and assuage doubt – 'to bring everybody along' – held the day, and the ANC assumed the task of trying to harmonize and distil from antagonistic interests economic policies that could win wide endorsement. If the scope for triumphalist action was limited in the political arena, it seemed almost non-existent in the economic one – at least to the top echelons of the ANC. Reinforcing that sense was the fact that the organization had paid scant attention to economic policy in exile. Its main reference point until the late 1980s had been the developmentalism that had characterized most post-colonial projects since the early 1950s, with anticipated Eastern bloc largesse being an important factor. By 1989, this had been softened into a professed commitment to a mixed economy, with the state still seen as a central economic actor. Soon, the collapse of the Eastern European variant of socialism, the end of the Cold War, the strutting ascendancy of neoliberalism and an increasingly graphic sense of the veto powers wielded by capital had all but erased those erstwhile markers.

During the 1990–3 negotiations, the ANC scampered to make up lost ground, but it relied on weak advice. Its historical neglect of economic policy left it prone to the counsel of business and mainstream foreign experts that set about schooling ANC leaders in the 'realities of the world'. The residue of left-Keynesian economic thinking (generated mainly from within the internal mass movement) had not entirely dissolved, but its persuasive power was fast waning. As South Africans celebrated the 1994 election results, there was already firm evidence that post-apartheid economic policy would conform to the pronouncement, seven years earlier, by Anglo American Corporation's Clem Sunter: 'Negotiation works. Rhetoric is dropped, reality prevails and in the end the companies concerned go on producing the minerals, goods and services.'[5]

In fact, the penny had dropped earlier for some ANC leaders. In 1991, Nelson Mandela was already telling an audience of business people in Pittsburgh, USA, that:

> ... the private sector must and will play the central and decisive role in the struggle to achieve many of [the transformation] objectives ... let me assure you that the ANC is not an enemy of private enterprise ... we are aware that the investor will not invest unless he or she is assured of the security of their investment ... The rates of economic growth we seek cannot be achieved without important inflows of foreign capital. We are determined to create the necessary climate which the foreign investor will find attractive.[6]

By 1996, as we shall see, the ANC government's economic policy had acquired an overt class character. It was geared to service the respective prerogatives of domestic and international capital and the aspirations of the emerging black *bourgeoisie* – at the expense of the impoverished majority's hopes for a less iniquitous social and economic order. This was a moment-ous shift for a party with a strong working class constituency, closely allied with the SACP and COSATU, and replete with avowed socialists in its lead-ership ranks. It also betrayed the ideological ambivalence of an organization in which pragmatism was steadily superseding principle as it sought to steer South Africa clear of the precipice.

The following section tracks the evolution of ANC economic policy which, in sweeping and telling terms, was consummated in the ANC gov-ernment's 1996 macro-economic plan, the Growth, Employment and Redistribution (GEAR) strategy.

Smoke and mirrors

When the ANC was unbanned in 1990, it had no economic policy, a pecu-liar situation for an eight-decade-old liberation organization, despite the efforts internationally on the left to train a cadre of ANC exile economists. The 1988 ANC Constitutional Guidelines had committed the organization to a mixed economy. But that avowal hung in a policy vacuum and invoked vague passages of the Freedom Charter that had pledged that:

> The People shall share in the country's wealth!
> The national wealth of our country, the heritage of all South Africans shall be restored to the people;
> The mineral wealth beneath the soil, the banks and monopoly industry shall be transferred to the ownership of the people as a whole;
> All other industries and trade shall be controlled to assist the well-being of the people;
> All people shall have equal rights to trade where they choose, to manufacture and to enter all trades, crafts and professions.[7]

This is not to suggest that a blueprint should have been devised – far from it. But the outline of a coherent economic programme, based on sound analy-sis of both local and global economic realities, was necessary as a platform from which to bargain a new economic dispensation. In 1990, the organiza-tion had only slogans and broad statements of principle at its disposal. Nothing resembling an economic policy outline existed. Economic literacy among cadres – and leaders (only a sprinkling of whom had economic train-ing of note) – had never been a priority. Without anchor lines, the drift into orthodoxy would turn out to be unnervingly swift and comprehensive.

The ANC's first serious attempt to fill this vacuum came in the form of a 1990 'Discussion Document on Economic Policy', issued by its new Department of Economic Policy (DEP). In the main, the document echoed policy work done by COSATU's Economic Trends Group, which, until then, had been responsible for the most substantial efforts to chart a sustainable, progressive economic strategy. Central to the ANC document was the 'restructuring' of the economy, which, as economist Nicoli Nattrass noted, could 'include anything from extensive state intervention to conventional market-driven structural adjustment' (1994c:6).

The DEP document envisaged an active role for the state in planning industrial strategy and overcoming racial, gender and geographic inequalities. It stressed the need to restructure the financial sector that, it said, 'does not sufficiently direct savings into productive activity nor into critical areas of infrastructural development' and, instead, encourages 'a scramble for short-term speculative profit'.[8] Foreign investment would be funnelled into targeted areas of the economy. Basic needs would not be met through 'inflationary financing', but by marshalling domestic savings and raising corporate tax rates. Also advised was the unbundling of conglomerates in order to stimulate competition and allow entry by small and medium-sized enterprises into the economy. Calls from business for a low-wage economy in order to achieve 'international competitiveness' were rejected, while a central role would be reserved for organized labour in devising and implementing policy.

The overriding theme was 'growth through redistribution', a formula 'in which redistribution acts as a spur to growth and in which the fruits of growth are redistributed to satisfy basic needs'.[9] In the 1993 summary of economist Laurence Harris:

> In its original formulation this strategy took a form that would have been familiar to left wing Latin American followers of Prebisch in the 1950s and 1960s, emphasising that the state should take a strong role in redistributing income and wealth toward the masses, simultaneously developing domestic industry's production to meet the demand for increased living standards and essentially growing on the basis of that domestic market while seeking simultaneously to increase the competitiveness of export industries (1993b:95).

Economists such as Nattrass have contended that the 'growth through redistribution' route was chosen largely 'because it served the political purpose of uniting various constituencies within the ANC' – implying a certain degree of expediency and an awareness that the policy had a short shelf-life. One could argue the converse: that it reflected the influence of the left (mainly SACP- and COSATU-aligned) within the ANC at the time. Strengthening that leverage was the fact that there were two streams of economic debate occurring: one in and around the ANC and the other in the media, and in the more rarified settings of think-tanks and seminars. ANC leaders were involved in both realms, which would only intersect later once clear policy pronouncements were demanded of the organization. As a result, much of the debate occurred at the ideological level.

The 'growth through redistribution' approach was severely censured by mainstream economists and in the media. Attacks ranged from consternation about the 'socialist' undertones of the document to complaints about its alleged overtones of macro-economic populism.[10] The latter variant argued that it tended to: '... underestimate the negative effects on investment, overestimate the existence of spare capacity, and fail[ed] to predict the continuing high demand for imports and the inflationary impact of large deficits' (Nattrass, 1994c:9).

Critics warned that a state spending spree (geared at redistribution) would overheat the economy and bog it down in a morass of foreign exchange shortages, currency devaluations, rampant inflation, severe indebtedness and cuts in real wages. Chile (1970–3) and Peru (1985–9) were invoked as sobering examples of such folly. In short, the 'growth through redistribution' path was deemed unsustainable, with the *Mont Fleur* scenario[11] later likening it to the fateful flight of Icarus, cautioning:

> After a year or two the programme runs into budgetary, monetary and balance of payments constraints. The budget deficit well exceeds 10%. Depreciations, inflation, economic uncertainty and collapse follow. The country experiences an economic crisis of hitherto unknown proportions which results in social collapse and political chaos (Le Roux *et al.*, 1993:8).

Still, it is worth recalling the thinking behind the 'growth through redistribution' slogan. In a 1991 Development Bank paper, it was described as a growth path resting on both export promotion and inward industrialization, geared at significantly expanding domestic demand and social infrastructure. The Keynesian overtones were clear. In Kentridge's summary it contended that:

> ... the poor consume goods made with a higher labour component, in which direct import content is lower, and that spending by the poor not only multiplies the GDP more than that by the rich, but that it does so primarily among the poor. In short, growth from redistribution would boost output and employment more than a similar injection among the rich (1993:8).

Such thinking quickly withered before the criticisms it evoked, although the opposition was never elaborated into anything resembling a coherent intellectual critique. The ANC's May 1992 economic policy guidelines made no reference to the 'formula'. In workshops, activists were discouraged from referring to it. Over the next two years, the party's economic thinking would increasingly take aboard precepts of neoliberal dogma. Thus the need for macro-economic stability was equated with fiscal and monetary stringency, and party activists were lectured on the virtues of liberalization and privatization.

The plethora of corporate scenario planning exercises unleashed after 1990 had a telling impact.[12] The first was Nedcor/Old Mutual's *Prospects for a Successful Transition*, launched in late 1990 and completed in 1993.[13]

This was followed by the insurance conglomerate SANLAM's *Platform for Investment* scenario and the social-democratic *Mont Fleur Scenarios*. Meanwhile, other documents, such as that of the South African Chamber of Business (SACOB) – *Economic Options for South Africa* – were wheeled into the fray. Later, the South Africa Foundation's 1996 *Growth for All* document would fix the terms of the debate firmly on the right.

In reflecting on the scenario exercises, it is helpful to distinguish between their form and content. On the latter score, there was some dissonance in their prescriptions – although an overarching set of precepts was common to all. Most ubiquitous was the counsel that economic policy had to become grounded in relationships of trust, negotiation and consensus-building. Decoded, this implied imposing 'a kind of "coerced harmony"', analogous to the central dynamic applied in the political negotiations (Bond, 1996c:2). In Bond's view, 'the scenario exercises reflected the desire of the masters and carefully hand-picked participants to come up with a *deal – rather* than with good analysis' (1996c:3). Undergirding that process was a set of elementary truisms, notably the need for macro-economic stringency, restraint in efforts at social restructuring, an outward-oriented economy and a facilitating (as opposed to regulating) state. Their common thrust was to demonize as macro-economic populism any attempt to ground future economic policy in a mutually reinforcing dynamic of growth and redistribution.

Also important was the form of the exercises and the activities that accompanied them. The language was that of melodrama, laden with populist flippancies and cartoon-like metaphors.[14] Lavishly promoted (in books, videos, multimedia presentations and newspaper supplements), the impact was ensured by a frenetic assortment of seminars, conferences, workshops, briefings, international 'fact-finding' trips and high-profile visits by carefully chosen foreign experts – financed by business and foreign development agencies. ANC leaders were fêted with private 'orientation' sessions and confabs at exclusive game resorts. The ideological barrage was incessant and was amplified by the corporate-owned media, which gleefully attacked any signs of heterodoxy and dissonance in ANC thinking. By 1993, SANLAM's *Platform for Investment* document could justifiably gloat about the '... close working relationship between the ANC, the World Bank, the Development Bank of Southern Africa, the Consultative Business Movement, and other organisations which are painstakingly pointing out the longer run costs of many redistributive strategies'.[15]

Broadly indicative of the counsel arrayed in those interventions was SACOB's *Economic Options for South Africa*. It claimed that free enterprise was 'the remedy for poverty and ensured economic growth'. Economic reforms were needed to create optimal conditions for free enterprise to flourish. Deposited with the state was the duty of ensuring social and political stability, but within policy and other parameters that favoured capital.

In several respects, the document proved to be prescient. As summarized by Kentridge, it advocated 'the promotion of small business, the reduction of corporate tax, the maintenance and upgrading of the country's infrastructure, and a reordering of government spending priorities to tackle poverty, unemployment and the skills shortage' (1993:18). Welfarist elements were seen as a 'political accessory', appended to an economic strategy – 'necessary evils rather than the basis for creating a new set of social alliances, a new era for economic growth and the bedrock for social stability in post-apartheid society', in Mike Morris's view (1993b:9).

Slightly less orthodox were the Nedcor/Old Mutual scenarios. These stressed the need to achieve competitiveness in manufactured exports and envisaged two stages of recovery. The government would make large investments in social programmes and infrastructure, after which a manufactured export drive would commence, founded on a compact between business, labour and government. Noteworthy was the downplaying of the need for massive foreign investment.

It should be noted that around economic policy in general, South African capitalists were not (and had never been) of a single mind. There was broad agreement around the need for a market economy, but different fractions of capital demanded different adjustments that best favoured them. For example, large financial and mining firms were keen on wide-ranging liberalization that would allow them to globalize (alone, through joint ventures with foreign corporations and via offshore listings, for example). Manufacturing sector firms were ambivalent: those confident of their competitive potential favoured trade liberalization, while their more vulnerable counterparts were less enthusiastic.

Research projects launched by the IMF and World Bank elaborated the same overarching perspective. But, while the IMF issued customarily strident injunctions, the World Bank soon after the 1990 thaw had opened channels to the ANC and the trade unions, and enlisted researchers associated with the democratic movement in its projects. 'This is the only country in the world where we speak to the opposition', its representative later boasted.[16] The soil of conciliation and consensus was being diligently tilled. The World Bank's 1994 *Reducing Poverty* report became the public component of an intensive process of lobbying and 'trust-building' with the ANC and other popular organizations. It melded detailed analyses of South Africa's economic woes with somewhat restrained neoliberal directives that were often offset by incorporating aspects of progressive thinking.[17] In the World Bank's view, growth hinged on private sector-led expansion in labour-intensive sectors of the economy, with the state assuming a subsidizing (through incentives and credit) and facilitating role (through investment in health and education): 'South Africa's unequal legacy cannot be reversed solely by market reforms because those disenfranchised by apartheid will be unable to obtain the resources necessary to exploit market opportunities.'[18]

The *Reducing Poverty* report criticized the capital-intensive character of industry and heavy state subsidies for large-scale capital intensive projects, and claimed that 200 00 to 400 000 fewer jobs were created in the 1980s as a result of the African workers' wage increases. However, along with the reminder that growth required 'continuing fiscal discipline' and 'happier industrial relations', the Bank made the rather unfashionable point that labour should not 'bear the brunt of reduction in real wages'.[19] On that score, the Bank diverged from the IMF. The latter's *Key Issues in the South African Economy* document forcefully paraded the institution's customary arguments. Along with slashing the budget deficit, lowering inflation and maintaining macro-economic stability, liberalized trade and financial relations were posed as prerequisites for increased exports, foreign investment and access to credit. It warned against 'excessive' government expenditures on education, health, training and complementary infrastructure, while declaring that the 'remedy for structural unemployment is to increase the productivity of labour, to lower the real wage, or some combination of the two'. Although fallacious,[20] the argument found many a receptive ear. The National Manpower Commission's chair, Frans Baker, declared that while wage cuts were 'not necessarily' the answer, the ideal approach would be 'to let employers and unions negotiate wages in the face of the cold winds of international competition'.[21] In the business press, some commentators openly advised the speedy implementation of IMF-style structural adjustment:

> The IMF will want measures such as currency liberalisation, reducing government spending, cutting subsidies to blue chip companies, privatising state assets and busting the cartels in labour and other markets. Some will complain about a loss of sovereignty, but we would have undertaken these reforms years ago had we not been thwarted by vested interests ... we've been unable to make the reforms that will give us 6% growth. Perhaps the IMF will help.[22]

Drawing heavily on IMF thinking was the apartheid government's Normative Economic Model (NEM), released in March 1993. It was an attempt to add some coherence to the bedraggled and erratic economic policies pursued by Pretoria. After hopping the supply-side bandwagon in the mid-1980s, the apartheid government touted privatization, trade liberalization, spending cuts and strict monetary and fiscal discipline as the way forward. The conversion to free market economics, however, was equivocal. The zeal for privatization proved short-lived and tariffs were cut half-heartedly. Former finance minister Derek Keys later even advocated a strong government role in facilitating an investment-driven economic recovery

(Kentridge, 1993). In short, government economic policy turned out to be a pastiche of Thatcherite adjustments and statist legacies. The NEM was meant to substitute a more coherent policy framework.

The NEM bore the hallmark of a January 1992 IMF 'occasional paper' that had reversed the 'growth through redistribution' formula and proceeded by way of elimination to argue for adjustments that were in step with its standard directives to the South. Paving the way toward growth would be an ensemble of measures. It included corporate tax cuts, higher indirect taxation, wage restraint (and higher productivity), lower inflation, restricted capital outflows, budget deficit cuts, more spending on research and development and training, boosted manufactured exports, improvements in the social wage, restricting unions' positions in collective bargaining and corporatist relations between government, labour and business. In other words, it advocated a trickle-down model with government providing some support (through welfare measures and public works projects) to the 'short-term' victims of adjustments.

The ANC and COSATU unreservedly slammed the government model, and the NEM seemingly was ushered onto the sidelines of the debate. Even mainstream business journals concurred, suggesting that 'neither the model's scenario nor that of the IMF have any hope whatever of being achieved'.[23] Three years later, though, the ANC government's macroeconomic strategy would contain several of its elements.

In late 1993, there appeared the ostensibly social-democratic *Mont Fleur* scenario. In retrospect, it significantly assisted the march of orthodoxy – less because of its content than its central theme and the range of progressive (including ANC) economists and union figures that were drawn into the exercise. The scenario daubed heterodox strategic options in the dread colours of macro-economic populism. Striking was its disapproval of redistributive state spending. Importantly, the intervention came several months before the release of the MERG report, *Making Democracy Work: A Framework for Macroeconomic Policy in South Africa* – the outcome of a process which, since 1991, ostensibly had been the main site of ANC economic policy development.

ANC economic thinking had come to reflect, according to ANC economist Viv McMenamin, 'a shift away from policies which may be morally and politically correct, but which will cause strong adverse reaction from powerful local and international interests' (Kentridge, 1993:10). Its draft policy guidelines (released in April 1992) had already been stripped of references to higher corporate taxes, made no mention of restructuring or regulating the financial sector and mooted the possibility of privatization in the public sector – changes that betrayed the waning influence of the left in ANC economic policy-making. In the media, the labour movement was being portrayed increasingly as a narrow and relatively 'privileged' interest group, a view that resonated powerfully among the ANC's *petit bourgeois* constituencies (who, themselves, would be threatened by measures such as minimum wages). In years to come, their concerns would feature more loudly in ANC government policies.

The ANC's commitment to an export-oriented growth strategy was also assured, despite warnings from unlikely quarters such as GATT that: '... export-led growth, while beneficial to the balance of payments, is unlikely to immediately affect levels of unemployment, given the capital intensity of the export sector, unless labour-intensive downstream industries can be developed'.[24]

It was not only cajoling by business that led to the endorsement of an export-led growth path. The stance was promoted also by the COSATU-initiated ISP.[25] Improved manufacturing export performance had been acknowledged on the left as an important factor in addressing South Africa's endemic current account difficulties and its reliance on revenue from primary commodity exports. This required restructuring industries that had been declining since the 1970s and that produced a range and volume of manufactured exports that were negligible compared to Brazil and Mexico.[26] Some left economists still argued that a revived manufactured export capacity should not come at the expense of a growth strategy that also had to focus on restructuring, developing and expanding the *internal* market. That perspective was soon marginalized.

Unlike business, the ISP stressed that competitiveness derived not so much from lower input costs (such as cheaper wages) as from product quality and variety, speedy innovation, capital and labour productivity, and 'the endowment of widely spread skills' (Joffe *et al.*, 1994b:17). Special emphasis was placed on high-value-added products. Rather than subject industry to attrition by randomly removing protection, the ISP proposed 'a trade policy that attempts to sharpen the flow of incentives from the international market' within an overall industrial strategy.[27] The desired alchemy required from the state supply-side measures and a range of (dis)incentives that could make the market function better – 'a kind of liberal Keynesianism', as one of the team members joked. Many of the elements of the ISP plan could have *augmented* an industrial revival strategy geared also at servicing popular domestic needs. Instead, they were deployed in a framework that *pivoted* South Africa's economic revival on an export-led growth strategy. This was despite the team's admission that:

> ... entry in external markets is increasingly difficult, partly because of the growth of protectionist barriers in key large economies and partly because of heightened competition. At the same time, most of the developing world (including South Africa) is being forced to open domestic markets to imports (Joffe *et al.*, 1994a:91).

Rearguard actions

By late 1993, Kentridge would note that 'the language and tone [of ANC and business policy documents] are so similar that at times they appear interchangeable' (1993:26). From 1992 onwards, the ANC's policy resolutions had increasingly hedged progressive state regulation with provisos that were clearly designed to mollify business. This triggered angry reactions among grassroots constituencies and in COSATU.

During the political negotiations, consultation by the ANC with its membership and political allies was patchy and perfunctory, and the relationship between the negotiations and economic policy formulation virtually non-existent. Pressure from ANC and trade union activists had kept on the agenda demands such as restructuring the financial sector and progressive taxation – but only until 1992 when they were dropped from ANC resolutions. At the same time, the organization began mooting the need for property rights guarantees and privatization. Its rhetoric still orbited around a 'developmental state' that would 'lead, coordinate, plan and dynamise a national economic strategy' aimed at job creation and redistributing resources to the poor.[28] But enthusiasm for that approach was ebbing among leadership, even if activists still felt stirred by the rhetoric.

At a May 1992 ANC policy conference, activists pushed privatization off the agenda and softened the wording of other placatory pledges. But the gist of the post-1990 retreats was endorsed, thanks partly, as Nattrass has suggested, to the personal presence of ANC leaders Nelson Mandela, Walter Sisulu and Cyril Ramaphosa in the economic policy debates at the conference. The draft policy guidelines emerged substantively intact though semantically adjusted. Thus the word 'privatization' was replaced with an unwieldy phrase designed to soothe dissent.[29] The exception was the re-appearance of a call for greater control of financial institutions.

COSATU, especially, tried to oppose many of the developments surveyed here. Two counter-attacks in particular were devised. The first was a push to have a greater institutionalized role in economic and industrial policy-making. In late 1992, it issued an economic policy document that emphasized job creation and meeting health, education and housing needs. The broad thrust toward social transformation negated attempts to portray the federation as the guardian of a narrow set of interests.

Arguments that a social contract was needed to advance these objectives were winning ground in COSATU. Since the early 1990s, several affiliates had already put this into practice at industry and company levels – the National Union of Mineworkers' (NUM) 1992 profit-sharing deal with mining houses and the National Union of Metalworkers' (NUMSA) agreements with employers around restructuring the auto industry were two examples. COSATU's push for the creation of a National Economic Forum

(NEF) was in line with this thinking. Such a bargaining body would transfer decision-making on key economic issues into a forum where trade unions could wield influence. Key ANC figures, such as Trevor Manuel (the party's shadow finance minister), openly disapproved, claiming that macro-economic policy was the preserve of government, not the trade union movement. Still, the NEF was launched in October 1992, amid confusion about its role and the extent of its powers.[30] COSATU wanted it to function as a negotiating body; business wanted an advisory body. That tension would plague the body in its later incarnation, NEDLAC (the National Economic Development and Labour Council), which would officially become described as a '*consultative* structure'.

As important was the development of a Reconstruction Accord, which began in 1991. The aim was to make COSATU's electoral support conditional on the ANC adopting the accord as a government programme once it assumed power. COSATU saw this as a way of maintaining leverage over its ally. The accord would eventually mature into the RDP, which became a central plank of the ANC's 1994 election campaign.

'No alternative'

By late 1993, the ANC had agreed to a clause that would enshrine Reserve Bank independence in the constitution, effectively removing monetary policy from democratic oversight and accountability. The ANC also agreed not to usher the incumbent Reserve Bank governor (the conservative Chris Stals) into another line of employment – he remained head of one of the most powerful economic institutions in South Africa. It has been claimed that these moves were less ominous than they appeared. The constitutional clause, according to economist Stephen Gelb: '... was sufficiently vague that the relation between government and the Bank would continue to depend *de facto* on the personal styles and relationship of the Governor and the Finance Minister' (1999:12).

A similarly sanguine reading later would spur hopes that Stals's eventual successor (former labour minister Tito Mboweni) could refashion relations between the Bank, the finance ministry and parliament. That view, however, over-personalized the Bank's location in the economic and political system. In periods when finance capital is dominant, the structural relationship between a country's central bank and the wider financial sector tends to deepen. As economists Paul Bowles and Gordon White have shown, the central bank then more strongly 'reflects the interests and ideology of that sector'.[31] Constitutionally decreed Reserve Bank independence would end up entrenching and defending that relationship in South Africa.[32]

The Reserve Bank clause was not subjected to organizational debate before ANC negotiators agreed to include it in the interim constitution. Explaining the decision, Mandela later said: 'We argued for the independence of the

Bank ... not only because we are committed to the sound economic management of the country, but also because we want to send out a strong signal to
the international and local business and financial communities that we are
serious about this commitment'.[33] A precedent had been set for the unilater-
alism that would later characterize the introduction of the ANC government's
GEAR macro-economic plan in 1996.

Meanwhile, the ANC (in November 1993) had entered into a secret
$850-million loan agreement with the IMF to help tide the country over
balance of payment difficulties.[34] Attached to the loan was a statement of
intent which, in retrospect, reads like a précis of the GEAR plan:

> [A]n easing of monetary policy would have risked a further undermining of
> confidence and a resurgence of inflation ... the thrust of SA's monetary
> policy during the past year will be maintained ... despite the pressures for
> additional expenditure that will arise in transition, there is widespread
> understanding that increases in the government deficit would jeopardise the
> economic future of the country ... Given the importance of maintaining a
> competitive tax structure, [fiscal policy] will emphasise expenditure contain-
> ment rather than raising taxes.[35]

Clearly dominant was the belief that the choice lay between yielding to
orthodoxy or exposing the economy to the wrath of the markets – and
thereby putting the democratic transition at risk. Highlighting that possibility was the savage violence that engulfed hundreds of black townships as
apartheid police units and death squads staged massacres and assassina-
tions, and state-supported vigilante gangs, IFP and ANC activists transformed communities into war zones. The role of the apartheid security
apparatuses in the violence of the early 1990s would later be partially
revealed by the TRC. There is no doubt that the state also took an active
part in fomenting violent rivalries between contending organizations. The
conflagrations took a huge toll: whereas 86 people were killed monthly
during the uprisings of the mid-1980s, 250 were dying per month in the
early 1990s. Between the release of Mandela in February 1990 and April
1994 when South Africans finally went to the polls, 14 800 people were
killed.[36] The causes and the actors in the violence were multifarious. But
the ultimate message rang loud: moderation, stability and compromise
might avert a cataclysmic implosion.[37] On the economic front, business was
issuing the same counsel. The cumulative effect was to recast the correlation of forces.

Yet, the argument that the ANC had a gun held to its head alone fails
to account for the resolve with which its leaders embraced economic
orthodoxy and the subsequent perseverance of those choices. A more persuasive explanation has to add factors to those already mentioned. Among
them was the organization's inability to hold its own in (ostensibly)

technical discussions and debates on economic policy. This was a direct consequence of the democratic movement's historical neglect of the social and economic spheres. As Jonathan Michie and Vishnu Padayachee later reminded, the ANC '… did not at the beginning of the negotiations possess a ready institutional capacity on the economic policy front to counter the power and resources available to its main opponents and other institutions' (1997:229).

In fact, there was a patent absence of technically rigorous economists at the helm of the ANC's DEP. Business could successfully conduct a vigorous political and ideological struggle at a nominally technical level, deploying massive resources to great effect.[38] Conservative figures in the ANC drew heavily on business advice (paraded as being in step with 'global standards') and were emboldened to steer policy along more 'realistic' paths. The glee with which they employed fashionable economic jargon and issued deeply conservative counsel might have embarrassed some of their comrades but hardly harmed their political careers. After all, they were heeding the 'hard truths' that faced a developing country in a world that was being reshaped by neoliberal globalization.

All this occurred in a wider, debilitating context. The collapse of Soviet-style socialism and the crisis of Western European welfare systems (driven especially by the fate of Francois Mitterand's government in France) had badly winded not only radical demeanours but the sheer ability to think in terms of alternatives. Half-hearted attention was directed at other growth models (in Asia, for example), but the examinations were shoddy. Having neglected the economic realm for decades, the ANC's resistance levels were low, particularly in an era advertised as the 'end of history'. With the organization's earlier, makeshift reference points either crushed or badly dented, its appetite for risk was weak. The low road of accommodation to orthodoxy held great appeal.

Strengthening the allure was the long-standing but growing force of *bourgeois* and *petit bourgeois* layers within the ANC, a reality conveniently overlooked by many members and foreign supporters, who preferred to regard the SACP-engineered radicalism of the 1980s as an intrinsic feature of the organization. In reality, as academic Sipho Maseko has written, those classes 'emerged more prominently and significantly from the 1960s onwards', and especially in the 1980s and 1990s as the 'decompression' of class differences within African communities gathered steam. Moreover:

> … the African National Congress has since its inception sought to promote the interests of this class, as well as other classes. During the liberation struggle, particularly before the ANC's banning in 1960, it articulated an ideology favourable to the development of the black capitalist class.[39]

As Maseko reminded, the notion of 'black economic empowerment' (a post-1994 siren call of the ANC government) was first trumpeted by the National African Federated Chambers of Commerce (NAFCOC), founded in the 1960s. Along with the Black Management Forum, 'it popularised an idea misleadingly referred to as "black economic empowerment" – misleading because it suggested socio-economic improvement of the general black population, yet it called for the enrichment of the minority black capitalist class'.[40] Those aspirations were hardly anathema to an organization that staked considerable hope on the rapid growth of a black 'patriotic *bourgeoisie*' (a notion that, moreover, had a strong pedigree in post-colonial Africa and Asia).

These factors congealed into a naïve faith in the prospects of a compromise with domestic and international capital. In large part, that credence stemmed from the ANC's elliptical understanding of globalization (see below) and its consequent hope of reconciling drastic and conservative economic adjustments with the aim of reducing poverty and inequality.[41] The quest for policies acceptable to business proceeded as if the process was politically and ideologically neutral, and could be appended to a set of strategic (and politically palatable) social objectives.

Sought by the ANC was capital's support for the successful completion of the democratic transition and its commitment to launching the economy onto a growth track that would enable an ANC government to meet its socio-economic pledges. The compromise carried a steep price: trade and financial liberalization, a privatization programme, a regressive tax system, ultra-low inflation targets (above all, favouring financial capital) and a vast array of other, business-friendly adjustments. The tone was patently neoliberal, albeit leavened by rhetoric to the contrary and, more importantly, later also by commendable changes to the labour market and affirmative action policies in the workplace.[42]

Viewed from afar, the route chosen seemed to herald the re-integration into the global economy of a country that was being patronizingly classified as an 'emerging market'. But it carried no guarantee of success. Measured in the lives of ordinary South Africans, the toll exacted would be heavy.

What happened to MERG?

The fate of the MERG proposals illustrated the ANC's aversion toward economic policies that seemed to buck the 'global consensus'. The organization had set up MERG in 1991 to develop a new macro-economic model for South Africa.[43] It took on the task amid controversy over the strong contingent of foreign economists on the team and, more tellingly, resistance from members of the ANC's DEP, who feared that MERG was usurping their roles. MERG members, meanwhile, complained that their work was 'frustrated by DEP delaying or spoiling tactics' (Kentridge, 1993:56). The squabbling was a side-show. By the time the group presented its neo-Keynesian final report, *Making Democracy Work*, in late 1993, the proposals were well out of line with ANC thinking.

The report died a quick death, despite the acknowledgement by economists such as Nattrass that the recommendations were 'carefully costed and situated in what appears to be a sound macroeconomic model' (1994b:2). Central to the document was the argument that the economy could best be restructured through the labour market (improved training, education and skills-building, and higher wages) and through interventions aimed at improving the structure and operation of business. A new economic system would depend on a 'strong private sector interacting with a strong public sector', the authors noted (Macro-Economic Research Group, 1993:265). If the key proposals were implemented, the MERG model predicted annual growth of 5 per cent in 2004 and the creation of 300 000 new jobs a year. It presented a two-phase growth plan (comprising a 'public-investment-led phase' and a 'sustained growth phase') that tied growth to expanded and efficiently deployed savings and investment. A robust role was reserved for the state, including:

> ... state intervention in output and pricing decisions in the minerals sectors, regulation of the housing and building supplies market, tightening and extending controls on mergers and acquisitions, monitoring the behaviour of participants in oligopolistic markets, and creating supervisory boards (consisting of bank, trade union and other represented interests) for larger companies.[44]

MERG saw state investment in social and physical infrastructure (housing, school education, health services, electrification and road development) in the first phase accounting for more than half of growth, and triggering sustained, growth-inducing effects throughout the economy. In addition, it proposed that the state strategically apply a mix of incentives and regulations to restructure and improve industrial performance, and recommended a national minimum wage, pegged at two-thirds the subsistence level for a household of five. The argument was that a minimum wage would improve productivity 'by reducing absenteeism, illness and labour turnover', and provide the incentive for firms 'to undertake the necessary adjustments to make human resources more productive' (1993:163). Nattrass was among many economists to counter that 'the low-wage sectors will shed labour once the minimum wage is introduced' (1994b:5). The other aspect to ignite wrath was the proclaimed need for the state to 'provide leadership and co-ordination for widely-based economic development' and to 'intervene directly in key areas' (Macro-Economic Research Group, 1993:281). This included the argument that no coherent macro policy could be implemented without more control or oversight over the Reserve Bank.

Not surprisingly, *Making Democracy Work* was savaged in the media and by mainstream economists, responses that some ANC leaders reportedly shared.[45] Some of its key proposals would be exhumed in COSATU's *Social Equity and Job Creation* document two years later. It was, by then, too late. The left had failed to politically defend MERG and advance its proposals within the ANC. Whatever the shortcomings of MERG's left-Keynesian framework, it was the most coherent progressive scenario available. Instead, it was seen to threaten the emergent consensus being assembled (on the economic front and in the political negotiations) as well as put at risk the career ambitions of ANC DEP figures who were acutely aware of which way the economic policy winds were blowing. It was impolitely set aside. Two years later, the ANC government's GEAR strategy would apply the final nails to the coffin.

A battle lost

The perspectives presented in the MERG report fell victim to a dominant discourse and a balance of forces that had tilted ineluctably rightward, so much so that President Nelson Mandela could, at the 1994 COSATU congress, invoke the examples of low-wage Asian economies and tell delegates that 'unless we sacrifice, [unless] we have that determination to tighten our belts ... it is going to be difficult to get our economy to grow'.[46]

The left had been in retreat on the economic policy front. The ANC had endorsed financial and monetary stringency, chosen a restricted role for the state in redistribution and supported the restructuring of trade and industrial policies in line with an export-led strategy. Economic revival would be market led and geared at achieving sustainable growth by attracting foreign and encouraging domestic investment. Exchange controls would be removed, tariff and non-tariff protection to industries lifted, and supply-side support provided to help stimulate industrial renewal. Social and industrial unrest would be checked through social accords, co-determination agreements and restructured labour relations.

The pat view was that the ANC 'saw the light', thanks to the determination of business to 'patiently and systematically educate blacks into the economic realities of the world'.[47] Nattrass suggested that as 'the ANC leadership began to worry about ensuring long-term sustainable growth – and hence also its long-term political future, its policies became more pro-business', with the future finance minister Trevor Manuel 'instrumental in this process' (1994c:20).

Brandished against the left and, increasingly, even traditional social-democrats was the argument that capital had become irrepressibly nomadic in the era of globalization. This left South Africa with no choice but to seek economic growth by adopting neoliberal policies. Such explanations assigned to orthodoxy the status of a self-evident 'truth', which was hardly borne out by international experience. The many variants of capitalism practicised across the globe disproved the notion that the neoliberal version constituted a kind of platonic ideal. The Chinese hybrid was grounded in familial and communal networks of production and distribution. It was vastly different from the individualistically grounded Anglo-Saxon models, They, in turn, could hardly be confused with the paternalistic *chaebol* (conglomerates) of South Korea, or with the bondage of corporate loyalties that underpinned the Japanese version. In each of these variants, the state adopted a distinct set of duties and powers in relation to the economy.

Moreover, the claim that the era of globalization has rendered the state powerless drew its authority much less from empirical evidence than from sheer repetition. No doubt, globalization constituted (as it still does) a seriously complicating dynamic. But the ANC adopted a specific and deeply conservative interpretation of it, one that formed the ideological bedrock of policy packages that would conform brazenly to the Washington consensus. It is therefore useful to revisit the globalization debate that the ANC so listlessly engaged with in the 1990s. ·

Tectonic shifts

The world shifted on its foundations in the final quarter of the twentieth century. The political-ideological divisions of the Cold War era had enabled developing countries to achieve shifting degrees of latitude (and even imperial support) for the pursuit of 'alternative' development models. The first tier of NICs in East Asia (South Korea, Taiwan and Singapore) arose in that context, as did the second tier (Malaysia, Thailand and Indonesia). In all instances, their achievements were closely linked to US largesse and support that was purposefully inserted into the most hotly contested region during the Cold War.[48] In Africa, several countries won space for their developmental experiments thanks to the West's nominal indulgence and the USSR and China's support (albeit uneven and inconsistent). Those relationships, too, were definitively shaped by the Cold War. The same applied to the Middle East and North Africa. The post-war world system, therefore, was 'tri-dimensional' (comprising the welfare capitalist West, the 'sovietism' of the Eastern bloc and the developmentalism of the Third World), with each 'nation state' acting as a basic unit in that system (Amin, 1997:6).

That system has disappeared. The geo-political and economic fields of the world today result not only from the end of the Cold War but from the collapse or deep erosion of the three development models that shaped the world's societies over the past 50 years. Deprived of their respective development paradigms, progressive movements everywhere have been thrown into disarray as their ideological moorings seemed to dissolve and their strategic options were narrowed. Vexing them is 'the apparent failure of all programmes, old and new, for managing or improving the affairs of the human race' (Hobsbawm, 1995:563). The task of mustering a viable progressive response is complicated further by a generalized retreat from 'old politics'. This is visible in the withdrawal of citizenries from participation in the formal political processes (evident in lower voter turnouts),[49] in the unexpected popularity of political contenders whose prime attraction lies in their disavowal of 'traditional' politics, and in the disaggregation of the left into so-called new social movements guided by identity politics that tend to gravitate less around ideologies and programmes than around 'an amalgam of slogans of emotions'.[50]

None of the main models for organizing economies seem capable of ensuring both sustained growth, full employment and universally humane living standards. Visions based on the elimination of private enterprise and the rule of the market, and their replacement by state ownership and central planning or by social ownership of production and distribution, have disintegrated. Their antithesis – that of the *laissez-faire* society ruled by market forces – has proved to be bankrupt.

More surprising and worrisome, in Hobsbawm's judgement, is 'the disorientation of what might be called the intermediate or mixed programmes and policies which had presided over the most impressive economic miracles of the century' (1995:564–5). In contrast to the other models, these programmes *were* successful. Though hardly impervious to criticism, they did produce rapid development, stimulate sustained economic growth, improve living standards and dramatically reduce social inequalities. Yet, they have been beaten into retreat – not only by the political/ideological vagaries of the day but by their apparent inability to manage the structural problems that have emerged. As Webster and Adler have noted, 'there is a seemingly universal trade-off between equality and employment' (1999:5). In the USA, rising employment and job flexibility goes hand-in-hand with greater polarization and poverty, while in Western Europe soaring unemployment is only partially off-set by the remnants of social security systems.

At the level of the world system, the late twentieth-century era of globalization corresponds also to increasing contestation between the major capitalist powers – a development closely linked to the absence of a global economic hegemon. Despite its military, cultural and diplomatic dominance, the US has not been able to maintain the hegemony it enjoyed in the economic realm during the third-quarter of the century. As a result, the world economic system has become dangerously volatile, with growing and deepening economic rivalries taking hold between the US and the other powerful industrialized countries, mainly Western Europe, Japan and, of late, China (Burbach *et al.*, 1997). Globalization, in other words, is not singularly guided by some conspiratorial unanimity between Washington, Bonn and Tokyo. These powers themselves harbour *contesting* needs in relation to one another – hence, the fierce contests to acquire dominion over or privileged access to foreign markets, natural resources, productive opportunities, new technologies and the like.

It is on the resulting fields that the process of globalization has been breaching the boundaries of national productive systems, reshaping and incorporating them as segments of a worldwide productive system driven by the 'laws' of the free market. The tripolar world system has been replaced by a unipolar one, marked by the unprecedented extension of market economies across the planet (most of which have been restructured along free market lines), the global dispersion of production processes (dominated by transnational corporations, TNCs) and the ubiquitous circulation of financial capital. It is clear that profound changes have occurred. But a closer look at the exact character and implications of those changes steers one into murkier waters.

In purely descriptive terms, globalization can be defined as the world-wide spread of industrial production and new technologies, accompanied and promoted by the rapid and unimpeded mobility of capital and unfettered freedom of trade, and the global reach and authority of TNCs.[51] Still popular is the view that the adjustments associated with globalization are launching the world towards an era of unmatched global prosperity, as economies are 'rationalized' along free market lines. The recipe for success is said to lie in a submission to Washington consensus: a compilation of adjustments allegedly aimed at freeing the capitalist system from inefficiencies and contradictions attributed to the interventionist or regulatory activities of states. Countries that conform to these dictates will, it is claimed, share in rising volumes of global trade and investment, and eventually constitute more or less equal players in a single, integrated world economy.

Defining the lives of the majority of the world's population is a less fanciful and immeasurably more distressing reality. Measured strictly in macro-economic terms, neoliberal structural adjustments have registered modest but uneven results. Inflation rates and state deficits have stabilized or declined. In some instances, growth rates have improved. But in all cases, social indicators have deteriorated, with the levels of inequality, joblessness, child mortality, fatal diseases and social dislocation rising.

Inequalities between countries and regions are increasing at a staggering pace. According to the UNDP's *1999 Human Development Report*:

> The fifth of the world's people living in the highest income countries has 86 per cent of world gross domestic product (GDP), 82 per cent of world export markets, 68 per cent of foreign direct investments and 74 per cent of world telephone lines. The bottom fifth, in the poorest countries, has about

one per cent in each sector ... Industrialised countries hold 97 per cent of all patents worldwide ... The income gap between the richest fifth of the world's people and the poorest fifth, measured by average national income per head, increased from 30 to one in 1960 to 74 to one in 1997.[52]

In 1960, the richest 20 per cent of the planet earned 30 times the income of the poorest 20 per cent; three decades later the ratio had swollen to 61, and by 1997, the richest fifth of the world was pocketing 78 times the income of the poorest fifth.[53] By 1994, 1,3 billion people were earning less than one US dollar a day (70 per cent of them women), while the numbers of homeless, undernourished and severely impoverished citizens have soared, prompting the Worldwatch Institute to warn that 'following a business-as-usual course in the future could doom half of humanity to absolute poverty by sometime between 2050 and 2075'.[54]

Preventable diseases and illnesses such as measles, cholera, meningitis, kwashiorkor and diarrhoea have re-appeared with ravaging vigour in regions where, two decades ago, they had almost been extinguished.[55] Environmental destruction proceeds at a devastating pace with effects that sweep across national boundaries. Inequalities have soared also within the world's most prosperous countries, each of which today harbours its own *de facto* 'Third World' underclass of discontents. In the United States, for example, the ratio between blue collar wages and top management salaries stood at 1:41 in 1975; two decades later it had widened to 1:189. Between 1977 and 1989, the incomes of the wealthiest 1 per cent of Americans rocketed by 104 per cent, while that of the poorest 5 per cent dropped by almost 10 per cent, increasing the number of poor Americans from 22 million to 32 million (Krugman, 1995:135). Food riots and looting rebellions punctuate the chronic social and political instability that besets many developing countries (and are answered with increased repression) while many desperate citizens seek refuge in the ideologies and networks of ethnic, religious and nationalist chauvinism.

New production technologies and systems are causing economies to shed jobs much faster than they can replace them, encouraging the widespread belief that one of the fundamental goals of both socialist and social-democratic projects – full employment – has become a 'pipe dream'.[56] Unemployment is now regarded as a structural (not a cyclical) feature as manufacturing jobs are lost at alarming rates in many industrialized countries. In the USA, 'from 1979 and 1992, productivity increased by 35% while the workforce shrank by 17%' (Rifkin, 1995b:18). By 1994, only 17 per cent of workers were active in manufacturing, compared to 33 per cent in 1950.[57] Some of these jobs have been transferred into the service sector: by the 1980s, more Americans were employed in McDonald's than in the steel industry (Vadney, 1987:391). Structural or not, the trend is not restricted to the industrialized countries. Mechanization in Brazilian automobile factories, for example, has caused massive labour redundancies, despite the comparatively cheap cost of labour. Emerging is what labour analyst Gerard Greenfield has termed a 'permanent crisis of "labour flexibility"'. Scanning post-1997 Asia, he has described this development as the outcome of:

> ... over a decade of national and international policies, strategies and processes of exploitation and control [that] have demolished the institutional expressions of workers' collective rights ... while creating new mechanisms for the suppression of workers' social and economic rights. This includes the casualisation of work and the decline of regular employment, downward pressure on wages in the name of 'competitiveness', increased working hours, the removal of 'rigidities' such as unemployment security and welfare rights, and the repression or co-optation of trade unions.[58]

Perversely, periodic economic crises (such as those that spilled across the world after the Asian crash) have served employers well in that respect. In the name of 'national reconstruction', they have effected large-scale retrenchments and severe wage cuts, while also restructuring their labour needs and pushing home regressive changes to national labour laws and regulations.[59]

Globally, trade unions totter on the horns of a dilemma. The co-determinist relations nurtured with union movements were based largely on the possibility of achieving full employment and the state's capacity to distribute adequate benefits (in the form of monied and social wages) to labour. Both those attractions are under severe attack. The goal of full employment has receded before the conviction that higher levels of unemployment have become a structural feature of the global economy, despite trenchant critiques of this view. Trade unions can adopt a defensive posture within that old corporatist framework in a bid to limit the damage – an option preferred by the state and capital since it tempers renewed instability and institutionalizes the subservience of a powerful social formation. Or they can choose the route of attack and assume an overt oppositional role (in concert with other social forces). All the while, however, retrenchments, declining union memberships and attacks by the state and business are likely to sap the strength of the labour movement. The danger in both instances is that the most powerful social force of the past century might be rammed onto the sidelines.

New wine in an old bottle?

A rich debate continues around the definition of globalization, its alleged novelty and the forces or developments propelling it. Much of it orbits around the uniqueness of economic changes that are customarily grouped under the heading 'globalization'. Conventional wisdom sees it as a unique and recent development destined to yield an integrated world economy in which benefits are spread more equally than ever before. Disputing this is a skeptical tradition. Paul Hirst (1996), for instance, reminds that globalization began centuries ago, while Saskia Sassen (1997) and David Harvey (1995) provide compelling evidence that the world economy of the late nineteenth century in some respects was as open as today's. In David Marquand's summary: 'The heaving, masterless, global economy of the 1990s differs from its benign and stable predecessor of the 1950s and 1960s, but it has a great deal in common with that of the 19th century and something in common with that of the inter-war period.'[60]

During the *belle epoque* of 1870–1914, the world economy was, by some measures, as globalized as it is today.[61] In fact, the ratio of capital flows to GDP then was greater than at the end of the twentieth century. FDI increased at such a formidable pace that by 1913 it amounted to more than 9 per cent of world output (Arrighi, 1997:2). Money, goods and people crossed borders virtually at will, while international financial speculation raged thanks to the laying of submarine intercontinental cables. By the end of the nineteenth century, trading floors in 'Chicago and London, Melbourne and Manchester were linked in close to real time', as Hirst has reminded (1996:3). States' abilities to introduce and manage national economic policies were severely constrained by the gold standard, while the sway of a ratings agency such as Moody's was so great in 1920 that it rated bonds issued by 50 governments across the globe.[62] It is more accurate, therefore, to speak of the current or latest stage of globalization – for it is not a new phenomenon *per se*. The transformations associated with it are 'new in degree but not in kind', in Arrighi's analysis (1997:2).

On the financial front, though, that assertion seems over simplified. Today's financial speculation is much more heavily leveraged by borrowing than it was a century earlier. The personal capital of wealthy families in Britain and Europe was a chief source of nineteenth-century short-term capital flows in and out of bond and equity markets. Essentially, this was long-term portfolio capital in search of higher rates of return. Today, a growing proportion of global capital is leveraged, most notably in the case of hedge funds. In other words, new transactions are financed with the anticipated – but unrealized – gains of earlier transactions, creating a rickety house of cards where each new layer rests on another layer of speculation.

The ratio of trade to output has grown massively, with imports and exports constituting a bigger share of economic activity than before. On the investment front, a signal shift is the rise of TNCs that now account for a much larger share of productive investments and dominate international consumer markets on an unprecedented scale. TNCs account for about one-third of world output and two-thirds of world trade. Hinting at the scale and power of TNCs is the fact that about one-quarter of world trade today occurs *within* these corporations. In Noam Chomsky's formulation:

> In the US about 40% of what is called 'trade' is actually internal to a firm – like Ford Motor Company shifting something for assembly in Mexico, and shipping it back across the border; it's not trade in any serious sense ... One fairly conventional estimate in technical studies is that about 15% of trade may be called free in some sense (1998).

But the most dramatic changes have occurred in world financial markets. The volume of trading in currencies, bonds and equities since 1980 surged five times quicker than the GDP of the industrialized economies. Foreign exchange transactions, especially, have grown to stellar proportions. By 1992, these transactions were 60 times bigger than world trade; by 1998, some $1,2 trillion a day was changing hands in these 'casino capitalism' deals. According to some calculations, this staggering amount is one-fifth larger than the combined foreign currency reserves of the world's central banks (Gray, 1998:62). In Sassen's view, these transactions represent 'in many ways the only true global market' (1996:40). Billions of dollars more are staked daily on an ever-growing array of complex, speculative investments. Yet, strictly speaking, the rise in both productive and speculative forms of investment is not *global* in sweep – the bulk of it is confined to the industrialized economies and, significantly, occurs within regional blocs.

The definitive features of the current epoch of globalization therefore reside in TNCs' share of investment, output and trade, and in the massive expansion of purely financial activities. Both developments are made possible by technological innovations: production and transport systems that enable the segmentation and dispersal of production across the globe, and information and communication technologies that allow financial transactions to occur at the speed of light, 24 hours a day. But it is a mistake to attribute the 'financialization' of the world economy and the dominance of TNCs to new technologies. They are better understood as tools that enable profound and necessary adaptations in the mode of accumulation to occur. Late twentieth-century globalization is not just another stage in the headlong advance and qualitative refinement of capitalism – it is an ensemble of adjustments that respond to structural weaknesses in the system. Technological innovations have abetted these corrective exercises. Viewing globalization as a 'natural' outgrowth of new technologies therefore is to hitch the cart before the horse.

Another long downturn
Long-wave theorists such as Giovanni Arrighi have detected in capitalism's history at least four 'systemic cycles of accumulation', each of which lasted several decades and was marked by swift and relatively stable growth in

world trade and output. Each, however, also ended in an upsurge of purely financial transactions, 'heightened inter-state competition for mobile capital, rapid technological and organizational change, state breakdowns and an unusual instability of the economic conditions under which states operate' (Arrighi, 1997:3). In a nutshell, each of these long cycles ended in a crisis of over-accumulation and in the breakdown of the institutional mechanisms on which the earlier expansion of trade and output had been based. There is compelling evidence that capitalism entered such a phase in the early 1970s and that the neoliberal adjustments defining globalization currently emerged in reaction to that downturn.

Plaguing the world economy since the late 1960s (although the oil crisis of 1973 is commonly used as a marker)[63] has been a *long-term* and *system-wide* economic downturn that registered profoundly in the most advanced capitalist countries. Compared to the preceding two decades of post-war growth, the economic system had entered a long trough of relative stagnation. 'Throughout these economies,' Robert Brenner has demonstrated, 'average rates of growth of output, capital stock (investment), labour productivity, and real wages for the years 1973 to the present [1998] have been one-third to one-half of those for the years 1950–1973, while the average unemployment rate has been more than double'. Industrial production in the industrialized countries declined steadily. After growing at an unusually high rate of 3,6 per cent from 1950 to 1973, per capita GDP growth fell to 2 per cent in the next 15 years – a 45 per cent drop. Causing this was massive over-capacity and over-production in manufacturing in the industrialized countries since the late 1960s. In Robin Blackburn's summary: 'Once rival complexes of fixed capital were locked in national confrontation with each other, with no easy escape into alternative lines of production, profits fell dramatically and in tandem across the whole advanced capitalist world.'[64]

One reaction was to lower input costs, by depressing wages and shifting production to low-wage zones.[65] This was achieved through assaults on organized labour (exemplified in the Reagan and Thatcher eras) – betraying the class dimension of the current epoch of globalization. It was also abetted by advances in transport and production systems that made it easier to segment production, with components manufactured and then assembled into final products in different countries. Naturally, it also required unfettered access to national economies – through the lifting of trade barriers and erasing of investment conditionalities. Neoliberal ideology (codified in the Washington consensus) would serve as a battering ram on the latter front.

Another simultaneous and overarching reaction was to withhold productive investment, a route fraught with danger, however. New outlets and opportunities for profit-making constantly had to be realized in order to prevent the devalorization of capital. Issuing massive loans to developing countries became one important antidote. Indeed, the Third World debt served as a crucial source of ballast for capitalism – with Africa, perversely, serving as an important life-buoy. In 1996, its debt burden amounted to $320,6 billion, which translated into more than $400 for every man, woman and child living on the continent. Three decades earlier, Africa owed about $3 billion debt; by the early 1980s, the figured had rocketed to $142 billion. The bulk of this debt (73,5 per cent) was owed to bilateral and multilateral creditors.[66]

Another route was the time-honoured one of exporting capital in the form of FDI. Between 1983 and 1989, global FDI flows rose almost 29 per cent annually – considerably faster than world GDP increases (Sweezy & Magdoff, 1992:10–11). By 1996, these flows totalled $350 billion annually; two years later, they had soared another 40 per cent to $640 billion. Much of the impetus came from cross-country mergers and acquisitions, while the bulk of the FDI was concentrated in the developed world markets as investors zeroed in on new opportunities that matched their comparative advantages.[67]

Smaller amounts (though massive when viewed from the recipient countries) were directed at some developing countries where low wages, growing consumer markets and sufficiently sophisticated infrastructure created opportunities for profit-making either in the local economy or, more commonly, on the export front. As the second generation of Asian 'tigers' matured in the 1990s, it was no surprise that rising shares of FDI ended on their shores. But UNCTAD's cheery 1996 summary that 'every developing region saw an increase in inflows ... even the 48 least developed countries experienced an increase'[68] hid the highly uneven distribution of FDI in the developing world. A third of all FDI flows in 1996 to Asia, Latin America and Africa went to one country: China. Of the FDI directed at Latin America, more than half was directed at three countries – Brazil, Mexico and Argentina. Africa's share of developing country inflows more than halved, from 11 per cent during 1986–90 to 5 per cent during 1991–6, dropping to 3,8 per cent in 1996.[69] UNCTAD's conclusion was sobering: 'Africa has not participated in the surge of FDI flows to developing countries'.[70]

That trend has continued. Global FDI reached $400 billion in 1997, but 58 per cent of it went to industrialized countries, and just 5 per cent to the transition economies of Central and Eastern Europe. Of the FDI that went to developing and transition countries in the 1990s, more than 80 per cent went to just 20 countries, mainly to China.[71] By 1998, Africa's share of global FDI has dropped by another $1,1 billion to $8,3 billion – or slightly more than 1 per cent of total FDI. What is revealed, in other words, is the highly polarized nature of the global economy, with Africa linked to it mainly as a zone for resource extraction and through its debt relations with the advanced capitalist countries.

Hidden in these figures also is the changing composition of FDI, which, increasingly has been directed away from manufacturing and toward services – especially the communications, financial and insurance, and advertising sectors and the media. In 1966, a mere 4 per cent of US FDI went toward the banking, finance and insurance sector; by 1990, the figure had soared to 24 per cent (Sweezy & Magdoff, 1992:16). That statistic alerts us to one of the dominant exit routes of capitalism in the current, long downturn: retaining capital in its financial form.

Since the early 1970s, world financial markets have undergone a stupendous increase in scale and complexity. The financial futures market[72] gained prominence in the early 1970s, first in New York and then in other Western financial centres. By 1990, it was no longer a novelty, but a giant of international finance, with 'open positions (the value of the contracts traded on these markets) [totalling] $1.2-trillion worldwide' (Sweezy & Magdoff, 1992:3). Interest and currency swaps were scarcely known in the 1970s, but by 1991, $2,5 trillion worth of these deals were being struck. Another index of the 'financialization' of the world economy was the boom in international banking. Traditionally, one of the main functions of cross-country banking had been to facilitate trade. In the mid-1960s, as Paul Sweezy and Harry Magdoff have showed, 'the volume of [this] banking activity amounted to around 10% of the volume of world trade of the market economies' (1992:2). Two decades later, it was *exceeding* the volume of international trade and became 'tied in with a host of new methods of financial speculation and manipulation' (1992:2). Declining profits in manufacturing and extractive industries had encouraged investors to keep capital in its liquid form and to hunt profits in the financial realm. A huge demand was created for new forms of transactions. Advances in information technologies abetted the process. Crucially, free passage for speculative investments had to be engineered across the globe. Neoliberal ideology and its institutional guardians obliged on that front.

Money, long regarded as subordinate to production, has become an end in itself, despite the obvious fact that production remains the main engine of capitalist expansion. In its liquid form, capital now speeds across the globe in search of profit, severely complicating and even upending national economic strategies that are locked into attempts to overcome balance of payments upheavals.[73] In David M. Gordon's summary:

As the rate of return on fixed investment in plant and equipment has declined and as global economic conditions have become increasingly volatile, firms and banks have moved toward paper investments. The new and increasingly efficient international banking system has helped to foster an accelerating circulation of liquid capital, bouncing from one moment of arbitrage to another. Far from stimulating productive investment, however, these financial flows are best understood as a symptom of the diminishing attractiveness and uncertainty about prospects for fixed investment (1988:59).

A slight digression is called for. An upsurge that began as one of several reactions to the systemic downturn steadily acquired its own momentum and hermetic logic. It spun out of control. As the aftershocks of the Asian crisis crashed across the world in 1998–9, the need to rein in the monster became manifest. Talk grew of a new international financial architecture, as did support for the re-introduction of capital controls. But the strongest proponent of free capital flows remains the US – and for good reason. In Robert Wade and Frank Veneroso's judgement:

> For the high-consuming, low-saving [at 15% of GDP in 1998, the lowest of all the advanced industrialised countries] US economy this is the most important foreign ecnomic policy issue of all; on this depends its capacity to attract savings from the rest of the world in order to finance high investment – and remain the dominant economy (1998:41).

In order to remain effective, therefore, these remedies required the liberalization of economies on a global scale. It occurred on the trade front (allowing exports from the industrialized countries unhindered access to new markets), the fixed investment front (enabling TNCs to set up operations on acceptably hospitable terms) and the speculative investment front (lifting capital controls to allow unhindered passage in and out of economies). Technological developments enabled these transit routes to be followed with zeal. They did not predetermine them. The impetus for today's phase of 'globalization', therefore, resided in the structural dynamics of the capitalist system – specifically, as Brenner reminds, the periodic crises spawned by: '... the unplanned, uncoordinated and competitive nature of capitalist production, and in particular individual investors' unconcern for and inability to take account of the effects of their own profit-seeking on the profitability of other producers and of the economy as a whole' (1998:8).

Globalization, in such analysis, 'reflects less the establishment of a stable and new international regime of capital accumulation than an aspect of the decay of the old social structure of accumulation' (Gordon, 1988:59). Compressed into the doctrine of neoliberalism, the adjustments associated with globalization are aimed primarily at altering the terms of economic interaction between the dominant industrialized powers themselves, as well as between them and other national and regional economies. Translated into national economic strategies, this has produced the fetish of export-led industrialization and growth. Free trade has become a sacred ingredient of neoliberal doctrine, yet it is honoured more in the breach than through observance. Since the mid-1980s, as Kevin Watkins has observed, 'the enthusiastic commitment of northern governments to free market principles has been second only to their enthusiasm for protectionist practices' (1994:61), while Noam Chomsky (1998) has reminded that, under the reign of free market capitalism, constraints on trade have increased:

> This period, since the early seventies, has been described as a period of sustained assault on free markets by the head of economic research at the WTO in a technical study of his. He estimates the effects of Reaganite barriers at about three times the level of other industrial countries ... A UN development report estimates that, annually, the Third World loses about half a trillion dollars from various forms of 'first world' protectionism and market intervention.

The uneven or 'eclectic' application of injunctions that are said to define the very essence of globalization is not accidental: it discloses not only its discriminatory and polarizing character but also the intense rivalries shaping it. Globalization represents a profound paradox: its homogenizing and integrating thrust leads, at the same time, to ongoing polarization at the global level. As Burbach *et al.* have noted, globalization '... is both centripetal and centrifugal. It concentrates and integrates capital, commerce and trade in and between the metropoles, while at the same time casting off industries, peoples and even countries it has no use for' (1997:5).

Most of the economies of the world (and, in Africa's instance, an entire continent) function at best as marginal adjuncts to accumulatory processes that remain anchored in the industrialized cores of the system. Within the logic of neoliberal globalization, countries of what used to be called the periphery are integrated into the world system insofar as they can, in an auxiliary mode, service the accumulatory requirements of the dominant economic actors (be they states or multinational corporations). Researcher Dot Keet has suggested that globalization therefore represents not an irrevocable march towards a single integrated world economy, but rather the establishment of '... a complex combination of national (and sub-national and even very local) economies in different degrees and forms of interaction with one another, and varying degrees and modes of integration into, or participation in the larger whole' (1998:2–3).

Keet's prognosis ushers into focus two crucial aspects of globalization. Firstly, these various economies are articulated to one another within the overarching frame of polarization at the global level. This means that even if developing economies of the semi- or pre-industrialized variety can more effectively be linked or integrated, most of them will be languishing on the remote peripheries of the world system, comprising what Samir Amin has called the 'Fourth World'. However, that status potentially also presents them with some space in which to pursue *modest* development paths that could answer to some of the social needs of each constituent – particularly if those efforts occur in the context of regional (and even more far-flung) networks and alliances. Secondly, one of the ways in which the rivalries that accompany – and shape – globalization are being played out is through the creation of new regional blocs that are appended in subordinate fashion to the major economic powers. We are witnessing a highly selective trend of relinking potentially dynamic or attractive economies to the axis of the world system. The European Union's reshaping of the Lome Agreement, the USA's forays into Africa and its bid to extend the North American Free Trade Accord (NAFTA) into South America are examples of this process.

The crisis of accumulation described earlier also required rolling back the institutionalized gains of the working classes in the advanced capitalist countries and stalling similar victories in the developing world. Those arrangements hampered the introduction of new, flexible and cost-reducing forms of labour and the need to depress wage costs. Viewed in this manner, the neoliberal ideology that came to define the current stage of globalization looms into clearer focus.

In summary, the capitalist system (anchored in its advanced cores) required a series of formative responses. These had to:

- Reduce the social costs attached to accumulation, by dismantling welfare systems and neutralizing organized labour.
- Greatly ease the penetration of other markets by re-adjusting trade regimes.
- Enable large corporations to more easily escape the constricting terms of production (in their 'home zones' and further afield).
- Unfetter the global circulation of surplus capital.

The current phase of globalization, therefore, cannot be divorced from the roles of the dominant states in the world system (the USA in particular) in augmenting the expansionist projects of national and transnational groupings of capital. At the same time, this does not mean that globalization is nothing more than a 'promotional gimmick', as David Harvey (1995:8) has remarked playfully, to sell necessary adjustments in the world system.

Acolytes of neoliberalism and their adversaries on the Left tend to conflate the objective and subjective dimensions of globalization. The former claim that only one variant of globalization can exist (the neoliberal type) and that it heeds a set of 'economic laws' that, once applied, will create level playing fields for all contestants in a single integrated world economy. The latter risk rejecting globalization *in toto* as the outcome strictly of an imposed economic doctrine. In that view, even the ostensibly *neutral* features of globalization are deemed 'reversible'. Both approaches are mistaken. The introduction of innovations such as fibre optic cables, advanced labour-saving technologies, super computers and sophisticated transport systems cannot be reversed. Yet the character of globalization is not singular and pre-ordained; its neoliberal form reflects the balance of forces in the economic, political and cultural/ideological fields globally *and* nationally.

The myth of the free market and the weak state

Free market ideologues portray globalization as a veritable force of nature that crushes in its path the 'distortions' and 'aberrations' that prevent the supposedly self-regulating logic of free markets from operating. Central to this doctrine – which harks back to Adam Smith's 'invisible hand' – is the belief that the state encumbers efficient and robust economic activity. Such deception is not new. Half a century ago, Karl Polanyi laid to rest that vintage fallacy in his classic study *The Great Transformation*:

> It was not realized that the gearing of markets into a self-regulating system was not the result of any inherent tendency of markets ... But rather the effect of highly artificial stimulants administered to the body social in order to meet a situation which was created by the no less artificial phenomenon of the machine (1944:140).

In fact, the free market economy requires prodigious degrees of state intervention: introducing economic and social adjustments, ruthlessly enforcing them through bureaucratic *fiat*, re-organizing the body social and the body politic, as well as defending the adjustments against the reactions of social forces. As Polanyi discovered, the free market requires the muscular support of the state, while the regulated market emerges by its own accord as organized social forces try to counter or temper the destructive effects of a *laissez-faire* system:

> The road to the free market was opened and kept open by an enormous increase in continuous, centrally organised and controlled interventionism. To make Adam Smith's 'simple and natural liberty' compatible with the needs of a human society was a most complicated affair. Witness the complexity of the provisions in the innumerable enclosure laws; the amount of bureaucratic control involved in the administration of the New Poor Laws; ... This paradox was topped by another. While *laissez-faire* economy was the product of deliberate state action, subsequent restrictions on *laissez-faire* started in a spontaneous way. *Laissez-faire* was planned; planning was not.[74]

As Robin Murray foresaw in a seminal 1971 essay, 'weaker states in a period of internationalization come to suit neither the interests of their own besieged capital nor of the foreign investor' (1971:84–108). The state, therefore, has not become impotent nor has capital become disarticulated from it. The reproduction of capital still occurs within the framework of regulations and adjustments introduced and managed by states. This is not to replay the hoary notion that the state is a mere tool of capital but to insist that a tenable understanding of globalization demands emphasis on the relations and struggles among social forces (which 'did not shift to some hyperspace beyond the state') and on the 'nation-state's continuing central role in organizing, sanctioning and legitimizing class domination within capitalism' (Panitch, 1994:22).[75]

The neoliberal programmes that have defined globalization have not so much rolled back the state as redefined its key priorities. This has taken the form of redirecting state resources away from the social welfare system towards law and order functions (the link is obvious) and increased subsidies and support for business, while removing the state's role as 'employer of last resort'. In essence, neoliberalism represents an attack not on the state *per se* but on the manner and interests according to which state resources are allocated in society.

It is no coincidence that the IMF and World Bank have tended to bookend their economic prescriptions with programmes of institution-building and 'good governance'. Neoliberal policies require a powerful, centralized and effective state – not to manage national development projects, but to neutralize and/or co-opt those social formations that under normal circumstances mediate relations between the individual and the market. Key among them are trade unions and other social movements.

This is not to belittle the encumbrances states now encounter, but to recast their conundrum. A re-organized world economy is not simply rendering states powerless. Yet, it is impossible to deny that many states appear to have been divorced from the social roles and responsibilities assigned to them over the past half-century – a status that reflects the class character of globalization.[76] Today, they bow before the prerogatives of capital, redirecting resources away from developmental or welfare functions and toward the private sector – as active agents in the deeper polarization of societies.

Perhaps the biggest problematic of our time, following Samir Amin's analysis, is that 'the link between the arena of reproduction and accumulation and that of political and social control' is disappearing in countries that have undergone extensive economic liberalization (1997:12). The central axis for ordering societies over the past 200 years – that of state power – is being radically redefined. Yet, as Hobsbawm correctly insists:

> ... the state, or some other form of public authority representing the public interest, [is] more indispensable than ever if the social and environmental iniquities of the market economy [are] to be countered, or even – as the reform of capitalism in the 1940s [showed] – if the economic system [is] to operate satisfactorily (1995:577).

Yet, at face value, the fates of individual economies are no longer decisively shaped by national governments, but by the opaque mechanics of financial markets, the profit-maximizing migration of TNCs, and the strictures and interventions of transnational institutions such as the IMF, World Bank and WTO. From this vantage point, it is not surprising to find advocates of the 'developmental state' in South Africa protesting its impotence. Removed, it seems, from the ambit of the nation-state is the ability to craft, implement and administer development paths that answer, in the final instance, to popular needs.[77] In certain respects, its powers have been radically pruned (unable to defend domestic industries against foreign incursion or regulate capital flows); in others, its roles have been profoundly reshaped (facilitating economic restructuring and policing the reactions of increasingly desperate citizenries).

But rivalry and contestation are part and parcel of globalization, with the planet as a whole now representing the field upon which differing interests and needs are pursued. The linkages and forms of integration that result depend on the balances of forces at play. The unfolding path of globalization is being determined not simply by the operation of objective factors but also, crucially, by social, political and economic struggles that are waged at the sub-national, national, regional and global levels. However debilitated they might have become, states have not become purely instrumentalized, subject to neoliberal dictates in the way apples obey the law of gravity. They are prone to a complex array of forces and processes that encourage – and often impose – economic and developmental trajectories that conform to the needs of the dominant economic powers. But their obeisance is not predetermined or inevitable.

Many African countries justifiably could claim to have had little option but to submit to IMF-decreed structural adjustment programmes, for example. But the complicity of national élites in their enfeebling adjustments and the benefits they seek to draw from them has been a consistent factor. All the more so in South Africa's case, where the leverage of the IMF and World Bank is minimal and where the level of economic development (stagnant though it had become in the early 1990s) provides manoeuvring space unavailable to a country such as Ghana.

Thailand's decision to lift capital controls (which precipitated its mid-1997 crash) is a case in point. In the four years prior to the Thai crisis, 'net portfolio investment or speculative capital inflows came to around $24 billion … while another $50 billion came in the forms of loans via the innovative Bangkok International Banking Facility' (Bello, 1998a). Even though the surge of Japanese investment after the 1985 Plaza Accord had dropped off by the mid-1990s, Thailand boasted one of the highest savings rates in the world, as Robert Wade has shown. Its need for massive inflows of foreign capital was, in a word, moot. The IMF – and Washington – brought considerable pressure to bear on the Thai government to lift capital controls. 'Our financial services industry wanted into these markets', the chair of president Bill Clinton's Council of Economic Advisers later admitted.[78] But Thai economic élites also had a strong hand in the eventual decision to relent. They succumbed to hubris, confident that they could bat on the same pitch as the élites of the advanced capitalist countries. Deeper integration into world financial markets seemed to be their ticket to ride. The outcome was disastrous.[79]

South African capital has long entertained similar hopes. The country's largest conglomerates had come close to exhausting local avenues for expansion, having built in the process massive and unwieldy corporate empires that straddled any number of sectors. A comparative international isolation achieved, on the one hand, by the anti-apartheid opposition and structured, on the other, into an inwardly-biased economy was at odds with the liberalized, transnational routes of capital accumulation being threaded across the globe. South African capital had been shunted onto a neglected siding of the world economy. Many local corporations faced the prospect of serious and sustained devalorization of capital – a calamity as ominous as the political crisis and, importantly, one intimately linked to it, as argued in previous chapters. For conglomerates most active in the financial and mining sectors, economic liberalization was essential if they were to wrestle free of a national economy that offered little scope for sustained expansion. In short, they suffered a pressing need to 'globalize'.

As it transpired, a new government that had paid hardly any attention to economic policy prior to 1990 and whose main paradigms of development had been shattered by the events of 1989 in Europe and the dissolution of 'Third World developmentalism' proved to be eminently understanding of their conundrum.

Notes

1 *Sunday Times*, 1 May 1994.
2 *Sowetan*, 5 March 1990.
3 Labour consultant Duncan Innes, quoted by Kentridge (1993:3).
4 Based on a disputable reading of the Freedom Charter's phrase: 'The mineral wealth beneath the soil, the banks and monopoly industry shall be transferred to the ownership of the people as a whole.'
5 The quote is drawn from Sunter's 1987 book, *The World and South Africa*, cited by Bond (1996c:4).
6 'Continuation Lecture', University of Pittsburgh, 6 December 1991, quoted in Gelb, S., 1998, *The Politics of Macroeconomic Policy Reform in South Africa* (conference paper), 16 January, Cape Town, p. 13.
7 See Karis and Carter (1977:206).
8 ANC Department of Economic Policy, 1990, 'Discussion Document on Economic Policy', p. 12, cited by Nattrass (1994c:7–11).
9 *Op. cit.*, p. 8.
10 The notion was first popularized, according to some accounts, by economist Terrence Moll, who later, in the service of Old Mutual, would author the ultra-conservative *Growth for All* document for the South Africa Foundation.

11 One of several scenario-building exercises, the 1993 *Mont Fleur* enterprise involved mainstream and progressive economists.

12 See, for instance, Bond (1996c).

13 For a critique, see Bond (1996c).

14 The *Mont Fleur Scenarios*, for example, translated the country's economic options into the flights of ostriches, flamingos, lame ducks and Icarus – illustrated by cartoons.

15 Cited in Bond (1996c:7).

16 Isaac Sam, *Business Day*, 15 August 1994. The Bank went further – leading one of its teams, for instance, was Geoff Lamb, a former SACP member.

17 Most significant were its *Reducing Poverty in South Africa: Options for Equitable and Sustainable Growth* (1994), and *South Africa: Paths to Economic Growth* (1993) documents.

18 Isaac Sam, *op. cit.*

19 *Ibid.*

20 As economist Neva Seidman Makgetla put it, 'at least since Keynes, no serious economist would use it to explain joblessness of the order of half the labour force, as in South Africa' (*Business Day*, 10 August 1994).

21 *Sunday Times*, 17 July 1994.

22 Editorial, *Business Times*, 21 August 1994.

23 *Finance Week*, quoted by Bond (1996c:10).

24 As argued in a 1993 study by GATT staff, cited by Bond (1996c:8).

25 Its extensive recommendations do not bear repetition here; see Joffe *et al.* (1994a).

26 See Samir Amin's summary of the economy's status, 'South Africa in the global economic system', *Work in Progress,* No. 87 (March 1993).

27 Former ISP co-director, Dave Lewis, quoted in *Business Times*, 10 July 1994.

28 ANC, 'Draft Resolution on Economic Policy', p. 3, quoted by Nattrass (1994c:15).

29 'Privatization' became 'reducing the public sector in certain areas in ways that will enhance efficiency, advance affirmative action and empower the historically disadvantaged while ensuring the protection of both consumers and the rights of employment of workers'; ANC, 1992, Department of Economic Policy, *ANC Policy Guidelines for a Democratic South Africa – as Adopted at the National Conference (May 28–31)*, p. 24.

30 The key negotiations on macro policy in the NEF, according to at least one account, were led by former unionist Alec Erwin, who 'consistently adopted a conciliatory and defensive posture towards government and business'; author's interview, December 1996.

31 Quoted in Marais, H., 1999, 'Banking on change', *Siyaya!,* No. 4 (Autumn), Cape Town, p. 36.

32 SACP deputy-general secretary, Jeremy Cronin, was correct in dismissing the notion of independence: 'They have close personal and historical ties with the corporate, and particularly the financial sector. The "independent" policies of the Reserve Bank closely reflect the strategic interests of this privileged minority'; 'Exploding the myths of the neoliberal agenda', *Business Day*, 9 November 1994.

33 'Mandela on the record: What the SA business community can expect of and from the ANC', *Finance Week*, 31 March 1994, quoted by Gelb (1999:12).

34 Strictly speaking, the deal was signed by the TEC (the country's caretaker government at the time) of which the ANC was a member.

35 Excerpt from the 'Statement of economic policies', reprinted in *Business Day*, 24 March 1994 and quoted by Gelb (1999:12–13).

36 Hamber, B., 1998, 'Who Pays for Peace? Implications of the negotiated settlement for reconciliation, transformation and violence in a post-apartheid South Africa'

(paper), Johannesburg, pp. 4–5. By comparision, some 5 400 people were killed in political violence in 1985–9.

37 There was continuity between this phase and the low-intensity conflict strategy employed from the mid-1980s onward and marked by the increased use of covert and unconventional forms of state violence. Overt violence continued, but there was a clear rise in clandestine variants carried out by apparently 'unknown' persons or groupings. State agencies provided support to forces that opposed or undermined anti-apartheid formations, principally the IFP and KwaZulu Police, although the support was extended also to vigilante groups, criminal gangs and paramilitary outfits operated by local warlords and chiefs. Those 'injections' meshed with a complex of other organic contests and conflicts (Hamber, *Ibid.*). One prime effect was to discourage organized forms of resistance and to exacerbate destabilizing dynamics in communities.

38 Neither the *Mont Fleur*, Nedcor or NEM scenarios were of high technical quality.

39 Sipho Maseko, 'The real rise of the black middle class', *Mail & Guardian*, 21 May 1999. He omits to mention that the SACP's 1962 Road to Freedom programme was also openly hospitable in that regard. See Chapter 8.

40 *Ibid.* As Maseko notes, the rise was dramatically boosted in 1986, 'when the PW Botha administration passed the Temporary Removal of Restrictions on Economic Activities Act, a law initially intended to last for 10 months – until June 1987 – but which was extended several times until it was overtaken by the events of 1990'.

41 Belatedly, an SACP strategy and tactics document would later note that 'we have not, as an ANC-led liberation movement, collectively thought through the implications of the new world situation for our national democratic revolution'; SACP (1995:4).

42 Introduced from 1995 onward, the new labour laws reflected the countervailing weight of the trade union movement *and* the political need to address key demands of this, the other most powerful social force in the country. See Chapter 8.

43 Its tasks also included training black economists and supporting COSATU on economic issues. MERG later became the National Institute for Economic Policy (NIEP).

44 As summarized by Nattrass (1994b).

45 For an illuminating debate on the MERG report, see the essays by N. Nattrass, R. Kaplinsky and J. Sender in *Journal of Southern African Studies,* Vol. 20, No. 4 (December 1994), pp. 517–45.

46 *Sunday Times*, 11 September 1994.

47 The *Financial Mail*'s admonishment in 1990, quoted by Kentridge (1993:4).

48 Important, too, were the roles of Japan and China. For a terse chronicle of the rise of the two generations of 'Asian Tigers', see Anderson, B., 1998, 'From miracle to crash', *London Review of Books,* Vol. 20, No. 8 (16 April), London, pp. 3–7.

49 In the USA, for example, the number of blue-collar workers casting votes in presidential elections fell by one-third between 1960 and 1988 (Hobsbawm, 1995:581).

50 Hobsbawm's caustic sentiment (1995:567). The trend has acquired many labels and triggered an avalanche of debates, to which the following texts are a useful introduction: Laclau and Mouffe, *Hegemony and Socialist Strategy* (1985), Hall and Jacques, *New Times* (1989), Osborne, 'Radicalism without limit?' (1991), McRobbie, A., 'Looking back at new times and its critics' in Morley and Chen (1996).

51 For a fascinating account of the origins of *laissez-faire* economics, written from a conservative vantage point, see Gray (1998).

52 UNDP, 1999, 'Globalisation in figures' (media release for *1999 Human Development Report*), July, New York.

53 Elliott, L., 1998, 'Why the poor are picking up the tab', *Mail & Guardian* (15 May), p. 19, citing figures and estimates from the UNDP.

54 Worldwatch Institute, 1990, *State of the World*, p. 148.

55 Likewise, rare diseases such as Grazer (known in Africa as Noma) that, until its recent reappearance, had last been visited upon children in the Nazi death camps; see O'Kane, M., 1998, 'Debt: The plague that kills millions', *Mail & Guardian* (15 May), p. 18.

56 For a critique of this sentiment, see *ILO Global Employment Report*, October 1996.

57 For a critique, see 'How jobless is the future?', *Left Business Observer*, No. 75, 16 December, 1996.

58 Greenfield, G., 1998, 'Flexible Dimensions of a Permanent Crisis: TNCs, Flexibility and Workers in Asia' (paper), Hong Kong. See Brenner (1998) for a detailed analysis of how strongly the restructuring of labour markets featured among the corrective measures to the post-1970 downturn in the advanced capitalist countries.

59 For a distressing overview of such forays in Asia, see Greenfield, G., 1999, 'Who's Unemployed Now? Technocratic "solutions" to the unemployment crisis' (paper), Hong Kong.

60 *Ibid.*

61 See, for example, the excellent account of that period in Hirst, P. & Thompson, G., 1996, *Globalisation in Question*, Polity Press.

62 Sassen, S., 1996, *Losing Control? Sovereignty in an Age of Globalisation*, Columbia University Press, New York, pp. 42–3; cited in Arrighi (1997:2).

63 The oil crisis of 1972–3 was an important factor, although this is disputed by Sweezy & Magdoff (1992). It saw massive amounts of oil profits inserted into the circuits of Western financial institutions at a time when profitable productive investment opportunities appeared to be waning. One of the most compelling surveys to date of the current phase of 'uncontrolled globalization' is Amin (1998).

64 Blackburn, R., 1998, 'Themes' (editorial), *New Left Review*, No. 229 (May/June), London, p. iv.

65 Indeed, those adjustments along with the steep devaluation of the US dollar in the 1980s served as a platform for the USA's impressive recovery in the 1990s.

66 See Elliott, L., 1998, 'Why the poor are picking up the tab', *Mail & Guardian* (15 May), Johannesburg.

67 UNCTAD, 1999, *World Investment Report 1999*, New York.

68 UNCTAD, 1997, 'Overview', *World Investment Report 1997*, New York, p. 20.

69 UNCTAD, 1997, *World Investment Report 1997: Transnational Corporations, Market Structure and Competition Policy*, New York, p. 56.

70 *Ibid.*

71 UNDP, 1999, 'Globalisation in figures' (media release for *1999 Human Development Report*), July, New York.

72 Essentially, betting on what interest rates will be at a future date.

73 John Holloway has argued that 'this is not an "internationalisation" or "globalisation" of the economy ... but a change in the form of the global existence of capital' (1994:41).

74 Polanyi (1944), cited by David Marquand, 1996, 'The Great Reckoning', *Prospect* (July).

75 Or in Leo Panitch's terse phrasing: 'Capitalist globalisation is a process which also takes place in, through, and under the aegis of states; it is encoded by them and in important respects even authored by them; and it involves a shift in power relations within states that often means the centralization and concentration of state

powers as the necessary condition of and accompaniment to global market discipline' (1994:14).

76 Some nation-states have failed to exist in anything but name, resembling 'a score of empty labels', in the 1949 prediction of anti-communist Russian Ivan Ilyin, without 'an uncontested territory, nor governments with authority, nor laws, nor tribunals, nor army, nor an ethnically defined population'. Cited by Hobsbawm (1995:567).

77 For an instructive summary of the state's role in the growth paths of first- and second-tier NICs in the region, see Ghosh (1997:1–19).

78 Nicholas D. Kristof and David E. Sanger, 1999, 'How U.S. wooed Asia to let cash flow in', *New York Times* (16 February), New York.

79 For terse analyses of the origins of the Asian Crisis, see Gill (1999), Wade and Veneroso (1998) and Bello (1998b).

CHAPTER SIX

The whiplash of history

The ANC was no different from other national liberation movements in anticipating a boundless vista of possibilities once it seized power. Central to this (in mobilizing terms, understandable) hope was the singular objective that had animated anti-systemic movements since 1848: the seizure of state power. Most of them envisaged transformation as a two-stage project: state power followed by far-reaching social and economic transformation, with the state serving as the prime lever for the latter. Embedded in the two-stage theory, however, was a great deal of naïvety – for it assumed that political victory unlocked a rich realm of national sovereignty and autonomy from where inevitable consolidations and advances would be launched. As numerous other liberation movements discovered, this assumption was blind to the realities of the world system. In Immanuel Wallerstein's caustic summary, such faith:

> ... took the theory of sovereignty at its face value, and assumed that sovereign states are autonomous. But of course they are not autonomous and they never have been ... All modern states, without exception, exist within the framework of the interstate system and are constrained by its rules and its politics. The productive activities within all modern states, without exception, occur within the framework of the capitalist world-economy and are constrained by its priorities and its economics ... Shouting that one is autonomous is a bit like Canute commanding the tides to recede (Wallerstein, 1996).

The ANC can hardly be accused of trumpeting its autonomy from the rooftops since coming to power. On the contrary, the alibi for the development path adopted since 1994 is precisely that of denuded state autonomy and sovereignty. Blamed in the main is globalization, prompting academic Philip Nel to suggest that the:

> ... emphasis on the loss of sovereignty makes it possible to shift some of the blame for domestically unpopular policies to faceless international forces

(while convincing) doubters that what is happening is to a large extent inevitable (1999:23).

In his political report to the ANC's 1997 national conference, Nelson Mandela repeatedly referred to globalization, particularly to the integration of capital markets that 'made it impossible ... [to] decide national economic policy without regard for the likely response of the markets'. Opening parliament in February 1998, Mandela could declaim that 'there is no other route to sustainable development' other than the market-led policies adopted by his government. Rejecting the possibility of a stronger role for the state in the economy, trade and industry minister Alec Erwin, for instance, could declare:

> A country such as South Africa, which started its economic reform in the 1990s, was prevented from using such interventionist methods by World Trade Organisation rules. Accordingly, we therefore tend to implement policy packages that are similar to those of the other developing countries.[1]

Ignored was the fact that the policy packages of other developing countries are varied – in the cases of many Asian countries, richly so. The growth paths of China and the two generations of NICs in Asia remind us that no single formula exists for economic growth. In the words of World Bank vice-president and chief economist, Joseph Stiglitz, 'here was a cluster of countries that had not closely followed the Washington Consensus prescriptions but had somehow managed the most successful development in history' (1998:2).

Played down was the possibility of contestation in concert with other countries. Forgotten was the fact that no successful liberation movement – particularly those with authentic revolutionary credentials – has not been confronted with a formidable range of obstacles, some of them ruthlessly and violently imposed. Limits to change are hardly novel.

In South Africa's case, the idealism that had animated the struggle against apartheid swiftly yielded to acquiescence that was, at best, reluctant and, at worst, enthusiastic. Perhaps the biggest surprise of the South African transition was not the development path that would be chosen, but the fact that economic policy outlines from the early 1990s onwards so studiously – and successfully – were emptied of elements that might violate the strictures of orthodoxy.

All GEARed up – but nowhere to go

A prime characteristic of post-1994 economic policies has been the desire to create a favourable environment for market-led economic growth. With considerable justification, government believes it has shown 'commendable determination' on this front (Mandela, 1998:5). Adopted in June 1996, the GEAR strategy remains the centre-piece of South Africa's growth path and, consequently, its broader development path – insofar as the latter is premised on core, economic priorities that establish the key *terms* on which development and reconstruction can be pursued.

After being drawn up in 'somewhat secretive conditions' (Gelb, 1999:16), GEAR was released after perfunctory 'briefings' of a few top-ranking ANC, SACP and COSATU figures. The 'COSATU and SACP leaders, according to one participant, were shown only the section headings' (Webster & Adler, 1999:16). 'I confess even the ANC learnt of GEAR far too late – when it was almost complete', Mandela would later admit.[2] In the later view of Gelb (who had participated in the plan's drafting):

> Close affinity with the 'Washington Consensus' characterised not only the substantive policy recommendations of GEAR, but also the process through which it was formulated and presented publicly ... This was 'reform from above' with a vengeance, taking to extreme the arguments in favour of insulation and autonomy of policymakers from popular pressures (1999:16–17).

That process was at odds with the ANC's hallowed (though, as argued, less than sterling) tradition of democratic practice. Finance minister Trevor Manuel followed through and immediately declared the plan 'non-negotiable' in its broad outline, although the government was willing to negotiate 'the details with our social partners'.[3] Such were the levels of discipline the ANC maintained over its long-standing ally that the SACP dutifully issued a woolly media release endorsing the objectives of the plan. Its verdict that the strategy resisted 'free market dogmatism' and 'envisage[d] a key economic role for the public sector, including in productive investment', tested credulity.[4] (Only a year later did the SACP harden its stance, calling for the scrapping of GEAR and its replacement by a 'coherent industrial policy').[5] It was left to COSATU to vituperate. Addressing an SACP seminar, the federation's Zwelinzima Vavi declared GEAR unworkable and unwinnable. COSATU also protested that the plan's prescriptions did 'not take into account the state of development in the economy and the need for massive spending on infrastructure and development'.[6] Strangely, it did not release a detailed response to GEAR – despite having commissioned such a study from National Institute for Economic Policy (NIEP).[7]

The disarray of the left was palpable. Although bristling with SACP and COSATU leaders, the ANC's National Executive Committee (NEC) gave GEAR the thumbs up. Again, the principle of unity in the face of presumed adversity won the day. In the months following, the SACP more stridently aired its discontent while COSATU thickened its voice. But dividing critics was an appropriate strategic response. Should they reject the plan *in toto* and, if so, how and to what lengths? In both COSATU and the SACP, a pragmatic view won the day: public opposition would be trumpeted in a bid to persuade the ANC government to revise specific features of the macro-economic plan. Thus, COSATU's sixth national congress rejected GEAR but did not demand that the government rescind it.

Engine work

The rush in which the document was unveiled partially explained its startling lack of rigour, a point confirmed a year later in an astonishing remark by deputy director-general of finance, Andre Roux, that more research was required into the link between economic growth and job creation.[8] The rush, however, did not explain the specific set of choices expressed in GEAR.

Drawn up by a coterie of mainstream economists,[9] and apparently based on a Reserve Bank model similar to that used for the apartheid government's NEM proposals a few years earlier, GEAR's prescriptions lit the faces of business, which could not fail to recognize its neoliberal character. There has been much handwringing over the applicability of that adjective, much of it unnecessary and disingenuous. A 1996 government document (*Gear, the RDP and the Role of the State*) sent out to provincial leaders admitted that 'in isolation certain measures in GEAR are similar to many neoliberal packages'.[10] The document's claim that this was 'because there is an objective character about certain economic relations' was nonsensical, for reasons already stated.

Like motherhood and apple pie, GEAR's stated objective defied criticism. It would achieve, claimed the government, growth *with* job creation *and* redistribution, superficially reconciling it to the RDP. But rather than determine how that could be achieved *without* unleashing unmanageable fiscal laxity and monetary instability, GEAR predicated the quest on fiscal and monetary stringency.

Although the comparison was seldom drawn explicitly, the superficial correspondence between GEAR and the apartheid government's NEM was telling. According to Adelzadeh, GEAR represented 'a recourse to the policy goals and instruments of the past apartheid regime' – a harsh but plausible judgement (1996:2).

GEAR promised to increase annual growth by an average of 4,2 per cent, create 1,35 million new jobs by the year 2000, boost exports by an average 8,4 per cent per annum through an array of supply-side measures, and drastically improve social infrastructure. This 'integrated approach', the document predicted, would achieve an economic growth rate of 6 per cent by the year 2000 and create an average of 400 000 jobs annually. A sustained growth rate 'in the 5,6 or 7 per cent range' was forecast, while redistribution would emerge from 'job creation and more focused public expenditure', according to finance minister Trevor Manuel. The document made plain the assumptions at the heart of the strategy:

The higher growth path depends in part on attracting foreign direct investment, but also requires a higher domestic saving effort. Greater industrial competitiveness, a tighter fiscal stance, moderation of wage increases, accelerated public investment, efficient service delivery and a major expansion of private investment are integral aspects of the strategy. An exchange rate policy consistent with improved international competitiveness, responsible monetary policies and targeted industrial incentives characterise the new policy environment. A strong export performance underpins the macroeconomic sustainability of the growth path (Department of Finance, 1996:21).

The rancour that greeted GEAR stemmed from the methods chosen to achieve these targets. The plan hinged fundamentally on an implausibly massive increase in private sector investment. This would be elicited by:

- A renewed focus on budget reform to strengthen the redistributive thrust of expenditure.
- A faster fiscal deficit reduction programme to contain debt service obligations, counter inflation and free resources for investment.
- An exchange rate policy to keep the real effective rate stable at a competitive level.
- Consistent monetary policy to prevent a resurgence of inflation.
- Liberalized financial controls, including the eventual complete lifting of exchange controls.
- A privatization programme that would see the complete privatization of 'non-essential' state enterprises and the partial privatization of some state-run utilities.
- A liberalized trade regime that would see most tariffs and other forms of protection drastically reduced (and, in several cases, completely removed) by the early part of the next century.
- Tax incentives to stimulate new investment in competitive and labour-absorbing projects.
- An expansionary infrastructure programme to address service deficiencies and backlogs.
- Wage restraint by organized workers and the introduction of 'regulated flexibility' in the labour market.

Stripped to basics, GEAR sandwiched government between two stringent and fundamental prescriptions. Fiscal austerity (reflected in a determination to drive the budget deficit down to 3 per cent of GDP by the year 2000) would be pursued to reduce the total public sector debt, which stood at 56 per cent of GDP in 1996.[11] Resources spent on interest payments should instead go towards increased social spending. Meanwhile, as a share of GDP, tax revenue would not exceed a ceiling of 25 per cent (later increased to 26,5 per cent). Increased government revenue would be predicated on higher economic growth (and, in the short term, on improved revenue collection), while growth would hinge on the private sector's hoped-for reaction to deficit pruning and other alluring adjustments. Shunned was the argument that, 'if deficit reduction were desired, the most effective way to achieve it would be through faster economic growth' (ILO, 1996:33).

The corporate sector hailed GEAR as 'investor friendly' and praised the manner in which it 'responds to many of the concerns expressed by business'.[12] Most observers concurred with that view. Business journalist Jenny Cargill noted that 'the government has met most of [business'] macroeconomic demands' and went on to remark that 'it is certainly difficult to identify social equity as an explicit feature of the strategy'.[13] Little wonder that Mbeki could later bait critics at a media briefing, inviting them to 'call me a Thatcherite', which one journalist declared 'an apt comment on the overall direction of GEAR'.[14]

In line with its title, three key tests have to be applied to GEAR. Would it trigger growth, would it stimulate job creation and would it increase socio-economic equality? Sadly, the verdict is negative on all three counts.

Boosting growth

GEAR's growth projections (from 3,5 per cent in 1996 to 6,1 per cent in 2000) hinged on increases in private investment and net non-gold exports, as well as substantial (delayed) state expenditure in social infrastructure.

The strategy unloaded the duty of economic salvation squarely onto the shoulders of the private sector – not only as the source of private investment but through partnerships in the public sector (created by a programme of privatization). Those partnerships would enable the state to meet its infrastructural and other obligations while, simultaneously, trimming state expenditure.

The document's calculations showed import expenses (over the five-year GEAR period) depressing the fiscus by –0,2 per cent, while state spending was scheduled to add a fiscal stimulus of only 0,5 per cent. It follows that achieving the projected 4,2 per cent average annual growth would require a huge fiscal stimulus of 3,9 per cent (or 93 per cent of the total stimulus) from private investment. Thus, as Adelzadeh warned, 'the projected growth rate is almost completely dependent upon the rapid success of government policy in stimulating private investment' (1996:6).

Conveniently ignored was the fact that one of the models used in GEAR's drafting contradicted the eventual plan – by showing that fiscal stringency would depress private sector investment and economic growth. According to Gibson and Van Seventer's Development Bank model, 'if the goal is to reduce the public sector borrowing requirements as a share of GDP, the result must be a fall in income, output and employment, all other things being equal' (1995:21).

What specific measures were proposed to ensure business met its assigned duty of productive investment? The answer was 'none'. Presented instead were a set of adjustments aimed at creating an optimal climate for private investment. Most important were a reduced fiscal deficit, a commitment not to increase corporate taxes and a low inflation rate.[15]

By buying into the argument that a fiscal deficit of 1996 proportions[16] 'crowds out' private investment, GEAR posed state spending as an impediment to economic growth. Summarized, the 'crowding out' argument holds that when the state borrows to finance a deficit, it competes for funds with the private sector. This is said to reduce investor confidence, drive up interest rates and slow growth.[17] Consequently, GEAR aimed to reduce the fiscal deficit (to an average 3,7 per cent), which would lead to lower real interest rates (average 4,4 per cent), boost investor confidence and trigger a dramatic rise in private investment (average 11,7 per cent). Yet, testifying to its shoddy logic, GEAR's insistence on an ultra-low inflation rate effectively demanded a high interest rate policy. (The inflation rate in 1996 was 7,4 per cent).

In fact, the entire sequence rested on rickety assumptions. Most obvious was the danger that a deteriorating balance of payment situation (which the document correctly saw as an enduring difficulty) would lead the Reserve Bank to intervene by further hoisting interest rates, thereby interrupting the purported chain reaction (Adelzadeh, 1996). As the Asian Crisis spilt onto South African shores in 1998, the Reserve Bank did just that – by hiking interest rates above 20 per cent and severely depressing economic activity. With the 'independence' of the Reserve Bank entrenched in the constitution and the Bank shielded against parliamentary oversight, the government had no authority to demand that the Bank desist from such responses.

The need to slash the deficit has become an article of faith for supporters of orthodoxy, who see a fiscal deficit in the region of 5–6 per cent of GDP as anathema to a sustainable growth strategy. Yet, even the World Bank does not offer unambiguous succour for this view. In an apparent *lapsus ceribri* in 1993, the Bank allowed for instances where a fiscal deficit of even 12 per cent might be acceptable, as long as it was integral to a growth pattern.[18]

This is not to argue that the size of the fiscal deficit is irrelevant, which it is not (incurring a large debt burden to finance the deficit and an unacceptably high inflation rate are two possible and important consequences). But it does acknowledge that there is considerable controversy about the presumed need to cut state expenditure to a *particular* level irrespective of the stage of the business cycle, whether this does act in fact as a trigger for private investment, and whether it does not become counter-productive (by depressing levels of demand). A Keynesian approach stresses the latter danger, since 'it is the ability to sell what is produced that guides investment decisions'.[19] Gibson and Van Seventer calculated that 'a 1% reduction in the deficit before borrowing ... will reduce the average growth rate by about 1.5% for each year' and concluded that 'while fiscal discipline is attractive, it is expensive in terms of forgone output and lost jobs'.[20] Elsewhere, the two economists warned that 'if the goal is to reduce public sector borrowing requirements as a share of GDP, the results must be fall in income, output and employment, all other things being equal' (Gibson & Van Seventer, 1995:21). They had reached that conclusion using one of the models on which GEAR allegedly had been based. Commenting on other, similar inconsistencies in the plan, Nicoli Nattrass concluded that there were:

> ... so many 'shift parameters' in GEAR's integrated scenario projection that its 'technical' status is severely compromised. The growth and employment outcomes are in large part the product of a set of optimistic guesses about the likely effects of the economic policy package (1996:38).

Rather than see investment as a direct function of investor confidence, for instance, a more empirically valid approach would view it as 'primarily determined by *profitability* of investment and the complementarity between investment by the state *and* the private sector' (ILO, 1996:29). Adelzadeh has reminded that, internationally, greater attention was being paid to:

> ... the role that public productive expenditures on infrastructure (such as investment on roads, transportation and housing) and social services (such as education, health care and welfare) play in promoting not only a country's economic well-being and growth, but also in encouraging private investment (1996:8).

In that approach public expenditure 'crowds in' private investment by helping create a structural bedrock for sustainable growth. This would appear particularly apt for an economy that requires structural changes to achieve comparative advantage in the world economy, *and* where the government is committed to overcoming or at least lessening social inequalities.

In contrast, GEAR viewed such public spending as part of the problem and only envisaged significant increases in public capital expenditure very late in the day – toward 2000 when it could be 'afforded'. Yet, it was bereft of measures that could increase the likelihood of large-scale, *sustained* productive investment by the private sector. Its central pillar, as Cargill noted, 'rests on a leap of faith'.

Even if the presumed need to reduce the deficit were inviolable, methods other than cutting state spending were available – including more progressive corporate tax rates, the use of differential rates of value added tax (VAT) on luxury consumption and a capital gains tax. GEAR recoiled from such options and instead offered an array of tax breaks to business.

What about the inflationary impact of deficit spending? As the ILO pointed out, there is no automatic correlation between inflation and fiscal deficits. Thus, if the deficit were financed through money creation,[21] higher inflation might result. But, unlike most developing countries, South Africa has a developed private sector market for government bonds that allows it to side-step the inflationary effect by financing the deficit 'in a manner that does not increase the money supply in excess of the rate of output growth' (ILO, 1996:34).

The monetarist obsession for managing relatively minute shifts in the inflation rate borders on the pathological. In Cambridge academic Ha-Joon Chang's view, it is 'misinformed' and serves the interests of the financial sector to the detriment of industry.[22] South Africa's inflation rate has not been high. It reached a peak of 15,3 per cent in 1991 before dropping to 7,4 per cent in 1996. Yet, GEAR explicitly made reducing the inflation rate one of the main objectives of monetary policy, without demonstrating how this would impact on other factors. The cross-country evidence on the relationship between inflation and growth certainly does not support the view that the relationship is negative.[23] The fixation added another fly to the ointment – by demanding that the Reserve Bank apply contractionary, *growth-inhibiting* measures whenever the inflation rate seems poised to step out of line.[24]

A broader point on macro-economic stability should be borne in mind. In dominant discourse, the monetarist view has become crudely contrasted with 'macro-economic populism' (unbridled deficit-led social spending), as if these are the only alternatives. There are other options, as economist Vishnu Padayachee has argued. Macro-economic balances can be assessed, maintained or restored over chosen periods (for instance, a ten-year reconstruction cycle). This allows for the positive results of particular policies to work their way into improved growth rates, rather than doggedly enforcing the often arbitrarily chosen macro-economic targets throughout the cycle. Whether or not the economy is growing has to affect the decisions. Within a sustained growth environment, certain macro-economic (im)balances can temporarily be stretched beyond the strictures of stringency if key social and economic indicators (such as employment figures, spending power and investment rates) are positive. In the South African debate, however, such perspectives were regarded as heretical.

GEAR's other main features require brief mention. The strategy correctly assumed a continued drop in the share of foreign revenue provided by gold exports. Thus it aimed to boost manufactured exports and trigger a staggering 23 per cent increase in the export:GDP ratio within four years. Adelzadeh saw this target as 'unrealistic and unattainable', particularly because 'the government has not developed a carefully formulated and precisely targeted industrial strategy geared to those sub-sectors that have potential for export growth' (1996:14). The allegation was harsh, since industrial strategy is supposed to rank among the more advanced *policy* areas of the ANC government. Yet, GEAR provided no detailed linkage between its macro-economic adjustments and industrial policy. Furthermore, growth in export:GDP ratios registered by other countries prompt scepticism about GEAR's 23 per cent target – between 1970 and 1994 the average figure for the Organization for Economic Cooperation and Development (OECD) countries was 6 per cent, for Brazil 5 per cent and South Korea 4 per cent. The scepticism is amplified when one considers that neither GEAR nor current industrial policy provides for an active state role in targeting sectors, and that the time lag in achieving comparative advantage through human resources development makes *rapid* export growth unlikely.

On exchange controls, GEAR wisely resisted the 'big bang' approach but called for the gradual, complete removal of those controls. Foreign investors would gain easier access to domestic credit, with wholly foreign-owned firms able to borrow up to 100 per cent of shareholder equity. Exchange controls were to be eased for local residents as well, allowing institutional investors (insurance companies, pension funds and unit trusts) to obtain foreign assets of up to 10 per cent of their total assets. The concession amounted to government-sanctioned capital flight – in a strategy that rested on encouraging domestic investment. The promised, ongoing relaxation of exchange controls for residents has momentous implications.

The steady abandonment of financial controls effectively rendered a strategy such as GEAR hostage to the vagaries of finance capital. By allowing the uncontrolled penetration of domestic financial markets by foreign capital and encouraging the migration of local capital, patterns of investment were to be swept out of the ambit of government policy.

GEAR's restructuring of taxes was manifestly non-progressive. In 1996, 37 per cent of tax revenue was derived from indirect taxation (VAT, which as currently structured discriminates against low-income earners) and so-called 'sin taxes' (levies on tobacco and alcohol that have a similar, discriminatory effect) with the likelihood of increases. There were several options to achieve greater progress, including a capital gains tax (the absence of which enables companies to lower their effective tax rates by converting income into capital gains),[25] a tax on luxury consumption and a tax on unproductive land (Adelzadeh, 1996:9). Reportedly, a tax on capital equipment was mooted, but rejected.[26] Instead, personal and corporate taxes were to be reduced and tax holidays proffered for selected investments. Overall, revenue was slated to increase by way of more effective tax collection.[27]

Once scrutinized, GEAR seemed to hover between different worlds. Rhetorically, attempts were made to align it with the socially progressive objectives of the RDP – but the central pillars of the strategy were fashioned in accordance with standard neoliberal principles. This was alarming for several reasons. There is no example internationally where neoliberal adjustments of the sort championed by GEAR have produced a socially progressive outcome. Despite its overall objective of attaining 'growth with job creation and redistribution', GEAR set no redistributive targets and demurred on the linkage between growth and income redistribution. Moreover, it failed to integrate its main elements: for instance, the impact of restructuring government spending on employment and redistribution was side-stepped, while the relationship between the plan and industrial policy was left undeveloped. GEAR offered no direct causal link, as ANC MP Rob Davies noted, 'between the measures proposed' and the achievement of its 'growth and employment targets' (1997:2):

> These results depend on assumptions that lie beyond the macroeconomic policy measures proposed, viz. that the new policies generate 'confidence' among domestic and foreign private investors, who respond by significantly increasing investment ... Whether investors really do respond to policy packages of this nature in this way, rather than to a record of growth and profitability, is clearly much more debatable (1997:2–3).

In similar fashion, much of the economic logic of the plan wilted in the light of scrutiny[28] – but to little effect. For, far from constituting a cogent strategy, GEAR was designed for other purposes. Its overriding aim, according to Gelb:

> ... was to signal to potential investors the government's (and specifically the ANC's) commitment to the prevailing orthodoxy. In 'marketing' the strategy, senior Department of Finance officials made explicit its close parallels with the approach of the international financial institutions, while emphasising at the same time the idea that GEAR was 'homegrown' in South Africa (1999:15–16).

Harvest time

South Africa's economic policies were being managed, as a *Financial Mail* article put it, by 'ANC politicians who have graduated from freedom fighters to the real new world'.[29] That real world, though, was looking decidedly unpleasant.

By mid-1998, the modest 1994–6 recovery had ground to a halt, with total real output for the year stuck at 1997 levels. Applying a new accounting framework, Statistics South Africa in 1999 revised the weighting of sectoral contributions to GDP and returned a marginally rosier picture[30] – GDP growth was deemed to have been 0,5 to 1 per cent higher than previously estimated. The adjusted figures put 1997 GDP growth at 2,2 to 2,7 per cent (GEAR aimed for 2,9 per cent), 1998 growth at 0,5 to 1 per cent (GEAR predicted 3,8 per cent) and 1999 growth at 1,2 per cent (against GEAR's 4,9 per cent).

The main sources of the minor improvement in GDP growth were instructive. They lay in the greater weight in the GDP basket accorded to three sectors:

- Transport and communication (share of GDP in the 1995 base year rose from 7,4 per cent to 8,9 per cent between 1993 and 1998).
- Finance, real estate and business services (up from 14,5 per cent to 16,4 per cent).
- General government services (up from 13,8 per cent to 16,2 per cent).

Opposite trends held in the traditionally mainstay sectors of the economy:
- Agriculture (down from 5,3 per cent to 3,9 per cent).
- Mining and quarrying (down from 9,7 per cent to 7 per cent).
- Manufacturing (down from 25,2 per cent to 21,2 per cent).[31]

In short, the relative output of goods-producing sectors continued to decline, while that of service sectors was on the rise. Yet, the new figures were presented with unalloyed delight by finance department officials shortly after the June 1999 elections. Finance director-general Maria Ramos claimed that the economy was more buoyant and resilient than previously believed. The new data supported expectations of better growth, she said, and proved that South Africa was benefiting from globalization.[32] Most exciting to government officials was the deduction that the debt:GDP ratio for fiscal year 1997/8 would be 48 per cent (not 55,6 per cent as on the previous data) and that the fiscal deficit for 1998/9 could drop to 2,9 per cent of GDP (not the initial estimate of 3,3 per cent). Government said the changes would enable it to increase capital expenditures – a welcome decision, though achieved at grave cost.

By 2000, the government's defence of GEAR had acquired Orwellian overtones, with President Mbeki informing parliament:

> Many major indicators point to the excellent work that has been done to place our country on a strong growth path. All indicators also signal that during this year, our economy will register much more vigorous growth than it did last year. Of great importance in this regard, indicating the resilience, the effective restructuring and therefore the improved international competitiveness of our economy was the success we achieved in withstanding the effects of the East Asian economic crisis of the late 1990s.[33]

The 'strong growth path', Mbeki referred to was in fact 1,2 per cent GDP growth in 1999, slightly up from 1998's 0,6 per cent figure. Save for a stabilizing balance of payments situation and an obsessively maintained low inflation rate (in late 1999, headline inflation reached its lowest level in 30 years – 5,2 per cent), the cheery announcement rested on threadbare evidence. By 1999, real GDP per capita was 2,6 per cent lower than in 1996.

Non-agricultural output growth had dropped from a rejuvenated 3,9 per cent in 1995 to 0,1 per cent in 1998, while manufacturing output shrunk by 1,7 per cent in 1998 before growing by 0,2 per cent in 1999. Private domestic investment was sluggish, and FDI had plunged sharply. Forecasts for 2000 were happier – with a Reuters survey predicting 3,5 per cent GDP growth and manufacturing output expected to rise more sharply. The fate of the predicted upturn, though, would hinge centrally on private investors' willingness to reverse their antipathy toward productive investments, and on the absence of more volatility in the world economy.

GEAR's architects had hoped private sector investment would rise by more than 9 per cent annually in 1996–8, before soaring by 13,9 per cent and 17 per cent in 1999 and 2000 – with heftier public investment occurring on the back of those surges. At this fundamental level, the plan failed dismally. Real private sector investment dropped sharply – from a 6,1 per cent growth rate in 1996 to –0,7 per cent in 1998. Overall, the sector's share of total fixed investment fell from 73 per cent to 68 per cent (Adelzadeh, 1999:2). Most of this investment was in the category 'machinery and equipment' – according to the Reserve Bank, 'in all likelihood a reflection of the continuous process of substituting capital for labour'.[34] Except in the mining and construction sectors, 'the private sector held back its fixed investment spending in all the other major sectors of economic activity', the Reserve Bank noted. It attributed the trend to weak domestic demand conditions, poor prospects for an immediate recovery in export demand, falling output volumes, greater under-utilization of production capacity and the high user cost of capital.

In 1999, domestic private fixed investment declined further – by 5,5 per cent against the 1998 figures. Trade union leaders continued to speak of an 'investment strike' by South African capital, but government remained bereft of the will and, supposedly, the means to counter that reluctance. As a result, FDI acquired a new allure, especially after FDI levels in 1997 had soared to US$1,7 billion. Much of the government's loyalty to GEAR came to hinge on the hope that foreign investors would step into the breach. But the destinations of the inflows should have tempered the optimism. They were lured mainly by privatization ventures (notably the selling of a 30 per cent stake in the telecommunications giant Telkom in 1997) and the unbundling of large local conglomerates. The other main destination for FDI was the capital-intensive oil and energy sector.

Unfortunately, the agreeable climate crafted for those investors failed to sustain 1997's FDI inflows. In 1998, FDI plunged to dismal levels – $371 million, four times lower than 1997's $1,7 billion and a little more than half the 1996 level, according to UNCTAD. This placed South Africa behind Nigeria, Egypt, Tunisia, Algeria, Zimbabwe and Angola as the continent's top FDI recipients.[35] Like most other developing economies,

South Africa was discovering that the 40 per cent and more boom in global flows of FDI during the 1990s was a boon mainly to the industrialized countries. In a bid to bend investors' ears, Mbeki in early 2000 set up a special investment council, comprising top multinational executives.[36] The only potentially authentic points of leverage government created for FDI increases were the market-driven spatial development initiatives (SDIs)[37] and the accelerated privatization of big-ticket state assets.

Notable was the increasing share of FDI that went toward mergers and acquisitions in South Africa. This kind of investment rose by 19 per cent in 1995 before rocketing by 160 per cent in 1996 and 130 per cent the next year (when it constituted almost 60 per cent of FDI). As Adelzadeh reminded:

> Mergers and acquisitions bring the possible benefits of improved productivity (through processes of rationalisation, the introduction of new technologies and overhaul of management and even production systems). But they do not on the whole increase productive capacity in the economy. Neither do they typically create jobs. On the contrary, [they] tend to be marked by rationalisation of labour inputs – in other words, job cuts (1999:4).

The changing composition of capital inflows was stark. Since 1995, the country witnessed a dramatic rise in net short-term capital inflows, most of it destined for the bond and equity markets. Their value increased five-fold since 1996, overshadowing FDI. Their volatile nature hit home in 1998 when almost $1 billion left the country in the third quarter, triggering serious exchange rate instability and prompting a series of interest rate hikes that badly depressed economic growth but also encouraged greater short-term inflows.[38] This revolving door phenomenon was being abetted dramatically by the relaxation of capital controls, as COSATU has warned:

> The first three-quarters of 1999 saw a net outflow of foreign direct investment (FDI) of R3,3-billion ($550-million). During the same period, net portfolio investment inflows of R46,7-billion ($7,6-billion) occurred. Foreign investment flows outside the fields of FDI and portfolio transactions experienced a net outflow of R21,6-billion ($3,5-billion) during this time. This suggests that our policies, particularly the high interest rate regime, are attractive to volatile portfolio investment, but does not encourage FDI, which is much more valuable for technology development and job creation. This trend also raises questions around the efficacy of exchange control liberalisation in the stated goal of attracting productive investment.[39]

Meanwhile, local corporations were showing a strong propensity for offshore investments, a tendency facilitated by the lifting of capital controls. South African firms made $2,3 billion of outward investments in 1997; the corresponding figure for 1996 had been a mere $57 million. Foreign portfolio holdings of South African corporations swelled to R60 billion ($9,8 billion) between 1994 and 1999, while Anglo-American Corporation and South African Breweries were allowed to shift their primary listings to the London Stock Exchange.

The reasoning for allowing those moves is worth noting. Government economic policy is in signal respects premised on large, sustained flows of FDI into the country. But foreign investors eyeing post-1994 opportunities found an economy dominated by sprawling local corporations, leaving little space for bulky foreign entrants. By encouraging offshore investments, government hoped to create 'space' in the economy for foreign investors (and, it must be added, black economic empowerment consortia), since firms shifting abroad are pressured into selling off non-core local operations in order to raise investment capital. Foreign investors took the opportunity (evident in the large share of FDI acquisitions), but without robust local demand to trigger further, new investments, the rush soon waned.

Some business economists have been less prone to denial on this issue. 'It is unrealistic to expect a huge interest in South Africa in the form of foreign direct investment without a rise in domestic corporate investment preceding it. The authorities should face up to the reasons for the lack of success and address them energetically', Gensec Asset Management noted in late 1998. The antidotes proposed were predictable, however: erase 'government dissaving', reduce the budget deficit to zero, put big-ticket state assets (such as the electricity utility Eskom) on the auction block 'on an unprecedented scale', reduce personal and company taxes, increase VAT.[40]

Secreted in that advice was further evidence of just how wide-rangingly regressive the ANC government's economic policy was. Analysing the tax system, Gensec found that the contribution of personal income tax to total taxes had risen from 37 per cent in 1979/80 to 57 per cent in 1987/8, and 74 per cent in 1997/8[41] – with a corresponding drop in corporate tax contributions. In the 1999/2000 budget, this process was accelerated with a 5 per cent cut in the corporate tax rate.[42]

Business, meanwhile, chided that the adjustments were being applied with insufficient resolve. Some business economists accused government of 'decision-making paralysis', arguing that 'countries that have taken aggressive corrective action against a bad backdrop have fared best'.[43]

In this realm, non-racialism seems alive and well. Thus, the president of SACOB, Humphrey Khoza, could, in a 1998 speech, call on all southern African countries to implement packages entailing:

> ... fiscal discipline, appropriate monetary policies, trade liberalisation, flexible labour markets, privatisation and restructuring of the public sector, commitment to provide modern (appropriate) infrastructures, appropriate

social and educational policy, effective border control measures and efficient public sectors, and constitutionally guaranteed property rights and no controls over foreign capital flows.[44]

Yet, different sentiments emanate from different branches of capital. While there is virtual unanimity around the call to substantially relax the labour regime, areas such as trade liberalization elicit different responses depending on the vulnerability of the sector to foreign competition. Likewise, an insistence on driving the inflation rate further into the lower single digit bracket is most pronounced among financial institutions.

By 1998, the finance minister was conceding that 'the results, in the short term, have not always reached the targets we set for ourselves', and adding that some of the targets could become 'even more elusive'. But, he declared, it was 'precisely at times like this that our resolve and commitment is tested' (Manuel, 1998a:3) – as millions of poor South Africans duly were discovering.

'Not hiring'
The experience of 'jobless growth' from 1994 to 1996 had brought home the realization that economic growth does not necessarily ease unemployment.[45] GEAR therefore presented specific job creation targets. It predicted 1,35 million new jobs by 2000,[46] of which 833 000 would be created through GEAR adjustments – 308 000 through higher economic growth, 325 000 through 'changes in the flexibility of labour markets' and 200 000 through 'government-induced employment' (mainly infrastructural development and public works programmes).

GEAR's failure is agonizing on this front. More than half a million (non-agricultural) jobs were lost between 1994 and 2000 in a trend that dates to the 1980s. Causing it is the introduction of labour-saving technologies, increased out-sourcing, and a marked turn towards using casual and contract labour. Some 200 000 more jobs are believed to have been lost on the country's farms as farmers mechanized production and retrenched workers in order to forestall the effects of new legislation aimed at improving farmworkers' job security and working conditions.

The official (non-agricultural) unemployment rate stood at 22,9 per cent in 1999, according to Statistics SA. Once unemployed workers who had not sought work in the month prior to polling were included, the 'expanded unemployment rate' rose to 37,6 per cent (up from 31,5 per cent in 1994). Testifying to the structural nature of this trend, 69 per cent of unemployed workers have never held a formal job, according to a COSATU survey. Unemployment rates are most severe among Africans (4,2 million were out of work) and especially among young Africans (1,9 million under the age of 29 were jobless), according to the 1999 *Bulletin of Statistics* released by Statistics SA in March 1999.[47]

Hardest hit are the sectors that contribute about 80 per cent of total formal non-agricultural employment: manufacturing, mining and quarrying, construction, and transport and electricity. According to COSATU:

> The service sector, particularly financial services, has experienced modest growth in employment. Gold mining alone accounted for some 40% of all formal job losses between June 1996 and March 1999. In the six months to March 1998, job losses in the industry came to almost 100,000, or over a quarter of jobs lost throughout the economy in the two years to March 1999 … Manufacturing on the other hand contributed 36% of job losses in the period. It experienced the sharpest decline in the year to March 1998, when it lost 75,000 jobs (COSATU, 2000).

These statistics only hint at the personal and social tragedies being generated. Gauteng housing and land affairs department research in four informal settlements found that, by late 1998, between 16 per cent and 40 per cent of households surveyed *often* were unable to feed their families, while between 47 per cent and 68 per cent were never able to save any money. The highest figures came from communities where unemployment had increased (CASE, 1998a:9, 32, 56, 81).

No less alarming are the economic effects. Given that black workers' wage packets tend to be shared extensively within family and kin circles, each job lost diminishes consumer demand – hitting sales of semi-durable goods (especially furniture and appliances), groceries, shoes and clothing. The Gauteng survey found that low-income households spend up to 75 per cent of income in these categories.

For the gold mining industry, NIEP research has found that the sacking of an average semi-skilled miner costs the economy R83 000 ($13 400) a year; for a skilled miner, the figure climbs to R132 000 ($21 300). The calculations measure the social burden created by the loss of the miner's consumption expenditure (that supports businesses and creates demand through a multiplier effect), as well as lost tax payments and the disappearance of remittances that support dependants. These effects are extensive. About 47 per cent of workers on South Africa's gold mines are migrant labourers who, on average, send about 60 per cent of their income to their countries of citizenship (mainly Lesotho and Mozambique). The loss of this income depresses both South African exports to neighbouring countries and the economic climate in those countries, NIEP found.[48] In wider perspective, the 65 000 miners retrenched in 1997:

> … cost society about R5,5-billion – or 0.8% of national GDP. Because the economy absorbs only a fraction of this unemployed labour, the social cost to the economy in the following year was roughly R8,8 billion (using a simple multiplier of 1.6 and an inflation rate of 6%, in addition to assuming that

10% of these retrenched miners would have been absorbed into the economy). So, in 1998, the social cost associated with miners retrenched in 1997 was equal to 1.2% of national GDP. That figure does not include miners sacked in 1998 (Nicolau, 2000).

Government has stuck to the belief that the structural adjustments made ('clearing away dead wood to allow the new to grow', as trade and industry minister Alec Erwin once put it) eventually will solve the unemployment crisis. But it is unclear where these jobs will be created. In finance minister Trevor Manuel's 1998 view, 'the prospects for a recovery in employment in manufacturing are strong' (Manuel, 1998b:3). There was little, if any, evidence to buttress this claim – certainly not from business leaders, who have stated repeatedly that the manufacturing sector would not become a key source for job creation in the near future. Thus, in 1989–96, the manufacturing sector spent R30 billion ($5,7 billion at 1996 exchange rates) on additional plant and equipment (over and above the upgrading of old machinery); during that period some 145 000 jobs were shed in the sector while output rose only marginally.[49]

By 2000, Manuel had revised his earlier, sunny prognosis, declaring that 'government, labour and business can pontificate and collectively lament the absence of jobs, but they aren't capable of creating jobs'.[50] Salvation was now being sought in the small business sector, which had to be relieved of some of the obligations imposed by the new labour regime.[51] The hopes and duties unloaded onto small business inflated steadily as the government's willingness to impinge on the prerogatives of organized capital shriveled.[52] Manuel's 2000/1 national budget therefore sported handsome tax cuts for small businesses, while the land reform policy was revised to focus more on aiding (black) small farming enterprises.

The job potential of the small business sector remains under-researched in South Africa. However, studies by the US Census Bureau's Center for Economic Studies suggest the enthusiasm should be tempered:

[S]mall isn't beautiful. Small firms pay less than large ones, are less likely to offer health, pension, or child care benefits, and are often more dangerous to workers. With few exceptions, they're not all that innovative technologically. And now it emerges that in manufacturing at least they are not the job machines they are reflexively praised for being.[53]

Basing their findings on scrutiny of a 16-year span of manufacturing activity in the United States, Martin Neil Baily, Eric Bartelsman, and John Haltiwanger found that the smallest plants (with fewer than 20 workers) showed a paltry contribution to total productivity growth, while the next range (20–49 workers) fared only slightly better.[54] A similar OECD study, found that small businesses do create jobs, but also destroy them at prodigious rates. Expanding existing firms were found to be more fruitful sources of job creation than start-up enterprises.[55]

Also evident was a new-found fondness for the informal sector. Addressing COSATU's central committee in June 1998, Mbeki challenged the view that 'the economy is not growing and that this stagnant economy is shedding jobs'. Nothing was being reported of the so-called 'grey economy' of informal trading and other small-scale enterprises that, he claimed, had resulted in both job creation and growth.[56] Manuel followed suit, alleging that 'much of the employment growth that is occurring' was not being captured in conventional statistical measurements (1998b:3). Erwin, a former trade unionist, adopted a more levelheaded approach. Because some job losses were being caused by casualization and sub-contracting, the actual number of jobless workers might be lower, but those trends also carried the 'serious ... danger of creating further divisions of rights and income inequality in the labour market' (1999b:4–5).

The 1995 October Household Survey calculated that 1,1 million were either employers or self-employed in the informal sector, 413 000 worked as employees in that sector, while 129 000 people held down full-time formal sector jobs while also moonlighting in the informal sector. About 86 per cent of them were African and 7 per cent coloured.

Informal sector activities are numerous and varied, ranging from street sellers to small-scale manufacturing, although the most common activities are retail and service-oriented, and a relatively small proportion of the self-employed are in manufacturing. Competition is intense, with most informal 'entrepreneurs' providing similar services or selling identical products. The absence of affordable transport means that activities are spatially concentrated in areas with narrow commercial horizons. Diversification and risk-taking is inhibited by the lack of access to finance and credit.

Statistics SA figures indicated that 80 per cent of the country's growing informal sector is survivalist and that most citizens active in it live below the poverty line. Average wages in this sector were below R500 ($110) a month. Neither did the sector appear to represent a hidden generator of growth – it contributed US$6,7 billion (at 1995 exchange rates) to South Africa's GDP annually – about 7 per cent of the total value added to the economy. Citing SALDRU studies, the *Poverty and Inequality in South Africa* report (UNDP, 1998) later noted that:

> ... average monthly net return to the self-employed was R826 ($130), while the median monthly income was much lower at R200 ($32) ... A minimum of 45% of the self-employed are earning an income lower than the Supplemental Living Level (SLL) poverty line, set at R220 ($35) per month ... the sector contains a high proportion of the working poor who would readily take up employment in the formal sector.[57]

The report also found that the most disadvantaged among the self-employed were African women aged 15–24 in rural areas; of them, 80 per cent earned less than the supplemental living level. Analysts have also disputed the portrayal of the informal sector as South Africa's entrepreneurial hub, pointing out that workers lack job security and most forms of benefits while working long hours in poor conditions. The purported benefit to the economy and society was also undermined by most of the enterprises' failure to pay taxes and their bypassing of social security and other laws.

Soberingly, the ILO has concluded from its cross-country surveys that 'no economy has successfully industrialised or boosted its productive employment primarily or largely through a massive expansion of informal own-account or petty activities' (ILO, 1996). It also warned against conceptually stratifying the labour market into formal and informal sectors, saying it creates an ideological framework that falsely pits a so-called 'labour aristocracy' against the un- and underemployed. These dualisms:

> ... tend to lead to debates about the merit of removing or exempting the 'informal' from regulations and of providing credit or subsidies to small-scale (informal) units on a preferential basis, paradoxically introducing arbitrary distortions into the market structure ... in reality, nothing is quite so simple. Increasingly, even large-scale firms resort to 'informal' forms of employment, through sub-contracting, out-sourcing, use of casual labour and so on (ILO, 1996:11).

The upshot is that the formal and informal sectors cannot neatly be separated; as more firms resort to flexible labour practices, the distinction tends to blur. Moreover, having full-time employment – whether in informal, semi-formal or formal settings – is not necessarily an antidote to poverty. Wages earned by most farm and domestic workers, for example, do not enable them to escape impoverishment. Thus, the National Speak Out on Poverty Hearings encountered testimony of female fruit packers earning a monthly wage of R340 ($55), of which R140 ($22) was spent on transportation.[58] Indeed, the ILO has found a strong correlation between poverty and wage employment in South Africa, which reflects a downward pressure on wage demands in the context of high unemployment.

A rock and a hard place

The government had trapped itself between a rock and a hard place. A more directive role on the job creation front would require repudiating both the ideological principles and many of the details of its macro-economic strategy. But, having liberalized the capital account and deepened the economy's reliance on both short- and long-term capital inflows, such a shift would, it believed, launch the economy along a turbulent path. It therefore opted for the low road – shielding GEAR from substantive discussion (let alone revision), while staging a long-delayed presidential Jobs Summit in late 1998.

In the run-up to the event, the ANC's authority over its two main allies again was on vivid display. So, too, was its tactical acumen. After several bruising backroom confabs with ANC ministers, COSATU and the SACP agreed not to raise the GEAR strategy at the summit. Their reward was to be government's support in resisting business' calls for greater labour market flexibility. Sweetening the 'deal', meanwhile, was the left's sense that the government was willing to relent on some of GEAR's prescriptions. Perhaps not coincidentally, the government also announced plans to massively boost public infrastructure spending. If carried through, this could increase gross domestic fixed investment three- to five-fold.

For a few months in late 1998, a buoyant optimism again circulated in left ranks. The mood seemed to have some basis. The economy was reeling in the wake of the Asian crisis, as the currency sank to record lows and investors abandoned the South Africa market and headed for safer shores. At a tripartite alliance summit staged in September 1998, government ministers were assailed by critics, before agreeing to a final statement that announced the arrival of a 'paradigm crisis for the simplistic 'one-size-fits-all' strictures of the so-called "Washington Consensus"'. Approved by the meeting was a paper that declared:

> ... the present crisis creates both the possibility (and the necessity) for the progressive movement to question what was until the most recent period the unquestioned economic global paradigm. We have, in engagement with many other international forces, to find our own solutions to the crisis (Anon, 1998).

Moreover, the meeting agreed on the need to apply 'contra-cyclical measures' to defend the economy against the effects of global instability 'and avert the danger of recession'. At the same gathering, a toadying paper claiming that all theoretical debates in the ANC-led alliance had been settled met with rancorous response and had to be withdrawn.[59]

The tide seemed to be turning. Instead of ganging up against a government policy, why not weld a common front and wrest concessions from business? This tactical flourish was midwifed by former trade unionist Alec Erwin (also a member of the SACP, where he is eyed with a mix of dread and befuddlement). Eighteen months later, COSATU and the SACP would still be wiping the egg from their faces, complaining that many of the agreements struck at the Jobs Summit had scarcely left the starting blocks. Save for the lowering of interest rates and a promise to review some tariff reductions, none of the 'contra-cyclical measures' saw the light of day. In response, COSATU staged a series of protests and strikes against job losses.

Far from being, in Mandela's words, 'perhaps the most important event since our first democratic elections', the Jobs Summit did not address the structural dynamics inducing job shedding and blocking job creation. Instead, what might be termed 'superstructural' adjustments were devised to be grafted onto an unchanged macro-economic framework.

Projects agreed to included a tourism enterprise programme to promote the entry of small and medium-sized firms into the sector, plans to build up to 150 000 low-cost housing units (with financing from government and business), the creation of youth brigades to promote youth employment, a buy-South Africa scheme (pushed by the labour movement), and measures aimed at promoting small businesses. Also accepted was the need for a 'counter-cyclical package to compensate for the effects of lower growth and the current international crisis'.

In more detail, the summit agreed that:

- Some funds generated by privatizations, as well as direct government contributions, would go into a National Empowerment Fund. The Fund would mainly assist black South Africans in launching small and medium-sized business ventures.
- About R1 billion ($160 million) would go to public works programmes in 1998/9, increasing to R1,8 billion by the year 2000 or 2002.
- A dedicated fund would be set up to help finance growth in the tourism sector, which government believed could create 300 000 new jobs. The private sector was expected to contribute matching funds.
- Workers would donate one day's wages annually to a special job creation fund.
- The effects of tariff reductions would be monitored and possibly reviewed in industries where jobs are threatened by trade liberalization.
- A series of tourism projects would be designed to link into the trade and industry department's SDIs (with the potential of creating 130 000 jobs, according to government).
- Business would train 5 000 new apprentices over three years in travel and tourism.
- A 'social plan' aimed at avoiding further job losses would be designed.

Other, more far-reaching proposals from COSATU did *not* survive the pre-summit consensus-seeking confabs:

- The Civil Service Pension Fund should switch to a pay-as-you-go financing system, which would release billions of rands (the summit agreed only that a task team would examine possible changes to the levels of government's contributions to the fund).
- Prescribed investments should be introduced. All retirement funds and the life assurance industry should be required to invest 10 per cent of their asset base in government bonds, dedicated to social investment and employment.

- A 55 per cent tax on annual incomes above R400 000 and an excise tax on luxuries could be considered (the proposal was not accepted).
- Industrial training should be financed with a 1 per cent levy of payroll instituted from May 1999 and increasing to 4 per cent over a three-year period.

To be sure, the measures agreed to could *contribute* to an effective job creation strategy. But they did not constitute the pillars of such a strategy. Their utility depended on other, more fundamental adjustments in the macro-economic and industrial policy arenas. In one, critical assessment, the summit 'turned out to be much more of a political spectacle than an economic operating room':

> Business was able to demonstrate its concern for society by agreeing to fund training and skills-development projects and labour cemented its credentials by temporarily ceding ground on the GEAR battlefront. The broad thrust of the Summit was towards consensus-building and circumspect moves to *soften* the unemployment crisis.[60]

Other assessments were harsher. In unionist Edward Cottle's view, labour 'made no gains for the working class through this process ... While the COSATU central committee set out a militant programme of struggle, the leadership chose to ignore its mandate. Not a single campaign ... ever got off the ground' (1999:78). Although advertised as a potential breakthrough for the labour movement, the Jobs Summit instead became an episode in the gradual weakening of labour's influence in the socio-economic realm. 'By committing the labour movement to merely "tinkering" with the system, the ruling class has politically reduced labour to dealing with collective bargaining issues', Cottle lamented.

Still hovering over the labour movement – and workers in general – is GEAR's call for 'regulated' labour flexibility and wage restraint. In Manuel's 1996 words:

> As South Africa proceeds with trade liberalisation and adapts to international competition, downward pressures will be placed on unskilled wages. If this is not accommodated by the labour market, then unemployment will rise.[61]

Manuel went on to remark that 'it is likely that wage bargaining in unionised sectors has contributed somewhat to the slowdown of employment' – a sentiment that harmonized sweetly with business' demand for a two-tier labour market (segmenting better-paid, organized workers and low-wage unskilled entrants into the job market). Even the extension of collective bargaining subsequently came under sustained attack. Yet, industrial council agreements covered only 10 per cent of South Africa's workforce in 1999 and only 1 per cent of that 10 per cent worked for employers who had agreements imposed on them through extensions of collective bargaining. 'No-one can seriously argue that this is a prime cause of unemployment in South Africa', said COSATU's Kenneth Creamer (1998:4). Reasoned argument and statistics, however, have a minor impact in what has become a dogged ideological battle.

The finance minister was merely repeating GEAR's assumption that employment levels are determined largely by the real wage rate. Thus the trend of jobless growth could be reversed by introducing (among other adjustments) wage restraint and flexibility, and selective deregulation of the labour market. This thinking is questionable on several grounds. According to the ILO, South Africa already has a flexible labour market where 'even large-scale firms resort to "informal" forms of employment, through sub-contracting, out-sourcing [and] use of casual labour' (1996:12). The ILO found that 82 per cent of firms use temporary labour and 45 per cent contract labour (see Adelzadeh, 1996:19). Moreover, '[m]any workers have little employment protection, retrenchments are fairly easy and widespread, [and] notice periods are short or non-existent' (Adelzadeh, 1996:19).

The economy is also characterized by considerable wage flexibility, with wages in certain industries fluctuating dramatically. The ILO found that in sectors 'such as metal goods, footwear, paper products, furniture and plastics, average black wages relative to subsistence actually fell' between 1984 and 1992 (1996:194–5) – despite the legislative gains notched up by trade unions. The ILO's research led it to conclude 'that the available studies have not demonstrated either that real wages have been rigid or that they have had a strong negative effect on employment' (1996:188–96). Finally, there is the often-ignored reality that job creation does *not necessarily* reduce poverty if employment is created mostly in low-wage jobs.[62]

Yet, GEAR saw regulated flexibility in the labour market as a key element of its job creation strategy. This could entail, for instance, exempting categories of workers from aspects of labour regulation, reducing real wage increases in the private sector to 0,7 per cent per annum, opting for sector-based standards rather than introducing a national minimum wage and extending industry-wide agreements to non-parties only if job losses are avoided. Some of the anticipated adjustments could violate labour laws, but Manuel mused that 'laws could be changed, if necessary'.[63] Again, comparative studies have revealed a more complex picture. In the East and South-East Asian economies, as Ghosh noted, 'a number of mechanisms which span policies across sectors have been used, rather than labour market policies alone' (1997:18).[64] These include strong public investment in housing, education, transport and agriculture, as well as price controls on basic goods (especially food), which have the effect of subsidizing elements of the wage basket.

Empirical evidence, though, has proved a flimsy barrier against a flood of highly ideological sentiment. The Johannesburg Chamber of Commerce and Industry's 1999 survey of member companies revealed that over 60 per cent of them *believed* the labour laws introduced since 1995 would further shrink the labour market, reduce productivity and retard new investment. The small business sector, especially, indicated it would reduce dependence on labour by cutting staff, mechanizing and using contractors.

COSATU's organized power has prevented the evisceration of post-apartheid labour laws. In early 2000, the labour ministry's review culminated in proposals for minor revisions to the legislation – most of them aimed at aiding small businesses. Whether the ministry could hold that line would depend on the persuasive weight of the finance ministry (which desires more profound changes) and the arbitrating judgements of the president's office (which now packs much more policy-making muscle). Perhaps temporarily selected – given COSATU's countervailing power – is a middle road along which concessions from labour would be rewarded with gains such as boosted public infrastructure spending, bigger public works programmes and the like.

Linked and edging into focus are signs of a more long-term bid to recast the balance of forces in the rickety form of corporatism constructed in the 1990s between the state, capital and labour, with the latter reduced to a junior partner. This enterprise calls for a mix of coercion and consent, not (given COSATU's power and its status as a prized political ally) an outright assault. Propelling it is an admixture of motives. They range from the ideological conviction that the left's visions of transformation and the mechanics of such a project are anachronistic, to the pragmatic view that current conditions force greater reliance on a well-lubricated market and that a carefully managed 'alliance' between state and capital should form the axis of a transformation project.

Consent would be nurtured through revised, accord-like arrangements that extend beyond the labour and into the developmental spheres. This would not be mere smoke and mirrors – genuine concessions would be made, even if they turn out to be skimpier than hoped for. The coercion gradually would be achieved by more emphatically drawing and patrolling the line against COSATU's efforts to shift the trajectory of South Africa's development path. Centrally, this demands that organized workers' right to strike – and protest – be demonized as a form of 'wrecking' that sabotages economic progress by scaring off investors. The remarks Mandela directed at striking workers in 1995 today seem less surprising than they did at the time:

> Let it be clear to all that the battle against the forces of anarchy and chaos has been joined. Let no one say that they have not been warned. All of us

must rid ourselves of the notion that the government has a bag full of money. Mass action of any kind will not create resources that the government does not have. Some of those who have initiated and participated in such activities have misread freedom to mean license. They have wrongly concluded that an elected government of the people is a government open to compulsion through anarchy.[65]

Ideologically, this process is well underway, as workers' demands are counterposed to the plight of the unemployed and the poor. Practically, it entails using (and even creating) potential conflicts to force unions to choose between possibly debilitating strikes or settle on below par terms. The process is basically Pavlovian: business and the government dig in against strike-backed demands on high-profile issues, while union leaderships are expected gradually to discover the futility of stand-offs (as public sympathy wanes and the costs of prolonged resistance register). Many of these features were on dramatic display in the 1999 public sector wage dispute, during which a government minister accused unions of 'infantile leftism' and 'narrow trade unionism'.[66] Propagated was a caricature that contrasted workers' demands with the transformation of society. A year later, Manuel would implicitly repeat that message when his allegedly 'pro-poor' national budget included sub-inflation wage increases for the public service.[67] Meanwhile, government has all but absolved itself from the duty of creating jobs. In January 2000, Manuel told journalists: 'I want someone to tell me how the government is going to create jobs. It's a terrible admission but governments around the world are impotent when it comes to creating jobs.'[68]

Ahead lie not a series of explosive battles but a long sequence of skirmishes intended to prune and domesticate union power. The goal, ultimately, is to construct a form of corporatism that orbits mainly around the state and capital – along the lines established achieved under Tony Blair's 'Third Way' in Britain. As shown in Chapter 8, the process is analogous – not identical – to the 'Third Way', not least because Blair's Labour Party came to power *after* the British labour movement had been thoroughly emasculated during the Thatcher era. For a host of reasons (including the risk that it could suffer serious political damage itself), the ANC government is unlikely to launch an outright assault on COSATU in the foreseeable future. More probable is a tactically astute approach that, in theory, could provide COSATU with some leeway to rewrite the script of this enterprise.

COSATU's failure to bend the government's arm on GEAR should be read, therefore, not as an index of impotence but as a reminder of the *limits* of its influence. Like the SACP, it has been unable to shift the paradigm of government's economic thinking. It is left in an unenviable position. The principal foe of this officially socialist trade union federation is capital. But adroitly running interference for that adversary is an ally – the ANC in government – that remains the political repository of popular aspirations. That its rhetoric often is contradicted by its deeds is, in a sense, beside the point. The discontent churned up by an unemployment rate of 37,6 per cent, of poverty levels that match those under the final years of apartheid and of widening inequality is still radically muffled and disorientated by a party that monopolizes the discourse of transformation. That it has assumed the role of facilitating and supervising a phase of modernized capital accumulation in South Africa is beyond dispute. That it does so with the support of powerful layers of its membership also seems clear. But other sections of the party remain opposed to this course of events; for COSATU and the SACP (and many other critical supporters), they remain the well from which hope is drawn.

Emboldening such optimism is the fact that COSATU can hardly claim to have been short-changed since 1994 – despite the barbed words and stiffened back of its ally. For the government's chief violations of neoliberal orthodoxy have occurred on the labour front – most obviously via a trio of labour laws that answered many of the workplace demands of the labour movement.[69] Ironically, those very gains would be turned against organized labour – as gains achieved at the expense of the unemployed and poor. The claims are plainly disingenuous, but they do reveal the lens through which the ANC now apprehends COSATU, in particular: less as an ally bonded by common principles and visions than as a formidable social force that features prominently in the arithmetic of political power. Hence, the finance minister's attack on COSATU's 'outmoded' visions could pass unchastened by his colleagues and superiors, while the president, a month later, would refrain from criticising the federation in a state of the nation speech.[70] COSATU (and the SACP) has not excelled in the face of such 'good-cop, bad-cop' tactics.

Yet the notion that 'COSATU has about as much power and influence as yesterday's newspaper'[71] is far off the mark. Albeit trimmed back, the federation's countervailing power figured in an unexpectedly restrained set of labour law revisions government outlined in early 2000, slowed efforts to fast-track the privatization programme, and prompted the introduction of a capital gains tax in the 2000/1 budget. Trapped in the force field of the ANC, COSATU (and the SACP) finds itself in a situation where the parameters of permissible moves are sternly policed, but in which limited advances *can* be achieved. The enduring hope of engineering a patent 'working class bias' in the ANC hardly fits this scenario. Neither, under current conditions, do the prospects of definitively tilting the development path in a more popular direction. Imprisoned by its own history – and by deference sustained with hope – COSATU (like the organized left in general) is still to find a way of recasting that contest. Its Mexican counter-parts can offer it grim but sobering reflections on a similar experience. A long and painstaking process of rebuilding is required if it is to avoid that fate.

Defending orthodoxy

Overall, government's defence of GEAR has come to rest on three contentions – one political, the others economic and social. Politically, the GEAR plan is presented as an elaboration of principles and perspectives contained in the RDP. Two variants of this argument occur. The more pliant one holds that the overriding goals of the RDP and GEAR are identical – attacking poverty and deprivation. GEAR 'simply seeks to set out clearly and unambiguously the key economic requirement for achieving [the RDP] goals', as Manuel has put it (1996:2). By launching the economy quickly into a new growth cycle, GEAR 'provides a foundation to underpin accelerated RDP delivery' (Manuel 1996:4).

But ANC government leaders have also gone further, arguing that the specific measures in the GEAR plan are merely refinements of positions established in the RDP. As Thabo Mbeki put it in mid-1998:

> In clear and straight forward language, the RDP identified a high deficit, a high level of borrowing and the general taxation level as, to quote the RDP again, 'part of our macroeconomic problem' … Comrades also appear to have forgotten that, having noted the fiscal crisis, characterised in part by a large budget deficit, and having called for new macroeconomic ratios, the RDP did not then go on to say what these ratios should be. For some strange reason, when work is then done to translate the perspective contained in the RDP into actual figures, this is then interpreted as a replacement of the RDP by GEAR.[72]

The claim had some basis. As shown, a great deal of consistency can be found in the ANC's economic thinking from 1992 onwards. As for the RDP, despite its overriding progressive character, on macro-economic matters it was both elliptical and timid. Gelb is correct in noting 'consistency in the ANC's position on macro policy between 1993 and 1996 or between the RDP and GEAR'.[73] Also, the main structures created in 1994 to implement the RDP perforce operated within those macro-economic parameters. Thus, the RDP Fund was funded (as the government's RDP White Paper prescribed) not by increasing overall expenditure, but by 'reprioritizing' departmental budgets. RDP funding, in other words, was contingent on 'fiscal discipline'. As Gelb has reminded, 'the RDP Office was set up within the executive in a way that allowed it very restricted influence over fiscal policy, and no influence over monetary issues or other aspects of macro policy' (1999:16). This pecking order became more explicit in early 1996, when government shut down the RDP Office and dispersed its functions among other, 'conventional' line departments, with the RDP's 'command centre' shared between the deputy president's office and the finance ministry.

Government's economic contention holds that the allegedly identical goals of the two documents can only be achieved 'in the context of sustained economic growth, a stable macroeconomic environment and a thriving competitive sector' (Manuel, 1996:1). Chastened by the economy's failure to respond to the treatment, government officials since 1997 preferred to stress GEAR's contribution to economic stability and the achievement of 'sound fundamentals'. Manuel's 1996 declaration that 'it was employment creation that became the central focus of the macroeconomic strategy' (1996:1) subsequently has been replaced by claims that the plan steeled the economy against the upheavals and instabilities that rocked emerging markets after 1997.[74] In the finance ministry's view, the liberalizing and deregulatory adjustments codified in the GEAR plan were not negative factors, but key ingredients of a successful defence against those upheavals:

> Since our own savings levels are inadequate, we have to attract foreign savings. However, we do so in a rapidly globalising world where capital moves relatively freely across borders ... We are a small open economy and must therefore recognise that we shall remain caught in this vortex of rapid capital movement until we can successfully address all of the structural difficulties ... The lessons we draw from all these experiences is that what matters are sound economic policies and solid economic institutions (Manuel, 1998a:2–3).

Which brings us to the 'social defence' of GEAR. In COSATU's view, it is 'blindingly obvious that it is not possible to have a developmental budget within an anti-developmental economic framework' (1998:2). Commenting on the 2000/1 budget, COSATU highlighted one of GEAR's central strictures: a conservative tax regime that prolongs a trend of decreasing corporate and rising personal tax contributions. Companies' contributions to total tax revenue plummeted from 27 per cent (in 1976) to 18 per cent (1990) to 11 per cent (1999). Over the same period, mines' contribution fell from 9 per cent to 2 per cent to less than 0,5 per cent. Personal taxes' share soared, meanwhile, from 25 per cent to 30 per cent to 42 per cent (COSATU, 2000). The 1999/2000 budget handed out more corporate tax cuts – according to the Institute for Democratic Alternatives in South Africa (IDASA), some R2,5 billion ($400 million) or roughly three times the funds allocated to land reform projects.[75]

Overall, tax-based government revenue is limited to 26,5 per cent of GDP. Along with the successful efforts to drive down the budget deficit, this has limited the funding pool available for social (and economic) spending. Yet, the government is adamant that 'achieving fiscal discipline has not been at the expense of delivery'.

In 1999, it provided a social pension of R470 per month to about two-and-a-half million citizens (including 700 000 who qualified for disability pensions). More than eight million children have been immunized against measles, five million against polio, and government claims that seven out of ten children are fully immunized.[76] About three-quarters of the one million dwellings promised in 1994 have been provided, albeit mainly in the elementary form of serviced plots of land.

That could not have been achieved if social spending was being gutted. Indeed, in the period 1996–9, the government was able to cut deeper into other line functions – especially in defence and in economic spending categories. But there was a limit to attrition on those fronts. Although improved tax collection, too, is a finite variable, it has swelled government coffers and provided more leeway in budgetary decisions. Meanwhile, caps on public service wage increases have also been translated into government 'saving'. As a result, social services expenditure (measured as a percentage of total non-interest spending) actually rose from 58 per cent in 1995/6 to about 61 per cent in 1999/2000.

Yet, the figures deceive. Recall that government has been reducing overall spending in line with its fiscal policy. In other words, steady or slightly rising social spending *measured as a percentage of total spending* has not automatically translated into *real* increases for social delivery line functions. *Real*, year-on-year social spending (as a percentage of non-interest expenditure) fell by 2,6 per cent in 1999/2000 and another 1,2 per cent in 2000/1.[77] A closer look at specific spending categories confirms this trend. Old-age pensions and disability grants only kept up with inflation in two years since 1995, while the nominal value of the child support grant has not changed since its introduction in 1998 (that is, it declined in real terms).[78] Funding for land restitution and land reform, on the other hand, rose impressively since 1996.

On the whole, the government has been able to avoid eviscerating social spending, instead cutting back incrementally. If GDP growth revives and tax collection continues to improve, it should be able to continue in this manner for the next decade – possibly even increasing social spending periodically. In a context that requires massive boosts in social (and economic spending), this leaves the government on something of a treadmill. Nonetheless, the social achievements surveyed below testify to the sometimes sterling efforts of social service departments to fulfil their duties to society. Without exception, this has been done in a tight fiscal context and against a backdrop of bewildering organizational changes that were needed to modify state structures to perform tasks they previously had been explicitly designed to prevent.

A snapshot of delivery

By the ANC's count, it has made good on more than 60 per cent of its 1994 election promises, as the following snapshot of delivery successes by mid-1999 shows:[79]

- In 1994, some 30 per cent of South Africans lacked access to a safe supply of water near their homes; today, after three million people have benefited from the government's water supply programme, that has been reduced to 20 per cent.
- In 1994, less than 40 per cent of South African households had electricity; by 1999, after more than two million connections, 63 per cent of households were connected to the electricity grid.
- In 1994, about a quarter of homes had telephones; after 1,3 million connections, 35 per cent were linked to the telephone system at the close of the century.
- On average each day since 1994, another 1 300 homes were electrified; another 750 telephones installed; and another 1 700 people gained access to clean water.
- The primary school nutrition programme reaches about five million children, while about 10 000 classrooms have been built or repaired.
- Pregnant women and children under six years qualify for free medical care, and 638 clinics have been built since 1994.
- The government developed the capacity to provide 15 000 houses every month. The housing subsidy scheme contributed to the building of 630 000 by March 1999. Almost 40 per cent of approved subsidies were registered to women.

Achievements like these have emboldened Mbeki to claim that 'it would be difficult to find examples elsewhere in the world where a negotiated transfer of power took place, where such progress was achieved in so short a period of time to redefine the nature of the new society' (1998e:4). Although hyperbolic, the claim has some merit. By no means has society been 'redefined', but in quantitative terms substantive changes have been wrought. Sadly, once bean-counting is replaced by closer scrutiny, the achievements shed much of their lustre.

Thousands of electricity and water connections are cut off each month because users cannot afford the service fees. Three out of four newly installed telephone lines in rural areas were disconnected each month in 1999 because users could not pay their bills.[80] The housing tally reflected both built (brick and mortar) homes and the transfer of title deeds for tiny serviced plots of land.[81] As much as 50 per cent of government housing subsidies was going toward non-physical inputs and consultancy fees, while many of the houses built were declared sub-standard by the (previous) housing minister because they had been poorly constructed or were smaller than the minimum size designated by government. According to the Development Action Group (DAG), the total housing backlog passed the 3,7 million mark in 2000.[82]

A May 1999 study by the Department of Water Affairs admitted that many of its vaunted water provision projects had crumbled into dysfunction or disrepair. According to the South African Municipal Workers' Union (SAMWU) as many as two million of the water taps installed were not working properly, although the department denied 'that more than half the infrastructure provided is not working'.[83]

Repaired townships classrooms are still overcrowded, while teachers buckle under increased workloads as the education department is forced to lower its salary bill. Matric pass rates have dropped steadily since 1994 – along with subsidy cuts and bursary shortages, this is one of the factors causing university enrolment to plummet in all but a few institutions. School fees have rocketed and in some provinces those students fortunate enough to get textbooks can wait until midway through the school year before receiving them. The education system has proved one of the difficult areas to transform. Not only does it require the overhaul of the entire education system (deracializing it, aligning it to skills needs in the broader economy and society, developing new curricula and teaching materials), but the huge, apartheid-bequeathed discrepancies in the availability of teaching sites, materials and personnel have had to be redressed. Complicating matters further has been the severe decay of an ethos of teaching and learning at many institutions. Candidly, education minister Kader Asmal in July 1999 declared the system 'in crisis' and announced its comprehensive overhaul.

Land reform lagged furthest behind the 1994 targets. Of the 54 000 land claims lodged, fewer than 100 had been settled in favour of claimants by late 1999 (involving 167 534 hectares of land and about 70 000 people). 'Restitution has turned out to be much more complex than was originally realised', the land affairs department's 1998 annual report admitted. According to the National Land Committee (NLC), less than 1 per cent of South Africa's farmland had been redistributed to poor, black households by mid-1999. The target set by the ANC in 1994 was 30 per cent. Land redistribution policy was definitively shaped by the counsel of World Bank and other technocrats (who persuaded government to opt for a market-driven voucher/grant approach) and by the decision to afford constitutional protection of property rights. Furthermore, the land reform budget was consistently cut after 1996.

In 1999, the land affairs department shifted tack, suspending a R16 000 ($2 600) land resettlement grant per household and opting instead to put black small farmers on their feet as part of a rural development strategy – in line with the small business fad that has taken hold in government. At the expense of its potential to reduce poverty (by providing the means for subsistence to the poorest layers of society), land reform has been recast to service the development of putative nodes of rural economic growth. The focus has shifted from providing some of the rural poor with a bedrock for survival, to aiding farming entrepreneurs. A further category of victims would be farmworkers seeking to gain secure land tenure rights (Hussy, 2000). Health clinics are severely understaffed and, particularly in rural areas, lack even the most basic medicines. 'We have fewer doctors, fewer beds, fewer resources and more patients than ever before', the principal surgeon at one of Johannesburg's largest public hospitals has complained, as patients flock to established hospitals.[84] The country's health system has become more resolutely split – between a public health service buckling under the AIDS endemic and an inadequate primary health care system on the one hand, and a private, market-driven medical scheme counterpart managed by financial capital on the other.

The stress lines seem doomed to give as the AIDS toll mounts. By 2000, almost four-million South Africans were HIV-positive with the prevalence rate exceeding 22 per cent nationally and passing the 40 per cent mark in some (mainly mining) communities. Yet, HIV/AIDS ranked low among government's priorities until late 1998 when a more vigorous prevention campaign was launched. As the country approached the threshold of a pandemic early in the new century, many of the developmental gains since 1994 seemed destined to disappear, with unprecedented social and economic consequences. Perhaps the most dramatic failure of post-apartheid social management has occurred in this front, despite the fact that a comprehensive HIV/AIDS national plan had been endorsed by the cabinet in 1994.[85] In early 2000, it was revealed that the health department had failed to spend 40 per cent of the 1999/2000 HIV/AIDS budget for prevention, counselling and care, while funding for AIDS service organizations was cut by 43 per cent in 2000/1.[86] Government has withheld funding for the provision of AZT treatment to pregnant, HIV-positive mothers – first arguing that the cost (R80 million or $13 million annually) was 'unaffordable', then claiming that AZT was 'too dangerous' to administer (see Marais, 2000).

But it is equally and demonstrably true that millions of South Africans can detect evidence of improvements – or, at least, genuine efforts to fulfil promises. It is partially on that groundwork that the ANC's ongoing popularity and electoral supremacy rests. Citizens are appreciative of the slow but determined efforts to convert a civil service encrusted with indifference into a real servant of the public and prize the new policy frameworks that have been erected on the abandoned work sites of apartheid. Mitigating the anger and disappointment triggered when services are disconnected due to non-payment is the recognition that the electricity grid or a tarred road has reached a previously neglected rural area, that a dilapidated school has been repaired, that a health clinic finally has been built.

More specifically, the ANC government has been especially adept at dispensing gains to a variety of constituencies, classes and interest groups. Though less evident in social life, women's rights enjoy constitutional and legislative protection. The Labour Relations Act, the Employment Equity Act and the Basic Conditions of Employment Act constitute the legislative pillars of a new post-apartheid labour market that benefits millions of workers. Affirmative action legislation has been passed, aiding the career opportunities of the black middle classes. Under the banner of black economic empowerment, the government enthusiastically promotes the ascent and growth of an African corporate class, as well as wedging space and building institutional support for the growth of a small- and medium-scale African entrepreneurial class. Some analysts have reflected on the emergence of 'a new generation of black companies, with a high dependency on state fiat for its sustenance'.[87] Meanwhile, established corporates operate within a decidedly market-friendly economic framework and with substantial state largesse.

At the same time, the society remains tragically polarized – not least along the lines of income and access to services – while the gulf of structural inequality appears to be widening. Aping government and business economists, the media measure the health and vitality of the economy against GDP growth figures, marginal variations in the inflation rate, the existence of 'sound economic fundamentals' and the like. In that paradigm, a shrinking budget deficit (pushed well below the 3 per cent of GDP mark in 1999) is celebrated as an edifying accomplishment, while rising capital inflows are paraded as proof that the economy has 'turned the corner'. Meanwhile, a national budget that extends tax cuts to the top 50 per cent of income earners is advertised as a 'pro-poor' budget, confirming the cognitive dissonance that plagues mainstream discourse.

The dull ache of deprivation

Virtually every social indicator betrays the extreme inequalities that define South African society. Measured by the Gini coefficient,[88] it was the third most unequal society in the world in 1996 (with a Gini coefficient of 0,584), according to the World Bank (1996). Based on census data, some South African calculations have pegged the Gini coefficient at even worse levels – 0,69 – although this could be because 'poor households [probably] underestimate their incomes to a greater extent than do wealthy households'.[89]

The final 15 years of the apartheid era saw significant redistribution of income from the poor to the rich: between 1975 and 1991, the income of the poorest 60 per cent of the population dropped by about 35 per cent. By 1996, the gulf between rich and poor had grown more vast. The poorest quintile (20 per cent of the population) received 1,5 per cent of total income, compared to the 65 per cent pocketed by the richest quintile and the 48 per cent netted by the richest 10 per cent. Also startling was the extent of poverty: in 1995, the poorest half of households earned a mere 11 per cent of household income.[90]

South Africa's rate of poverty (a measurement of the extent of absolute poverty) is 45 per cent, which translates into 3 126 000 households or more than 18 million citizens living below the poverty line (pegged at a monthly income of R353 or $57). In mainly rural provinces, the figure rises above 50 per cent. Access to basic services is similarly unequal:

- Only 6,2 per cent of South Africans have received higher education, 16,4 per cent have completed their schooling while one in five have no formal education.
- Slightly more than half the population live in formal housing.
- Fewer than half have running water in their homes, while 19,8 per cent use a public tap and more than one-tenth of the population relies on water collected from dams, rivers or streams.
- Only 29 per cent of South Africans have a telephone (landline or cellular).
- Only half the population have a flush or chemical toilet, while slightly more than half have refuse removed at least once a week.

A closer look reveals more precise contours of inequality and poverty. The experience of extreme poverty is dramatically concentrated among Africans: 57,2 per cent of Africans live below the poverty threshold, compared to 2,1 per cent of whites. The poorest 40 per cent of citizens remain overwhelmingly African, and female and rural. According to Statistics SA, twice as many female-headed than male-headed households are in the bottom quintile (26 per cent compared to 13 per cent). When race and gender are aggregated, the figure rises to 31 per cent of African, female-headed households in the lowest quintile, compared to 19 per cent of African, male-headed households.[91] Overall, the poverty rate among female-headed households is 60 per cent, compared with 31 per cent for male-headed households – underlining the need to target (especially African) women in welfare, job creation, training and small business development programmes.

Unemployment, too, is highest among African women (52 per cent, measured by broad definition),[92] followed by African men (42,5 per cent). The labour absorption rate differs widely between population groups: for men, it ranged between 35 per cent for Africans and 68 per cent for whites in 1997, while for women it ranged between 22 per cent for Africans and 44 per cent for whites. Urban men were most likely to find jobs (40 per cent of those of working age were formally employed in 1997), while non-urban women had the worst job prospects (only 15 per cent had jobs in 1997).[93]

Rural/urban inequality is momentous, with African and coloured median incomes in rural areas about half that of their counterparts in urban areas. Indeed, most of the poor live in rural areas, where the poverty rate is 71 per cent. According to the *Poverty and Inequality in South Africa* report (1998), it would require R28 billion merely to increase the income of those South Africans living below the poverty threshold. Fully 76 per cent of this money would have to be spent in rural areas.

The same report revealed huge discrepancies between the country's provinces when measured by the human development index (HDI). The Western Cape and Gauteng, as well as the white and Indian population groups, fall within the HDI range equivalent to 'high human development'. Northern Province falls within the HDI range equivalent to 'low human development' (UNDP, 1998:5). In that province, almost two-thirds of residents cook with wood fires, while only 18 per cent have running water in their homes and 7,5 per cent have a telephone. More than one-fifth of residents have no toilet facilities. In the Eastern Cape, 78 per cent of children live in poor households, compared with 20 per cent in Gauteng.

Factory of crime

It should come as no surprise that amid such violently induced deprivation, crime has become commonplace and 'democratized', prompting one writer to suggest anxiously that 'urban crime has become a replacement for the civil war that never happened'.[94] Most forms of property crime increased in the 1990s, among them common robbery, residential burglaries (266 817 cases reported in 1998 – 17 per cent higher than 1994) and theft.[95] Violence often accompanies ostensible property crimes, as shown in the rise in armed robberies (53 per 100 000 people in 1998) and vehicle hijackings. In 1998, 188 out of every 100 000 South Africans were victims of armed robbery (the 1997 ratio was 151).[96]

Police figures showed that only one in seven murders ended in conviction, while for every 50 hijackings reported only one conviction resulted. One in 13 reported rapes, one in 34 armed robberies and one in 50 car thefts ended with the perpetrators serving jail sentences.

Booming in South Africa's foundering economy are insurance corporations and a $10 billion private security industry whose 5 000 firms employ 130 000 people. Most of them are poorly paid black men. Meanwhile, security walls, sealed-off residential blocks and fortress-like cluster housing complexes have redrawn the geography of cities and towns, separating 'insiders' from 'outsiders'.

For scores of South Africans, property crime functions not only as a method of survival but as an entry route into the circuits of consumer capitalism (and mainstream economic activities).[97] Indeed, many criminal enterprises are exemplars of entrepreneurship. Their most successful representatives excel at innovation, display an uncanny nose for market opportunities, and revel in displaying the rewards of their initiative – acting as living advertisements for their endeavours and determination. It seems reasonable to suggest that the entrepreneurial excellence the government wishes to ignite in the (legal) small business sector already is prevalent in criminal activities. According to one police officer:

> The typical Gauteng hijacking syndicate was a textbook model of a networked firm, in which specific functions were outsourced and labour markets were as flexible as product demand … Businessmen dream of an organisation this sensitive to market signals.[98]

The goods pass back into the underground market place, where poorer consumers are able to acquire, replace or upgrade consumer goods at bargain rates. Reinforced in this netherworld are both the values of consumerism and the ability of poorer citizens to participate in that system. Although ignored in official discourse – where crime is abstracted from its socio-political and economic contexts – property crime helps sustain consumer capitalism in a society that deprives the bulk of society from sharing in its ostentatiously advertised fruits. In many depressed communities, circuits of illegal accumulation have become integral to social and economic reproduction. As journalist Ferial Haffajee has observed:

> In this subverted economy, car theft, drug and cellphone syndicates provide employment and career paths. Its downstream industries are chop shops and specialist stolen goods networks, where it is possible to furnish a home from the pickings of crime. Eldorado Park is not a glitch, but a universal. Economies like these are replicated across the country.[99]

Thousands of gangs serve as alternative family forms in communities where family and other traditional structures have been shorn of their stabilizing functions. On the Cape Flats, some 80 000 people belonged to 130 gangs at the turn of the century. Criminologist Wilfried Scharf has argued that state violence under apartheid contributed indirectly to gang growth in those Cape Town townships 'by preventing or impeding informal mechanisms of social control that had previously retarded gang-formation and gang activity'.[100] Gangs ballooned 'in African townships only when the street committees had been weakened and when the people's courts had been smashed by the police'.[101]

Testifying to the frayed social fabric were the 24 875 cases of murder reported in 1998 – up by 1,2 per cent on the previous year, but down by 7,3 per cent on the four previous years. In early 1999, the country's murder rate was 55,3 per 100 000 people (down from 69,5 per 100 000 in 1994), while attempted murders fell from 70,7 per 100 000 to 66,7 in the same period.[102] Public insecurity is generated largely by the perceived risk of 'random' crime, yet:

... the majority of intentional injuries and fatalities occur during inter-personal disputes between people who know each other and not, as it is often commonly believed, in attacks by unknown criminals during pre-meditated robberies and the like (Hamber & Lewis, 1997:5).

In 1998, the country's first national victim survey found that the main incidents of crime occurred at the home and that the victims knew their attackers. Half of all sexual offences and 30 per cent of assaults took place in respondents' homes. 'Domestic violence is a factory for the culture of violence in our society', the report said.[103] Hospital records in the late 1990s showed an average of 2 500 people were being treated daily for violence-related injuries. Women, particularly African women, bore the brunt of the violence – more than 50 000 rapes were reported in 1999, a figure women's organizations said captured only a fraction of the reality.[104]

The statistics only hint at the levels of social dislocation and malfunction generated under the apartheid system and prolonged subsequently. For millions of South Africans, the pain of poverty and deprivation is transformed also into the horrors of routine abuse and violence at the hands of friends, kin and loved ones. The victims are predominantly women, young and old. The personal agonies defy description. They also register on the larger fields of politics and society – for the trauma caused by emotional proximity to a murder, rape or violent assault undermines many of the rudiments of healthy social relations, both between people (as individuals or groups) and between citizens and the state. As summarized by Hamber and Lewis, certain elemen-tary assumptions about the 'self and the world' are up-ended:

... the belief in personal invulnerability ('it won't happen to me'); the view of the self as positive; the belief that the world is a meaningful and orderly place, that events happen for a reason (and) the trust that other human beings are fundamentally benign (1997:9).

Affordable and accessible counselling and support services are at a pre-mium, despite the warnings of psychiatric workers that 'as a country, South Africans are exhibiting symptoms which add up to Post-Traumatic Stress Disorder'. British psychiatrist Dr Mark Nathan has warned that 'there is so much mental trauma in this country that as a psychiatrist it is difficult to distinguish classic psychiatric symptoms from a situation where people have simply reached the end of their tether'.[105]

Here, one encounters one of the lasting 'accomplishments' of apartheid: the virtual dissolution of a caring society, despite the valiant efforts to sus-tain networks of social support. In this almost Hobbesian scenario, it is the poor who are turned unto and into themselves, while the privileged cavort or huddle behind bolted doors and electrified fences. To some extent the law and order panic of post-apartheid South Africa reflects the extent to which these horrors have become 'democratized', spilling beyond the zones of the poor. Backlit by a capitalist ideology that equates consumption with prestige and wealth with self-worth – yet denies the vast majority even a taste of its fruits – it is a scenario that defines (and ruins) the lives of millions. It is here that Mbeki's claim of a 'new society' stands most resoundingly indicted, for the formative dynamics of inclusion and exclusion, of privilege and deprivation are not being altered.

Also violently shoved beyond the perimeters of 'decent society' are African youth. They have become thoroughly demonized, though the assumption of an allegedly terminal alienation among them is not borne out by research. Deprived of understanding, empathy and validating roles in economic and social life, youth have been sideswiped into a twilight zone and blacked-out with scorn, stereotypes and neglect. Fewer than five in every 100 school-leavers find work, while a 1998 survey of schools revealed that normal teaching in some schools occurred on about 10 per cent of annual schooldays. Yet, marshalled around them – and rubbed in their faces – is the most pervasive and ostentatious example of consumer capitalism on the African continent. In the late 1990s, *kwaito* music – a brash, often crass, compression of hip-hop, house music and 1980's South African pop styles – came to signify the no-man's land of African youth and the clash of desire and denial it has to endure:

> This music that you find vulgar and offensive means more to the youth of this country than you can imagine. It is a mirror of our lives … It asks questions like: Who are we? Where do we fit in? Where are we going? The struggle culture offered one answer to that question: Liberation. Today, we have our doubts (Hill, 1999:12–13).

Contours of inequality

Statistics paint a world of averages, patterns and contours. They cannot, as Colin Bundy has written, convey the realities of intense poverty and inequality: 'its texture: the dull ache of deprivation, the acute tensions generated by violence and insecurity, the intricacies of survival and all its emotions – despair, hope, resentment, apathy, futility and fury'.[106]

The 1995 South African Participatory Poverty Assessment found that, inscribed in South Africa's indices of deprivation, were millions of citizens plagued by continuous ill health, extraordinary levels of anxiety and stress (and the accompanying realities of violence and abuse vented mainly on women and children), harsh and dangerous work for low income, and pervasive demoralization and fatalism. A defining characteristic is the sense of impotency and of an inability to alter the conditions of life. Yet, all this is matched by the courage and perseverance with which South Africa's poor attempt to hold at bay these ravages. Describing her life to the *Speak Out on Poverty Hearings* in 1998, Emma Mahkaza told commissioners:

I am having seven children and nothing to depend on. I am making bricks and sometimes it rains and then I can't do it. And I collect food and take it to people. I fetch wood and collect cans of cold drink and sell them. When I am without food then I go next door and if they don't have, then the children will have empty stomachs and I cry. Yesterday I left with my children fast asleep because they will ask me what we are going to eat. I am very thin, because when I bought a bucket of mielie meal, I won't eat at all if I am thinking of the children. They say: 'Mum, you are going to die'.[107]

Inequality of income distribution between race groups is considerable. Whites earn more than half the total income, although they only constitute 13 per cent of the population. Africans, on the other hand, earn just more than a third of total income but make up three-quarters of the population. It is not surprising, therefore, to find that 65 per cent of white households slot into the top income quintile (or fifth) while only 10 per cent of African households earn incomes sufficient to hoist them into that category. (For Indians the figure is a surprisingly high 45 per cent and for coloureds a very low 17 per cent.) Viewed from the other end of the scale, one finds 23 per cent of all African households in the poorest quintile, compared with 11 per cent of coloureds and 1 per cent of Indians and whites.

Statistics, of course, can be viewed through different ideological lenses. In its official pronouncements, the ANC government highlights the racial contours of poverty and inequality. Reviewing these indicators in June 1998, Mbeki declared:

It helps nobody, except those who do not want change, to argue that the difference in income between a senior black manager and an unskilled black worker is as high as the difference in income between an equivalent senior white manager and an unskilled black worker and, therefore, that like many countries, we are now faced with the challenge of class differentiation rather than the racial differentiation that is the heritage of white minority rule (1998d:5).

To be sure, the perception of a ballooning black élite is exaggerated. The national census of 1998 showed nearly 50 per cent of white workers occupied management jobs, while 73 per cent of blacks operated as unskilled or artisan workers. Only 11 per cent of the working black population were managers or legislators.[108] Between 1995 and 1997, the number of black senior managers in the private sector rose by only 2,3 per cent, while middle managers increased by only 1,6 per cent. In the public services, whites in 1997 still held 62 per cent of management positions although they only comprised 21 per cent of overall staff. A slightly better balance pertained in senior management, where Africans held 47 per cent of posts and whites 43 per cent.[109]

Although still small in overall numbers, the African middle-class has grown impressively – by almost 80 per cent in the period 1991–6, pushing the number of households in that category from 220 000 to 400 000. (By comparison, there were just fewer than one million white middle-class households in 1996 – Whiteford & Van Seventer, 1999:36.)

The government might prefer not to dwell on this reality, but an uneven deracialization of inequality is occurring, although it must be noted that this process began before the ANC assumed power. Between 1975 and 1991, large income disparities opened among Africans as class and social structures were reshaped. A more differentiated class structure emerged among Africans as the middle class and professional stratum swelled and a tiny economic élite found its feet (see Everatt, 1999).

Cementing that trend in the 1980s were rising wages earned by skilled workers, fewer job opportunities for unskilled workers and the easing of apartheid proscriptions in the economy that allowed more African entrepreneurs to emerge. Homeland bureaucracies played an important role in the process. They were transformed into burgeoning élite, with ministers and officials often utilizing their positions in, or links into homeland government structures to build up lucrative business ventures (in retail, transport, construction, property and agriculture). In some rural areas clusters of African entrepreneurs emerged, a trend that has accelerated dramatically in urban townships.

By 1991, the mean income of the lowest-earning 40 per cent of African households had declined, while that of the richest 20 per cent of African households (representing 5,6 million people) soared by 40 per cent. According to the World Bank, this made 'them the most upwardly mobile race group, as black professionals, skilled workers and entrepreneurs benefited from the erosion of apartheid'.[110] Between 1991 and 1996, according to a 1999 study by economists Andrew Whiteford and Dirk Van Seventer:

> Within each population group the poorest 40% of households have been the biggest losers in terms of income decline. Each successively wealthier income class [sic] has done better than the previous class … The average income of the poorest 40% of African households declined by 21% … while the richest 10% of African households have enjoyed an average income increase of 17%. The decline in income of the poorer households can be explained in terms of a decrease in formal employment among Africans (1999:21).

According to the ILO, inter-racial inequality constituted 65 per cent of general earnings inequality in 1980; by 1993, it had dropped to 42 per cent (1996:21). Racial inequalities of income remained large (in 1996, white per capita income was nine times bigger than that of Africans), but a 'significant redistribution of income towards previously disadvantaged population groups' had occurred in the period 1991–6, Whiteford and Van Seventer noted. Their study also found inequality *within* population groups increasing, with the Gini coefficient 'within the African community [rising] from 0.62 in 1991 to 0.66 in 1996' (1999:37). Other, earlier studies detected the same trend, but found lower levels of inequality within population groups. Thus, an income and spending survey by the predecessor of Statistics SA found that levels of income disparity between African households (measured by the Gini coefficient) rose from 0,35 in 1990 to 0,51 in 1995.[111]

Between 1991 and 1996, whites' share of total income dipped from 59,5 per cent to 51,9 per cent, while the proportion of white households in the richest 10 per cent of the population fell sharply from 95 per cent to 65 per cent. Africans' share of total income rose from 29,9 per cent to 35,7 per cent, while the proportion of Africans households in the top 10 per cent of income earners climbed from 9 per cent to 22 per cent. Overall, the poorest 40 per cent of South Africans earned less than 4 per cent of income in 1996, while the richest 10 per cent pocketed more than 50 per cent (Whiteford & Van Seventer, 1999:38).

Subsequent developments will have propelled those processes further. They include the deracialization of state institutions and (although at a slower pace) access to management positions in the private sector, the improved employment and entrepreneurial prospects of sections of the middle classes that were previously excluded and suppressed, and the phenomenon of black economic empowerment. Meanwhile, ongoing job losses and depressed wage rates continue to skew income distribution, prompting a troubling conclusion from Whiteford and Seventer:

> Are these trends in the labour market likely to continue, further fuelling rising inequality? On the basis of employment projections published Whiteford *et al*, the answer has to be yes. That study predicts that the employment of highly skilled persons will continue to rise while the employment of less skilled persons will decline, resulting in rising unemployment. Unless there is a fundamental shift in the path along which the South African economy is moving, there is little hope for a reduction in inequality and income poverty.[112]

The indicators bring to mind vividly the fear, expressed in 1976 by former SACP leader Joe Slovo, of a situation where 'the national struggle is stopped in its tracks and is satisfied with the co-option of a small black élite into the presently forbidden areas of economic and political power' (1976:141). At the turn of the century, the deracialization of power and privilege indeed was occurring on terms that reinforced the structural foundations of inequality.

Notes

1 'Interview with Alec Erwin', *Global Dialogue*, Vol. 4, No. 1 (April 1999), Johannesburg, p. 19.
2 'Business unconcerned as Mandela yields to political expediency', *SouthScan*, Vol. 12, No. 34, 1 September 1997.
3 This style of decision-making would persist. After the finance minister announced the fixing of a 3–6% inflation band target, parliamentary finance committee chair, ANC MP Barbara Hogan, complained about the lack of engagement and transparency that preceded the decision. See 'Govt criticised over inflation target band: Politicians, economists and unionists say there was not enough consultation', *Business Day*, 1 March 2000.
4 SACP statement, reported by SA Press Association, 14 June 1996.
5 SACP media statement, 10 June 1997.
6 COSATU media statement, reported by SA Press Association, 14 June 1996.
7 The study was presented to COSATU, which apparently used it to brief top leadership (author's interview October 1996).
8 'Govt pessimistic about job creation', *Business Day*, 13 May 1997.
9 Including Iraj Abedian, Brian Kahn, Stephen Gelb, Andre Roux, Andrew Donaldson and Ian Goldin.
10 Cited in Davies, R., 1997, *Engaging with GEAR* (draft), Cape Town, p. 3.
11 Whether this was unacceptably high remains moot; in OECD countries the average at the time was 72% of GDP.
12 *Business Times*, 16 June 1996.
13 'Growing pains?', *Democracy in Action* (August, 1996), p. 27.
14 *Business Times*, 16 June 1996.
15 The other key variable – political stability – lies somewhat beyond GEAR's grasp.
16 Officially measured at 5,4% of GDP, although finance department officials claimed it stood closer to 5,8%.
17 The argument was forcefully advanced in the South African Foundation's ideologically-charged *Growth for All* economic strategy document, although NIEP claimed there was 'no empirical evidence to suggest' that this process 'has ever occurred in South Africa' (1996:6).
18 See the World Bank's *Paths to Economic Growth* (1993:5). The suggestion was not repeated in the Bank's *Reducing Poverty in South Africa: Options for Equitable and Sustainable Growth* document (see pp. 48–52).
19 Bill Gibson and Dirk van Seventer, 'Economics has changed since the days of Robinson Crusoe', *Business Day*, 28 July 1995.
20 *Ibid.*
21 For instance, if the government sold bonds to itself via the Reserve Bank.
22 'Bank's monetary policy "misinformed"', *Business Day*, 13 June 1997.
23 See Ghosh (1997:9).
24 In 1999, the government decided to move toward a policy of 'inflation targeting' – basically, fixing a band within which the inflation rate could vary. Incongruously, SACP leaders treated this as evidence of greater flexibility around GEAR's prescriptions. In early 2000, the target band was fixed at a low 3–6%.
25 A capital gains tax was eventually introduced in early 2000. Interestingly, it drew little more than murmurs of protest from the business community.
26 The aim would be to encourage investment in labour-intensive enterprises. However, this could backfire and merely discourage productive investments.
27 Interestingly, the 1997/8 Budget's attempts to introduce such regressive taxation were rejected by the parliamentary finance committee in May 1997.

28 A detailed critique appeared in the first edition of this book (1998).
29 'Spare us from this collectivist twaddle', *Financial Mail*, 21 May 1999, Johannesburg. The article labelled critics of GEAR as 'naïve believers in the ability of government intervention – even worse, activism – to get an economy moving'. Months later, finance minister Trevor Manuel would repeat that exact sentiment in a *Sunday Independent* interview (16 January 2000).
30 Incorporated into calculations for the first time is government infrastructure provision (roads, bridges, dams, etc.), while informal activities in the respective sectors are allegedly better measured. The latter include the (private) commuter taxi industry, use of firewood, microlending and traditional health practices.
31 Mark Orkin, 1999, 'Service sector contributions reflect growth', *Business Day* (22 June).
32 'GDP defies expectations', *Business Day* (22 June 1999).
33 'Mbeki bullish on economy, names top advisers', *Mail & Guardian*, 4 February 2000 (http://www.mg.co.za).
34 SA Reserve Bank, 1998, *Annual Economic Report 1998*, Pretoria, p. 10.
35 'Foreign direct investment plummets', *Business Day*, 28 September 1999.
36 Invited onto the council were the chairpersons or CEOs of Citigroup Inc., the Soros Fund Management, Alliance Capital Management International, Investor AB of Sweden, British–Dutch Lever, Mitsubishi Corporation of Japan, Ashanti Goldfields of Ghana, Tata of India, Petronas of Malaysia, D-Group of Britain, Commerzbank of Germany and Daimler-Chrysler.
37 The trade and industry ministry claims the 11 local SDIs could create as many as 104 000 jobs.
38 High interest rates act as a magnet for short-term capital.
39 COSATU, 2000, 'Public response by COSATU to the 2000/2001 budget' (March), Johannesburg. Dollar figures are calculated at the average of 1999 exchange rate.
40 'Revisit GEAR, review the tax system', media statement from Gensec Asset Management, 21 October 1998.
41 *Ibid.*
42 The response from economic élites was cynical. Investment levels failed to rise, but the rich set up close corporations in record numbers in order to pay less tax; see 'Corporate tax reductions lead to more close corporations', *Business Day*, 22 February 2000.
43 SG Frankel Pollak Securities' Nico Czypionka in 'An economy that is tip-toeing on a knife-edge', Financial Mail, 26 February 1999.
44 'Foreigners will not invest if requirements are not met', *Business Day*, 21 July 1998 (an edited version of a speech to the Zimbabwe National Chamber of Commerce).
45 According to the Reserve Bank, only 12 000 new jobs were created in 1995.
46 This represents employment growth of 2,9 per cent, while the labour force grows annually by 2,5 per cent.
47 Reported in the *Mail & Guardian*, 15 April 1999.
48 Nicolau (2000). The amounts were calculated at 1998 prices, while the dollar figures were calculated at 1998 exchange rates.
49 'No one has really thought about new bill's effects', *Business Day*, 31 October 1997.
50 'Left blamed for economic failures as Manuel woos foreign investors', *SouthScan*, Vol. 15, No. 1, 14 January 2000.
51 That process began in early 2000 when the labour ministry announced a modest set of revisions to labour laws enacted since 1994. More far-reaching changes were in the offing, however.

52 These include the activities of Khula Finance (which approved R57 million in loans to small businesses in 1997/8) and the 1998 launch of the KhulaStart programme, aimed at providing small amounts of credit to rural communities, with an emphasis on women. Also established have been information and counselling services for new small businesses.

53 Reported in 'Busting myths: small biz no job machine, downsizing not so magical', *Dollars & Sense*, No. 66 (October 1994).

54 In a paper titled 'Downsizing and Productivity Growth: Myth or Reality', Centre for Economic Studies Working Paper 94–4, US Census Bureau.

55 The findings were published in the July 1994 issue of the OECD's *Employment Outlook* publication.

56 'Virtues of "grey economy" questioned', *SouthScan*, Vol. 13, No. 14, 10 July 1998.

57 Dollar figure calculated at 1998 exchange rates.

58 SANGOCO, CGE & HRC (1998) *The People's Voices: National Speak Out on Poverty Hearings – March to June 1998*, Johannesburg, p. 16. The countrywide hearings were organized by the SA National NGO Coalition, the Commission for Gender Equality and the SA Human Rights Commission.

59 'First cracks appear in official macroeconomic strategy', *SouthScan*, Vol. 13, No. 22, 30 October 1998.

60 'Job creation projects planned as more losses loom', *SouthScan*, Vol. 13, No. 23, 13 November 1998.

61 *Sunday Times*, 23 June 1996.

62 The US experience in the 1980s is sobering. Low-wage jobs grew substantially during the decade, but poverty levels increased dramatically, with 10 per cent of the population experiencing a 16 per cent drop in real earnings (Hobsbawm, 1995:573). In South Africa, many of the poorest rural households participate in poorly paid employment which indicates that they are poor because of their low wages (ILO, 1996).

63 See *Business Times*, 16 June 1996.

64 See also Gordon (1988:51).

65 Cited in Gall (1997:214).

66 See 'Outspoken government attacks on unions as strike action spreads', *SouthScan*, Vol. 14, No. 17, 20 August 1999.

67 The budget also cut social spending by 1,2 per cent in real terms – a minor detail, barely observed in the media, which chose to equate middle and upper income earners with 'the people'.

68 Quoted in 'Left blamed for economic failures as Manuel woos foreign investors', *SouthScan*, Vol. 15, No. 1, 14 January 2000. The original interview appeared in the *Sunday Independent*, 16 January 2000.

69 These are the Labour Relations Act, the Employment Equity Act and the Basic Conditions of Employment Act.

70 The reference is to Manuel's 9 January 2000 interview in the *Sunday Independent* and Mbeki's gingerly constructed address to parliament in early February. See 'Mbeki polemicises on race, talks up economic performance', *SouthScan*, Vol. 15, No. 3, 11 February 2000, which described the speech as 'the latest installment of [Mbeki's] "good-cop, bad-cop" routine' in which he 'pulled punches against some recent targets, but let fly against others'.

71 SG Securities political analyst Gary van Staden, quoted in 'COSATU still backs ANC despite discord', *WOZA Today* (Internet newsservice), 24 February 2000.

72 Mbeki (1998b:4). He was speaking in his capacity as ANC president.

73 Gelb (1999:13). He is wrong, though, in claiming that 'GEAR in other words did not represent the abandonment of the RDP'. The progressive – and some instances leftist

– tilt of the the RDP on social policies was made to shrivel or disappear in the overriding economic policy framework. Housing policy was a prime example of this.

74   See, for example, Manuel (1998a).

75   The cut also favoured rich individuals, who were able to shift personal income to
lower-taxed corporate entities – recreating, according to one analyst, 'a form of tax
arbitrage practised in the 1960s and 1970s (and) widely felt to offer unfair advantage to high earners'. See 'Of course it's an election budget. So what?', *Financial
Mail*, 19 February 1999.

76   Figures cited by Trevor Manuel (1998) 'Address to the Societe Generale Frankel
Pollak 21st Annual Investment Conference' (24 February), Johannesburg, p. 2.

77   Department of Finance Budget Review 1998 and 1999, Pretoria; 'Development
elements of give-and-take budget outflank critics', *SouthScan*, Vol. 15, No. 4,
25 February 2000. The 2000/1 budget also saw a 21 per cent real increase in
defence spending – see 'The Poor remain vulnerable', IDASA Budget Information
Service, 23 February 2000 (http://www.idasa.org.za).

78   'Submission to the Portfolio Committee on Finance on the 2000/01 Budget',
IDASA Budget Information Service, 2 March 2000, Cape Town, p. 3.

79   Based on *ANC Election Manifesto*, 1999, Johannesburg; 'ANC's achievements and
failures', *SouthScan*, Vol. 14, No. 11, 28 May 1999; and finance minister's Budget
Speech 1999.

80   'Drive to get Africa in touch' , *Mail & Guardian*, 12 March 1999.

81   'R6bn housing ripoff', *Sunday Times*, 14 March 1999. Almost all were built by
private developers, underwritten by state subsidies schemes.

82   'Housing fund cut by R200m', *Business Day*, 24 February 2000.

83   SAMWU general secretary Roger Ronnie, 'Govt must supply affordable water'
Business Day, 17 March 1999; (then) water affairs minister Kader Asmal, 'Stepped
tariffs no help to poor', *Business Day*, 25 March 1999.

84   Quoted in *The Star* newspaper, 19 March 1999.

85   For a critical analysis, see Marais, H. (2000) *To the Edge: An Examination of South
Africa's National AIDS Response 1994–1999*, Centre for the Study of AIDS,
Pretoria. See also Chapter 9.

86   'Government develops maverick AIDS theme, hits at drugs giants', *SouthScan*,
Vol. 15, No. 6, 24 March 2000.

87   Cargill, J. & Brown, A. (1999) 'Black economic empowerment – The next leg of the
journey', *Business Map, 1999, SA Insider: South African Investment Report* (1998),
Johannesburg, p. 46.

88   The Gini coefficient is a number between 0 and 1 that indicates the level of income
inequality within a population. A value of 0 indicates perfect equality (everyone has
the same income), while a value of 1 indicates perfect inequality (one person or
household has all the income). As the Gini coefficient becomes larger and closer to
1, the extent of inequality increases.

89   Whiteford and Van Seventer (1999:17–18). A similar 1994 study had put the Gini
coefficient at 0,68; see Mcgrath, M. & Whiteford, A. (1994) 'Disparate
circumstances', *Indicator SA*, Vol. 11, No. 3, Durban, pp. 47–50.

90   'South Africa is still suffering inequalities from racial capitalism', *Parliamentary
Bulletin*, 14 April 1998. The Bulletin was based on a paper by Professor Sampie
Terreblanche of the University of Stellenbosch.

91   Statistics SA figures, using the 1995 Income and Expenditure Survey and cited in
Mbeki (1998a:2).

92   The broad definition includes anyone who is unemployed and is available to start
work within a week of being polled.

93   Statistics SA figures released in October 1998; see 'Detailed picture of labour losses', *SouthScan*, Vol. 13, No. 23, 13 November 1998.
94   Mike Nicol, *The Star*, 3 July 1996.
95   Unless otherwise stated, the statistics cited were reported in the following issues of *SouthScan*: Vol. 14, No. 13; Vol. 14, No. 10; Vol. 14, No. 9; Vol. 14, No. 2; Vol. 13, No. 25.
96   A survey by the Institute for Security Studies found that black South Africans were more likely to become crime victims than whites in all major cities, with Johannesburg the only exception. Almost three-quarters of whites surveyed had been victims of crime in the preceding four years, the survey found, compared to 58 per cent of blacks; 'Blacks fear crime most', *SouthScan*, Vol. 13, No. 19, 18 September 1998.
97   It serves as an alternative zone in which capital can be raised in a context where banks and other financial institutions regard most black start-up loan applicants as 'high risks'.
98   Police investigator, quoted in 'Hijackers responsive to market demands', *Business Day*, 11 August 1998.
99   'Crime is the only business providing jobs', *Mail & Guardian*, 15 May 1998. The ironically-named Eldorado Park is a mainly coloured township in Johannesburg.
100 Scharf, W., 'The resurgence of urban street gangs and community responses' in Hansson, D. & Van Zyl Smit, D. (eds) (1990), *Towards Justice? Crime and State Control in South Africa*, Oxford University Press, Cape Town, p. 244.
101 *Op. cit.*, p. 252.
102 'Incidence of murder drops over five years', *Business Day*, 1 March 2000.
103 'Crime at all levels revealed', *SouthScan*, Vol. 13, No. 25, 11 December 1998. 'People don't talk anymore. They kill. And we're starting to see kids acting this way', according to Marilyn Donaldson, a trauma clinic counsellor (author's interview, March 1997, Johannesburg).
104 Although there appears not to be empirical evidence to back the often cited statistic that a rape is committed every 83 seconds in South Africa.
105 Quoted in *Sunday Independent*, 21 July 1996.
106 Bundy, C., 'Development and inequality in historical perspective' in Schrire (1992:25).
107 SANGOCO, CGE & HRC, 1998, *The People's Voices: National Speak Out on Poverty Hearings – March to June 1998*, Johannesburg, p. 17.
108 'ANC's achievements and failures', *SouthScan*, Vol. 14, No. 11, 28 May 1999.
109 Figures cited by Mbeki (1998d:5).
110 Whiteford, A. 'The poor get even poorer', *Mail & Guardian*, 18 March 1994.
111 Figures cited in 'Poor still no better off', *Financial Mail*, 19 September 1997. See note 89 for an explanation for the discrepancy in Gini coefficient figures.
112 *Op. cit.*, p. 38. The employment study referred to is Whiteford, A., Van Zyl, E., Simkins, C. & Hall, E., 1999, *Labour market trends and future workforce needs*, Human Sciences Research Council, Pretoria.

CHAPTER SEVEN

Rudiments of an alternative

At the turn of the century, the post-apartheid growth path is not squaring the circle of poverty eradication, job creation and economic growth. Poverty levels remain extreme and available indicators suggest that income inequality is widening. Saddled almost exclusively with the burden of adjustment are the country's poorest citizens, some 20 million of whom live below the poverty line. Changing that state of affairs is not just a matter of social justice but of economic sustainability, as well as political and social stability.

By 2000, a targeted poverty reduction strategy had slipped further down the rungs of government priorities. Adhered to instead was a classic trickle-down approach in which 'government is resolved to minimise its intervention in the economy and restrict its actions to those that aim to create an economic climate that is conducive to private sector led growth'.[1]

The 2000/1 national budget confirmed that stance by handing out R9 billion ($1,57 billion) in tax cuts to middle and upper income earners in the hope this would boost savings and investment. Social spending suffered a 1,2 per cent cut in real terms, while targeted poverty programmes absorbed less than 0,7 per cent of total non-interest spending. Ignored in the budget were plans to establish a basic income grant scheme – essentially a kind of 'dole' that could serve as a safety net for the country's poorest citizens. According to welfare minister Zola Skweyiya's calculations, the scheme would cost about R7 billion ($1,1 billion) annually (or three-quarters of the tax cuts contained in the 2000/1 budget). Yet, there was fiscal space for such a venture: the budget deficit had been driven down well below the 3 per cent of GDP mark.

At the same time, it transpired that the welfare department had spent less than 1 per cent of the R204 million ($32 million) allocated for poverty relief in the 1998/9 financial year. In 1996–9, fully R516 million ($83 million) was returned unspent to state coffers.[2] This prompted Skweyiya to admit that 'the welfare system has failed those who most need its support; the poorest of the poor'.[3] The same could be said of the economic system in general. The presumed need to set out an alluring stall for international markets reigns supreme despite the lacklustre interest and desultory performance of the economy. More than half a million non-agricultural jobs were lost between 1994 and 2000, amid every indication that the trend would continue. Meanwhile, labour supply continues to grow by about 2 per cent annually (or 487 000 potential workers). Yet, the government is lost for a response. In finance minister's Trevor Manuel's words:

> I want someone to tell me how the government is going to create jobs. Workers can go on a general strike day after day and you're not going to create jobs. It's a terrible admission but governments around the world are impotent when it comes to creating jobs ... Government, labour and business can pontificate and collectively lament the absence of jobs, but they aren't capable of creating jobs.[4]

The sentiment is borne out by the fact that funding for public works programmes was set to shrink by 14 per cent in 1999–2003 (in terms of the finance ministry's medium term expenditure framework). The Umsobomvu (job creation) trust set up in 1998 received no new funding injection from the government in the 2000/1 budget, prompting IDASA to note that 'it would appear as if government largely depends on the funding contributions of labour and business to boost this trust'.[5] In Manuel's view, job creation would have to occur mainly in the small business sector. Yet, government support for the sector has not increased in line with the hopes pinned on it.

Government's reasoning remains trapped in a web of misreading – most obviously the notion that the global context has enfeebled the state, and forced a trade-off between social spending and market-friendly supply-side measures (or, differently phrased, equity and efficiency). To be sure, not all government departments roundly accept that dichotomy. But their persuasive weight is limited – by the powerful, super-ministry status of the finance ministry and by the fact that the president's office wields a formidable hand in policy-making.

There is ample evidence that national states have not been shorn of the ability to regulate their economies, design appropriate social policies and build critical infrastructure for development.[6] States retain substantial power to create and manage *distinctive social and economic arrangements* for growth and poverty eradication. That capacity is not limitless – the state cannot assert an absolute autonomy *vis-á-vis* capital. This is because the institutions and apparatuses of the state, as Nicos Poulantzas noted, 'do not possess' their own 'power' but 'express and crystalise class powers' (1975:70). This does not mean that the state is purely 'instrumentalized'.[7] Rather, its policies and activities are profoundly influenced by the ways in which it seeks to locate itself within a system of interconnected – but also competing – capitals at the domestic and global levels. In other words, the state retains the ability to display degrees of relative autonomy, the extent and character of which depend on how it modulates and adjusts its relations with domestic and international capital. Typically scorned in 'polite' company, the recognition of this relative autonomy underpins the increased emphasis in mainstream economic thought on the social roles of the state, a shift that coincided with the global upheavals triggered by the Asian crisis.

A post-Washington consensus?

By 1998, the one-size-fits-all ideology of the 'Washington consensus' seemed to be on the skids, as some of its intellectual vanguard toyed with the notion of promoting diverse variants of capitalism, while others saw merit in reviving of the regulatory functions of the state.[8] Thus, World Bank chief economist Joseph Stiglitz would venture that 'expanded social spending can be a very effective way to engineer fiscal expansion', adding that 'spending on social programs keeps almost all the money in the country, potentially leading to a larger output "multiplier"'.[9] Yet, as Dani Rodrik has pointed out, the 'Washington' consensus was hardly dead:

> The old Washington consensus emphasized the standard things: fiscal discipline, unified and competitive exchange rates, deregulation, financial liberalization, trade liberalization, privatization, essentially price and market reform together with macro stability … Interestingly, this new Washington consensus has not dropped any of the items from the old consensus. What the new consensus is doing instead is adding other things on, which is partly driven by the sense of malaise and a sense that something is not going right (1999b).

More forthrightly recognized, too, is one of the prime lessons of economic history this century: that the successful capitalist economies developed distinct brands of national capitalism. Although widely propagated, the Anglo-American model was not, as a rule, mimicked. Rodrik (1999a) has shown that South Korea and Taiwan, during their high growth phases, observed only half of the ten key adjustments propagated by John Williamson, who coined the phrase 'Washington consensus'. 'They were not star pupils of what was going to become an eventual consensus', as Rodrik put it (1999b).

Central to all these instances were legitimate domestic institutions, social and political stability, massive investment in infrastructure and in education and training (thereby answering the need for a skilled labour force). In the case of Asia, stability was not a given – it was introduced, often through repressive means. Importantly, the outcome was a series of (tacit and explicit) social compromises.[10]

It is worth recalling, too, that the post-war welfare states of Western Europe were not assembled without tumult. Their emergence and refinement were accompanied (and shaped) by intense class struggle. In Europe, the rewards extended beyond the main social forces (capital and labour) to the general population – in the form of social safety nets and expanded welfare systems. In Asia, those safety nets were weak. In so far as they existed, they were the outcome of earlier state interventions (including the transfer of assets via land reform) and high rates of economic growth that broadened access to basic services and the means for economic survival. On the whole, the state was – and remains – weakly active in social security provision.

Although highly selectively, some of those lessons seem bound to feature in the post-Washington consensus. However, all indications are that liberalization on several fronts will remain the beacon. Key will be a persistent push for labour markets and trade liberalization. Supervision of financial capital flows probably will be enhanced and supplemented with more credential regulation and better prudential standards – as part of an 'orderly' push for capital account liberalization. Perhaps the signal shift will be on the social side, thanks to greater appreciation of the need for social safety nets.[11]

Those attempts at reconsolidation will occur, however, in a context where the character of globalization has become more hotly contested. Tensions have become magnified between the World Bank and the IMF, while deeper rifts have opened between the USA, Europe and Asia about the types and the extent of alterations required for a post-Washington consensus. Some of French prime minister Lionel Jospin's assertions have hinted at the erosion of élite consensus: 'Capitalism is its own worst enemy ... The (post-Asian) crises we have witnessed teach us three things: capitalism remains unstable, the economy is political, and the global economy calls for regulation'.[12]

The upshot for a country like South Africa is that even more manoeuvring space has become available – particularly if, in concert with other countries of the South (and North), it seeks to exploit the tensions between the main economic powers. Yet, in South African's case, resistance has been supplanted by lamentation. Consider the words Thabo Mbeki directed at US businesspeople in 1997:

> With regard to economic reform, there are many issues that are of common concern, including the liberalisation of trade, the reform of financial, commodity and other markets, the functioning of multilateral institutions, and development assistance and resource transfers from the developed to the developing world. We are interested that these matters be discussed in an atmosphere that recognises the legitimate interests of the poor.[13]

While hardly dismissive of the negative effects of globalization, the government has remained drawn toward an idealized prospect of equal partnership and mutual reward. A document issued by Mbeki's office in 1998, for example, declared that Africa had to 'create the conditions for becoming part of the globalisation process', reminding that 'this will essentially depend on the competitiveness of its economies and the adoption of successful industrialisation strategies'.[14]

The quest for more equitable participation in the global capitalist system in fact is an updated version of the long-standing ideal of 'catching up' with the industrialized countries, a quest that definitively shaped most of the post-colonial projects in Africa and Asia after 1945. Not only does this notion have dubious purchase in the current world system, but it neglects a central and persistent feature of the world system – in Samir Amin's words, its 'immanent tendency ... towards polarisation into centres and (variegated) peripheries', a state of affairs in which 'the centres "restructure" themselves while the peripheries "are adjusted" ... Never the opposite'.[15]

South Africa is attempting an updated version of those earlier, Southern projects by combining some 'developmentalist' postures with wide-ranging obedience to reigning economic ideology. The 'developmentalist' frame can be summarized as:

(1) a determination to develop productive forces and diversify production (notably to industrialize); (2) a determination to ensure that the national state should lead and control the process; (3) the belief that 'technical' models are 'neutral' and can simply by reproduced; (4) the belief that this process does not involve popular initiative as a starting point but simply popular support for state actions; (5) the belief that this process is not fundamentally in contradiction with participation in the international division of labor even if it involves temporary conflicts with the developed capitalist countries (Amin *et al.*, 1990:113).

Save for point (2) and the oppositional thrust of point (5), the post-apartheid path bears close resemblance to this framework. It deviates mainly in the decision to jettison the leading *economic* role of the state and replace it with a resounding – though, as yet unrewarded – faith in the market. Calling this a public-private partnership at the macro level is accurate only to the extent that the description conveys a partnership between the state and capital in which the role of the state is largely subordinate and facilitatory.

Being attempted, in other words, is a modernized version of a 'national bourgeois project' in which the black capitalist class gradually comes to feature more prominently. It is a hazardous undertaking. On the one hand, the most powerful South African corporations are determined to expand beyond the national territory in which they arose. They demand not only government's leniency but also its support (by refraining from imposing investment requirements and other forms of reciprocation in the South African sphere). Among the factors that saw government allow firms to list offshore was the need to create entry spaces for foreign investors and black economic empowerment ventures in a highly monopolized local economy. In order to finance their moves offshore, firms would have to sell non-core assets – that could then be acquired by new investors. Also at play was the assumption that these 'South African' firms, once listed abroad, could gain easier access to capital (and serve as potential sources of local investment). Historical experience elsewhere has rubbed the gloss off such hopes, as Arthur MacEwan has noted:

> [A]s important segments of capital become more international in their orientation, they are less willing to support the types of state policies which would yield national growth. Industrial policies and programs to develop the national labour force, for example, are of little interest to firms committed to and dependent on overseas operations; indeed, in so far as those policies and programs carry a cost – as they always do – such firms are likely to oppose them (1994:13).

The hopes staked on the transformatory potential of a black 'patriotic bourgeoisie' seem destined to remain unsatisfied. The global division of labour relegates the so-called 'patriotic bourgeoisie' of a country such as South Africa 'to carry out its development in the compradorized subordination that the expansion of transnational capitalism imposes on it' (Amin et al., 1990:115). Rather than serving as a vehicle for achieving greater developmental sovereignty, the national bourgeoisie is much more likely to operate in a structurally submissive and supportive role to international capital.

Plotting a way out

Judged against the government's own transformatory goals, the current development path appears to be headed toward a dead-end. Alternatives are available. They do not require surrendering to reverie or wistful idealism. They are eminently feasible in the context of an unstable global economic system, the contests that accompany bids to reconfigure the Washington consensus, and growing anxiety world-wide about the social and political upheavals that have been primed by twenty years of neoliberal policies.

A revised development path will entail (in fact, require) renewed social struggles to shift the balance of forces in favour of changes that authentically benefit the poor; but the same holds if the current path is persevered with. The idea that a new, gentlemanly class compromise can be engineered by stakeholder élites is both fanciful and out-of-joint with the South African reality. This implies the risk of sporadic instability that will test the ostensibly consensual features of the post-apartheid order. No doubt, such hazards rank among the factors that discourage the revision of the development path (and help explain the timorous resistance mounted by an organization such as COSATU). Yet, the effect of a blocked process of change is to postpone much graver instability into the future – at which point discontent might become convulsive and desperate enough to defy not only the state's authority but also that of the organized left. A shift to repressive management then becomes almost guaranteed.

One of the beloved shibboleths of the 1990s was the claim that progressive critics were not proposing alternatives. It does not require a romantic predisposition to recognize that the RDP, despite its shortcomings, outlined a framework for realizing many of the ANC's historical social pledges. Since then, research institutions, academics and progressive NGOs have produced a welter of empirically based and often highly detailed critiques and alternatives. Some have been taken aboard by large formations such as COSATU and translated into policy proposals. Others were commissioned directly by government departments that, on occasion, seemed embarrassed by the findings.[16]

At hand is a rich array of alternative proposals. Among them are COSATU's recommendations for boosting economic growth, job creation and redistribution.[17] They hinge on a set of integrated (short- and long-term) policies that would link macro-economic, labour market and industrial policies, and a comprehensive social security system. The proposals urge that:

- The fiscal deficit should be allowed to fluctuate within a band, depending on the size of the social deficit and the level of unemployment.
- A prescribed asset requirement should be imposed on the financial sector, including on worker provident/pension funds, to raise capital for social investment.
- State expenditure should be increased to improve social infrastructure (such as health services and education).
- There should not be downward pressure on wages and a two-tier labour system should be resisted.
- A universal basic income grant of about R100 ($15) a month should be introduced – which higher income categories will pay back in the form of a tax levy (with the highest income earners paying back double that amount as a 'solidarity tax').[18]

More broadly, COSATU has called for a 'blend of demand management and appropriate supply-side initiatives', with the former aimed at boosting demand for domestically produced goods and services. This would require lower interest rates, a more flexible but still responsible fiscal policy (that allows for stronger, redistributive state spending), attaching stronger condi-tionalities to investments, and a trade policy that aligns tariff adjustments to their effects on industries. The supply-side measures would seek to lower costs, improve quality and promote product and process innovation in local goods and services.

COSATU also assigned to the state an important role in employment cre-ation, economic activity and service delivery. This role extends beyond public works programmes and includes aligning privatization ventures to 'the explicit goal of retaining and, where possible, expansion of jobs'. It also proposes active labour market policies to create and save jobs, including the introduction of 'social plans in every industry to manage the economic restructuring process in a manner that is sensitive to job creation'.[19]

The broad paradigm shift should be obvious: measures aimed at eco-nomic growth are slotted into a wider reform package that also tries to answer the need for a drastically expanded social safety net. As apparent is the society-wide scope of the proposals, which puts a lie to the 'labour aris-tocracy' argument so often flung at COSATU and its affiliates.[20] That said, one can examine in more detail the logic and feasibility of proposals of this kind, which, broadly-speaking, earn the tag 'left-Keynesian'.[21]

An investment strategy

The first area is that of *macro-economic policy* and specifically the need for an *investment strategy*. Dani Rodrik's conclusion, based on a study of high-growth economies since the 1960s, is instructive (1999a). He found that openness to the global economy could garner economic benefits in the form of imports of investment and intermediate goods not available domestically at comparable cost, the transfer of knowledge and technology, and access to foreign savings. Ultimately, though, *domestic investment makes an econ-omy grow.*

As domestic private investment continues to decline, the government has looked more expectantly to FDI to kick-start and sustain growth. It is highly unlikely that those hopes will be realized. Research by economist Chris Edwards has shown that, in ideal circumstances, South Africa can hope for foreign financing of 5 per cent of its GDP. (FDI flows to Malaysia and Singapore between 1967 and 1986 averaged 4,6 per cent and 6,8 per cent of GDP, respectively, despite the fact that they ranked among the top recipients of FDI among semi-industrialized countries.) Thus, as Edwards contends, 'investment equivalent to about 25% of GDP will have to be found from domestic sources if a rate of growth of 6% a year is to be sustained' (1998:56). Moreover, economists have failed to demonstrate a positive correlation between short-term capital flows and FDI; indeed, since 1997, South Africa's experience suggests that an inverse relationship applies.

The primary challenge for government, therefore, is to devise new ways to lever higher levels of *domestic* private investment and to boost state investment. Progressive adjustments to *monetary policy* form one leg of a realistic route.

A broad consensus has emerged around the need to revise monetary policy. In late 1998, for instance, economist Iraj Abedian (who had helped draft the GEAR plan) blamed the policy for 'high and rising real interest rates that are throttling economic growth; an appreciating and unstable real effective exchange rate; and an economy on the brink of recession'.[22] Indeed, the advantages of lower interest rates are patent. According to Edwards, they would: '... reduce the interest burden of the government's debt, would allow ... greater public sector investment in infrastructure and basic needs and would therefore boost the level of effective demand in the economy'.[23]

For more than a decade, the Reserve Bank has ignored those benefits, preferring to treat high interest rates as a way to discourage credit-taking, swell the savings pool and thereby boost investment levels. The outcome speaks for itself: in the context of growing unemployment, both savings and investment levels fell. At the same time, the high interest rate regime further inflated government debt, thus creating even more pressure for severe fiscal contraction.

An alternative approach is hardly heretical. In it, savings are seen as a function of income and investment. In economist Edward Osborn's words, 'everyone understands, except possibly bankers, that savings are a residual function of income'.[24] Low interest rates cheapen the cost of capital needed for investment and thereby can stimulate greater levels of (private and public) investment that, through multiplier effects, generate higher aggregate income. In other words, more *investment* boosts employment opportunities, increases income and swells savings – ideally, setting in motion a virtuous cycle. Economic and job creation growth then becomes investment- and *not* savings-led. The advantages of a low interest rate regime for small business growth are obvious.

In addition, lower interest rates would discourage high levels of short-term capital inflows, thereby lessening the economy's vulnerability to the instability they engender. Since high real interest rates function as one of the prime attractors of such inflows, the Reserve Bank's monetarist policies are partially responsible (along with the relaxation of capital controls) for the substantial rise in these flows. When they reverse, as happened in mid-1998, the Bank is forced to raise interest rates even further in a bid to counter ensuing exchange rate volatility, thus creating a vicious circle: short-term inflows resume, setting the stage for another bout of instability. Lower real interest rates can help break this cycle, particularly if capital controls are also judiciously tightened.

Mainstream economists respond with three contentions. Firstly, they argue that short-term capital inflows can increase savings. That this, in fact, happens in the South African context is not clear. Moreover, there exists no evidence that short-term inflows have spurred productive investment levels. A second assertion is that short-term inflows are needed to boost the country's foreign reserves. This has validity, insofar as it recognizes the need to plug the foreign reserves gap. Recall, though, that the argument is not to 'ban' short-term capital, but to discourage – through various mechanisms, including low interest rates – large, speculative rushes that disrupt stability.

The third objection is that low interest rates cause higher inflation. Certainly, sustained inflation rates in the 20 per cent plus range should be avoided. But the obsession for ultra-low inflation is easily demystified. In Stiglitz's view, 'controlling high and medium-rate inflation should be a fundamental policy priority but pushing low inflation even lower is not likely to significantly improve the functioning of markets' (1998:6–7). Economists disagree on the exact threshold, but there is strong evidence that once inflation breaks into single digits, minor shifts do not place significant, extra burdens on poor households.

The trade-off between a growing economy and increased employment and income levels, on the one hand, and moderate inflation levels, on the other, cannot be summarily dismissed. Studies by NIEP have shown that the average annual cost of the Reserve Bank's monetarist stance was 'foregone gross domestic product growth (of) between R9-billion and R13-billion' in 1990–5.[25] Those findings confirmed warnings contained in a 1994 World Bank study on South African policy options, where it was cautioned that:

> … disinflation to low inflation rates implies a significant cost to output … Our work also shows that attempts to get inflation further below the 10% mark would imply a trade-off between income redistribution, growth and inflation rates.[26]

In similar vein, Stiglitz (1998) has found that countries tend to enter a high inflation/low growth trap once they cross the threshold of 40 per cent annual inflation. Moreover, a 44-country study between 1980 and 1988 found no evidence:

> … to support the notion that a low rate of inflation has in the past and in various countries been associated with improved growth rates; to support thus the statement that low or zero inflation is an essential or very important condition for high and sustained growth, or that government action to reduce inflation would be very likely to have such an effect.[27]

The chief beneficiaries of a monetarist stance are financial networks that, after all, are net lenders – not borrowers – of capital. Therefore, the benefits of a high interest rate/low inflation regime accrue mainly to a specific, powerful branch of capital, with the negative effects off-loaded onto other branches and the broader public (through lower economic and employment growth, and the higher cost of credit). Small businesses suffer especially.

But there is a constitutional hitch. The 1996 constitution prohibits government 'interference' in the Reserve Bank's operations by guaranteeing the institution's 'independence'. As a result, one of the most powerful economic institutions in the country stands insulated against parliamentary oversight. It is required to appear ('from time to time') before the parliamentary standing committee on finance and to stage regular discussions with the finance ministry – but neither entity has any institutional leverage over the decisions of the Bank.

The constitution also declares that the 'primary object' of the Bank 'is to protect the value of the currency in the interest of balanced and sustainable economic growth'.[28] This suggests that, if the pursuit of fuller employment requires measures that compromise price stability, the Bank is constitutionally required to prioritize stability. The outlining of the Bank's primary tasks in the constitution seemed shortsighted, to say the least. (In the United States, for example, the Federal Reserve Bank is legislatively required to pursue the joint objectives of full employment and price stability – see Edwards, 1998:65.)

Politically, it would be difficult to revise the constitutional clause even if the required parliamentary majority and political will were mustered. But such a potentially antagonistic move could be avoided by fostering greater operational harmony between the Bank and government. While there are signs of greater co-operation between the Bank and government, the consensus remains deeply conservative. In early 2000, the inflation target was set at a low 3–6 per cent. Asked why a slightly higher level was not chosen, Reserve Bank governor Tito Mboweni replied: 'That is massive economic populism. How can someone argue that when high inflation reduces the risk appetite of investors?'[29] A more democratic form of oversight is required, perhaps in the form a triangular process of consultation between the parliamentary finance committee, the Reserve Bank and the cabinet.

In isolation, such measures would insufficiently shield the economy against disruptions generated by short-term capital flows. At the moment, government remains committed to the gradual, complete lifting of *capital controls*. There is a pressing case for revising that stance.

Three, mutually compatible arguments have been advanced for the relaxation of capital controls in South Africa:

- The flimsier the controls, the more likely capital inflows (long- and short-term) become. These flows can ease balance of payment problems.

- A highly monopolized local economy (with conglomerates straddling sectors) left little entry space for foreign investors and black economic empowerment ventures. Firms wishing to go offshore would, in most cases, have to sell non-core assets to finance the moves, thus creating space for newcomers, including foreign investors. By relaxing controls, those processes could be encouraged.
- Most importantly, the removal of capital controls became seen as a pre-requisite for increased FDI; in other words, a positive correlation is alleged between short-term inflows and FDI.

The latter contention is difficult to sustain on the basis of cross-country evidence. A 1998 study by Rodrik showed short-term flows had no effect on either economic growth or FDI, prompting Stiglitz to comment that 'one should not be surprised at the empirical findings that ... short-term capital flows do not support higher economic growth'.[30] According to South African economist Iraj Abedian:

> ... it is obvious, yet seldom acknowledged, that there is a trade-off between attracting portfolio investment and foreign direct investment. The latter requires low domestic real interest rates so as to make investment projects viable ... It is thus ironic that the Bank often cites the balance of payments deficit as a reason to maintain high real interest rates. Yet, its monetary policy attracts relatively large inflows of foreign portfolio investment that are reversible in a flash.[31]

Several countries have successfully maintained or applied controls – among them Chile, China, Malaysia, Singapore and India. Indeed, in the case of China and India, the controls are generally acknowledged to have sheltered those economies against the so-called 'Asian meltdown'. In the case of China (and to a lesser extent India), capital controls have not prevented FDI.[32] None of these countries can be accused of autarky. Also gaining favour internationally is a Tobin Tax (first proposed in the 1970s) in terms of which a 0,25 per cent tax would be levied on all speculative transnational investments.[33]

The South African government supports the regulation of financial markets (including hedge funds), but insists that this must occur as part of a redesigned international financial architecture. Lifting its hopes have been calls from the World Bank for 'tighter financial regulation and, where necessary, restrictions on capital flows'.[34] Despite much banter, there is little prospect that such changes (if they are made) will impede the passage of speculative capital around the globe, and in and out of the South African economy. Instead, the US, United Kingdom and IMF strongly favour ongoing liberalization, as South African representatives discovered when they attended the IMF's annual general meeting in late 1998. Mooted in that year – at the height of the global financial upheavals – was a revision to Article I of the IMF's constitution, according to which one of the Fund's purposes would become the 'the orderly liberalisation of capital'. In addition, a revision was proposed to Article VIII, assigning to the Fund: '... the same jurisdiction over the capital account of its members as it has over the current account. This means, in effect, that the Fund shall oversee and approve any capital account restrictions.'[35]

Still in the wings, despite being beaten back by progressive NGOs worldwide in 1998 and 1999, is the mainly US-driven determination to negotiate a Multilateral Agreement on Investment (MAI) that would prevent states from 'discriminating' between foreign and domestic investors. Although the MAI is commonly understood to apply only to FDI, it also covers the movements of liquid forms of investment (Wade & Veneroso, 1998).

Looking to the IMF or G-7 group of industrialized countries for movement on this issue entails a forlorn wait. But so mighty is the ideological resistance against capital controls that the South African government is unlikely to violate convention, despite the volatility caused by speculative capital flows. By 1999, all exchange controls applying to foreigners had been lifted; in early 2000, the finance minister announced that remaining controls on South Africans would continue to be removed.

The government does not have to sit on its hands. If unilateral controls seem destined to incur unacceptable punishment from the markets, a multilateral response can be mustered through an alliance with other countries of the South – most obviously in Asia, but also in Latin America. For example, Chile, hardly an emblem of heretical economic policies, demands that investors deposit a portion of their funds with the central bank for a minimum period (and without interest) before being able to deploy those funds. The aim is to slow the revolving door of financial speculation, especially of hedge funds and portfolio investments.

In considering what types of controls could work, it must be noted that it is much easier to set the terms for incoming capital (as Chile does) than to patrol the departure of capital. Tightening of controls should also be accompanied by steps to reduce transfer pricing, double-, under- and over-invoicing and other furtive means of exporting capital used by South African firms even in periods when controls did apply. Also, administrating these steps is not an effortless task; it requires brigades of skilled bureaucrats. In weighing the costs, the objective should serve as the chief guide: to enable government to adopt market-steering mechanisms that can help shift the development path onto a more equitable and just track.

The role of budget deficit targets

A further area of workable adjustment is the relaxation of *budget deficit* targets. Here, it is essential to recognize the ideological sleight of hand that enables the finance ministry (and business) to equate 'fiscal responsi-bility' with 'fiscal austerity'.[36] In Chapter 6, we dealt with the 'crowding out' argument against relaxing the deficit. The prime demurral remaining is that higher debt servicing costs would eat into funds available for increased spending and launch government on a not-so-merry roundabout where it keeps increasing the budget deficit and its debt to meet social obligations.

The argument is corrupt on several scores. If it occurs as part of an over-all economic and development strategy, increased state expenditure in infrastructure and in expanding the social wage acts as a spur to economic growth, private sector investment and social equity.

Hence the notion of a virtuous cycle that can be achieved by allowing the budget deficit to fluctuate in a pre-determined band, thereby removing the risk of 'macro-economic populism'. The deficit target would then be linked to stages of the business cycle, levels of private sector investment and GDP growth. The case for such an approach is strengthened by the fact that government has at its disposal two ways of reducing its debt obligations: a low interest rate regime (given that most of its debt sits with domestic creditors), and restructuring the Civil Service Pension Fund back to a pay-as-you-go system.

The latter option requires explanation. Agreed to in 1993 was a 'sunset clause' that protected incumbent civil servants from retrenchment. It formed part of the bid to placate insecurities that might have stoked 'counter-revolutionary' mobilization. While much has been made of its effects on efforts to transform state structures that were left replete with old bureaucrats, the *fiscal* cost of that appeasing gesture turned out to be its most debilitating side-effect. Expensive voluntary retrenchments and golden handshakes became the only broom with which the new govern-ment could clean out the civil service bureaucracies. Linked to this was one of the most far-reaching oversights (or compromises) of the negotiations period: leaving intact the 1989 conversion of the Civil Service Pension Fund from a pay-as-you-go system into a fully funded entity. This guaranteed full payouts to however many civil servants chose to leave the service.

One effect was to hugely inflate government debt, thereby dramatically strengthening calls for fiscal stringency. In 1994, that debt stood at R189,9 billion ($31,1 billion); by March 1999, it had ballooned to R375,9 billion ($61,6 billion). Fully 96 per cent of this debt is owed to South African creditors. Crucially, 40 per cent of the debt load is absorbed by the Civil Service Pension Fund, which swelled from R31 billion ($5 bil-lion) in 1989 to R136 billion ($22,3 billion) in 1996.[37] (Strictly speaking, the 40 per cent is owed to the Public Investment Commission, which invests state pension funds.) As part of the Jubilee 2000 debt campaign, churches and NGOs have been arguing that the debt can be cut by shifting the pension fund back to a pay-as-you-go system. This would reduce debt obligations and release a large 'social dividend'.

Industrial policy

A second area calling for progressive adjustment is *industrial policy*, which has to be synchronized closely with macro-economic restructuring. The current, broad framework already offers several opportunities for more directive steps. South African corporations' penchant for offshore investments, for example, presents the government with some leverage. It could tie approval for offshore listings and large foreign investment forays to directed investments and other conduct in the domestic sphere. This would require that the government acts as a gatekeeper for offshore investment, with the trade and industry department (and *not* just the finance department and Reserve Bank) being centrally involved.

Incentives built into investment promotion and industrial development programmes (particularly the SDIs) should explicitly favour job creation. Regular employment audits are needed to monitor the performance of the benefiting firms and the programmes themselves. (The supply-side driven Motor Industry Development Programme is a case in point: superficially successful, it has abetted the dramatic 'rationalization' of the local components sector, which has shed nearly 10 per cent of its workforce since 1995 – see Nicolaou, 1999, pp. 19–20.) Conversely, the substitution of capital over labour should incur disincentives or even penalties.

At the heart of such an approach lies the need for a 'developmental nexus between profits and investment', which the East Asian economies excelled at. Rather than limit government's role to designing and supervising supply-side support, it entails redirecting profits into re-investment, while helping to ensure profits accrue from those ventures (through directed credits, tax incentives and co-ordination of investments) (Khan, 1999:25).

Many of the details of South Africa's export-oriented growth path deserve critical re-examination, in light of evidence that 'an open trade regime, on its own, will not set an economy on a sustained growth path' (Rodrik, 1999b). Seldom acknowledged, for instance, is the fact that the South African economy showed a significant export bias even before it was launched along a more vigorous export-oriented path. Between 1960 and 1994, its non-gold, non-agricultural export:GDP ratio hovered around the 22 per cent mark – high compared to the OECD countries. There, the ratio of exports to total output in the same period averaged at 15 per cent. In India, Brazil and South Korea, the ratio was below 20 per cent.[38]

Rather than serve as a mechanism to enhance competitiveness through attrition, tariff reductions need to fit into a more coherent and sequenced package of measures that include skills development, job protection (and creation), the enforcement of anti-dumping regulations and improved customs control.

The pace and sequencing of reforms are crucial. Thailand and China began to liberalize trade after having invested heavily in skills-building and education. In contrast, South Africa seems to be following the Latin American examples, where trade liberalization occurred amid tepid commitment to skills and education. Huge job losses were one result.

The strictures of the WTO inhibit some corrective actions. But it is also true that, in some sectors, South Africa has lifted tariffs at a faster pace than required by WTO agreements. The claim that government's hands are entirely tied rings a little hollow. Tactical alliances with other blocs and countries of the South can be welded into platforms of resistance. Besides business organizations, these should include other civil society formations.[39] No doubt, those efforts will be complicated by disagreement (for example, around labour and environmental standards). But the international trade arena is also riven by tensions between the major mercantile powers, as the 1999 Seattle round of the WTO showed. This has wedged open manoeuvring space for allied or networked engagements by countries of the South at the international level (see Marais, 1998b). Despite attempts to achieve greater convergence of policies and standards, it is essential that South Africa joins and animates campaigns for rules that are flexible enough:

> ... to allow selective disengagement from multilateral discipline ... The purpose of such an 'escape clause' mechanism would be to allow countries greater breathing room, under well-specified contingencies and subject to multilaterally approved institutional procedures, to fulfil domestic requirements that may conflict with free trade.[40]

Also lacking is a more advantageous balance between production for export and domestic markets – in order to boost the economy's ability to absorb surplus labour. In fact, the country's industrial policy seems caught in a paradox. It is geared towards swelling trade flows that are based on (largely) capital-intensive exports and an influx of labour-intensive imports – against a background of rising unemployment and poverty. Given the emphasis on high-value-added products, export production tends to bypass un- and semi-skilled labour. This is underscored by the high rate of job losses in export-oriented sectors that have shifted resolutely to capital-intensive production. The trend is not new, but it was allowed to continue in the 1990s. A key factor has been the under-pricing of capital relative to labour – by way of a complex of tax and other measures that have lowered the user cost of capital. According to the Katz Commission, they included the absence of substantial capital taxes, skewed depreciation rules, investment allowances and, importantly, a monetary regime that buttressed the value of the rand (thereby preventing the cost of imported capital equipment to rise dramatically).[41]

Higher worker productivity alone will not reverse the bias toward capital-intensive production, which also tends to be reinforced by higher wage demands. Needed are measures that increase the cost of fixed capital in order to shift factor demand toward job creation – among them a reformed tax system.

Tax policy has a further, important role in this regard – not simply on the concessionary side but as a method to redirect surpluses into productive investment. The levying of a capital gains tax from 2001 onward could serve as a step in that direction, especially if the resulting revenue enables the government to increase public investment spending.[42] In addition, pre-scribed asset ratios for pension funds and assurance companies deserve to be examined through less ideological lenses.

In summary, trade and industrial policy remains blurred. It is haphazardly articulated to the macro-economic framework. The incentives marshalled reflect too heavy a bias on the supply-side, neglecting important demand-side needs. Insufficient attention has been brought to bear on designing and managing appropriate types and degrees of targeting that could absorb surplus labour and trigger investment/profit/reinvestment cycles. Also, it lays too light an emphasis on physical investment, although this shows signs of changing under the SDIs, private sector-driven as they are. Meanwhile, monetary and fiscal policies are at odds with an effective trade and industrial policy. A restrictive monetary policy primarily serves the interests of the finance sector – not industry – while tight fiscal policy limits government support for trade and industrial initiatives. There is vast room for improvement.

The labour market

The piecemeal dismantling of the post-apartheid *labour regime* and a push to depress wages must be prevented. The guiding principle has to be the recognition that the 'transformation of the apartheid labour market, characterised by segmentation, inequality and exploitative relationships' is integral to broader social transformation (Creamer, 1998:4). Achieving this will require making up a lot of lost ground on the ideological front – for the defence of a progressive labour regime typically is misrepresented as a sheer bid to guard the 'privileges' of organized, employed workers. Workers' demands for wage increases that match or exceed the inflation rate commonly are presented as evidence. Yet, the claim does not survive inspection. Wage depression triggers higher wage demands from the organized workforce because of the ways in which wage packets cross-subsidize the income of unemployed and low-wage dependants. The reason is simple, as COSATU's Neil Coleman has reminded: 'It puts enormous pressure on workers to push for a higher take-home pay to support the growing number of unemployed in the extended family' (1999b:43).

Nevertheless, business will continue to answer wage demands by intro-ducing labour-saving technologies and by resorting to sub-contracting and other flexible options. There is no evidence that wage restraint *per se* will halt those moves. In fact, it is much more likely to embolden a drive to pummel wage rates down further.

There is an abundant supply of studies that contradict the notion that South Africa's labour market is inflexible, and they have been acknowledged publicly by the government.[43] But equally widespread are perceptions to the contrary. Government set about addressing these in early 2000 by unveiling limited revisions to some of the labour laws passed since 1994. Although limited, the changes herald the possible realization of one of the GEAR strategy's prescriptions: a move toward 'regulated flexibility'.[44]

For most of the ANC government's first term in office, COSATU was able to stall regressive adjustments in this area. Indeed, it was on this front that its political alliance with the ANC did bear fruit – but at a steep price. It involved a trade-off that saw the government temporarily hold the line against business' demand for greater flexibility at the 1998 Job Summit. In return, COSATU agreed to have its alternative macro-economic proposals struck from the Summit's agenda and loyally muffled its opposition to the GEAR strategy during the 1999 election campaign.

But progressive labour standards cannot be successfully defended in isolation from other changes to macro-economic and industrial policies, as outlined. The same holds for the protection and creation of jobs. Meanwhile, the ideological assault against the post-apartheid labour regime showed no signs of abating. Facing the labour movement at the turn of the century was the danger that it might fail to demonstrably marry its defence of labour rights to its bids to achieve wider socio-economic transformation.

Social security

A final area of crucial adjustment is *social security*.[45] Compared to most developing countries, South Africa has a relatively advanced non-contribu-tory social security system (like old age, disability and child support grants). But the system provides thin and uneven protection that fails to reach most of the poor. Worse, it is delinked from other strategies to eradicate poverty through asset redistribution, structural transformation of the economy, affordable service delivery and education. As such, it fits the conservative definition of a social 'safety net': limited income transfers aimed at prevent-ing some of the poor from plunging into outright destitution.

The concept of a social wage goes considerably further. It is not aimed at containing but at reducing poverty, redistributing wealth and opportuni-ties, and drawing more South Africans into productive economic activity – by linking a revamped social security system into a broad development strategy. It was outlined in the RDP and again in COSATU's 1997 September Commission report.

A basic income grant scheme would form an important pillar of a new social security system. As part of a ten-point plan to reform the country's social security system, the scheme by late 1999 had won the support of the welfare department, although the finance ministry chose a carping attitude. The goal is suitably ambitious: 'Every South African should have a minimum income, sufficient to meet basic subsistence needs, and should not have to live below minimum acceptable standards'.[46]

The scheme could take several forms. The welfare department seems drawn towards a mix of cash grants and non-cash 'service' grants for the poor – with a price tag of R7 billion ($1,1 billion).[47] The danger is that the cash portion would have to be means-tested (to determine eligibility). This would not only be difficult and costly to administer, but it invites fraud and corruption. Another version, which COSATU tabled at the 1998 Job Summit, could avoid such snarl-ups. It entails a universal basic income grant of R100 ($16) a month for each citizen. Payment would occur via direct deposits through the banking system. But everyone earning more than a certain monthly income would pay the grant back through the income tax system. High-income earners would pay back double the grant, as a form of 'solidarity tax'. COSATU estimated this would cost the government R23 billion a year (assuming 75 per cent take-up), although a portion of the expense would be recouped through the tax system.[48]

Many questions still surround the scheme – not least the welfare department's capacity to implement it. But the most difficult challenge would be to integrate it both into an overhauled social security system and a more equitable development strategy. For that to occur, the grant scheme could not be a 'stand-alone' initiative, but would have to function as a component of wider adjustments of the kinds outlined above. Yet, even if that failed, the grant could provide vital support to the survival strategies of the poor.

Bear in mind, though, that the duty of providing the entire spectrum of social wage benefits cannot fall solely on the state. Required is a combination of public, non-profit and private sector endeavours within the ambit of a state-led strategy. A first step toward such a concerted initiative would be to draw the private sector into a tighter regulatory framework.[49]

Shifting gears

All these require a stern paradigm shift from a wistful faith in dominant economic ideology to a strategic response that is based on ample empirical evidence that:

> Economic openness is part of a development strategy – never a substitute
> for development strategy … The relationship between growth rates and

indicators of openness – levels of tariff and non-tariff barriers or controls on capital flows – is weak at best. Policy makers therefore have to focus on the fundamentals of economic growth – investment, macroeconomic stability, human resources and good governance – and not let economic integration dominate their thinking on development.[50]

Leftist readers will have noted – probably with disapproval – that none of these adjustments are predicated on a bid to move beyond capitalism. In fact, none herald a challenge to that system *per se*, although some could serve as seedbeds for such a venture. In the South African context, and against the current global backdrop, such a project seems cast in a long time frame – 'seems', because as historians know, history is fickle, and no less so in an epoch in which an apparently triumphant capitalist system is impregnated globally with deep structural contradictions. The global balance of forces, however, still favours the quest to muffle and deflect the consequences of those contradictions.

In such an era, and given the bone-crunching poverty and suffering that defines the lives of half the South African population, the paramount task is to fashion a development path that neither reinforces that fate nor postpones salvation into the distant future. Required, in other words, is the art of the possible. As hopefully demonstrated, an expanse of possibilities *do* exist. But thus far, intellectual persuasion and deferent engagements have served progressives poorly in their bids to influence government economic policy. This brings into focus the politics of an alternative, which the next chapter surveys.

Notes

1   Budget Information Service, 2000, 'The poor remain vulnerable' (23 February), IDASA, Cape Town.
2   'Welfare department "lacks capacity" to use R500m', *Business Day*, 2 March 2000.
3   'Officials blamed for unspent poverty relief', *Business Day*, 29 February 2000. Skweyiya was not welfare minister during the period mentioned. The post was held by Geraldine Fraser-Moleketi who, subsequently, was 'promoted' to public services minister. The cabinet announced later that the entire affair had been caused by an 'auditing error' and that department had, in fact, spent most of its poverty relief funds – see 'Welfare cleared of not using poverty funds', *The Star*, 30 March 2000.
4   Quoted in 'Left blamed for economic failures as Manuel woos foreign investors', *SouthScan*, Vol. 15, No. 1, 14 January 2000.
5   'Submission to the Portfolio Committee on Finance on the 2000/01 Budget', IDASA Budget Information Service, 2 March 2000, Cape Town, p. 6.
6   See, for instance, Rodrik, D. (1997) 'Sense and nonsense in the globalisation debate', *Foreign Policy* (Summer); Rodrik, D. (1996) *Why do more open economies have bigger governments?*, Working Paper 5537 of the National Bureau of Economic Research, Cambridge, Massachusetts; Weiss, L. (1997) 'Globalisation and the myth of the powerless state', *New Left Review*, No. 225, pp. 3–27; Scholte, J.A. (1997) 'Global capitalism and the state', *International Affairs*, Vol. 73, No. 3, pp. 427–52.

7 Ironically, it is in neoliberal thought that the notion of the instrumentalized state is most acute. There it is accorded the role of a purely facilitating apparatus for capital accumulation.

8 See, for example, Stiglitz (1998).

9 Stiglitz (1998).

10 For a compressed comparison of the economic development routes of the Asian 'tigers', see Castells (1998:270–6).

11 The prognosis is drawn from Rodrik (1999b).

12 Quoted in Wade and Veneroso (1998:29).

13 See Mbeki, T. (1997) *Address to 'Attracting Capital to Africa' Summit*, Chantilly (USA), April 19. Document included in Foundation for Global Dialogue (1998) *South Africa and Africa: Reflections on the African Renaissance*, Occasional Paper No. 17, Johannesburg, p. 36.

14 The document was issued after Mbeki attended meetings of the World Bank's Forum for Development in Africa; quoted in Nel (1999:23).

15 Amin, S., 'Social movements in the periphery' in Wignaraja, P. (ed.) (1993) *New Social Movements in the South: Empowering the People*, Zed Books, p. 79.

16 An example was the burying in mid-1999 of two personnel audit reports that had identified serious personnel and skills shortages in the public service, and therefore conflicted with government's aim of cutting at least 35 000 public service jobs. The deputy director-general who had supervised the audits subsequently was replaced as government's chief negotiator with public sector unions. See 'Audits which undermined cuts theme are quietly buried', *SouthScan*, Vol. 14, No. 19, 17 September 1999.

17 These can be found at http://www.COSATU.org.za.

18 For an outline of COSATU's basic income grant proposals, see Coleman (1999a:45).

19 Quotes are drawn from 'Summit must not die in sterile debate', *Business Day*, 10 July 1998.

20 It must be added that this expansive social commitment has seemed more evident at this abstract level than in action, where the federation often has ignored or paid only lip-service to other popular initiatives (the Jubilee 2000 debt campaign is one example). For a candid survey of these trends by a National Union of Metalworkers unionist, see Sikwebu (1999:6–11).

21 Much of what follows fits the general tenor of ANC intellectual Joel Netshitenze's 1998 discussion paper, *The State, Property Relations and Social Transformation* – yet, the policy imprints of that thinking remain indiscernible. This 'mystery' is discussed in more detail below.

22 'Monetary policy costing us dearly', *Business Day*, 27 November 1998.

23 Edwards (1998:62). Recall that the bulk of government's debt is owed to domestic institutions.

24 Edward Osborn in 'The fuss caused by Roche', Reuters news service, 9 October 1999.

25 *Op. cit.* The figures are in constant 1990 rands. For 1995, this translated into about 5 per cent of 'lost' GDP growth. This does not mean that an inflationary monetary policy would, necessarily, have added 5 per cent GDP growth; that outcome would depend on a confluence of several other factors. The method (used by Paul Krugman to calculate the cost of the 1979–84 disinflation programme in the USA) merely quantifies foregone growth.

26 Cited in Adelzadeh, A., 'Quest for monetary options', *Mail & Guardian*, 30 May 1997.

27 Cited in Khan, F. (1999) *SANGOCO Economics Project Base Discussion Document* (paper prepared for SA National NGO Coalition), Cape Town, p. 28.

28 *The Constitution of the Republic of South Africa*, Act 108, 1996, para. 224,1.

29 Quoted in 'Tougher times are on the way', *Business Times*, 5 March 2000.

30 Quoted in 'Globalisation must be managed carefully', *Business Day*, 22 June 1998.
31 Abedian, I., 'Monetary policy costing us dearly', *Business Day*, 27 November 1998.
32 For an analysis of the debate and its stakes, see Wade and Veneroso (1998).
33 For more on the Tobin Tax, see www.tobintax.org. Several variations have been proposed. German economist Paul Spahn, for instance, advocates a two-tier tax. This would entail a very small baseline levy on all transactions within a set band of acceptable rise-and-fall, along with a highly punitive tax on transactions that exceed those rise-and-fall limits. The baseline levy would generate government revenue, while the higher tax would punish excessive speculation (but leave less volatile transactions largely unaffected). The original Tobin Tax proposal calls for a small, flat tax on all speculative transactions.
34 Getz, M., '"Blip" hits global economy', *Business Report*, 3 December 1998.
35 The phrasing belongs to Wade and Veneroso (1998:34).
36 Finance minister Trevor Manuel has grown fond of this mendacity. In his 2000/1 budget speech, he tried to invoke *Das Kapital* to underscore the vagaries of fiscal irresponsibility – defined, of course, as any policy that defied the random 3 per cent of GDP deficit target selected by government.
37 See Meer, F., 'It's not right that SA is still paying for past wrongs', *Sunday Times*, 11 July 1999. Dollar figures are calculated at average 1999 exchange rates.
38 Figures cited in Khan (1999:21).
39 It is a fallacy that trade negotiations exclude civil society. Business organizations feature prominently. On occasion, South Africa has allowed nominal involvement by the labour movement. But roundly excluded are other civil society groupings – churches, human rights, women's and environmental organizations.
40 The proposal is Dani Rodrik's, the summary is by Khan (1999:23). See Rodrik (1999a).
41 See *Interim Report of the Commission of Inquiry into certain aspects of the Tax Structure of South Africa*, 1994, Pretoria, pp. 254–5.
42 A capital gains tax was announced in the 2000/1 national budget.
43 Several ILO reports reached that conclusion. A South African study of the impact of the Basic Conditions of Employment Act on the small business sector made a similar finding – see Godfrey and Theron (1999).
44 'Minister soft-pedals on revisions to labour laws', *SouthScan*, Vol. 15, No. 3, 11 February 2000. The labour ministry was likely to be hard-pressed defending the minor changes against a finance ministry that envisaged more extensive revisions.
45 This section draws on Khan (1999).
46 Quoted in 'Safety net for the poorest of the poor', *Mail & Guardian*, 21 January 2000.
47 In a state of the nation speech in early 2000, Mbeki did not mention the scheme, but emphasized the need to 'improve the quality of our social spending' and pledged to 'continue to allocate significant resources to address [social security] needs as best we can' (see Mbeki, 2000). Neither did it feature in the finance minister's budget speech weeks later. The fate of such a scheme, therefore, still hung in the balance.
48 For an outline, see Coleman (1999a:45).
49 For more on this aspect, see Khan (1999:34–5).
50 Rodrik (1999a), quoted in Khan (1999:14).

CHAPTER EIGHT

The politics of an alternative

Power is spread diffusely through society. No development strategy, therefore, can be mounted strictly or even mainly on the basis of intellectual persuasion that wins the agreement of élites. The concept of élite-pacting might explain how certain compromises are *achieved*, but not how they *endure*.

Conversely, the prospects of an alternative hinge on a tenable understanding of how power and consent is reproduced in post-apartheid South Africa. That implies explaining how – and to what extent – political and ideological authority is being extended across the surface of society.[1] The starting point, obviously, is to shift analysis well and beyond the crude frame of a 'sell-out' or 'betrayal'. Equally apparent will be the choice to enlist some of the Italian Marxist Antonio Gramsci's theoretical insights in this exercise.

Glancing back

By the early 1980s, South Africa's economy was outgrowing its dependency on cheap, unskilled (and semi-skilled) black labour and was running aground in a morass of other constraints. Apartheid education badly limited the supply of educated, skilled black workers. Domestic demand was fast approaching its imposed limits. Access to foreign financing and new technologies was hampered by international boycotts and sanctions, and by puttering economic growth. The latter factors, along with the capital controls that were re-introduced in the mid-1980s, stood in the way of expansion abroad. Compounding the problems was the burgeoning militant resistance and seemingly chronic political and social instability. An exit from this 'crisis' had to be found. In academic Andrew Nash's phrasing:

> ... to overcome these barriers, big capital needed a government which
> expressed the aspirations of the majority, but only in the limited and modi-

fied form made possible by the repression of the mid-1980s revolt, the international context after the collapse of Stalinism, and the gradual transformation of the liberation movement itself as it became increasingly dependent on the support (or neutrality, or unwillingness to aid the apartheid state) of bourgeois institutions.[2]

The trajectory of post-apartheid South Africa broadly answers to those prerogatives. To be sure, some of the economic adjustments made are anchored in structural changes and policy shifts that preceded the ANC's ascent to power in 1994. In reinforcing and refining that continuity, government's economic policies are geared at enabling domestic capital to wrestle free of a thicket of constraints. The attempts to align the South African economy to orthodoxy and integrate it deeper into the global system, therefore, did not spring only from the *objective* pressures emanating from the system. They were propelled also by the *subjective* requirements of domestic capital.

Yet, the ANC government also had (and still has) to address contesting interests and demands – principally those of the African majority, which had organized itself into a formidable array of popular organizations. Not least of these was the ANC itself. So, the configuration of adjustments that constitutes the post-apartheid development path was not preordained by some 'law of necessity'. It is a provisional outcome made possible by, in Stuart Hall's words, 'the relations of forces favourable or unfavourable to this or that tendency' (1996:422). That is to say, there was no *direct* line linking economic causes with political effects.

Those relations of forces were shaped by a range of dynamics in various realms. They included the geopolitical shifts occasioned by the end of the Cold War, the ideological and strategic impact of the collapse of Eastern bloc socialism, and the ideological ascendancy of neoliberal economics (and the related restructuring of the global division of labour). Among them, too, were the moves made to establish an adequate platform of stability for a post-apartheid system, the organizational and strategic weaknesses of popular formations, and the decompression of class differences among the African majority generally and within the ANC specifically.

It is on this terrain that an 'unstable balance' is being created, a balance that is underpinned by an evolving alliance of classes and interests, and that is expressed in the ensemble of policies and practices that constitute South Africa's development strategy. It does not (yet) represent a hegemonic victory for any particular alliance of forces – *but neither is it a stalemate.*

This tentative equilibrium manifestly favours domestic (and international) capital. But it also rests on measures that are hospitable and beneficial to a range of other layers – among them the broad middle classes, the African *petite bourgeoisie* and, to lesser extents, the organized working classes and sections of the African poor. Crucially, this 'balance' has not been unilaterally and coercively imposed: it is made possible by the resolute cultivation of consent.

This line of analysis necessarily draws into focus the strategies, activities and features of those formations that seek to achieve a development strategy that, in the first instance, can address popular needs. On the one hand, the current failure to accomplish this betrays the weakness of a popular hegemonic project. On the other hand, it testifies to the comparative vigour of another hegemonic project – a work in progress that is proving more adept at creating a (tentative) '"unity" of classes' on the basis of 'specific economic, political and ideological practices' that enable the ruling class to *lead* and not just *dominate*.[3]

Hegemonic struggles

The struggle between two classes is usually the struggle between two hegemonic projects. The basis of each is a set of (ideological) principles, ideals and activities that assume the status of 'common sense' and that enable that class 'to escape the confines of its own corporate interests and to enlarge its political action to the point where it can understand and advance the aspirations of the subordinate classes' (Pellicani, 1981:30). This popularized worldview cannot be reduced to mere 'legitimation, false consciousness, or manipulation of the mass of the population' (Bottomore, 1983:202). As an ideological map it has to enable a class to co-ordinate its own class interests with those of subordinate groups in order to obtain their active consent. In Bottomore's summary, 'the material basis of hegemony is constituted through reforms or compromises in which the leadership of a class is maintained but in which other classes have certain demands met' (1983:202).

Naturally, this cannot affect essentials and, in the last instance, the fundamental interests of the dominant class have to prevail. But it has to be equipped with an elasticity that allows subordinate classes to align themselves to the hegemonic project – *and benefit from it*. The ideological platform upon which consent is built therefore has to be 'constructed at the intersection of ... multiple subject positions which, though *over-determined* by class struggle, cannot be said to be directly determined by it or reducible to its effects' (Mercer, 1980:126).

As a practical example, one might consider the reign of Thatcherism in Britain. Indeed, Margaret Thatcher could be said to have operated squarely in the Gramscian mode, as David Coates has argued:

> In the heyday of her dominance, Thatcherism re-established the link between values and policies in UK public life ... Like all successful political forces in democratic societies, Thatcherism took many of the central *values and aspirations* held by us all (values of liberty and individual rights, aspira-

tions for prosperity and progress), tied them to a series of *operating principles* (in her case, overwhelmingly the principle of the unfettered market), and then steadily, resolutely and with great self-confidence, applied that operating principle, in the pursuit of those values and aspirations, to *policy area after policy area* (1996:73).

Hegemony, state and civil society

The hegemonic struggle is waged primarily on the terrain of relations and institutions that comprise civil society. In Gramscian theory, civil society is not rigidly set apart from the state. Rather, the state and civil society are seen to be interlinked in complex ways. This allows for an understanding that locates civil society in rules, transactions and struggles that connect the state and society (Beckman, 1993), creating a 'complex "system" which has to be the object of a many-sided type of political strategy' (Hall, 1996:429).

Related is another, central premise of Gramsci's concept of hegemony: the realization that the state does not represent the site of pure, concentrated power in society. Neither is it simply a set of administrative and coercive institutions through which a dominant class imposes and defends its prerogatives over the subordinate classes. Instead of functioning as the central instrument for precarious domination via coercion and material force, the state is central to the *ideological* conquest of society. One of its most important functions, in Gramsci's words, 'is to raise the great mass of the population to a particular cultural and moral level or type which corresponds to the needs of the productive forces for development, and hence to the interests of the ruling class' (1971:258). In Hall's interpretation of Gramsci's thinking on the subject:

> It is the point *from which* hegemony over society as a whole is ultimately exercised (though not the only place where hegemony is constructed). It is the point of condensation – not because all forms of coercive domination necessarily radiate outwards from its apparatuses but because, in its contradictory structure, it condenses a variety of different relations and practices into a definite 'system of rules'. It is, for this reason, the site for conforming (that is, bringing into line) or 'adapting the civilisation and the morality of the broadest masses to the necessities of the continuous development of the economic apparatus of production' (1996:428, emphasis added).

The state is then revealed as a 'strategic field' that is 'constituted, condensed [and] materialised through a complex … interplay of economic, political and ideological forces' (Mercer, 1980:119–20). Implicit is a recognition that contradictions of the state do not stem merely from conflicting interests within the ruling class, but are created also by tensions between it and the dominated classes.

The dominion of a ruling class therefore is grounded in the ability of the state to nurture the active consent of broad sections of society, in concert with other social forces. It is not the sole marshalling agent of consent, but it is an essential one. Not a *thing* to be captured, smashed or overthrown but a 'complex formation', the state is the zone or field where 'the bloc of social forces which dominates over it not only justifies and maintains its domination but wins by leadership and authority the active consent of those over whom it rules' (Hall, 1996:429). That achievement marks the 'moment' of hegemony – a rare feat and one of indeterminate duration. Such periods represent the achievement of unity that is sufficient for a society 'to set itself a new historical agenda, under the leadership of a specific formation or constellation of social forces' (Hall, 1996:424). It is also more than a loosely structured alliance of social classes. As Pellicani has indicated, it is a unique 'cultural, economic, political and moral phenomenon' – which means that the hegemonic period:

> … lasts as long as the ruling class is able to ensure the cohesion of the system of alliances on which its rule is exercised, and [enlarged] to include the other classes, thus satisfying in one way or another their moral and material interests (1981:32).

Other interpretations go further to argue that what leads in a hegemonic period is no longer a 'ruling class' but a 'historic bloc'.[4] This is an important distinction because it recognizes that, although class remains a 'determining level of analysis', whole classes cannot unproblematically and directly be translated:

> … on to the political-ideological stage as unified historical actors. The 'leading elements' in a historic bloc may be only one fraction of the dominant economic class – for example, finance rather than industrial capital; national rather than international capital. Associated with it, within the 'bloc', will be strata of the subaltern and dominated classes, who have been won over by specific concessions and compromises and who form part of the social constellation but in a subordinate role … Each hegemonic formation will thus have its own, specific social composition and configuration. This is a very different way of conceptualising what is often referred to, loosely and inaccurately, as the 'ruling class' (Hall, 1996:424).

A work in progress

One can detect in post-apartheid South Africa the evolution of an ascendant hegemonic project of growing sophistication and vigour. Its many facets converge in a refined and expansive discourse[5] of concessions, affirmations, traditions and innovations that together cultivate an enveloping (though incomplete) sense of common interests and consent. As the following sections show, the project is equipped with imposing advantages.

Essentially, it entails modulating capital's 'modernizing' drive in ways that enable the allocation of gains also to other social layers – not least an emergent African *bourgeoisie* and the black middle classes. The fact that it encompasses pledges, activities and professed ideals that seem to benefit a wide range of classes and interests does not obscure its overriding bias toward the generalized desiderata of capital. These include a rules-based system of governance geared at efficiency, stability and growth, a manifest commitment to a market-driven economic system, and the ability to foster and sustain social unity.

But more crucial is its bias toward the requirements of specific fractions of capital (centrally, banking and financial institutions) and of large corporations (in a variety of sectors)[6] whose accumulatory needs require both substantial liberalization and active state support for expansion abroad. Prominent among the prerogatives of the former is capital account liberalization and a positive monetary policy. The latter require that the state desist from directive interventions in their investment decisions, as well as provide a political-ideological and economic framework that enables them to internationalize their activities in pursuit of higher returns than the national economy seems to offer. Servicing these demands, for example, is the emphasis on foreign – as opposed to domestic – investment as a catalyst for growth. Also ushered into view is a specific, but generally overlooked function of the African renaissance discourse, which locates bids at international and especially *continental* expansion within a project of pan-African revival. The extent to which these imperatives have come to define the post-apartheid development path is detailed in Chapters 5 and 6.

Naturally, the endeavour also encompasses other essential elements that can address the needs and demands of the subordinate classes. Also, it contains profound features that could enable it to resolve the problem of fashioning an *ideological unity* that registers across the field of society.

At the outset, it should be noted that the project is also imbued with weaknesses and contradictions. Not least is the fact that its fate hinges on the ability to maintain – and overcome – an unsteady balance between servicing the requirements of the classes that stand at its axis, and addressing the interests of a range of subordinate forces. Confronting it, too, are more specific challenges that deserve some elaboration.

The project is being managed primarily *out of* the state – but within a complicated context. Firstly, the state still contains pockets of unabashed reaction and is riddled with internal conflict and contradictions. This complicates the process of engineering consent *within* the state. In addition, the ability to foster popular consent *via* state activities is spasmodic and is undermined by state institutions' operational travails (for instance, in dispensing welfare services or supervising the construction of enough new houses or managing an effective law and order system).

Secondly, some of the 'symbolic language' deployed in the project also has divisive effects. At one level, there are proficient efforts to manufacture consent across disparate sections of society – the hallmark of a potentially successful hegemonic venture. On this front, the accent on 'efficiency', good governance and 'realistic' policies combines with state-supervised efforts to distribute or facilitate gains to as many layers of society as possible. Simultaneously, the *uneven nature of those gains* requires that the 'allegiance' of the African majority also be shored up through other means – among them the justifiable emphasis on race (concretized, for instance, in affirmative action policies) and the obvious need to acknowledge and rail against patterns of poverty and inequality. This complicates the affinities of white élites.

Thirdly, many of the reference points of this work-in-progress (the history and traditions of the Congress movement, the Freedom Charter, the RDP, etc.) are implicit indictments of it – since they can also be made to highlight departures from a popular development path. An alternative hegemonic project could deploy these references to greater effect.

Finally, two organizations that potentially could function as the fulcra of a popular hegemonic project – the SACP and COSATU – are joined in a political alliance with the ruling party. The fact that this generates huge ambivalence in those organizations is more obvious than the possibility that ructions could be triggered in the ruling party and government if that ambivalence is overcome.

How far has the dominant hegemonic project progressed? An answer is aided by the schematic distinction Gramsci drew of three, key phases of maturity: the 'economic corporate', the 'class corporate' and the hegemonic stages, as outlined by Hall (1996:423). In the first, common but parochial interests become manifest and serve as a springboard for action. But the protagonists are oblivious to the need for, and possibilities of engineering wider class solidarities. South Africa clearly has surpassed that stage. The 'class corporate' phase sees the achievement of such solidarities – but only in the economic realm. The *moment* of hegemony is approached when this alliance transcends:

> ... the corporate limits of purely economic solidarity, [encompasses] the interests of other subordinate groups, and begins to 'propagate itself throughout society', bringing about intellectual and moral as well as economic and political unity, and 'posing also the questions around which the struggle rages ... thus creating the hegemony of a fundamental social group over a series of subordinate groups'.[7]

By 2000, South Africa appeared to be hovering between the 'class corporate' and 'hegemonic' stages. As always in history, there is no guarantee that a hegemonic moment will be reached or, if it is, be maintained for long.[8] At the same time, the status of a contesting project that heeds as priorities the visions and more radical injunctions of the Freedom Charter and 'original' RDP document seems much less hale. The final sections of this chapter will consider why that is so and offer preliminary thoughts on how this state of affairs might be altered.

First, though, it is necessary to examine the ways in which an intellectual, moral, political and economic collective will is being marshalled across society for a project that is recasting – but not transcending – South Africa's insider/outsider mould. Importantly, these facets of hegemony operate with great potency inside the ANC as well.

Building blocks of hegemony

The ANC's history confirms its adeptness at nurturing and consolidating loyalty and consent. By the mid-1980s, the party had established its status as a government-in-waiting and confirmed its supremacy over the internal opposition. The route towards a 'better life for all' (the party's later election slogan) had come to pass through the broad church of the ANC, where the specific meanings different constituencies attached to that goal seemed to achieve harmony. Through deed and affirmation, it lodged itself in the popular imagination as *the* vessel for redressing all manner of grievances and for realizing a rich assortment of ambitions and interests. Paradoxically, the apartheid system assisted in this process. Its ideology of exclusivity summoned a counter ideology of inclusivity. The unifying and inclusive character of the ANC therefore stood in a dialectical relationship to a system that violently tried to enforce the converse.

Key to these feats was an ideology of struggle and ideals that was supple enough to accommodate and entertain contradictory impulses, and persuasively present shifts as distillations of a consistent, historical vision of change. In the 1990s, especially after 1994, an inclusive ethos became projected across society, where it formed a mantle of reconciliation, consensus-making and nation-building. Putative commonalities and shared interests were highlighted in a crucial quest for stability. The perspectives were widely embraced and propagated by the main political parties, organized business and the vast majority of the media. They also enjoyed what one might term 'organic authenticity', in the sense that they resonated (and were made to make 'sense') among most ordinary South Africans. A rich stock of spectacles and gestures amplified that endorsing mood. Sports events (such as the Rugby World Cup and the African Nations Cup), startling images of white army generals saluting president Nelson Mandela or of the new South African flag billowing beneath air force helicopters at the 1994 presidential inauguration, or Mandela sipping tea with the widow of apartheid architect Hendrik Verwoerd were examples

Even more dramatic was the translation of this mood of appeasement and 'unity' into government policies – as manifested in economic policies but also in the market-friendly tilt of the housing and land reform programmes. From 1994 onward, the RDP was converted into a powerful adjunct of this overall process.[9]

The RDP remade

As a government programme, the RDP by late 1994 bore the stretchmarks of a bid to accommodate the divergent interests of contesting social and economic forces. So much so that conservative commentators could approvingly remark that 'all signs now are that our policy makers see that the objectives of the RDP are wholly compatible with the three words [privatization, liberalization and convertibility] which so interest the money men'.[10] Made to embody the conciliatory principles that underpinned the political settlement, the RDP was seen by the ANC government as a partnership of:

> ... everyone, every organisation, every opinion-making group that can contribute ... that's the protection this government needs to ensure that if anything goes wrong, it will be our collective responsibility.[11]

However radical the original intentions that had spawned the programme, its birthing process also reflected this 'collective' ethos. The outcome of wide-ranging consultation, the original RDP 'base document' was an attempt to harmonize a rich variety of demands and concerns. As a result, it was no seamless blueprint. The product of many hands and minds, 'the policy framework was beset by enough fragmented voices, multiple identities and competing discourses to leave even postmodern analysts confounded' (Bond, 1999). Later promoted as a national endeavour, around which contrasting interests could converge, the RDP was pruned of most of its earlier, radical outgrowths and promoted as a unifying, national endeavour that allegedly transcended parochial interests. As a road map of transformation, it promised to lead just about everyone to their respective promised lands. Some observers would go further and declare that 'with a little ingenuity, anything can be made to fit in with the goals of the RDP' (Rapoo, 1995:5). Not quite, for the RDP's overriding *goals* were unequivocal. No matter the ingenuity applied, massive job losses could not be reconciled with the goal of creating jobs and moving towards full employment. Likewise, the guarantee of a living wage could not be made to fit a reality in which many employed workers live in poverty, nor could a commitment to reduce income disparities be deemed to have been realized when such disparities increased.

Central to the 1993 RDP 'base document' was a vision of transformation that hinged on a mutually reinforcing dynamic between basic needs provision, economic growth, vigorous civil society participation and initiative, and a democratized state geared at servicing the needs of all citizens. In essence, the document answered to the description 'left-Keynesian', although some aspects expressed more radical impulses – the provision of certain basic goods and services through non-market mechanisms, the partial decommodification of low-income housing and the like. Yet, according to a participant in the drafting processes:

> ... the broad presumption was that when the market failed, as it so often did in South Africa, the state would step in to both force capital to follow a long-term rational, non-racial capitalist logic, and to facilitate access to basic goods and services, to environmental and consumer protection, or to industrial and technological development. This was ultimately no profound challenge to the market, but rather an affirmation of its hegemonic role in the ordering of society. Corporatism in this spirit pervaded the document (Bond, 1999).

While emphatically mapping the ultimate destination – 'a people-centred society which measures progress by the extent to which it has succeeded in securing for each citizen liberty, prosperity and happiness' – the document established a 'comfort zone' between conflicting forces and interests, by lending itself to different interpretations. This eclecticism became even more pronounced in government's RDP White Paper (released in late 1994). So, too, were the more constrictive terms on which growth and redistribution would be pursued.

The left tried to arrest the retreat from the 'original' RDP and reclaim ownership of the programme. It criticized departures from the 'base document', and cherished the 'explicitly non-capitalist logic' and 'substantially socialist reforms' outlined in that draft (Bond, 1994c). The closure of the RDP office in 1996 and the introduction of the GEAR plan a few months later hardened its sense of betrayal.

Mistakenly, though, it contrasted a 'pure' RDP with the version that had emerged from the hands of government. But, as noted, even earlier drafts had spoken in many tongues, prompting labour analyst Karl von Holdt to detect (in 1993 already) a tendency in which 'any issue which might suggest a serious conflict with the interests of the rich and powerful has been smoothed over' (1993:25). No doubt, the 'base document' had contained a wealth of signposts for a more progressive development path. As clear was the fact that most of them had been sideswiped by 1996.[12]

But seldom featuring in the defence of the 'base document' was the fact that it also had advocated strict limits on state spending, endorsed a drive towards international competitiveness and approved calls for an 'independent' Reserve Bank. It had precious little to say on monetary policy, ignored issues such as the apartheid debt, did not achieve even a nominal integration between macro-economic and industrial policies, and failed to articulate its proposed land reform programme to a rural development strategy.

In so doing, the realm of the 'purely economic' was ceded to small bands of technocrats and their political defenders. Steadily, the terrain of economic policy was depoliticized and desocialized, and turned into the stamping ground of technical experts. Under the penumbra of the edict 'there is no alternative', conservative economic policies came to prefigure and over-shadow the social ideals of the RDP.

What the left also failed to latch onto was that not only had the RDP been eviscerated of its original ideals, its *function* in the transition had been altered dramatically. In its revised form it became neither the paragon of, nor a mere sop to the transformatory demands that had brought the ANC to power. It had mutated into something altogether different.

As implemented by government, the RDP exemplified the desire to dis-tribute gains as widely as possible without raising the anxiety levels of capi-tal – hence its one-size-fits-all character. The make-over vividly expressed the compromises that came to shape post-apartheid South Africa's develop-ment strategy – trade-offs that seemed spurred by the obvious need not to jeopardize stability, but that also reflected a balance of forces that favoured capital. The RDP became a distillation of that state of affairs.

Closely related is the programme's other, subsequent function: as an *ideological* reference point that seems to confirm the political-historical continuity between the Freedom Charter and the realities of post-apartheid South Africa. Its political resonance as a programme of mooted transforma-tion prevents it from being discarded formally, even though it has been shorn of *literal* meaning. In the context of the transition, the RDP has become a form of shorthand for the values and principles that animated the anti-apartheid struggle, thereby signifying continuity. The fact that govern-ment references to it have grown rarer and more selective only highlights this function.[13] It has been inserted into a constellation of 'democratic' interests where the self-help activities of working class residents, the unbundling exercises of corporations and the courting of foreign portfolio investors are portrayed as equal expressions of a postulated 'unity of purpose'. The variegated interests of capital and of the subaltern classes are not only blurred, but *made to appear contingent on each other*. No longer the chief compass point of a development strategy, the RDP now functions as an accessory of an ascendant hegemonic project.

Facts on the ground

Such flourishes would dissolve in the face of reality, were it not for the visible gains that accrue to a variety of classes and constituencies. The scope of these accomplishments is commonly misread – both because observers have understated the extent of tangible delivery and because they tend to measure it mainly in terms of quantifiable benefits distributed to the coun-try's poor and marginalized social layers.

Scanning post-1994 South Africa, an unjaundiced eye cannot but detect evidence of the wide range of benefits allocated to specific classes – the organized working classes, the existing and emerging African middle classes, and the aspirant African *bourgeoisie*. (The largesse extended to incumbent élites does not require repeating.)

The gains of organized labour are a case in point. Won through a marshalling of trade union power, the Labour Relations Act, the Employment Equity Act and the Basic Conditions of Employment Act rank among the more dramatic gains since 1994. Although hardly impervious to left-wing critique, many of the historical demands of the labour movement have acquired legislative force in these Acts. Indeed, much of the *concrete* basis for the endurance of COSATU's alliance with the ANC rests in the Acts.

The Employment Equity Act resonates even wider, with its affirmative action thrust confirming a determination to address the 'national question'. Ideologically, its impact cascades far beyond the workplace, since it authenticates the ANC's status as the historical guardian of African nationalist ideals and the post-apartheid state's determination to advance those ideals. The impact is powerfully legitimating.

Pertinent, too, is an expanding range of measures to aid African entrepreneurship. They also present evidence of a 'unity of purpose' that extends beyond the state and includes major capitalist organizations (that contribute to small business funds, mount skills-building ventures and stage entrepreneurial training). Affirmed, at the broadest level, is the historical-ideological continuum between the ideals and commitments expressed in struggle, and the reality of post-1994 South Africa. Also highlighted is a commonality of interests that seems to join the fate of the African *petite bourgeoisie* to that of capital. Addressed, at a narrower level, are the pronounced interests and demands of the African *petite bourgeoisie*, whose weight and sway inside the ANC continues to grow.[14]

Building a 'patriotic' bourgeoisie

Like other successful liberation organizations of the post-World War Two era,[15] the ANC has been keen to cultivate a 'patriotic' (African) *bourgeoisie* under the banner of black economic empowerment. This sub-project of the 'national democratic revolution' is expounded on the grounds that transformation within a capitalist system will be sold short if the heights of the economy remain exclusively in white hands. The rise of African capitalists therefore is also deemed to address a facet of the 'national question'.

Vested in the rise of an African capitalist class is the expectation that racial solidarity (in this case with the African poor) would eclipse class solidarity and become the wellspring of a 'patriotic' capitalism. Its profit-seeking activities could be harmonized with an overriding commitment to help improve the living standards and opportunities of the African poor.

Needless to say, such notions sit squarely in the African-nationalist tradition. Tellingly, it is a proposition that also fits comfortably in the SACP's 'colonialism of a special type' (CST) thesis.[16]

But measured in terms of productive investments, job creation, income growth, redistribution and working conditions, black economic empowerment firms show little sign of making headway on that front. Part of the reason lies in the character of the ventures:

> Black companies have had difficulty in establishing a presence at the operating level of business, and particularly in manufacturing. Instead, they have opted for the investment holding company model, trying to make a large number of investments, with a high level of borrowed finance to build their businesses (Cargill & Brown, 1999:48).

The highly leveraged financing formulas adopted have put a premium on rapid profitability. One result has been that the selection of key business activities and the operational and managerial ethos of these firms are seldom distinguishable from those practised by white-controlled companies. The same holds generally for firms controlled by holding companies in which trade union investment companies are prominent stakeholders. Yet, the notion that a different ethos would govern the decisions of black capitalists survives. According to Loyiso Mbabane, director of the Black Economic Empowerment Commission, 'we have to look at who manages us and who does the work of the enterprise. How many of them are blacks?'.[17]

Overall, however, black and white business leaders broadly share a common set of ideological principles – among them the need for austere fiscal policies, lower company taxes, capital account liberalization and a flexible labour market. In his African Life 1998 chairperson's statement, Real Africa group chairman Don Ncube, for example, decried government's alleged lack of commitment to the GEAR strategy and attacked the country's new labour laws.[18] Cyril Ramaphosa has castigated the 'unduly prescriptive' nature of the labour regime, while publisher Thami Mazwai has gone so far as to declaim:

> Unless I am missing something, it is the buyers, the investors, who must say that our labour costs are competitive and not COSATU, the sellers ... Regretfully, if our priority is jobs, we have to accept the going wage. This is the wage workers in other parts of the world will accept. What directors and CEOs earn is for another forum and cannot be part of the debate about what workers earn. Overseas, labour has learnt this the hard way; time we also swallowed the pill.[19]

Also puncturing the anticipation that black capitalists would add to their bottom line a sense of solidarity and duty toward the African poor is the comprador status of many ventures that are being harnessed into consortia by foreign multinationals keen on taking advantage of privatization moves.[20] An analogous point holds for the so-called national *bourgeoisie* in general. Indeed, Nicos Poulantzas was prophetic in detecting (in the 1970s already) the decline of national *bourgeoisies* and in replacing the concept with that of the 'internal *bourgeoisie*' which, in Konstantinos Tsoukalas's elaboration, denotes:

> ... the emerging and thereafter dominant fraction of a domestically operating capital which was already permeated by, and was thus reproducing, 'external' inter-imperialist contradictions ... [I]t is now even more true that the contradictions between fractions of capital within national states are 'internationalised'. As a consequence, the disarticulation and heterogeneity of national *bourgeoisies* is further accentuated. Indeed, it may be doubtful whether the very term corresponds to a specific social reality (1999:57, 60).

Such lines of analysis cast severe doubt on the notion that a national or 'patriotic' *bourgeoisie* can, of its own accord, muster the autonomy required to organize its activities in ways that privilege the needs and demands of domestic subaltern classes. This has nothing to do with the subjective will of individual capitalists, since the national (or, to follow Poulantzas, 'internal') *bourgeoisie*'s subjugated or attenuated role stems from its structural location in the domestic and the international capitalist system. It is therefore deprived of the ability to muster an effective autonomy *vis-á-vis* international capital. Yet, it can have an effect on the relations of the state apparatus of a specific national or domestic formation towards international capital. In the South African context, however, that effect appears to take the form of pressuring for deeper submission to prerogatives expressed in the form of alleged 'international norms'.

The fates of black economic empowerment ventures have not been all happy. By 1997, 28 black-controlled firms listed on the JSE had a market capitalization worth 9,3 per cent of the JSE's total. The figure had doubled within six months.[21] A year later, however, many of the companies succumbed to the depressed economic conditions. By the end of 1999, black control of market capitalization on the JSE had plunged to 6,8 per cent.[22]

That slump is likely to be temporary. Black economic empowerment requirements are now prominent in government tender, procurement and privatization policies. One result is a growing number of authentic and makeshift multiracial business partnerships that are paraded as empowerment ventures. Despite the setbacks suffered since mid-1998, they are expected to regain momentum as more packages of large state-sponsored contracts and licences are finalized, and privatization speeds up. The upshot will be a more intimate nexus between black capitalists and the state, perhaps analogous to the apartheid state's levering of the Afrikaner *bourgeoisie*. Along with the ANC's 'redeployment' of figures into the parastatal and private sectors, this potentially has the makings of a new élite stratum dependent on a network of business/political links. Interestingly, *Who Owns Whom* publisher Robin McGregor has argued that black capitalists need a *broederbond*-type network to propel their ascent more firmly. The possibility that a system of patronage might take root within the discursive ambit of black economic empowerment and the African renaissance cannot be ruled out.

The business-as-usual ethos and élitist nature of such 'upliftment' appears not to be endorsed by many ordinary citizens. Yet, the ideological impact of black economic empowerment is hardly negligible for the promotion of an African capitalist class reflects not only the aspirations of a small would-be élite but also the daydreams of many people. It speaks both to the tiny coterie of individuals able to capitalize on the opportunities created *and* to the private yearnings of millions more.

This is hardly surprising in a society where the ideology of consumer capitalism reigns supreme. Despite the devastation achieved under racial-capitalism, the principal compass points of South African society remain monied prestige and material comfort – a reality as evident in a top ANC politician's blushless defence of the right to 'get filthy rich' as it is in the dogged efforts of ordinary South Africans to participate more fully in consumer society. Publicly denigrated but privately envied, African élite advancement carries strong symbolic meaning. The achievements of a few rekindle the hopes of many more, even if the scale of their success is structurally destined to be minor. In such ways, black economic empowerment aids the nurturing of a collective moral, ethical and economic will in society.

Demonstration effects

The cramped contours of socio-economic change (surveyed in Chapter 6) would seem to encourage discontent. But organized expressions of dissatisfaction have been rare, despite the private grumbling of many. In June 1999, 10,6 million of 18,3 million registered voters cast their ballots for the ANC, handing it 66,3 per cent of the seats in the national assembly.[23] The fact that 1,6 million fewer South Africans voted for the party in 1999 than five years previously could hint at a protest 'stay-away' on election day. But this is not clear. Combined, the opposition parties attracted 2 million fewer votes than in 1994. This suggests that other, more pervasive factors caused the drop-off in voting.

One factor could be the apparent alienation from formal politics felt by youth of voting age, whose turnout on election day in 1999 was considerably lower that that of any other age group. Unlike 1994, voters also had to register for the 1999 vote and, indeed, about 80 per cent did (among the mainstay of ANC support, Africans, 82,5 per cent registered). Whereas upward of 90 per cent of voters 30 years and older registered for the election, only 48 per cent of South Africans aged 18–20 years registered. Among those 20–30 years old, 77 per cent registered (see Levin, 2000). According to Melissa Levin (2000), among youth 'we see signs of the global trend manifesting here in South Africa. Amongst youth, more men vote than women and urban provinces benefit from greater youth participation than rural ones.' Sadly, this phenomenon is poorly researched – so much so that the main polling exercise during the 1999 election campaign ('Opinion 99') glossed over youths' attitudes toward politics and the election. That lack of interest was in line with the generalized lack of interest shown for youth in South Africa in the 1990s.[24] Obscured is a massive challenge for the ANC and other political parties: by 2009, the bedrock of their electoral support will have to be built among successive generations of apparently disaffected youth.

The drop in ANC votes therefore could be attributed to the 17 per cent of African voters who failed to register (often for reasons beyond their control), the bulk of them youth. Significantly, opinion poll data suggested that the more marginalized sections of the African population (such as women, the rural poor and shanty-town residents) were, pro rata, as well represented on the voter's role as the rest of the African population of voting age.[25]

The ANC's election support testified not only to the enduring trust vested in the party but also to its remarkable ability to absorb spleen and deflect disappointment. Three months before the 1999 election, 75 per cent of eligible voters polled in a countrywide survey had listed joblessness as their main concern. A mere 18 per cent had approved of the government's performance in job creation, a 5 per cent drop from a similar poll conducted shortly after the heavily publicized Jobs Summit in 1998. Yet, those sentiments seemed not to register on voting day. This could be attributed to the fact that no viable political alternative appeared on the ballot paper. But that does not account for the fact that an overwhelming number of supposed discontents still bided their time in long queues to cast their votes for the party.

Some of the reasons for this faith have been touched upon. But also at play were the effects of diligent work by government (with the clamorous aid of business and the media) to exonerate its economic policies from the unemployment crisis and the economy's sluggish performance. The global financial crisis has featured prominently as an alibi. So, too, has the dominant reading of globalization as a juggernaut capable of inflicting withering punishment on a government that flirts with 'irresponsible' policies. Thus, the principled calls from grassroots ANC delegates at the 1997 Mafikeng conference for moves to make capital more 'socially accountable' can transmutate into a tractable pragmatism.

Less manifest is the role that ordinary people's lived experiences play in this deflective flourish. For, in their experience, it is not the ANC government that turns them away at factory gates or hands them pink slips with a day's notice,[26] but business – whose interests are not yet associated in the popular consciousness with government policies. In an ironic twist, the residue of a cod class-consciousness fostered during the anti-apartheid struggle today shields the ANC government against resentment at economic policies that manifestly favour capital.[27]

Tilling the turf of approval and consent further is an appreciation for accomplishments that are too often dismissed as insignificant. The failure to alter overriding patterns of inequality is tempered by the fact that millions of South Africans can detect around them evidence of improvements – or, at least, efforts to fulfil promises. Mitigating the anger and disappointment triggered when services are disconnected due to non-payment is the knowledge that, finally, the electricity grid did reach a far-flung village in the Eastern Cape or that the long-demanded water well has been dug. The efforts to direct a limited portion of the surplus to the poor trigger a resounding *demonstration effect* that is amplified by an awareness of the manifold difficulties encountered by a new state apparatus. Embedded in the consciousness of millions of South Africans is the sense that the road to freedom and a better life is neither short nor linear. Like the anti-apartheid struggle itself, it is seen to twist and turn. This is not fatalistic patience at play, but the residue of experiences accumulated through countless personal and collective struggles.

Not surprisingly, that sensibility is consciously affirmed as salvoes are fired at generic 'enemies of change' – corrupt bureaucrats, niggardly opposition parties and shadowy forces intent on wrecking the process of change. Flanking the finger-pointing are fatherly assurances, such as president Thabo Mbeki's remark to ANC supporters during the 1999 election campaign: 'Just because you have four children and can only afford new trousers for two of them this month does not mean you do not love the others.'

Reconciliation with a bite

The loyalty and deference shown toward the ANC government – and the indulgence of the development path it is supervising – therefore cannot be explained away as a 'false consciousness', as a mere hangover from history. Nor can the griping that accompanies it be interpreted as a potential seedbed of radical opposition. To the extent that the trust rests on affinities forged in history, on an awareness of the obstacles confronting the transformation of state apparatuses and on the genuine (though disappointing) evidence of improvements, it is authentic. Importantly, that confidence is not taken for granted but is constantly replenished – through new legislation,[28] public-private partnerships that seem to illustrate the awakening of business to its transformatory duties, praise for corporate assistance for development projects and adroit discursive shifts.

In such ways, a virtual equivalence is maintained between the ANC (and, in a more qualified sense, the post-apartheid state) and the interests of the African majority. The upshot is more than an association of interests with the party. For its supporters, the very fate of the African majority is lodged with the ANC. The result is quasi-mystical: a party that is seen to be larger than its structures and members, and that is entrusted with historic duties. This perspective was fervently nurtured in exile and in the (internal) underground; it has been diligently advanced since.

Yet, the allegiance does not translate automatically into party membership, which overall has dropped steeply since 1994, especially among African voters. A November 1999 HSRC poll found that only 10 per cent of African respondents belonged to a political party (compared to 24 per cent in 1994). The 1999 election turnout suggests that voters are still keen to register their political preferences at the polls, but without being active members of a political party. (Interestingly, membership of a range of civil society organizations remained fairly stable, which contradicts the widely held notion of demobilization in South African civil society since 1994.)[29]

Highlighted by that trend is the need constantly to top up the consent of the African majority. As shown, the dominant discourse since 1994 orbited around supposed common interests and destinies. By 1998, that phase of appeasement appeared to be winding down. In its stead came more hardnosed talk that focused forthrightly on persistent racism and on other divisions that fissure society.

The apparent shift speaks to the realities most Africans encounter in everyday life – where the hand of appeasement is routinely shunned, racism remains rife and privilege is guarded behind haughty indifference. In such a context, an overriding emphasis on reconciliation clashes too obviously with daily experiences and risks inviting alienation. Also, the overt indulgence of the demands of business needs to be balanced.

The result has been an *ambiguous* discursive shift away from appeasement at all costs. Thus, Nelson Mandela would earn cheers when he told parliament in early 1998: 'We cannot continue to imprison ourselves in the paradigm of large profits and only large profits as the driving force of business operations.'[30] So did former Gauteng premier Mathole Motshekga when he aimed barbed words at the black élite: 'Our historic mission is to liberate and develop the nation, not individuals or their pockets.'[31]

A harder line was adopted on affirmative action – not only in state institutions and the workplace, but also on the sports fields. Some business leaders have griped, but others seem to grasp the need to address popular sentiments, in much the same manner as they promoted a political settlement from the late 1980s onwards. The acumen displayed by IDC chair Christo Wiese is telling: 'Unless all South Africans can participate meaningfully in the economic life of the country, we will not be able to sustain a market-oriented political philosophy.'[32] In similar vein, the business press routinely praises government's economic policies and pleads for understanding of the popular pressures that weigh on the state.

President Thabo Mbeki (who succeeded Nelson Mandela in June 1999) has proved most astute at this discourse. In speeches, he smartly combines stirring attacks on racism with remonstrations against whites for refusing to voluntarily make sacrifices that could promote greater equity and reconciliation, and against the 'seemingly insatiable and morally unbound greed' of the black élite. 'Those responsible for or who were beneficiaries of the past absolve themselves of any obligation to do away with an unacceptable legacy ... We are not one nation, but two nations, and neither are we becoming one nation', he told parliamentarians in June 1998, elaborating on a speech a month earlier.[33]

Such themes have become the hallmark of government pronouncements, though few politicians have matched Mbeki's ability to tailor the same rebukes for different audiences. The speeches referred to above were a good example. To the African poor, they declared the ANC government's unflinching empathy with their plight. To white South Africans, they warned that the indulgence of their privilege and indifference could not continue unless some form of reciprocation was mustered. To the socialist left, they declared that the party's allegedly radical instincts were intact and would not be kept in abeyance for too long.

Not lost on leftists was the telegraphed nod to Marxist rudiments (in this case the base/superstructure model) when Mbeki concluded his June 1998 address with the comment that 'we must accept it will take time to create the material base for nation-building and reconciliation'.[34] The timing of that remark was not accidental, for it coincided with the drafting of a highly critical SACP discussion document that cautioned against stabilizing society around a non-racial ruling élite. This was 'likely to prove unstable and unsustainable', the authors wrote. 'In practice, it amounts to a 30 per cent-70 per cent solution – an attempt to overcome the present post-apartheid crisis by stabilising a new capitalist order around about 30 per cent of the population, while the great majority remain marginal in a "flexible", "unregulated" and substantially "right-less" second tier ... This path towards "national democratic" transformation is unjust and unworkable.' Weeks later, Mbeki proceeded to whip the SACP back into line.

Prominent, too, is an emphasis on notions of loyalty and patriotism, contrasted with those of betrayal and deviance. The subtext is a noxious affirmation that 'if you are not with us, you are against us'. The tone is populist, with invective directed at a gallery of targets: 'undisciplined' teachers, corrupt bureaucrats and businesspeople, élitist black business ventures and motley 'sinister' forces bent on scuttling the democratic revolution. Also at the receiving end are leftist critics, whose analyses and complaints are seen to be 'driven by a psychosis which dictates that a message of failure and pessimism must necessarily be communicated, overriding the nuisance of facts' (Mbeki, 1998b). Thus established are the terms both for inclusion into the fold, and for the indulgence of differences.[35]

But those terms remain flexible enough to suggest that the shift away from reconciliation and appeasement is neither inexorable nor entirely emphatic. No major capitalist organization has been made to endure the vitriol directed at the organized left. Instead, economic policies rank among the most profound gestures of appeasement made since 1994. There is little sign that this 'hand of peace' will be withdrawn in the near future. On the political front, the deepening *rapprochement* between the ANC and the IFP tells a similar story.

Bonds of race and identity
In society broadly, the discourse of reconciliation has succeeded in fostering consent and sapping resistance. There is little current evidence that its overhauled, more ambiguous format will not build on those accomplishments. But inside the ANC itself, the ideological basis for camaraderie also has required an overhaul. With the unifying impetus of the anti-apartheid struggle flagging, a new 'language' of unity was needed – one that could resonate among the different layers and interest groups that constitute the party's constituencies. Metaphorically, one can think of it as a canopy of values, avowals and ideals under which fellowship and trust is cultivated. To be effective as a bonding agent, the discourse has to 'speak' to the lived realities of individuals in ways that highlight what is potentially common and shared.

The attacks on racism and the accent on affirmative action have prompted some commentators to suggest that this new ideological glue has taken the form of a more chauvinist 'Africanist' discourse. That reading seems premature. An eventual recourse towards a jingoist 'Africanism' cannot be ruled out. But it should not be confused with explicit and necessary assaults on racial inequality and racism.

Instead, the ANC since 1996–7 has been refashioning a discourse of belonging and community by *updating* the African-nationalism variant prominent in the late 1940s and early 1950s. It is *vintage* in the sense that it establishes perimeters of inclusion and exclusion that are not strictly racial, while at the same time pivoting on the interests of the African majority. Also vintage is the attempt to locate it within the idea of pan-African destiny and solidarity. It is *updated* in the sense that it seeks to align a model of inclusive nationalism to the exigencies of a racially divided society and of the global capitalist order. In other words, it has to be flexible enough to accommodate prerogatives and interests that are out of joint with those of the African poor.

This task has been undertaken most strikingly under the banner of an African renaissance, which has acquired a potent *ideological function* inside South Africa. Trading on, and evoking powerful yet ambiguous notions of identity and belonging, it has all but replaced the dissolving epoxy of anti-apartheid ideology. Its emotional force was startlingly clear in reactions to Thabo Mbeki's 1996 'I am an African' speech to parliament. Its most obvious register is the re-awakening and fortification of what one might term an African-populist compound of nostalgia, lived experiences, romanticism, pride and hope. In so doing, it locally also provides a renewed basis for consolidating loyalty, trust and solidarity.

It exerts formidable appeal for South Africans who share histories – and current realities – of racial oppression and denigration. At the same time, the circle of inclusion drawn is tensile, offering entry to others as well. It offers a pliant ideological framework for inclusion and tolerance but at the same time contains a basis for censure and exclusion. None of this should suggest that the African renaissance is a kind of shadow play. The quest to unleash a continental revival is indisputably earnest and necessary. But *inside South Africa* it also performs a potent function – nurturing a basis for belonging and support.

The ideological function of the African renaissance

Coursing prominently through local African renaissance thought is a tension between two perspectives. In academics Peter Vale and Sipho Maseko's reading, the first can be defined as 'globalist'. Here, South Africa's economic interests are linked 'to Africa through the register provided by the meta-narrative of globalization with its seemingly endless vistas, shrinking horizons and economistic logic'. The second can be called 'Africanist', in that it seeks 'to unlock complex social constructions around African identity'[36] and tap into indigenous popular practices, 'the capacity for innovation, reinvention of traditions and resurgence of native skills' (Ela, 1998).

It hinges, in other words, on two highly dissimilar notions of modernity: the dominant, Western version (expressed in development and economic theories that arose from 'a pattern of social change peculiar to the specific paths taken by Western societies') and an embattled African variant (in which the co-operative spirit and 'the principle of reciprocity underpins economic ties within the mesh of social relationships') (Ela, 1998).

Rather than undermine the African renaissance's allure in the South African context, that contradiction lends elasticity. Lodged in a distinctive compilation of Afrocentric histories, identities, practices and realities, the discourse at the same time is explicitly welcoming to white domestic capital. The latter's role is not merely invited, but demanded: to establish South Africa as the 'anchor' for a 'chain of economies which, with time, might

become the African equivalent of the Asian Tigers ... through the development of trade, strategic partnerships and the like'.[37] This is not 'inclusion'
borne merely of convenience. White capital is assigned an integral role in
the revival not just of South Africa, but of an entire continent. It is a far
cry from the status of 'necessary evil' many had anticipated in a post-
apartheid order. Reciprocating, capital has embraced the African renaissance with relish.[38]

Mbeki can announce that Africa 'must be in the forefront of challenging
the notion of "the market" as the modern god',[39] but the template of the
African renaissance version popularized in South Africa remains that of a
modulated, friendlier version of globalized capitalism. It is within that
frame that a former communications minister could declare that he wants
'to wire Africa' by extending the IT revolution across the continent.
Likewise, it allows the Engen petroleum corporation to sponsor African
renaissance conferences and declare its intention 'to link the splendours of
Africa through a continuous network of Afrika-tourism routes from the
Cape to Cairo – a route colonialists failed to achieve, but which is within
our grasp' (Lodge, 1999a:98).

Corporate South Africa has proved equally accepting of other, more
authentically 'African' concepts that are woven into the African renaissance. *Ubuntu* is one of them. Essentially, an ethos of reciprocity and
mutual aid, it centres on the idea that people realize themselves through
others. Motivational speakers and consultants, corporate human resource
planners and advertising agencies eagerly assimilate the concept into their
attempts to help modernize and revitalize South African capitalism. The
African renaissance vision is eminently hospitable to such opportunism.

Alongside these supple notions of Africanism operates another with more
exacting entry requirements: a racially defined Africanism. It exudes strong
appeal in a society mutilated by white racism – thereby helping to envelop diffuse (and increasingly contradictory) specificities under the dome of a nominal but, in the South African case, heartfelt commonality: race. It is within
this narrower perspective that the ANC can court a former enemy which, a
decade ago, it had sought to eliminate from the political stage. Although
veiled by references to a shared rejection of apartheid, the basis of attraction
is plain in Mbeki's speech to the IFP's 1998 annual general conference:

> [W]e who were killing one another are brothers and sisters. Together we suf-
> fered under the yoke of apartheid oppression and together we shared one
> vision, the liberation of our country and our people ... for almost a century
> now, certain common things stood undisputed in this relationship,
> *njengezingelengele zoKhahlamba nemihosha yoThukela* (like the cliffs of the
> Drakensberg and the kloofs of the Tugela). These are things that stand
> durable and fundamental.[40]

It is in this sense that Vale and Maseko also describe the African renaissance as a mobilizing instrument, 'a double-edged agreement, as it were, which commits the South African state to democratic accord with its own people'.[41] Highly flexible without sacrificing its more concentrated and specific appeal, it manages to nod in numerous directions at once. Both its hegemonic function and its class character become overt. In the exposition of Vusi Mavimbela (a former adviser to Mbeki), for example, the success of an African renaissance depends on:

> ... a new proletariat ... emerging and unionised into new forms of trade unions ... the unbridled flourishing of countless small and medium-sized firms that promise to produce a strong propertied class ... an emerging large urban middle class comprised of the unionised workers, teachers, intellectuals, nurses, traders, artisans, civil servants, and so on ... This section of the middle class should also assume an entrepreneurial role, and become a crucial component of economic democratisation and sustainable economic growth. This middle class should also be understood and be seen as the driving force of civil society.[42]

Noteworthy is another contradiction. The pursuit of a common continental destiny is made to pivot on notions of South African *exceptionalism*. This is not simply a matter of pinpointing a vanguard catalyst. Made to stand at the heart of a project anchored in re-asserted affinities, commonalities and shared interests is a phenomenon (post-1994 South Africa) that is quite deliberately and explicitly counterposed to the rest of the continent. Alert to this dynamic, Ugandan academic Mahmood Mamdani has asked mischievously: 'When did the "African renaissance" begin? Was it in 1994 or earlier? It is a turnkey South African export to the rest of Africa?'[43] Indeed, the local ideological force of the African renaissance seems tied also to South Africa's desire to project itself as the first among equals on the continent. In one newspaper columnist's lordly mix of sporting and biblical metaphors:

> Africa screams for a brave African nation to step on to the plate [sic] and lead the continent out of the abyss. South Africa with its economic and political clout is the only country with the ability and the moral capacity capable of doing this.[44]

Whatever the merits of such claims, they harmonize with the South African self-image of distinctiveness and superiority *vis-à-vis* the rest of the continent – thereby resonating with the pervasive sense of *differentness* and superiority frequently encountered and remarked upon by visiting foreigners. Buried in that sensibility is one of the distinctive features of post-apartheid South Africa and contradictions in African renaissance discourse: virulent xenophobia towards Africans from elsewhere on the continent, an attitude fuelled by some government figures.[45] Heaped onto their shoulders is the blame for most of the country's ills – its high unemployment rate, rising crime, the proliferation of hard drugs on city streets, the spread of HIV/AIDS and even the low wages paid by small firms. No longer able to blame the apartheid government for their hardships, South Africa's poor have turned black foreigners into a convenient target for their frustrations. Indeed, xenophobia functions morbidly as another bonding agent among the poor. It also means that blame is deflected away from business and government – other Africans serve as scapegoats for travails in which they have no hand. By and large, government has chosen not to challenge those sensibilities. In some instances, on the contrary, it actively promotes them. Thus, 'anti-crime' sweeps decreed by the safety and security ministry point-edly target 'illegal immigrants' from elsewhere in Africa. Indeed, 80 per cent of the 'criminals' netted in such sweeps in early 2000 were 'illegal immigrants', with media reports casually conflating the two categories. According to the Southern African Migration Project, most 'immigrants' are in fact migrants who enter the country frequently and legally, and who are well-educated (two-thirds have tertiary education). Few intend settling in the country. Numerous studies have shown that they, in fact, are net creators of jobs in the informal sector. Yet, in 1999, government launched a 'get tough' policy against them – a stance that is not at odds with the African renaissance discourse. Again, the suppleness of that thinking is striking: it offers a basis for inclusion, while at the same time shoring up notions of difference and distinctiveness.

Taken together, the ideological elements scanned in the previous sections tap into and reshape what Gramsci called 'common sense' and which Hall has described as:

> ... the terrain of conceptions and categories on which the practical consciousness of the masses of the people is actually formed. It is already the formed and 'taken-for-granted' terrain, on which more coherent ideologies and philosophies must contend for mastery; the ground which new conceptions of the world must take into account, contest and transform, if they are to shape the conceptions of the world of the masses and in that way become historically effective (1996:431).

Battening down the hatches

Finally, it is necessary to examine what one might call more 'literal' or 'disciplinary' mechanisms for marshalling consent and discouraging organized dissent in two zones especially: the ruling party and government.

South Africa's system of proportional representation militates against the abilities of individual politicians to build and defend careers based on popular constituency support. The sentiments of residents of a specific area have a minor bearing on the political fates of members of parliament, for instance, since those politicians are only nominally linked to particular geographical constituencies.[45] Their careers rest largely in the hands of party leaders who assign places on the party's election lists.[46] That power is tempered by more democratic balloting at ANC national and provincial conferences. But there, too, careers depend on support mustered inside ANC structures. Even then, that support can come to nought.[47] The centralized pathways of power and accountability are reinforced by a constitutional clause that deprives a parliamentarian of her seat if she abandons her party.

The result is a party where the threat of penalty, the prospect of promotion or the very survival of a political career is determined much less by popular support than by the imprimatur of party leadership.[48] Democratic processes inside the party (and the political system in general) therefore fit into a matrix of rules and powers that sets stern limits on dissidence and nonconformity. The resulting, disciplined loyalty is largely self-administered; the wages of transgression are known to all, as a 1997 episode during an ANC caucus meeting illustrated:

> [ANC MP] Barbara Hogan kept prefacing her remarks with the phrase that she 'did not want to cause any trouble'. To his credit, Mbeki intervened and said he was worried that she felt it necessary to say this. Was there, he asked, a more general feeling that the ANC leadership did not welcome dissent? 'Yes-s-s,' the MPs whispered in chorus (Lodge, 1996:117).

Only in rare cases, in fact, is outright action by the *apparat* required to discourage 'delinquency'. When that happens, as Bantu Holomisa discovered, votes netted at an ANC national conference count for little. The former head of the Transkei homeland and, later, deputy minister of environmental affairs, was expelled from the party in 1995 – despite having been one of the five most popular ANC figures in balloting at the party's 1994 national conference.

This phenomenon harks back to organizational traditions and styles that, perforce, characterized the ANC in exile and in the underground struggle. Then, too, it did not rest on naked coercion: activists understood discipline and obedience as necessary conditions for the survival and triumph of the ANC during the struggle decades. Those sensibilities remain strong. The ANC is seen as larger than the sum of its parts – a mindset that explains the servile manner in which most censured figures accept their fates.[49]

Announced in early 2000 were plans to run an even tighter ship, by transforming the ANC into a trim election machine, drastically scaling back its head office and radically reducing the number of ANC branches. The party's policy desks would be merged into a trim think-tank that would co-ordinate policy formation. According to press reports, Thabo Mbeki 'wants to "wind down" the organization between elections and "wind it up" again ahead of them ... Mbeki and his team believe a much smaller, less bureaucratic party would make and implement policies faster'.[50]

The parameters of obedience are flexible; space for criticism and hetero-doxy is shaped by intra-party dynamics in the ANC. But vested, in the final instance, with party leadership are powers that engender self-enforced dis-cipline and compliance, and that militate against the emergence of open, organized blocs and platforms that can promote specific interests. Formidable degrees of consent, loyalty and unity are the outcome. Potential centrifugal dynamics are restrained. The party achieves greater internal stability and control, while the leadership at the same time acquires consid-erable latitude for policy shifts. The result is a party that, at once, seems rooted in a codex of principles and traditions but is also capable of remark-able manoeuvrability.

Efficiency and order

The capacity for agility and control has been replicated in the executive, which was restructured smartly in 1999. Ostensibly, the aim is to enable better co-ordination so as to achieve economic growth, job creation, social development and security – that it to say, it is guided by the twin beacons of efficiency and order, goals commonly compressed into the phrase 'good governance'.[51]

Grandly expanded are the powers and size of the presidency. Its staff complement has been boosted to 334, thanks in part to its absorption of the deputy presidency. The president's director-general, Frank Chikane, has emerged as a key figure at Mbeki's side. Acting as *the* gatekeeper in the president's office, Chikane is also secretary to the cabinet and doubles as director-general to deputy president, Jacob Zuma. The latter's position, meanwhile, has been reduced to largely titular status. His brief is to 'fulfil tasks delegated by the president' and act as leader of government business in parliament. Seemingly more weighty is his role as head of a new ANC 'deployment committee'. That body is tasked with:

> ... vetting election lists and 'deploying' anointed members into provincial political roles and government departments, as well as into statutory bodies, parastatal firms and private sector companies. The committee operates under the aegis of the ANC's national working committee, which Mbeki successfully loaded with loyalists in 1998.[52]

Also created immediately after the 1999 elections was a new cabinet portfo-lio, that of 'minister in the office of the president', with the post assigned to one of Mbeki's most loyal lieutenants, Essop Pahad.[53] As the president's right-hand man, he performs multiple tasks:

> ... office manager, political adviser, go-between and fixer. When Mbeki wants to avoid saying something that may have a negative backlash, Pahad will make the statement and take the flak ... He is also responsible for liaison

with the ANC and its alliance partners, as well as [with] opposition parties (Jacobs, 1999:6).

Among the main – and provident – changes effected is the 'clustering' of government departments in order to co-ordinate policies and activities more efficiently. Six clusters, each with its own cabinet committee, have been set up. They group ministries and departments into six sectors: economic, investment and employment, governance and administration, social, crime prevention and integrated justice, and international relations.[54] Interestingly, only the intelligence ministry has not been 'clustered', although it seems to fit in both the latter two categories. The ministerial cluster committees are shadowed by a five-unit policy co-ordination and advisory services arm that vets new policy and drafts legislation before it is tabled at cabinet meetings.

Steeling the president's hand in policy-making further is another gatekeeping structure, the policy co-ordination and advisory services unit (PCAS). Based in the president's office and reporting to him, the unit splits into five chief directorates. In one analysis, the chief directors:

> ... have power at least equal to that wielded by ministers. While each minister has control over a single portfolio, each chief director is responsible for a cluster of ministries ... The likely outcome is that the PCAS will take the decisions behind-the-scenes, while ministers will sell PCAS policy to the public.[55]

Once a department drafts a policy, the line-function minister no longer submits it directly to the cabinet. It first goes to this unit, which advises the presidency on its feasibility and desirability. If it fails the test, the minister and his or her department are back at the drawing board. Only after the approval of the president's office has been won does it cross the path of the cabinet. Greatly boosted, as a result, is the president's power to monitor, fine-tune or veto government policies. Unlike cabinet ministers, the chief directors of the advisory unit are not accountable to parliament. No portfolio committee can summon them to explain decisions. They report to the president.

Among other striking changes has been the restructuring of the cabinet secretariat. In the past, a secretarial adjunct of the cabinet, its powers stand considerably magnified. It now functions as a co-ordinating body inside the president's office and is equipped with two arms. One handles administrative matters, the other vets policy initiatives.

The overall advantage is that new policies and draft legislation pass beneath the eyes of experts who can detect flaws, conflicts with existing laws or contradictions with other policies. At face value, too, the arrangements could prime robust debate as ministers square off against presidential bureaucrats. But the distribution of power within government means that ministers more often will decide that discretion is the better part of valour.

The upshot is that, for example, a labour ministry that proposes minor revisions to labour policies first has to ensure their survival in an opaque zone of concentrated power before being able to submit them to relatively open debate in cabinet. Even then, the ministry has to contend with a seldom-noted feature of the governmental balance of power. All ministries have to jockey for influence on the basis of their performances, their relations with the presidency and their ability to sway opinion in the cabinet – with one, sterling exception, the finance ministry.

The finance ministry is alone in its ability to fortify its authority primarily outside government, by invoking the reactions of the market to its policies. Thus, in the context of the broader economic-ideological context sketched in previous chapters, it has emerged as a super-ministry. A higher investment or credit rating from Standard & Poor, a pointedly supportive remark by an IMF chief or a bull-run on the JSE – these 'extraneous' factors dramatically boost the ministry's weight in policy jousting inside government. For this reason it seems less than accurate to attribute the finance ministry's ability to persist in unpopular and poorly performing economic policies *strictly* to the support of the presidency, since it is the only ministry capable of reproducing its power outside of government. Meanwhile, the influence of other ministries (and departments) is profoundly mediated through the president's office.

The president has also strengthened his influence over directors-general. In terms of legislation passed before the 1999 election, all newly appointed directors-general now sign their contracts with the president (before, contracts were signed with line-function ministers). The terms of those contracts have been adapted to the results-oriented and performance-based principles of managerialism.[56]

Also augmented is the power of central government in relation to the provinces. A compelling case can be made for this shift. Provincial audit reports released in 1997 gave only two provinces (Gauteng and Western Cape) relatively clean bills of health but warned that several others were on the verge of institutional collapse. So damning were the findings that a cabinet committee initially tried to prevent publication of the reports. Public service director-general Paseka Ncholo later suggested that the entire system of provincial government might have to be revised: 'From an administrative point of view the system is expensive, chaotic and unafford-able.'[57] The remedy chosen has been to create a more hands-on role for national government in provincial administrations.[58]

While this could address some technical difficulties, the political implications appear less salutary – prompting some analysts to suggest that provincial powers should be extended, not pruned. Provincial administrations' latitude for decision-making is tightly limited in the fields of health, educa-tion, welfare and safety and security. Provincial legislatures' scope for deci-sion-making is also narrow. Politically, in policy analyst Steve Friedman's view, provinces already are reduced 'to conveyor belts for the centre'. The current system:

> ... burden[s] provincial legislatures with tasks they cannot perform – such as speedily analysing complicated technical Bills – but assign them no real powers .... [T]he provinces will not work as long as they are representative bodies at election time, but turn into unhappy and inept foot soldiers of the centre the moment they are in office (1999:46).

In an electoral system based on proportional representation, the provinces potentially play an important role in replenishing faith and involvement in formal politics by serving as a less remote tier of elected government. It is at this level that a diversity of interests can be expressed more forthrightly within and around a ruling party. Provinces could also boost opportunities for citizens' groups to influence govern-ment policies and conduct – a 'luxury' few are able to exercise in rela-tion to national government.

By using the yardsticks of efficiency, smoother co-ordination and improved service delivery, sound arguments can be made for each of these adjustments. Also, the re-organization of power was not concocted in the presidency. Rather, it followed closely the recommendations of a public commission of inquiry into the operation of the presidency (the presidential review commission). Its final report pinpointed a need to overhaul poor policy formulation and decision-making systems in the cabinet. Lacking, it found, was adequate co-ordination between across national departments and between them and their provincial counterparts. Chief among its rec-ommendations was converting the presidency into 'the core of the system of governance' – a move that would follow a world-wide trend toward the cen-tralization of power, it claimed. In Essop Pahad's words:

> What we are seeking to develop in [South Africa] is not an imperial but an effective presidency. The measure of the success achieved is the carping that goes on on the sidelines. The burden of much of the criticism is that the presidency is too centralised and, apparently, both hands-on and remote at the same time. At least the implicit recognition that [South Africa] *has a firm hand at the top, rather than one allowing drift and confusion*, surely augurs well for the country's future.[59]

None of this, though, alters the insidious character of the re-organization of power, in the sense that it harbours potentially harmful consequences. Most obvious is the resemblance to 'delegative democracies' – hybrid political systems 'characterised both by the existence of formal representative structures and the concentration of power in the executive'.[60] Equally visible is the risk of a trade-off between efficiency and order, on the one hand, and authentic democratic participation and accountability, on the other. But by situating these adjustments on the terrain of hegemonic struggle, their wider utility can also be observed.

That the centralization of power helps ensure discipline and loyalty in the top tiers of the ANC, government and the state is clear. But it also boosts the technical ability to dispense gains more broadly across society within a constrained fiscal context. Government's fiscal policy does not allow room for much slippage and wastage on the social delivery front, especially when the budgets of social service departments are cut. At the same time, a demonstrable improvement in the levels and quality of benefits reaching the majority of citizens is essential for sustaining and extending popular consent. More cost-effective and efficient social service delivery meanwhile make it possible to offer tax cuts to higher-income earners without violating fiscal strictures, thus spreading state largesse across wider sections of the social surface.

Good governance

These moves sit squarely in the paradigm of good governance which, first and foremost, speaks of efficiency, enterprise and rectitude. It demands sound and robust systems, institutional harmony, oversight mechanisms and transparency. The desired outcomes include boosted co-ordination, streamlined policy-making and the ability to mount forthright corrective actions swiftly and smoothly.

Yet, the fit between good and *democratic* governance is not seamless. At the core of good governance formulas one discovers the value-free world of managerial 'science', gilded expertise and systems logics. It is structured around the sanctity of efficiency and order, and centres, as Neil Postman wrote in his book *Technopoly* (1993), on the belief:

> ... that the primary, if not the only, goal of human labor and thought is efficiency; that technical calculation is in all respects superior to human judgment; that in fact human judgment cannot be trusted, because it is plagued by laxity, ambiguity, and unnecessary complexity that subjectivity is an obstacle to clear thinking; that what cannot be measured either does not exist or is of no value; and that the affairs of citizens are best guided and conducted by experts.

That description is not tantamount to dismissal. The need for sound institutions, limpid plans and reliable systems is self-evident. But that commitment can allow important questions to go begging: how integral is popular accountability and participation to good governance, and is the public its subject or its object? In other words, how comprehensive – and 'automatic'

– is the overlap between good and democratic governance? For, once it is extended beyond formalities, democracy:

> ... pulses with caprice, ambiguity, unruly demands and objections – with the unexpected. If authentic, it tends to complicate the certitude and glacial logic of technocratic systems. Its ducks simply don't march in rows.[61]

Good and democratic governance are not synonyms, nor do they automatically conflate. The fit can be rough and unsettling. The national budget is an example. Clearly required is a framework that heeds certain principles of efficient economic management and that slots into an economic (and, ultimately a development) strategy. At face value, the process is not only technical but highly technocratic. Yet, every national budget is also an acutely political deed. It functions as a key instrument in the political management of society. Technocratic procedure then serves as a *vehicle* for a highly politicized exercise that involves making economic and political calculations and translating them into specific budgetary decisions.

All this occurs in rarefied and insulated settings where, supposedly, the requirements of good governance are best met. Democratic participation in the drafting of the budget is replaced with a *nominally* democratic process after the fact – in the form of perfunctory budget votes in parliament. Even when that process generates opposition and contestation, it is at best (or worst) reactive and disruptive. It does not shift to parliament the power to shape the economic, political and social logic of the budget. The imperatives of good governance appear to have been answered – but at the expense of democratic governance.

The fact that this occurs in a democratic system does not alter the judgement. A handful of elected political representatives will have participated in drafting the budget – along with bands of departmental unelected advisers and appointees – but the *process* is undemocratic, even within the paradigm of parliamentary democracy. Hence, COSATU and other progressive organizations' long-standing demand for democratic reforms to budget-making. Writ large in those calls is an awareness that 'good' does not necessarily equal 'democratic'. Good governance is an essential aspect of an efficient and equitable form of social management. But, indubitably, so is democratic governance.

Prospects of an alternative project

Couched in the frame of hegemonic struggle, the preceding sections aid a clearer understanding of the forlorn status of a popular challenge mounted under the stewardship of the traditional organizations of the left.

It is no accident that the 'rudiments of an alternative' growth path outlined in the previous chapter contain elements that answer to the description 'state-led Keynesianism'. This is not to dismiss the serious doubts that cloud the medium- to long-term feasibility of a Keynesian economic strategy in the current era of globalization. Yet, in a society that condemns so many of its citizens to wretchedness, some such instruments still have a role *as part of a workable alternative*. They do not constitute the sum total of an alternative.

Accompanying them will have to be strategies that shift informal economic activities away from their desperate, survivalist form and their status as sweat-shop adjuncts of the formal sector. The informal sector is here to stay. But it should not fulfil a netherwordly function in the restructured division of labour. Linked is the need for radical steps toward worker ownership and control of enterprises, the democratization of the workplace and moves toward forms of autonomous self-management. The scale of those innovations initially would be small. For the foreseeable future, they would not define the overall system. They would represent components of an economy that operates mainly according to market *mechanisms* but that comes to contain (hopefully growing) pockets of economic activities that defy market *logic*.

These are tall orders, which the South African left demonstrably has failed to deliver. Save for the realm of the labour market, at best it can claim to have inflected a feeble trickle-down growth strategy with faint progressive features.

Yet, large portions of the left for decades have occupied key positions in the ANC. The SACP has been bonded symbiotically to the ANC since the early 1950s; virtually its entire membership also belongs to the ANC. Its officials and cadres occupy top positions in government structures at national, provincial and local council levels (including seven cabinet minister posts). COSATU, meanwhile, officially joined what became the tripartite alliance in the early 1990s, after having declared its allegiance to the ANC in the late 1980s. More than a dozen former labour leaders sit in parliament, while many more have prime positions in provincial governments. They were self-consciously 'deployed' to carry workers' struggles into government.

Venting disappointment or anger, strictly at the ANC government compounds the question few South African leftists have confronted with rigour. How is it that a liberation organization stoutly linked to a socialist trade union federation and in many ways shaped by a long and intimate relationship with a communist party could so rapidly and resolutely adopt the practices and implement policies of right-wing social democracy? The next sections try to examine the left's failure to definitively influence the post-apartheid development path.

The gravity field of national liberation

The main organizations of the left remain caught in the gravity field of national liberation, which still matches some of the conceptions associated with the Bandung era.[62] Indeed, the strategies of the ANC-in-power represent a fascinating mix of the 'old' and the 'new'. Its modernizing thrust has been touched upon and is examined more closely below. But equally striking are the ways in which it applies principles and practices associated with *traditional* national liberation movements in service of a *modernizing* agenda.

One of those practices was the unequal relationship established between victorious liberation organizations and other (relatively) autonomous popular organizations – with the energies and resources of the latter harnessed and directed by the former. The post-war era presented a legion of examples where liberation movements assumed a leading and directive role in relation to the popular sector. The central, guiding principle was the notion that the transformation process, in Samir Amin's summary, 'does not involve popular initiative as a starting point but simply popular support for state actions'.[63]

Related was the fixation on state power, with the state understood not in Gramscian terms,[64] but as a potential fortress of unadulterated power.[65] That perspective militated against the need for an authentic plurality of forces that could become allied in struggle without surrendering their autonomy or their ability to act in the interests of their respective constituencies. Instead, it relegated those forces to the status of instruments, tools whose utility resided in the role they could assume in the quest for state power. Those that resisted this instrumentalization were denounced as 'reformist' or, worse, 'objectively collaborationist'.

Within a discourse that all but equated the masses with the main liberation organization (and it, eventually, with a new, liberated state), the steps at first seemed quite acceptable, if not outright fortuitous. As experiences elsewhere remind, as long as a successful liberation movement could retain and extend hegemony after decolonization or democratization, the costs seemed modest: the draining of progressive civil society and the weakening of authentically independent organizations. Once that movement's hegemony waned, however, the inclination and ability to resort to new forms of authoritarianism grew, as many post-colonial societies discovered.

In South Africa, the outcome has been much less extreme, yet profound. In 1990–1, the ANC moved to absorb (and, in some cases, dismantle) anti-apartheid organizations that had emerged organically inside South Africa during the 1980s:

> This was notably the case in the women's and youth movements where there had been strong grassroots organisations with their own distinct and diverse agendas, but which were folded into the ANC and then turned almost overnight into vehicles for mobilising their constituencies for the political agendas set at the centre (Connell, 1995).

All of them had been at least fellow travellers and, in most cases, active allies of the exiled ANC. But many had evolved not as internal adjuncts of the 'government-in-waiting', but out of grassroots and interest-based struggles waged by women, youth, students, black professionals, rural peasants and *petit bourgeois* groupings. The process met with some resistance at grassroots level, but on the whole occurred consensually. At play was what Jeremy Cronin has called a 'B-team mentality', which viewed the internal movement as a temporary substitute for the exiled ANC. Needless to say, it was also in the ANC that career paths beckoned tantalizingly and where political ambitions seemed most likely to be satisfied.

But such self-interest could not explain the high degrees of consent that accompanied the moves. That dated back to one of the ANC's most remarkable feats: the authority it had achieved over much of the internal popular movement by the late 1980s. Among the several factors that produced this situation, one deserves special mention.

The ANC had become adept at a key aspect of any hegemonic project: it managed to deploy an array of ideological precepts and symbols, and assert their pertinence to the lived realities of millions of South Africans. The Freedom Charter was resurrected and popularized as *the* programme for change; the liberation struggle was personified in the form of Nelson Mandela; the colours, flags, songs and slogans of the ANC became ubiquitous features of resistance activities. The idea of 'the people' was 'turned into a formalism whose singular consciousness was homogenized by the movement which spoke in its name', while a 'plurality of opinions' was 'negated by the singular notion of public opinion', as Robert Fine noted (1992:80). The armed struggle, too, functioned impressively in this process. Although armed attacks multiplied in the 1980s,[66] their efficacy lay less at the level of military strategy than as cathartic, galvanizing signifiers of resistance and as a symbolic refutal of the apartheid system's alleged invincibility. Overall, the ideological field through which millions of citizens experienced reality was dramatically altered. In short, the ANC, by the late 1980s, had succeeded in extending its authority across the broad popular movement.

The effect has not been wholly debilitating. A rich variety of organizations have survived (even if the terms of their survival are not entirely hearty). This is a reflection of the scope and depth of progressive civil society that had evolved in the dual context of a country that had reached a semi-industrialized stage by the early 1970s and where discontent and activism tended to mature into a variety of organized (anti-apartheid) formations.

The trade union movement did not succumb to absorption. Yet, its strongest organizations – those affiliated to COSATU – had since the mid-1980s entered the political and ideological force field of the ANC. In 1994, they went further – releasing top leaders to take up seats in parliament as ANC members and dispatching hundreds more into provincial and local government structures. The hope was that those emissaries would advance workers' interests from their new vantage points. That anticipation soon wilted, as party discipline compelled them to toe the ANC line or risk losing their seats. Tightening the grip of party discipline was the constitutional clause that prevents expelled party members from retaining their seats as independents. COSATU's Trojan horse in the ANC turned out to be little more than a pack animal for the ruling party.[67]

The SACP, meanwhile, is even more emphatically drawn into the gravity field. In fact, since the late 1920s it has understood its role along in such terms. The reasoning traces back to the SACP's so-called 'Native Republic' policy[68] of the 1920s, the related 'two-stage theory' (first winning and consolidating national liberation, then the struggle for socialism) and the colonialism of a special type (CST) thesis. It rests on deep theoretical foundations that remain shielded from earnest critique and re-evaluation.

Colonialism of a special type

The SACP in the mid-1990s declared the need to 'build socialism now' – in effect, putting to rest the 'two-stage theory'.[69] In late 1997, an alliance summit meeting affirmed the view that 'the present national democratic revolution struggle is not a mere platform, it is inherently valuable, and its core values will be integral to the kind of socialism both the SACP and COSATU hope to see'.[70] But that quest continues to occur under the *stewardship* of the ANC, an approach theoretically inscribed in the CST thesis.

In 1962, the SACP indigenized the 'two-stage theory' by defining the South African situation as CST:

> On one level, that of 'White South Africa', there are all the features of an advanced capitalist state in its final stage of imperialism ... But on another level, that of 'Non-White South Africa', there are all the features of a colony ... It is this combination of the worst features both of imperialism and colonialism, within a single national frontier, which determines the special character of the South African system (SACP, 1962:129).

The late Harold Wolpe noted that CST 'purports to rest on class relations of capitalist exploitation [but] in fact treats such relations as residual', according them 'little or no role in the analysis of relations of dominance and exploitation, which are instead, conceived as occurring between "racial", "ethnic" and "national" categories'.[71] Later, he would question whether 'the contention within the internal colonialism thesis that racial domination serves to bind the classes within each group to a common struggle'.[72]

But the CST theory in fact was a 'self-consciously pragmatic' effort to devise an 'ideological midpoint at which both nationalists and communists could meet' (Everatt, 1991). It served as the theoretical platform for the ANC/SACP alliance and, although appearing to reconcile the tension between national and class struggle, it asserted the imperative of the former, with the latter relegated to an ancillary role. Indeed, it is in the CST theory that one finds embedded the strongest roots of the ANC's dominion over the traditional left.

The decision to struggle under the mantle of African nationalism and within a multi-class ANC was not foolhardy. It created a basis for mobilizing disparate social actors into an encompassing front that eventually helped produce the deadlock of the late 1980s and cleared the path for subsequent breakthroughs. The marshalling of this broad front and the cementing of ANC authority over it enabled the democratic movement to meet one of the prerequisites for a negotiated settlement: the existence of a powerful political force capable of 'delivering' its constituencies to the bargaining table and sticking to an eventual deal.

But there were costs attached. One has been the muffling of ideological and strategic plurality in the broad congress movement, with the socialist left targeted especially. Here one observes the Janus-face of traditional national liberation struggles. Under their dome, sundry interests and forces can be enlisted in a common struggle. That this served the anti-apartheid struggle in potent fashion is beyond dispute. But differences and contradictions also became flattened under the canopy of inclusive identities: 'the people' or the 'oppressed majority', for instance. At times, the process encouraged outrageous propositions – such as Tom Mboya's description of the main liberation movement as 'the mouthpiece of an oppressed nation' whose 'leader embodies the nation'.[73] In the post-liberation phase, inclusivity increasingly is maintained at the expense of heterodoxy, strategic autonomy and contestatory activities. In short, the gravity field of national liberation has taken on an arresting function in relation to the ANC's main political allies.

Ties that bind

Since 1997, the boundaries of dissent in the tripartite alliance have been set more sternly by the ANC leadership. The manner of reprimand is illuminating. Leftist critics who complain of a too-slow process of transformation are lumped with conservatives as 'those who seek to spread the gospel of failure' or are accused of being duped by enemies of change. In words Thabo Mbeki addressed to COSATU's central committee in 1998:

> If I may speak frankly, in reality some within the movement who think they know, only know what we have been fed by those people who are opposed to our movement and to the fundamental transformation of our society (1998c:4).

Charges directed at the SACP have been even more scornful. Addressing the SACP's national congress in July 1998, Mbeki railed against:

> ... those who consider themselves to be the very heart of the left [who] in pursuit of an all-consuming desire to present themselves as the sole and authentic representatives of the progressive movement, seem so ready to use the hostile messages of the right and thus join forces with the defenders of reaction to sustain an offensive against our movement (1998b:8).

Vividly drawn in such declamations are the terms of unity, the limits of tolerance and the boundaries of permissible dissent within the ANC, the tripartite alliance and what occasionally is still referred to as the 'mass democratic movement'.

The prime (interlinked) functions of the alliance have become, in one respect, *therapeutic* and, in another, *disciplinary*. It is therapeutic in so far as it allows for debate and the voicing of dissent within a tightly managed context, thereby replenishing hopes that unpopular policies and practices can be contested and changed. That faith is not entirely unwarranted. The alliance was a valuable site for holding off challenges against the new labour regime and for retarding the privatization programme.

On other aspects of economic policy the limits are writ large. The ANC leadership assiduously steered the GEAR plan clear of substantive debate in alliance meetings until 1998, most often by deploying the time-honoured method of postponing meetings. When both COSATU and the SACP in frustration then amplified their dissent in public, they earned a matronly dressing-down:

> We must end the practice of claiming easy party victories for the cause of the revolution on the basis of having told lies about our own comrades. We must not engage in fake revolutionary posturing so that our mass base, which naturally wants speedy transformation and the fulfilment of its material needs on an urgent basis, accepts charlatans who promise everything that is good while we know that these confidence tricksters are telling the masses a lie ... It is incorrect to proceed from the assumption that contradictions among ourselves are best addressed by ignoring the possibility of an organised interaction among ourselves, however vigorous, in favour of media headlines (Mbeki, 1998b).

Highlighted in that quote is the structure's disciplinary role: funnelling contestation away from the public realm and into a discreet zone. What the average South African learns of an alliance meeting is, at best, a 'consensus' statement stressing the need for further debate. Harsh to say, but the alliance's formal features (meetings and summits) function as enclosures where steam can be vented and dissent sponged up. On the whole, its influence on policy decisions is feeble. Not even the outline – let alone some details – of forthcoming national budgets crosses its path, for instance. It serves as an instrument for the management of dissent, the corralling of opposition and the policing of unity. Structured on such terms, the alliance debilitates rather than advances the quest for an alternative development strategy that could serve popular needs more successfully.

Yet this whittled-down status is maintained with a high degree of consent, despite the private grumbling of some. One immodest example of this deference was the SACP's 1997 explanation for its (initially muted) resistance to GEAR:

> Our first objective has been to *keep the debate on macro-economic policy wide open*. We have taken up this objective both out of principle (*we want to set an example of comradely debate and discussion*), and out of concern with the actual content of GEAR. We fully appreciate the huge financial market pressures on government (*and therefore upon all of us*), and we appreciate the temptations that may exist to declare this or that policy 'non-negotiable', to show 'toughness' and 'determination'. But it is simply *not helpful* to declare any policy, particularly one that has not emerged out of an effective process, 'non-negotiable' (1997, emphasis added).

The cringing tone defies comment. But as startling are the shrunken horizons (keeping a debate 'open'), the prone affirmation of loyalty ('comradely debate and discussion') and the supplication that it is 'not helpful' for the ANC leadership to shut its ears to disagreement. To be fair, the SACP grew bolder in its proclamations in the months that followed, earning itself an unrestrained chiding at its 1998 congress.[74] But still dutifully adhered to subsequently has been the assertion that emerged from a 1995 Alliance Executives' Summit – that it is the 'ANC-led political centre [that is] capable precisely of co-ordinating and driving a political, social and economic transformation programme'.[75] Five years later, COSATU and the SACP are hard-pressed to provide more than flimsy evidence of their roles in 'co-ordinating' and 'driving' definitive features of South Africa's development path. Hence their pleas that the alliance be granted a stronger say in the framing of policies.

In late 1999, the ANC leadership seemed to relent when it agreed to set up a 'permanent political monitoring structure' with its allies, lifting spirits in the COSATU and SACP camps. But as analyst Steven Friedman warned:

> [B]oth may find that their 'victory' benefits the ANC and Mbeki far more than them. The 'monitoring structure' is so ideal an Mbeki vehicle that this may be by far the easiest 'concession' he has ever made to the ANC's partners. Mbeki's strategy in his dealings with the ANC's allies is to woo leadership figures; it is an activity at which he is adept ... The 'structure' therefore allows Mbeki to meet union and SACP leaders in a forum ideally tailored to his strategy and skills, hence his intention to chair it.[76]

The evergreen faith vested in the alliance, of course, has a long historical pedigree; it is not merely the offspring of habit. It is also shored up by other factors. One is the habitual counsel that the only alternative to a currently ineffectual alliance is its break-up, which tends to have a vitalizing effect on sagging confidence levels inside the alliance. Another is the fact that a surprising variety of political-ideological currents cohabit in COSATU and (more dramatically) the SACP. Orbiting deferentially around the ANC, the alliance enables those differences to gravitate toward and become 'reconciled' around centrist positions. Finally, the alliance serves as something of a life-support system for a party – the SACP – that has been unable to reclaim the influence it wielded inside the ANC during the 1970s and 1980s. That remark calls for some elaboration.

Wagging the dog?
By 1998, it was clear that the fence the party had sat on for much of the decade was collapsing. Revealed was a surprisingly heterogeneous outfit, marked by what deputy general-secretary Jeremy Cronin kindly has called 'a considerable degree of necessary ideological fluidity'. At play was more than just an 'old guard' versus 'young radicals' standoff. The party had become a hybrid of social democrats skilled at commuting between Thatcherite positions and popular affirmations, dyed-in-the-wool Stalinists, a band of left-wingers alert to the thinking of Gramsci, Samir Amin and Andre Gorz, and a rump of paint-by-numbers socialists.

That equivocal character, camouflaged by a common commitment to 'build socialism now', goes a long way towards explaining the ease with which the ANC leadership has contained an organization whose official programme constitutes an indictment of the unfolding trajectory of post-apartheid South Africa. Along with COSATU, the SACP remains bent on invigorating the tripartite alliance. But unlike its trade union ally, that feat threatens to highlight, rather than overcome, the more deep-rooted internal differences and deficiencies that have elbowed the party onto the sidelines of the transition.

Historically structured as a tightly-knit vanguard, the SACP since 1994 tried to distinguish itself as the torchbearer of progressive political and moral values, while consciously refraining from elaborating through research a corresponding development path and mobilizing around it. Selected was a route of influence that passed into the ANC or via it into state structures. Indeed, the party's presence is pervasive – in parliament, at all levels of government (including seven cabinet ministers) and throughout the state. Alas, head counts are a poor index of influence. At the same time, party leaders grew bolder in their analysis of the transition, generating critiques that cut closer to the bone:

Can we advance, deepen and defend the national democratic revolution without connecting in practice, class and national struggles? Do the April 1994 elections simply draw the veil over past capitalist accumulation and its present consequences? Or should we now, in the interest of social stability, just keep quiet about such matters? (Cronin & Nzimande, 1997)

But with the SACP no longer the tail that allegedly used to wag the dog, such stridency does not sit well with the ANC:

The idea that any of our organisations can build itself on the basis of scavenging on the carcass of a savaged ANC is wrong. This is because the death of the ANC, which will not happen, would also mean the death of the rest of the progressive movement of our country.[77]

Mapped in that intolerance is the holding pattern fixed for the party. Submitting to it means accepting a minor handmaiden status, leavened by the circumscribed right to engage in 'debate' that does not breach the perimeters of loyalty. Resisting it in too cocksure fashion carries the threat of expulsion from the alliance – and possibly into oblivion.

The SACP's (and COSATU's) ability to resist remains sapped by the events of 1989. The SACP was a party deeply schooled in the mythologies and Marx-esque ideology promoted by Soviet and Eastern European socialist states. In the early 1990s, many members withdrew – some because an unbanned ANC seemed a more suitable vehicle for political advancement, many others because the very idea of socialism seemed to have crumbled with the Berlin Wall. Yet, the communist party impressively kept growing, enlisting as members homegrown South African radicals that were still attracted to the idea of socialism, however muddled and elusive it had become. This must rank as one of the prime (and too often overlooked) successes of the SACP in the 1990s: salvaging from what could have been the dustbin of history an organized, socialist force.

But the real, lasting damage wrought by 1989 (on both Stalinist parties and those socialist currents critical of the collapsed systems) was less visible to the naked eye: a draining of both the confidence and imagination of the socialist left. The horizon of possibilities seemed to shrink, all the more so as the scions of neoliberal capitalism went on the offensive locally. Also, a left which had thought in terms of insurrections, military victories and the smashing of the apartheid state in the 1990s found few familiar landmarks in a terrain shaped by a negotiated political settlement, the assimilation of the liberation movement into the apartheid state, the creation of a government of national unity and all manner of subsidiary compromises.

Narrowing the SACP's options are other weaknesses, among them the lack of a strong mass base. Paid-up membership has dwindled to around 20 000, despite its impressive membership drives in the early 1990s. Its cadres are of uneven quality and generally operate without cogent organizational direction.

Unlike COSATU (which can still rattle nerves by threatening mass protests), the SACP's arsenal has been reduced mainly to the tools of reason and persuasion, instruments it once wielded with aplomb thanks to its strong organizational, intellectual and tactical influence inside the ANC. By the mid-1990s, that was already no longer the case. Even on this intellectual front, the party has been reluctant to build its own research capacities.[78] With some justification it has claimed that it could draw on intellectual and research resources in civil society, not least those servicing COSATU. Yet, networking with progressive NGOs and think tanks appear not to be a priority. Likewise, only patchy efforts have been made to build and actively link into wider progressive networks and campaigns. The upshot is that the SACP's main route of influence still passes through an organization (the ANC) and an alliance that stifles its autonomy and exerts considerable constraints on action.

The effects are plain to the eye. On the one hand, the SACP proclaims its duty to steer society beyond 'a self-satisfied and limited version of our revolution' in which a new capitalist order is stabilized 'around about 30 per cent of the population, while the great majority remain marginal', as a 1997 document put it (Cronin & Nzimande, 1997). On the other hand, its responses to concrete issues often are highly equivocal. Government's almost simultaneous announcements in late 1998 of a R30 billion ($4,8 billion) arms purchase package and its refusal to finance the provision of AZT treatment to pregnant, HIV-positive women (at a cost of R80 million or $12,7 million annually) drew only murmured misgivings from the SACP (and COSATU). In February 1999, the party praised a budget that cut corporate tax rates, re-affirmed government's bid to lower the budget deficit and committed government to further lifting capital controls. A year later it 'welcome[d] the emphasis on the eradication of poverty and inequalities' in a budget that cocked a cold shoulder at 40 per cent of the population, while doling out tax cuts to the middle classes and cutting social spending.[79] More broadly, an ANC replete with COSATU and SACP members was allowed to stage a perfunctory 15-minute debate on government's macro-economic strategy before endorsing its broad outlines at the ANC's 1997 national conference.[80]

Revealed by such incongruities is a party that tactically (and perhaps even strategically) has steered up a cul-de-sac. Trapping it there are residues of its own history (operating mainly through its host, the ANC, and an overbearing emphasis on the state as *the* citadel of power in society),[81] and its submission to the heavy hand of ANC discipline.

As a result, the party walks a thin line between abstracted critiques of the development path (and the paradigms of government policies) and 'comradely' engagements with the ruling party on specific points of dis-agreement. It can recognize the emergence of conflicting hegemonic pro-jects, as it did in a 1999 document by asking:

> Will post-apartheid change be, fundamentally, a reform (a structural adjust-ment), with some progressive and modernising national and democratic features, but that leaves the underlying gender, race, class, and other power inequalities of our society largely intact? Or will it be a profound national rev-olution, that radically democratises gendered, race and class power? The prin-cipal strategic re-alignment of social forces in struggle within our country is now increasingly pivoted around these two conflicting agendas (SACP, 1999).

Yet, the way forward was crudely mapped as a path between 'two different, mutually reinforcing, ideological dangers – a reformist opportunism, and a pseudo-revolutionary voluntarism' (SACP, 1999).

Shuffling the pack

There are strong reasons for not reading the constricting terms of the alliance as an 'aberration' generated by a temporary need to muster unity and manage dissent in the face of adversity. Much more persuasive is an analysis that locates those terms amid other, far-reaching adjustments and initiatives that together drive the dominant hegemonic project in post-apartheid South Africa. One key element of that project is the domestica-tion and assimilation of the key organizations of the socialist left into a neo-corporatist framework dominated by the state and capital.

Currently, the alliance serves this purpose well – as an arena in which dis-agreements can be aired, managed and contained. Importantly, its utility is not only *restrictive*. It is also a zone in which consent is nourished, via com-promises that benefit some constituencies (COSATU's membership, for instance) or that tilt some (non-essential) policies and programmes in a more progressive direction. It is, therefore, one of the essential instruments for achieving a requisite mix of confrontation, consultation and compro-mise with powerful organized forces.

Ironically, and in related fashion, an alliance that functions in this manner also helps further diminish the already depleted authority of a formal, corpo-ratist institution such as NEDLAC. As long as the alliance serves as an arena in which COSATU and the SACP demonstrably can register some gains, the appeal of NEDLAC's laborious and lengthy processes wanes. Where possi-ble, and for obvious reasons, both COSATU and the SACP prefer the option of winning their ally in government over to a position without having to con-tend with organized business sitting across the table.

But government also has widened bilateral access for business. Set up in late 1999 were bilateral economic working groups for 'big business', labour, black business and the agricultural sector. Their role, according to Mbeki,

was to forge a 'common agenda for economic growth and social development'.[82] Augmented in such ways is government's ability to side-step
NEDLAC on contentious policy issues and/or cultivate enough prior agreement before putting thorny matters before that institution.[83] Likewise,
Reserve Bank governor Tito Mboweni in late 1999 set up a new monetary
policy forum, despite the fact that NEDLAC already had a monetary and
finance chamber.

At face value, these various bilateral theatres seem to add up to a
balanced and equitable arrangement. Their usefulness for lubricating
decision-making seems obvious. But amid the evidence of a maturing nexus
between the state and capital (and the diminished authority of the ANC's
main *political* allies), the new schema is in line with a neo-corporatist framework with its multitude of accords, forums and working groups.

In this scenario, the working class-based left's acquiescence is maintained
on the basis of its own organizational and strategic weaknesses, its abbreviated ability to defend some prior gains and achieve minor new ones, and the
overarching context of public sentiment in which these skirmishes occur.
Ultimately, the arrangement still rests on the arithmetic of give-and-take
(after all, consent, not coercion, is the driving dynamic), expressed especially in a series of social accords in which the state and capital dominate.
Against such a reading, the 1998 Jobs Summit marked a turning point.[84] By
no means did labour emerge empty-handed, but the eventual agreements
were barren of its key proposals.

The resemblance to the Third Way experiments undertaken by social-
democratic parties in the UK and, to a lesser extent, France and Germany is
striking. Indeed, the ANC government has embarked on what might be
termed a 'third way of a special type' that shares many key assumptions and
prognoses, but is also inflected with a number of specifically South African
drawbacks and advantages.[85]

Third way of a special type

Though hardly identical, British and European Third Way advocates share
the conviction that it is no longer possible to revitalize or even recreate the
class compromises that had undergirded the post-war welfare systems. This
is because a key component of those class compromises is deemed to have
disappeared: the ability to organize workers into strong, coherent and 'centralised trade unions in the context of large, dominant and stable firms'
(Zuege, 1999:88). Spurring that shift has been the adoption of post-Fordist
forms of flexible production technologies and work organization, and the
allegedly steam-rolling effects of globalization. In Alan Zuege's summary:

> The integration and mobility of capital is said to pose severe limitations on
> the traditional range of options available to left governments, faced now with

the combined threat of imports from low-wage economies, relocation of international investment, and a spectacular growth in the volume of mobile financial assets. In such a global setting, aggressive national policies of expansion will result in benefits 'leaking' abroad and vigorous opposition from investors and financial markets (1999:89).[86]

In this view, the goal of full employment and an extensive state-managed welfare system has been rendered wistful; likewise, the prospects of updating the Keynesian formulas that had propelled those systems. Not far in the background hover conscious attempts to adapt and restructure national economies to the demands and exigencies of 'informational capitalism' (Castells, 1998).

The thinking draws on many antecedents, among them the neoliberal stance towards the state and, importantly, also the New Left critiques of the welfare state and 'orthodox' socialism that helped prime the 1968 uprisings – which helps explain the hybrid and inchoate character of the Third Way. It is a child born of many parents, a reminder that attempts to equate the Third Way with neoliberalism are inaccurate. Its relationship to neoliberal ideology is more instrumental than intrinsic.

This has led some analysts to see it less as a problem-solving programme or strategy and more as an 'interface between politics and public relations'. It enables a political leadership to assemble a set of policies, which, although not integrated and harmonious enough to constitute a programme, does create possibilities for addressing certain 'priority problems' on the basis of broad consent.[87] In other words, it functions as a discursive surface for fostering and advancing a hegemonic project – hence, British political scientist Anthony Barnett's telling description of the Third Way as 'corporate populism'. That phrase acquires clarity when one considers the emphasis on cobbling together new types of social accords. These are a prerequisite for bridging the two, contradictory visions that stand at the centre of the Third Way: the necessity for a mobile, enterprising and competitive society, and the need to achieve social inclusion. Investment in human capital (especially education and training), for example, straddles these two objectives. But a more far-reaching redistribution of income and resources is seen to pit one against the other. Which is why, in David Marquand's words, Tony Blair's Third Way exhibits a:

> ... social vision [that] is closer to Thatcherism than to any other tendency in postwar British history. Individuals compete. There are winners and losers. Having won in fair competition, the winners are entitled to their gains; indeed, they occupy the most honoured places in the social pantheon. As for the losers, their duty is to lick their wounds and return as soon as possible to the fray.[88]

Reserved for the state is an important role in helping ensure 'fair competition', in the main through supply-side interventions. To the extent that this does not clash with the prerogatives of capital, a restructured social security system (typically taking the form of 'workfare' innovations) features prominently.

Related – and as important – is the fact that Third Way theory and practice goes beyond the ideal of a relatively equitable class compromise that emerges from a stalemate between capital and the organized labour movement. Corporatism remains the linchpin, but its bedrock is radically altered – hence the description 'neocorporatism'. The sway and might of organized labour either stands diminished (and has to be kept that way) or it has to be substantially reduced. Instead of institutionally grounding expansive compromises around the state, labour and capital, labour is assigned a minor role alongside other 'interest groups'. These are webbed into a multiplicity of partnerships and accords that pivot on the state and capital. Thus Blair, when asked about possible concessions to the labour movement, can answer:

> The country is our heartlands. These issues about the so-called heartlands … sometimes people want me to adopt old-fashioned rhetoric. Well I won't. I will say nothing other than what I believe, which is that I'm delighted that we have business people and entrepreneurs that can today support the Labour party. And I never ever want to see that situation change again.[89]

In this sense, the Third Way is much less about class *compromise* than about class *struggle*, and about the restructuring of social relations in order to achieve growth, productivity and competitiveness in a new global division of labour that demonstrably favours capital. Turn-of-the-century South Africa exhibits many of the features of the Third Way experiments.

But the South African version is also imbued with specific and, in some ways, unique features – hence the description 'third way of a special type'. It shares an awed trepidation in the face of globalization and the sense of severely narrowed options. Also common is the difficulty in reconciling an overriding emphasis on growth, productivity and competitiveness with the need to effect social inclusion. Central to the ethos of government (and the state broadly) are the watchwords of efficiency, cost-effective delivery and good governance. As conspicuous is the re-organization of power in the executive and the ruling party, which centralizes power and allows for greater levels of co-ordination, efficiency and discipline to be achieved in pursuit of a modernized economy capable of holding its own in the global system. Simultaneously at play are levelling, populist rhetoric (that disguises some fault lines, like class, and allows other, like race, to be accentuated) and meritocratic sensibilities. Consider Mbeki's remarks to the United Nations general assembly in 1999:

[I]t is clear that there is no automatic or inherent mechanism within the operation of the markets to enable both capital and technology to make the sort of impact we are talking about on all countries of the globe. When we say this, we should not be taken to mean that we are contemptuous of all that has been said about what each country needs to do to create the conditions conducive to investment and technology transfers ... What we are saying is that the functioning of the markets does not and cannot exclude conscious interventions being made, both to increase economic opportunities and to raise the standards of living and the life possibilities of many in the world denied their human dignity by the scourge of poverty ... *Once more, the matter turns on the will of the political leaders actually to discover among themselves the moral and intellectual courage to do what is correct and necessary* (1999a, emphasis added).

In other respects, the South African version displays 'home-grown' features. A key feature of Britain's Third Way is the *de-ideologizing* of politics. This is an ambiguous process. Traditional categories of 'conservative' and 'progressive', left and right, seem to lose their purchase amid a complex of adjustments that encompasses those categories and appears to compress them into a new phylum – that of 'realism'. At the same time, there remains the conscious need to neutralize working class-based challenges in order to better service the prerogatives of capital (both domestic and international), which now 'calls the shots'.

In this process, class-based and other, previously pre-eminent organized interests are dissolved into a flattened ideological plane. Society is reconceptualized as the sum of the individuals living in it. Organized into collectives, individuals are deemed to constitute motley 'interest groups' or 'stakeholders' that can be woven into various forms of accords. Necessarily accompanying this *atomization* of society is a heightened accent on patriotism and liberal use of populist language and gestures.

Central to all this is the redrawing of relations between the social-democratic party and its traditional labour movement and working class-based allies. In their book, *The Blair Revolution: Can New Labour Deliver?*, Mandelson and Liddle were forthright on this score:

[W]hereas the old Left saw its job as to represent the unions, pressure groups and the working class, and the Right saw its role to protect the rich together with powerful corporate interests, New Labour stands for the ordinary families who work hard and play by the rules.[90]

This requires that the ruling party establishes a comfortable distance between itself and labour, thereby conjuring the illusion of fair play – since any vestigial class bias is thereby supposedly removed. In its place come various forms of partnership in an overall frame that is best described as 'stakeholder capitalism'. Overall, the advantage is to curtail the 'distorting' influence of traditionally powerful formations (chiefly, labour organizations) that threaten or undermine necessary adjustments that are needed to meet a set of new challenges.

However, 're-ordering' society in this manner is risky in a potentially unstable context. A pressing need exists in South Africa for new affinities and allegiances that can supersede the lines of historical division. Merely disaggregating society into individual units or subjects runs the risk of clearing the terrain for the emergence of new and old forms of organized chauvinism and reaction. Required, therefore, is an 'ideological glue' that can bond people along new lines – hence, one of the distinctive features of South Africa's Third Way.

At one level, the de-ideologizing of politics is occurring – most notably by arresting the countervailing power of working class-based formations. At the same time, there is a patent need to shore up stability by reproducing and reinforcing the loyalty (or at least consent) of an African majority that is largely denied access to the circles of privilege and opportunity. For obvious reasons, the unifying force of anti-apartheid discourse has all but dissolved. Replacing it with an emphasis on class-based inequality conflicts with the central role accorded to capital in the bid to modernize and transform South Africa.

Ironically, the country's history of racial division has bequeathed it a powerful and expansive group identity that resonates emphatically: race. Thus, South African politics is being *re-ideologized*, with 'the people' referring to an assemblage of individuals who are congregated under the umbrella of race. The enduring reality of racism lends this discourse considerable potency. By refracting it through the stout traditions of African nationalism and the shimmering vision of an African renaissance, it also acquires a 'progressive' character.

Taking care of business

The South African version differs in another, important respect. Britain's Labour Party was able to proceed on the scorched terrain left by almost two decades of Thatcherism. The labour movement had been pummelled into submission, which allowed that party to usher its traditional mainstay to the sidelines in party politics. Thus it could be 'modernized' on the basis of defeats administered by the previous regime. Obviously, the ANC government has not been bestowed with this 'luxury'.

In France and Germany, a more diluted (and aberrant) version of the Third Way has been attempted. Although under attack and plagued by structural changes in the global division of labour, trade unions retained their footholds in relatively sturdy, institutionalized forms of corporatism. It is from those platforms that they have been able to mount defensive actions

and retain a hand in the adjustments promoted by their respective governments. That state of affairs, too, does not pertain in South Africa. Not only
does it lack a solid, corporatist foundation for a managed class compromise,
but the imperative of stability restricts the extent to which the working class
movement can be subdued through a sustained series of confrontations. This
is why a much more complicated – and uncertain – route is being attempted.

The ideological groundwork for this manoeuvre is well underway.
Though not always with equal vehemence, both government and business
portray organized labour as a 'special' interest group, pitting its demands
against the needs of society as a whole. The mid-1999 public sector wage
dispute contained striking examples. In his first public reaction to the
standoff, President Mbeki told parliament:

> Nobody is saying anything about national defence, one of the things we need
> to look at, the building of schools and clinics ... There are constraints which
> mean we're not going to meet each and every demand ... and there are many
> competing demands with regards to public finances.[91]

Public services minister Geraldine Fraser-Moleketi followed suit, accusing
unions of practising a 'narrow trade unionism' and ignoring their broader
responsibilities to society, while some union leaders were likened to 'infantile leftists'. The reference was to Lenin's *Left-wing Communism – an
Infantile Disorder*, though the attack was more reminiscent of the 'loony
left' invective popular during Margaret Thatcher's reign in Britain.[92]

Importantly, those charges enjoy some purchase. On the one hand,
COSATU's influence on the broader social and economic policy terrain has
been trimmed back. Indeed, it is not unthinkable that government's hardline stance during the public sector dispute was partly informed by the
desire to highlight the alleged contradiction between workers' demands
and its own developmental responsibilities. On the other hand, COSATU
has not done enough to counter that view. According to Dinga Sikwebu,
education co-ordinator of NUMSA:

> COSATU has been unable to successfully link up with and strengthen other
> organisations. There has been no revival of the mass democratic movement
> ... COSATU does not appear to take the emergence of sector networks (for
> example, the rural development network) seriously. [It] also seems contemp-
> tuous of single-issue coalitions (for example, on debt) and other NGOs ...
> Although always strongly denied, a tendency has developed within
> COSATU to approach issues from a narrow 'workerist' perspective. What is
> its position on the R29-billion [sic] arms procurement deal, besides the few
> words on workers' jobs in the armaments industry? (1999:7)

The federation's official goal is to act as a catalyst for broader societal transformation – indeed, for socialism. But it has been caught in something of a

pincer movement that constrains this bid. In dominant discourse, worker demands are counterposed to society's needs. Tautologically, strikes are presented as evidence of the claim. COSATU general secretary, Zwelinzima Vavi, can stress that 'COSATU must retain the character of a broad liberation movement – anybody who thinks that COSATU can be isolated now is dreaming.'[93] But on the ideological front, COSATU (and the broader labour movement) appears unable to present or popularize compelling, contrary evidence. The upshot is that it already is being fitted for its subsidiary role in the scenario described above.

Wriggling free will not be easy. Many of the battles being fought by the labour movement have become defensive – against regressive changes to the labour regime, retrenchments and efforts to restructure the labour market along even more flexible lines. Indeed, the two-tier system COSATU is intent on preventing has been taking shape underfoot, as more firms blur the line between formal and informal employment – despite the regulatory system created under the Labour Relations Act.[94] At the same time, COSATU has 'lost members through job-shedding in sectors that form the core of its organisational base' (Sikwebu, 1999:10). The federation is seeking legislative amendments that would outlaw replacement labour and labour brokers, and secure the right to strike over dismissals. But in public consciousness, such defensive manoeuvres are easily contrasted with government's 'coherent and enlightened policies to effect transformation'.[95]

Hampering COSATU and the wider labour movement are other weaknesses. All unions have suffered high rates of staff turnover. Experienced shop stewards in particular are drawn constantly into supervisory and even managerial positions as part of firms' affirmative action programmes.[96] Unions cannot compete with the lucrative salary packages on offer. Hundreds of other leaders and officials have taken up posts in government and state structures.

Ironically, some frailties stem from the movement's successes.[97] Rising memberships in some sectors, the winning of basic rights and the creation of a multitude of bi- and trilateral forums increased the tasks of national offices. In most cases, they have coped poorly. Many have been leery or unable to introduce efficient staff and office management systems or communications strategies – leading to poor co-ordination, and aggravating tensions between rank-and-file members and leaderships. Shop stewards complain that they are 'tired of feeling like transmission belts for decisions taken elsewhere'.[98] Surveys have highlighted a widening rift between leaderships and rank-and-file members and suggest 'that a tiny minority within the federation fully understands the policies that are formulated' (Sikwebu, 1999:10). Along with an absence of authentic political debate in COSATU and its affiliates, Dinga Sikwebu has listed a distressing array of problems, including:

... an imbalance between mass campaigning and negotiations ... an inability to ensure proper co-ordination of the different forms of engagement, a lack of canvassing membership views when formulating positions, [and] little education of members on actual positions (1999:11).

COSATU and the wider working class-based left is hard-pressed to resist being tamed and bridled. But that process promises to be protracted – punctuated by occasional, spectacular showdowns, but defined more decisively by a series of managed skirmishes and embellished also by concessions to worker organizations. For reasons of stability, the project cannot proceed on the basis of dishing out cataclysmic defeats and humiliation to the labour movement. Required is that movement's *acquiescence to* the restructuring of power in society.

By no means is the success of this endeavour guaranteed. One of its crucial ingredients, for example, requires that the state be capable of facilitating the (re)allocation of resources and opportunities within a broadly consensual setting. In the context of low economic growth, and high (and rising) unemployment, that feat becomes difficult. The economy's limited capacity to generate (and the state's limited ability to direct the distribution of) the surpluses needed to nourish consent seems set to magnify tensions between class-based (and other) interests. All the while, compromises will have to be engineered and, in some circumstances, imposed – in line with the overriding need to assemble the trade-offs needed to foster such broad-based consent. Yet, viewed in isolation, each would seem to favour one set of interests over another and, consequently, run the risk of discharging new rounds of tension.

More overt forms of struggle seem inevitable. So, too, does the gradual uncoiling of the whip of coercion. Whether the targets stand or fall will depend on how effectively they perform on the ideological front – by winning over and sustaining public sympathy and support, through statement and deed.

A class compromise?

The South African left's visions of societal change had long hinged on Leninist notions of rupture and the seizure of state power. As the 1990s progressed, these were eclipsed by the notion that an ensemble of revolutionary or *structural reforms* could build socialism within a capitalist system, with those innovations eventually achieving a critical mass that would tilt society into a socialist transition.[99] Drawing especially on an essay by Andre Gorz (1973) and on the Russian Marxist Boris Kagarlitsky's book *The Dialectic of Change*, Canadian social scientist John Saul attempted to draw a distinction between structural reform and reformism.[100] He proposed two essential criteria for the former. Structural reform must:

... be allowed self-consciously to implicate other 'necessary' reforms that flow from it as part of an emerging project of structural transformation [and] must root itself in popular initiatives in such a way as to leave a residue of empowerment – in terms of enlightenment/class consciousness, in terms of organizational capacity – for the vast mass of the population, who thus strengthen themselves for further struggles, further victories (1993:91).

At the heart of Saul's formulations was not a quest for a class compromise but an attempt to transcend such a compromise. A spirited debate ensued, spanning numerous journal articles and essays.[101] Some critics questioned whether, as Ralph Miliband put it, 'an altogether different social order can be achieved by a smooth accumulation of reforms, so that one day we will wake up and find that we have been living in a socialist society without being aware of it' (Miliband, 1996:19). Supporters approached the future on a train of metaphors. But Saul's intervention resonated strongly in left thinking. Former unionist Enoch Godongwana, for example, advocated 'a turn from exchange-values to use-values in our conceptualisation of why we are restructuring the economy and society',[102] and urged the building of 'certain alternatives within the capitalist framework that will tend to undermine the capitalist logic'.[103] The ANC's Pallo Jordan argued for 'establishing a number of strategic bridgeheads which enable you to empower the working class and the oppressed, and from these bridgeheads you begin to subordinate the capitalist classes to the interests of society in general'.[104] According to the SACP's Langa Zita, this would entail transferring 'certain areas of economic activity away from the mediation of the market to society',[105] by decommodifying certain economic resources and services (such as housing, education, health and other basic services), and by establishing producer and credit co-operatives.

In COSATU, these views condensed in the form of 'strategic unionism'. As defined by union analyst Karl von Holdt, it involves a programme of radical reform: 'of the state, of the workplace, of economic decision-making and of civil society ... driven by a broad-based coalition of interest groups, at the centre of which is the labour movement' (1992:33).

As part of an intensive assessment of COSATU strategies and organization capacity, the 1997 September Commission attempted to spell out more clearly what, by then, had become known as 'social unionism'. Informing the exercise was an awareness that the federation, despite its success in institutionalizing a role for itself in partnership with the state and capital since the early 1990s, was not leaving a firm enough mark on the post-apartheid order.

The outcome was a heavy emphasis on 'institutionalized parterships' with capital and the state. At the broadest level, for example, the goal would be to transform the private sector into a 'stakeholder sector', driven by the interests of workers, civil society and shareholders. In turn, social needs would become one of the criteria determining investment and distribution decisions. At the level of production, this would be augmented by a co-determinist 'workplace strategy' aimed 'a shift from the shareholder company to the stakeholder company where workers are empowered to jointly decide production and distribution issues'.[106]

Also counselled was the creation of a 'social sector' that would comprise enterprises and capital collectively owned by, for example, trade unions and community trusts. The sector would seek to 'influence investment patterns, manage enterprises democratically and use profit for the benefit of workers and communities'.[107] Also advised were broad alliances with the voluntary sector and an 'active, interventionist state'. Together, the measures would create 'the foundation for a potential socialist transformation in the future', the report claimed.

In sum, the proposals were aimed at reviving and extending the tripartite and co-determination arrangements that had characterized much of the 1990s. Underlying this was a dual but contradictory objective: to stabilize society while, at the same time, trying to challenge the rule of capital. In essence, it amounted to a quest for a class compromise.[108]

An analogous but more conservative set of propositions has been made by Glen Adler and Edward Webster – essentially, that 'a class compromise ori-ented towards growth and redistribution can better provide the economic foundation for sustainable democracy'.[109] The compromise would be aimed at achieving 'non-zero-sum enforceable agreements between independent actors based on mutually accepted rules'.[110] Drawing on Adam Przeworksi (1995), they advocate a 'social democratic alternative to neoliberalism' as a way of safeguarding democracy and expanding socio-economic improve-ments. It would be based on two compromises.

The first involves the introduction of a 'social wage to all citizens', while the second would increase the influence of workers and their representa-tives 'over investment decisions and productivity gains, to ensure that surpluses generated by growth benefit the population as a whole'. On the flipside, capital would gain 'a more productive workforce and flexibility conducive to job creation, while committing itself to longer-term produc-tive investment', and the state would achieve 'economic growth, increased tax revenues and stability' (Webster & Adler, 1999:9). The thinking is similar to that found in a contentious 1996 ANC discussion document, 'The State and Social Transformation', which advised that:

> ... private capital must recognise that the democratic state offers the best possible environment for the realisation of the interests of capital. So the partnership between the democratic state and capital is mutually beneficial. The alternative is an environment of social and economic dislocation which is not conducive to the interests of the two parties.[111]

The groundwork for a class compromise allegedly has been created by a 'class stalemate'. Following Bond (1996c), they attribute the post-apartheid development path to an 'élite compromise' that has become bogged down in two difficulties. It is not delivering growth or generating employment 'and it is not clear whether it can ever do so'. Also, it was arrived at 'over the heads' of ANC supporters who now bear the brunt of the ensuing adjustments.[112] The stalemate has been created, Webster and Adler argue, by the failure of COSATU, the SACP and the voluntary sector:

> ... to impose their alternative economic ideas on either the state or domestic and international capital. Nor is the government and capital able to satisfy the economic demands of this constituency through GEAR. Neither can they crush the opposition. In other words, South Africa has entered a class stalemate ... where neither capital nor labour are able adequately to secure their interests by pursuing traditional demands through adversarial strategies and tactics (1999:20).

Whatever the possible merits of the trade-offs that could constitute a class compromise and the institutional arrangements that could cement it, the overall argument is flawed. As this and previous chapters have shown, South Africa already has progressed considerably *beyond* a class stalemate. The evidence is vividly expressed in the current development path. So much so that it requires prodigious imaginative powers to sketch the kinds of further concessions that could draw capital into a relatively constricting compromise. Moreover, as noted, the concept of 'élite pacting' is of questionable value when trying to understand the *endurance* of this state of affairs. A more compelling explanation is arrived at by situating South Africa's economic policies and broader development strategy within the context of hegemonic struggle and of the relations of forces. These manifestly favour an alliance of class and other interests that centres on powerful fractions of domestic and international capital.

Such is the sophistication and vitality of the dominant hegemonic project – and the corresponding frailty of an alternative, popular one – that a compromise of the kind mooted by Webster and Adler would have to be preceded first by a remarkable recovery by the labour movement, the SACP and the popular sector in general. But facing them is a long haul back. That passage seems destined to require renewed bouts of struggle that are guided by tactical acumen and organizational capacities that were shyly displayed in the 1990s. It will also require new and more robust alliances with other actors in the popular sector. Before exploring some of the main conditions for a revival, it is useful briefly to survey others trends as they have affected progressive churches, youth and women's groups, rural and landless people's organizations, NGOs and the like.

Organizations of the governed

In South African discourse, the popular sector is often – and mistakenly – referred to as 'civil society'. Compounding the confusion are various other definitions of 'civil society', its location and its role. Both the bafflement and the infatuation stemmed from three developments in the 1980s: the collapse of Eastern European socialism, leftist critiques of the welfare state and the ascendancy of neoliberal ideology.

As a result, 'civil society' came to reside very much in the eyes of its beholders. It was made to describe politically independent social movements, or 'a robust, locally-constituted voluntary sector' (Swilling, 1991:22), or everything from 'a little jazz collective [to] a multi-billion rand company' (Narsoo, 1991:25). Some included in it the institutions of capitalism, others conveniently excluded them. This yielded bewildering anomalies in progressive discourse, where, as Steven Friedman asked mischievously, 'the aim is no longer only to win state power but to limit it' – leading him to ask whether 'yesterday's populists and socialists [are] today's liberals and libertarians?' (1991:5).

The origins of these notions and the debates surrounding them were discussed at length in the first edition of this book. Suffice to say that the confusion persists. 'Civil society' is seen as a countervailing sphere where multiple interests and relations intersect and where freedom is realized – thus allowing capitalism to 'disappear into a conceptual night where all cats are grey' (Wood, 1990:66). Or it is extolled as the platform from which liberal-democratic rights and freedoms are defended, thereby casting it in explicit tension with the state. Or it is viewed as zone of corrective actions in a context where the state fails to live up to its developmental duties.

Needless to say, these conceptions cut to the heart of some of the dilemmas facing the popular sector. Disaffection with the old statist routes of transformation has coupled with the perception of the state as being withered away by globalization, yielding often inflated notions about the ability of community-based organizations (CBOs) and new social movements to step into the breach. The idea of the state as a (shrinking) fortress-like zone in the field of society lives on. Consequently, the complex interconnectedness of the state and civil society ends up being rendered in terms of externality and exclusion, thereby neglecting the interwoven ways by which power is exercised and reproduced.

In order to side-step the muddle, this section concentrates on a specific category of formations and organizations, which here are termed the 'popular sector'. This is an admittedly imprecise attempt to group together CBOs, social movements and NGOs that are self-consciously committed to transform society along just and equitable lines. In other words, they try to act as catalysts of change. They occupy a small part of the field of civil society, which is dominated by the institutions and activities of capital. Finally, it must be stressed that they are at once the *objects and potential subjects* of hegemonic struggle.

It would be an exaggeration to state that 'the masses of our people have withdrawn from the public space and have pulled back from popular involvement'.[113] Yet it is difficult to dispute that the 1990s were marked by considerable demobilization of popular organizations. This is not unusual in societies undergoing democratic transitions; as the political system becomes democratized, extra-institutional mobilizing and organizing tends to flag. In South Africa's case, this tendency was propelled by a range of other factors.

Conducted by political *élites*, the political negotiations offered few entry or marshalling points for grassroots-based organizing (as opposed to mobilizing). Members' enthusiasm dwindled, only to be sporadically revived when deadlocks in the negotiations prompted calls for mass action. The result was a steady depletion of organizational capacity at grassroots level. This was exacerbated as thousands of key activists and figures in progressive organizations left to participate in parliament and in the democratization and transformation of state structures. A great deal of institutional memory and experience departed with them. Especially pronounced was the exodus of key figures in the women's and trade union movements. The rewards, though, have been mixed: in Shamim Meer's view, 'it has been easier to get women and worker leaders on to structures than to get women's and workers' interests on to decision-making agendas' (1999).

After 1994, the process was fuelled by a pervasive mood of expectancy, as citizens looked to the democratic state to deliver on the demands that had fuelled the anti-apartheid struggle. Even the ANC was unable to positively answer the question churning in many activists' minds: What's our mission now? Denuded of active members, some branches existed in name only. The ANC Dobsonville branch in Soweto, for example, saw its membership plummet from 4 500 in 1993 to 27 in 1997. An ANC report in the Free State province in 1997 lamented 'a lack of collective leadership, of political direction, of contact with branches and a lack of resources'.[114] A November 1999 poll suggested the trend had continued: it found that political party membership among Africans had dropped from 24 per cent in 1994 to only 10 per cent.[115]

The spectating stance was aggravated by deep confusion about the roles of popular organizations, particularly in relation to the new state. The mainly oppositional idiom of organizing during the anti-apartheid era seemed to have been rendered inappropriate by the new political order, where they were being urged to move from 'resistance to reconstruction'. Former South African National Civic Organization (SANCO) president Lechesa Tsenoli judged the slogan 'undynamic and undialectical', since it presumed that the society had passed through a magic portal, beyond which the contradictions that had fuelled resistance dissolved into common endeavours.[116] But such remarks only highlighted the difficulties popular organizations would have in relating to the state in the context of a national reconstruction effort.

The state would stress that the success of transformation efforts required widespread popular initiatives in tandem with state activities. But it soon transpired that autonomous activities that involved criticism or contestation of government policies were not welcome. Thus, the voluntary sector came under fire from former president Nelson Mandela when he questioned their representativeness and accountability in a speech at the ANC's 1997 national conference. The call for 'dynamic partnerships' between the state and civil society remains shadowed by unanswered questions: What are the appropriate divisions of labour in such a relationship, and where lie the boundaries of dissent?

Most popular organizations have failed to arrive at an answer. Their histories have left them poorly equipped for a shift towards forays based on the principle of 'critical support'. This central weakness can be traced back to two core features of the anti-apartheid resistance. Efforts to exploit spaces and frailties in the state were denounced as collaborationist and rejected in favour of outright conflict. Hardly any experiences of engagements with and within state apparatuses were allowed to accumulate. Secondly, change 'was conceptualised as starting with a seizure of state power and from there the transformation of society would flow in a very centralised manner', in former trade union leader Enoch Godongwana's words.[117] Conceptually, civil society had virtually collapsed into the post-apartheid state. 'The irony,' SACP deputy general secretary Jeremy Cronin admitted, 'is that we fought for decades to arrive at a point where we seem unable to devise a clear strategy to move forward'.[118]

Once touted as a 'new social movement', civic associations have not risen to the challenge, prompting academic Jeremy Seekings to note that 'the civic movement has become fragmented and lacks coherence and a sense of direction and purpose' (1997). Trying to shift into 'developmental' mode, their activities were inevitably less dramatic (and, therefore, unlikely to replenish members' enthusiasm and commitment in the manner of the earlier phases of confrontational mobilizing). Magnified was a lack of organizational capacity (research, lobbying, management). With foresight, Monty Narsoo in 1993 had proposed that they adopt a 'programmatic' role, in which they would 'lobby, pressure, negotiate and form alliances to press for the programmes they want, and then, with other interests and institutions, state and private, monitor the implementation of those which are agreed' (1993:17).

But that has proved difficult. The mobilizing skills honed during the anti-apartheid struggle were poor stand-ins for the facilitation, lobbying and management abilities called for in Narsoo's prognosis. Plaguing civics further has been their relationship to the ANC. Nominally, SANCO is joined in a political alliance with the ruling party at the national level. But at the local level, servicing community demands often has required a non-partisan and politically non-aligned stance (CORE, 1999). The ANC's response has not been indulgent. Often the relationship has been complicated by power politics. In the run-up to the 1995/6 local government elections, some civic leaders became loud advocates of 'autonomy' and 'independence' after local ANC branches chose not to anoint them as potential councillors by nominating them as ANC election candidates.

Even more troubling is civics' faltering knack for representing broad community interests – a failing that draws this chapter's central theme into view. A study by the Community Agency for Social Enquiry (CASE) of Johannesburg communities has linked 'the flagging authority, legitimacy and representivity of civics' to their association with the most powerful local socio-economic élites amid 'increasing social differentiation' (1998b:17). In Tladi-Moletsane, a section of 'old' Soweto,

> ... both the civic and local branch of the ANC were run by the most powerful socio-economic group. Residents of informal settlements and backyard tenants rarely attended their meetings and had adopted attitudes toward them that ranged from indifference to outright hostility (CASE, 1998b:23).

The challenge, obviously, is to transcend that parochial status by engineering and promoting inclusive development activities based on wider local partnerships. That, in turn, calls for the creation of gateways 'between the groupings to cultivate the shared interests that could become the basis for common action' (CASE, 1998b:24). In the absence of such innovations, new structures organized along class, gender and employment status will continue to compete for scarce resources (all detected in the CASE study) and bedevil concerted challenges at the local level.

These are some of the troubling hindrances that affect the ability of mass- and community-based organizations to help determine the trajectory of transformation and to extend those efforts into government and the state. Many of them face both financial and political pressure to concentrate their work on 'delivery' and to do so with fast-track methods. This threatens to dilute the train of elements that, ideally, form the hub of voluntary sector organizations' ethos of development: 'people-centred' practice, consultation, participatory processes, capacity-building, experimentation, transferable skills and experiences, independent analysis and critiques that, ideally, can help challenge the social relations that confine the poor to the margins of society.

An undercurrent is the rise of 'technicism as a new, core trait of NGO endeavours' that, according to Shamim Meer, threatens to overwrite the 'political nature of development' with technical calculations and equations (1999). Driving this are voluntary sector organizations' efforts to compete against private sector firms for government contracts where the imperative is quick, quantified output.

Commenting on the RDP document in 1994, ANC MP Pregs Govender detected similar trends, where 'lots of numbers are thrown around, yet social relations are talked about in the abstract as broad statements'.[119] Far from being 'neutral', the ascendancy of the *technical* disguises the *politics* of development. Indeed, the logic of South Africa's development path bears some resemblance to the social policies advocated by the World Bank which, as Mexican sociologist Carlos Vilas has observed, isolate 'poverty from the process of capital accumulation and economic development' and reduce 'the solution to designing specific social policies' that target the 'poorest of the poor' while urging economic policies that structurally reproduce highly unequal social relations (1996:16). This is precisely the framework preferred by business. According to Ben van Rensburg of SACOB, government should not 'interfere' in the market and, instead, 'put in place poverty safety nets to assist those that are in dire straits until the economy improves to the point where the majority of citizens benefit from growth'.[120]

Should the current development path continue to limit government social spending, large parts of the voluntary sector could find themselves harnessed into such a containment role, acting as a shadow welfare/development arm of the state that helps absorb the worst excesses of poverty. This could inaugurate a shift from development (altering social relations and enhancing capacities for economic survival) to 'welfarism' (a makeshift social safety net aimed only at containing the spread of absolute poverty). The voluntary sector's role would then harmonize with neoliberal logic – in the sense that its activities become functional to an economic growth path that reinforces the patterns of inequality and deprivation in society.

It is not improbable that CBOs and other voluntary sector organizations that draw financial sustenance from the state (through tenders, contracts and other relations) will find themselves trapped in an unhappy paradox. Emerging on the one hand would be a greater political-ideological *intimacy* between them and the state. In itself this is not a problem – if it spawns vibrant engagements and practical activities. But it also carries the risk of a potentially drab relationship that lacks the necessary dynamism of difference and contestation that can give rise to the kinds of innovations and plurality of endeavours a successful popular project requires.

It is at the local level that the space for innovative challenges and new bids to foster consent around programmes that privilege popular needs seems most pronounced. Yet, they will have to negotiate many of the same complexities identified at the national level: the eruption of socio-economic differences, the increasing intersection of organized politics with *élite* strata, the complicated relationship with the ruling party and the deadening weight of the traditions of the past.

Plotting a recovery

In the context of manifold weaknesses, double-binds and foreshortened perspectives, the challenge for the South African left ultimately stands captured in Stuart Hall's description of hegemony as an accomplishment that:

> ... cannot be constructed or sustained on *one* front of struggle alone (for example, the economic) ... [Mastery] results from winning a substantial degree of popular consent ... It is this 'authority', and the range and the diversity of sites on which 'leadership' is exercised, which makes possible the 'propagation', for a time, of an intellectual, moral, political and economic collective will throughout society ... [It requires mastery of] organic ideologies, which are *organic* because they touch practical, everyday, common sense.[121]

In these respects, the left lags badly. The living conditions and emotional pain endured by the majority of South Africans are a testament to capitalism's failure to acquire a 'human face'. Yet, the values of that system pervade society. They are embodied in the celebrated forms of those 'that have made it' (whether corporate moguls or community gangsters), in national lottery winners that have beaten the trillion-to-one odds, in the virtual realities conjured in TV and radio advertisements that penetrate the homes of 90 per cent of the population, and in the fantasies of millions of ordinary people.

The alternatives seem ghost-like, bereft of examples, shorn of hope. They come dressed in stiff declamations and jargonized denunciations. They speak in the name of rights, demands and desires, yet somehow fail to speak *to* the lives of their audience. And all the while, as push becomes shove, they are prone to endorse the very deeds they claim to oppose.

A popular hegemonic project has to advance on several fronts *simultaneously*. One front would entail pursuing macro-level adjustments of the kinds outlined in the previous chapter. Another one would be oriented around more radical and 'transformative visions of worker ownership and control', including 'worker-initiated workplace democratization', different forms of self-management and co-operative enterprises, credit institutions and the like (Satgar, 1997). The same would apply, analogously, to other zones – school comittees, women's organizations, neighbourhood structures, grassroots housing initiatives, etc. In such an approach, the project acquires an 'eclectic' character and comprises, in Langa Zita's words, 'a combination of various forms of struggle through varied agency, within a context of appreciating the various levels of determination'.[122] Guiding it all the while is the need to project a *distinctive* appeal that draws its power not just from declarations and protest, but from positive examples that touch people's lives. That, in turn, requires a complex of breakthroughs.

As the most powerful progressive formation in civil society, COSATU has to practically add flesh to the tradition of social movement unionism. This entails *not* reducing the range of fronts it operates on, but extending its links with other progressive groupings and expanding its support and participation in popular campaigns – in other words, building a series of popular social alliances around palpable compaigns and activities. Such collaboration has been sorely lacking, with the federation often offering little more than lip service to important but under-resourced activities such as the Jubilee 2000 Debt campaign. The same challenge holds for the SACP. Obviously, there are limits to the potential roles of these organizations. But the choices must be made strategically: does a particular campaign enable advances in a critical area?

The second breakthrough is implicit in the first: transcending the constricting bounds of the tripartite alliance by buttressing intra-alliance engagements with campaigns that can help build and broaden popular consent across wide sections of society. Bids to reduce the government debt (by restructuring the civil service pension fund) or campaigns against a high interest rate regime hold potential appeal for a diverse range of classes and interests, for example.

The third challenge is closely related. A popular hegemonic project requires a political and programmatic axis. COSATU and the SACP, despite their weaknesses, still seem best positioned to serve as such a nexus. The more intimate relationship mooted between them (at the federation's sixth congress in 1997) therefore needs to become practically expressed. The implication is obvious: an *autonomous* organizational and programmatic platform has to be assembled – from where contradictions inside the ANC and the state especially can be magnified and turned to the advantage of a popular project. This does not require the break-up of the alliance, though it might eventually lead to such a split.

At the same time, the political anchor-point cannot operate on domineering lines. It has to provide or help achieve strategic coherence within a field of plural interests and activities – not as an overweening Big Brother, but as a catalyst and facilitator. This is not an anointed, vanguardist role; it is achieved through practice and its survives on the basis of democratic consent. Engagements in concert with other social actors therefore cannot hinge on prior unanimity around a prefabricated, watertight programme. The criteria need to be flexible, yet orbit around certain common principles and ideals. This is easier said than done. Such a route lacks the luxury of certainty and will not escape turbulence, surprises, embarrassments and disappointments. There will be differences and disputes. What the left has to discover is how to manage them positively. Reflecting of the UDF experiences would remind that its history is hardly bereft of pointers and tools. Fourthly, these endeavours cannot be limited to civil society. They have to proceed from an understanding of the interconnectedness of the state and civil society, and a vigilant appreciation of contradictions inside the state. So, for example, the important efforts to establish a basic income grant require close collaboration with the welfare department, which, like other social service departments, finds its work severely impeded by the dominance of the finance department. A multitude of contestatory entry points exist in the state. The same applies in relation to the ANC.

The converse, of course, also holds. It sees, in Vishwas Satgar's phrasing, societal transformation as 'not just the prerogative of the state and solely implementable by the state, but instead [also] at the grassroots, within civil society, where social movements and forces also have the power and responsibility to advance and deepen reform' (1997).

Fifthly, all of this demands a dramatic departure from the habits of the traditional socialist left, particularly those organizations rooted in Marxist-Leninist traditions. Whereas the frame of national liberation tends to accommodate and (temporarily) assuage conflicting interests, the socialist left lacks a similar 'hospitality'. National liberation projects are built on the basis of disciplined or domesticated pluralities; traditional left projects tend to impose much more exacting entrance requirements. As a result, they lack a prerequisite for successful hegemonic struggle: an inclusive discourse. Yet, without it, the axiomatic need to draw together traditional left forces and so-called new social movements cannot be met. This weakness is expressed in the mechanistic and often half-hearted ways in which relations with other social movements are conceived. In the absence of a 'language' of deed and avowal that envelops and unites, those engagements tend not to acquire an organic momentum. Hence, the laborious processes needed to assemble such links, networks and campaigns, their sporadic nature and the ease with which they disintegrate.

The prospects for such advances seem forlorn without a critical inter-rogation of the current utility of strategies and paradigms inherited from the past. That they aided the achievement of democracy is beyond dispute. But, as this chapter has argued, they also engendered weaknesses and limits that are visited most acutely on the left, which faces a long process of re-definition and rebuilding.

Notes

1   The words 'ideology' and 'ideological' as used in this chapter refer not to philo-sophical or political systems of thought, but to avowals, values and practices that 'are organic because they touch practical, everyday, common sense and they "organise human masses and create the terrain on which men [sic] move, acquire consciousness of their position, struggle, etc."' (Hall, 1996:431).

2   Nash, A., 1998, 'South Africa: Is the revolution over?', *New Socialist*. Vol. 2, No. 1 (March–April 1997), Toronto.

3   Hall (1996:423). The concept of hegemony used here corresponds to that found in Gramsci's later writings where it is 'applied to the strategies of *all* classes' and 'to the formation of all leading historical blocs, not the strategy of the proletariat alone', in Hall's phrasing (1996:425).

4   Distinct from a power bloc, which describes only the moment of force and coercion.

5   The words 'discourse' and 'language' are used here to refer to the social processes of making and reproducing sense. They are therefore intimately tied to power relations.

6   Prominent are mining, construction, information technology, financial services and some manufacturing and retail corporations.

7   Hall (1996:423). The quotations are drawn from Gramsci (1971:182).

8   This is why Gramsci preferred the word 'moment' to the word 'victory', which suggests a definitive triumph. Once achieved, hegemony has to be positively sustained. Even then, as Hall reminds, 'this extraordinary degree of organic unity does not guarantee the outcome of specific struggles' (1996:423).

9   The origins, details and eventual fate of the RDP were discussed at length in Chapter 6 of the first edition of this book.

10 Kevin Davie writing in *Business Times*, 9 October 1994.

11 Former 'RDP Minister', Jay Naidoo, quoted in the *Cape Times*, 4 July 1994.

12 For a critique of the RDP's overhaul by the ANC government, see Adelzadeh, A. and Padayachee, P. (1995) 'The RDP White Paper: Reconstruction of a development vision?', *Transformation* (February), Durban.

13 Thus Mbeki can invoke it in an attack on the SACP, and the finance minister refers to it repeatedly in budget speeches.

14 For an illuminating analysis of class formation in African communities, see Everatt (1999).

15 Sometimes referred to as the Bandung generation. The reference is to the famous 1955 conference in Bandung, Indonesia, where many of the key signposts of post-colonial projects were elaborated.

16 This is discussed in more detail below. For now, consider this assertion: 'The special character of colonialism in South Africa, the seizing by Whites of all the opportunities which in other colonial countries have led to growth of a national capitalist class, have strangled the development of a class of African capitalists … The interests of the African commercial class lie wholly in joining the workers and rural people for the overthrow of White supremacy.' See SACP (1962) 'The road to South African freedom: Programme of the South African Communist Party' in Various authors (1970:135).

17 '"Genuine" black model for SA due next year', *Business Report*, 19 October 1998.

18 'Ramaphosa's departure raises key black empowerment issues', *SouthScan*, Vol. 14, No. 5, 5 March 1999.

19 'Labour faces wages of unemployment', *Business Day*, 3 July 1998.

20 Poulantzas's definition of the comprador *bourgeoisie* rings true particularly in the South African context: 'that fraction of the *bourgeoisie* which does not have its own base for capital accumulation, which acts in some way or other as a simple intermediary of foreign imperialist capital'. In the South African situation, of course, the black *bourgeoisie* acts as intermediary not only for foreign capital but for dominant, white capital in several ways. It is used as a vehicle allowing access to state contracts and tenders and as a profit-taking route for finance capital, while its desired emergence and growth also facilitates the globalizing ambitions of capital

(as outlined earlier). Poulantzas's definition appears in *Classes in Contemporary Capitalism* (1978), Verso Books, London, p. 71.

21   See note 18.

22   'Black hold on JSE slips as Afrikaners strengthen', *Business Times*, 30 January 2000. Meanwhile, the demise of apartheid saw Afrikaner firms' share of JSE capitalization climb at its fastest rate in 30 years – soaring from 24 per cent in 1996 to 35 per cent in 1999, as they filled the gaps left by unbundled (English) corporations, some of which had shifted their core operations abroad.

23   Based on 1996 census data, there were an estimated 24,9 million South Africans of voting age. Other calculations put the figure at 23,5 million.

24   By far the best recent analysis of youth in post-apartheid South Africa is David Everatt's 'From urban warrior to market segment? Youth in South Africa 1990–2000' (paper), Johannesburg.

25   'Opinion 99' survey data cited by Lodge (1999b:58).

26   The pink slips are dismissal notices.

27   Note, for instance, that a 1998 poll found that fewer than 7 per cent of respondents could muster even an elementary grasp of the GEAR strategy and its implications.

28   The so-called 'transformation laws' passed in early 2000 are examples. They included the Promotion of Access to Information Act and the Promotion of Equality and Prevention of Unfair Discrimination Act. The latter marked a bold step to tackle the rampant and often violent discrimination that still defines South African society. It prohibits hate speech, as well as discrimination on the grounds of race, gender, sexual orientation, pregnancy, disability, age and language.

29   See 'Mass fall-off in African party political activity', *SouthScan*, Vol. 15, No. 4, 25 February 2000. Other research has suggested that church groups, local sports bodies, burial societies and *stokvels* (informal saving schemes) dominate organized civil society activities in many African communities – see CASE (1998).

30   'Empowerment drive becoming dominant theme', *SouthScan*, Vol. 13, No. 4, 20 February 1998.

31   *Ibid.*

32   *Ibid.*

33   'Mbeki champions poor against black and white élites', *SouthScan*, Vol. 13, No. 12, 12 June 1998.

34   *Ibid.*

35   Punctuating this discourse are occasionally Orwellian flourishes. Consider Mbeki's lament in a newspaper interview: 'I worry about the level of debate in the country. Truly, what I feel has happened is that the ending of apartheid government, and therefore the removal from our national agenda of a matter that had persisted for a very long time, has exposed a lack of depth in many people's thinking about the new challenges that face us. That worries me.' See 'Face to face with the president', *Sunday Times*, 6 February 2000.

36   Peter Vale and Sipho Maseko (1998) 'South Africa and the African renaissance' in *South Africa and Africa: Reflections on the African Renaissance*, Foundation for Global Dialogue Occasional Paper No 17, Johannesburg, p. 6.

37   Vale & Maseko, *op. cit*, p. 8.

38   For a detailed survey of South African investments and other economic activities on the rest of the continent, see Marais (1998a).

39   Quoted in Ferial Haffajee, 'Renaissance incorporated', *Mail & Guardian*, 2 October 1998.

40   Thabo Mbeki (1998) 'Speech by ANC President Thabo Mbeki to the Annual General Conference of the IFP', 18 July 1998, Emandleni, pp. 3–4.

41   *Op. cit.*, p. 6.
42   Vusi Mavimbela (1997) *The African Renaissance: A Workable Dream*, Foundation for Global Dialogue roundtable paper, July, pp. 31–2. The paper is generally regarded as distillation of Mbeki's thinking on the topic. Interesting is the appended acknowledgement that millions more survive on the basis of 'forms of economic production and ownership [that] are still largely rural and subsistent' (p. 32).
43   Quoted by Haffajee, *op. cit.*
44   Quoted by Lodge (1999a:98).
45   ANC parliamentarians are assigned 'constituencies', but voters living in those areas cannot express their (dis)approval of a specific politician in national elections.
46   The formulae for those decisions are also sufficiently flexible to disguise the motives for decisions that can be explained in terms of the need to achieve a balance in terms of gender, racial, ethnic and even internal/exile representation.
47   In mid-1999, for instance, former Gauteng housing minister Dan Mofokeng was struck from the ANC's election list, despite having cultivated a strong grassroots support base that positioned him as one of the most popular leaders at the ANC's 1998 provincial conference. The ostensible reason was a probe into alleged mismanagement and corruption. Almost a year later, the findings of that probe had not been released.
48   The ANC leadership also chooses the premiers in ANC-held provinces. The power is vested with the party's national working committee, acting through a committee headed by ANC chair Jacob Zuma. Previously, the person elected ANC leader in an ANC-controlled province automatically became premier.
49   Holomisa was an exception – he went on to form a new political party (the United Democratic Front) with the fallen National Party 'prince', Roelf Meyer.
50   'Mbeki wants a leaner organisation, and a super think-tank', *Financial Mail*, 31 March 2000.
51   For a critical overview, see Sean Jacobs, 'An imperial presidency or an organised one?' *Business Day*, 17 February 2000.
52   'Centralised administration means ministers are on short leash', *SouthScan*, Vol. 14, No. 20 (1 October 1999). Such deployments allow the party to extend its (disciplinary) reach into top tiers of the state (including nominally 'independent' statutory bodies) and into pockets of civil society. They are not always overt, nor is the 'deployment committee' always responsible for them. In early 2000, a government ministry invoked the intervention of a multinational CEO to ensure that a head-hunted journalist joined it as 'media adviser' – a sobering *vignette* of state-capital relations in post-apartheid South Africa.
53   Their friendship dates back to Sussex University in the UK, where they studied together.
54   For a survey of the sectors, see Howard Barrell and Barry Streek, 'The hidden face of government', *Mail & Guardian*, 12 November 1999.
55   *Op. cit.*, p. 7.
56   For a critical review of the 'new managerialist' approach in South Africa, see Paine (1999:44–51).
57   'Provinces doing little to train poorly skilled staff, committee told', *Business Day*, 23 April 1998.
58   The moves to restructure the provincial tier appear not to stem only from the technical problems revealed in the Ncholo reports. Inside the ANC, the need to limit occasionally disruptive intra-party jousting at the provincial level has seen the ANC's national leadership assume the power to appoint premiers in provinces governed by the party.

59   Essop Pahad, 'Imperial presidency the new "gevaar"', *Business Day*, 2 March 2000 (emphasis added). 'Gevaar' is Afrikaans for 'peril'. The reference is to the former apartheid regime's rhetoric of 'rooi gevaar' ('red peril') and 'swart gevaar' ('black peril') with which it sought to galvanize support among whites.

60   See Habib (1996:14).

61   Marais, H. (1999) 'Walking the tightrope' (editorial), *Siyaya!* (Autumn), Cape Town, pp. 2–3.

62   With an important twist. In South Africa, the standard formula of the era – development first, then democracy – was turned on its head. The reason was obvious: in the South African context, decolonization became democratization, the central historical demand of the ANC.

63   Amin, S. (1990) 'Social movements in the periphery' in Amin *et al.* (1990:113).

64   In Gramsci's famous formulation: '[W]hen the State trembled, a sturdy structure of civil society was at once revealed. The State was only an outer ditch, behind which there stood a powerful system of fortresses and earthworks: more or less numerous from one state to another' (1971:237–8).

65   In conceptions of struggle that converge on the seizure or destruction of the state, history is deemed to converge in the point of triumph, beyond which a kaleidoscope of new possibilities arch out. At the end of the century, it was easy to forget just how pervasive and appealing such perspectives were – in El Salvador it lasted until the *offensiva ultima* of 1989; in South Africa it survived until roughly 1987, when the dream of a people's war lay in tatters.

66   Up from about 23 in 1977 to 228 in 1986, according to political analyst Tom Lodge's count (1991:178). See also Lodge's 'The African National Congress after the Kabwe Conference' in Moss and Obery (1987).

67   How much longer COSATU would continue to regard the ANC as its most provident host is unclear. At its 1994 national congress, its most militant affiliate – NUMSA – tried to table a motion proposing the creation of a workers' party. The proposal was stillborn: no other affiliate was willing to second it. That vote of confidence is unlikely to be repeated indefinitely.

68   This was directly linked to the SACP's (called the CPSA at the time) membership of the Communist International (or Comintern), which at its second congress in July/August 1920 had adopted Lenin's Theses on the National and Colonial Question. Emphasized in them was the need for an alliance of national and colonial liberation movements with working class organizations. Handed down to the CPSA at the sixth congress of the Comintern in 1928 was a harder line: socialism could arrive only after a phase of bourgeois nationalism had passed, the so-called 'two-stage theory'. The dictum was not happily received by all South African communists, but it became a central part of the dogma that would define the party's strategy for the rest of the century. See Ellis and Sechaba (1992:17–22).

69   It could be argued that the SACP's promotion of insurrectionism in the 1980s constituted an earlier shift away from the two-stage theory, since success could have allowed the two phases to blur into one.

70   Tripartite Alliance (1997) 'Assessment of the Current Phase of Transformation' (discussion document), *African Communist* (Fourth Quarter), Johannesburg.

71   Wolpe, H. (1975) 'The theory of internal colonialism: The South African case' in Oxaal, I. *et al., Beyond the Sociology of Development*, London, cited by Bundy (1989:9–10).

72   Wolpe (1988:32). Class exploitation and national (racial) exploitation are entangled in South Africa. The theoretical challenge awaiting those activists and

organizations steeped in CST thinking is, as Colin Bundy (1993) has written, 'to determine when and how they overlap and complement each other, and when and how they are analytically different'.

73   Quoted in Cronin (1994:15).

74   The SACP has not been the sole target of such attacks. Standing in for Mbeki at Cosatu's 1999 congress, ANC chair and defence minister Patrick Lekota told delegates that public criticism of government policies smacked of a lack of 'revolutionary discipline'. Only 'consensus positions' should be aired in public, he said, adding that 'sharp and uncontrolled criticism merely confuses the masses'. See 'Outspoken government attacks on unions as strike action spreads', *SouthScan*, Vol. 14, No. 17, 20 August 1999.

75   'Strategic Perspectives' adopted by the Alliance Executives' Summit, 1 October 1995. The document makes for instructive reading – not least for its bold insistence that the 'national democratic forces' unproblematically represent a progressive bloc.

76   Steven Friedman, 'Mbeki forum won't tame the grassroots', *Mail & Guardian*, 14 January 2000. Friedman also noted that Mbeki's knack at handling leadership level debates and disputes has not been tested among contrary activists. In 1998, he used COSATU and SACP national conferences as podiums for laying down the line. On both occasions, he left the proceedings immediately afterwards. Tellingly, in 1999, he dispatched ANC national chair Mosiuoa (Terror) Lekota, who is much more skilled at handling grassroots dynamics, to address COSATU's national conference.

77   Mbeki (1998b). These were not mere words spoken in anger. The SACP's alleged role in blocking the election of two Mbeki-anointed candidates at the ANC's 1997 Mafikeng national conference was followed by a bid to launch a probe into the so-called 'red plot' – to no avail, although one of the alleged protagonists subsequently found his election prospects in the SACP were stymied. In June 1998 came an attempt (reportedly mounted out of the president's office) to remove Cronin from the ANC's national executive committee. This, too, failed.

78   As Cronin put it in 1996: 'I don't think we should be trying to come up with an economic strategy document, for instance, and anyway we don't have the capacity, remotely. That's why we're in the alliance.' Quoted in 'No room for rebels without a cause', *Mail & Guardian*, 22 November 1996.

79   'SACP Response to Budget Speech', media release, 23 February 2000.

80   Note that the conference did *not* endorse the GEAR plan per *se*, as some media reports claimed. Approved were the general goals of the plan and some of its underlying principles – such as the need for macro-economic stability.

81   SACP documents argue the contrary, noting that the state is not a fortress of pure power, for example. In practice, though, that (correct) reading is disavowed by its lukewarm bids to practically act as an ideological and strategic compass for broader social struggles.

82   'Mbeki polemicises on race, talks up economic performance', *SouthScan*, Vol. 15, No. 3, 11 February 2000.

83   Recall Stephen Gelb's view (in Chapter 6) that one of the GEAR plan's main flaws was its unilateral introduction by government.

84   Please see Chapter 6.

85   The description 'third way of a special type' is more than a tongue-in-cheek reference to CST. The claim that a programme of change has to service a presumed equivalence of interests that extend across society – and, that is to say, rests on a sublimation of class struggle – lies at the heart of Third Way thinking. As an analogy, consider these excerpts from the SACP's 1962 Road to Freedom pro-

gramme: 'As its immediate and foremost task, the South African Communist Party works for a united front of national liberation. It strives to unite all sections and classes of the oppressed and democratic people for a national democratic revolution to destroy White domination ... The interests of the Africa commercial class lie wholly in joining the workers and rural people for the overthrow of White supremacy.' See 'The Road to South African Freedom: Programme of the South African Communist Party', reprinted in Various authors (1970:113, 135).

86 As Zuege notes, a landmark reference point was the unhappy fate of Francois Mitterand's apparently anachronistic bid to revive a Keynesian strategy in France in the early 1980s. The French and German versions differ from the British variant most obviously in their readings of globalization. Britain's Labour Party takes it as 'a given and seeks to run with what it believes to be the grain of the global marketplace' – hence, its inclination toward flexible labour markets and low social costs. In contrast, the continental variants, at least rhetorically, begrudge the impact of globalization on their welfare and labour systems.

87 German political scientist Jochen Hippler, for example, has highlighted the vast manoeuvring space that theorists such as Anthony Giddens leave for politicians to make certain choices (and revise them, if need be). Seen as a 'map', the Third Way therefore contains fundamental principles and assumptions, but lacks precise steps and injunctions.

88 Marquand, D. (1998) 'The Blair paradox', *Prospect* (May), London.

89 Brian Groom, 'Blair fights on with modernising agenda', *Financial Times*, 16 March 2000, London.

90 Mandelson, P. and Liddle, R. (1996) *The Blair Revolution: Can New Labour Deliver?*, London, p. 18, quoted in Coates (1996:72).

91 Quoted in 'Cosatu discovers its weakness and Mbeki his strength', *SouthScan*, Vol. 14, No. 19, 17 September 1999.

92 *Ibid.* ANC government leaders have grown fond of invoking Marx and Lenin in defence of free market policies. In a 1996 tripartite alliance meeting, Mbeki appeared to impress some SACP figures when he tried to situate the GEAR plan within 'a Marxist metaphysics', as Jeremy Cronin later recalled. Taking his cue, finance minister Trevor Manuel has tried to defend his austere fiscal policies with references to *Das Kapital*.

93 Quoted in 'Outspoken government attacks on unions as strike action spreads', *SouthScan*, Vol. 14, No. 17, 20 August 1999.

94 A 1999 study by Andrew Levy & Associates found that 68 per cent of companies surveyed had outsourced labour in 1994–8; of them, 79 per cent had outsourced more than once. Almost all the workers affected were blue-collar. See Kelly (1999:37). In the clothing industry, 72 small firms used liquidation to restructure their labour forces in 1999. 'Workers were then re-employed as independent contractors by the same company, relaunched under a different name', one press report noted. See Shirley Jones, 'Sweatshops swamp bargaining councils', *Business Report*, 3 March 2000.

95 Renee Grawitsky & Barbara Adair, 'Showdown looms between govt and unions', *Business Day*, 7 March 2000.

96 Unions' losses have not necessarily been management's gain, because 'once unionists joined management, they often lost their credibility and were not given sufficient support in their new positions'. See *Business Day*, 6 July 1994.

97 A more detailed overview of the state of the union movement appeared in the first edition of this book, pp. 222–34.

98   For examples see issues of the *Shopsteward*, a magazine created by COSATU to improve communication with factory level workers and officials.
99   See the special feature 'Social democracy or democratic socialism', *SA Labour Bulletin*, Vol. 17, No. 6 (Nov/Dec 1993), pp. 72–99; and John Saul (1991) 'Between "barbarism" and "structural reform"', *New Left Review*, No. 188 (July/August), republished in his *Recolonization and Resistance in Southern Africa* (1993). See also Moses Mayekiso (1993) 'Nationalisation, socialism and the alliance', *SA Labour Bulletin*, Vol. 17, No. 4 (July/August); 'What's left for the Left?' *Work in Progress*, No. 89 (Special Edition, June 1993); Karl von Holdt (1992) 'The rise of strategic unionism', *Southern Africa Report* (November); 'Strategic objectives of the national liberation struggle' (discussion paper), *African Communist*, No. 133 (Second Quarter 1993); 'The present situation and the challenges for the South African left' (SACP discussion paper for the Conference of the Left), July 1993, unpublished.
100 Gorz (1973) and 'Thinking the unthinkable: Globalism, socialism and democracy in the South African transition', in Miliband, R. and Panitch, L. (eds.), *The Socialist Register* 1994, Merlin Press, London. For a cautioning response from Kagarlitsky, see his 'Letter to South Africa', *Links*, No. 4 (January–March 1995).
101 For volatile examples, see Callinicos, A. (1992) 'Reform and revolution in South Africa: A reply to John Saul', *New Left Review*, No. 195; Saul's reply in the same issue; Godongwana (1992); and Lehulere, O. (1996) 'Social democracy and neo-liberalism in South Africa', *Links*, No. 7 (July–October).
102 Paraphrased by Bond (1994:19).
103 Cited by Saul (1994a:40).
104 *Ibid.*
105 Cited by Patrick Bond, 'Election in South Africa', *International Viewpoint* (May 1994).
106 The September Commission report quoted in Collins and Ray (1997:13).
107 The phrasing belongs to Collins and Ray, *op. cit.*, p. 12.
108 Interestingly, Vishwas Satgar (1997) has also pointed out the subtextual reversion to a 'two-stage' outlook: 'Socialism is some kind of abstract future goal within this strategic perspective, which can only be achieved through a two stagism – social democracy then socialism.'
109 Webster, E. and Adler, G. (1999) 'Towards a class compromise in South Africa's "Double Transition": Bargained liberalisation and the consolidation of democracy' (paper), History Workshop of the University of the Witwatersrand, 18 September, Johannesburg, p. 1.
110 *Op. cit.*, p. 3.
111 Anon (1996) 'The state and social transformation' (discusion paper) reprinted in *African Communist* (First Quarter, 1997), Johannesburg. The paper is believed to have been penned by Vusi Mavimbela, a former adviser to Thabo Mbeki. For a stern critique, see Cronin and Nzimande (1997).
112 *Op. cit*, p. 19.
113 Sangoco (1996) *1996 NGO Week report,* p. 9.
114 'Deep divisions in directionless Free State ANC branches', *The Star*, 17 February 1997.
115 See note 28. Interestingly, membership of a range of civil society organizations remained fairly stable, which contradicts the widely held notion of demobilization in South African civil society since 1994.
116 Author's interview, November 1994.
117 Author's interview, October 1994. At the time, Gondongwana was general secretary of NUMSA. He later became economic affairs minister in the Eastern Cape province.

118 Author's interview, November 1994.
119 Quoted in Marais (1998:211).
120 Quoted in 'Relations sour between government and business', *SouthScan*, Vol. 12, No. 42, 14 November 1997.
121 Stuart Hall, 'Gramsci's relevance for the study of race and ethnicity' in Morley and Chen (1996:424, 431).
122 Quoted by Satgar (1997).

CHAPTER NINE

Shock of the new

For decades, South Africa represented perhaps the paradigmatic case of racist discrimination and racial discord. In the 1990s, unity and reconciliation became the beacons of post-apartheid South Africa, and a postulated 'rainbow nation' metaphorically described the desired outcome.

The need to construct an enveloping national identity that could subsume or at least muffle racial and ethnic antagonisms is self-evident. Without it there is the danger that diverse grievances and tensions could be opportunistically translated into racialist and ethnic reactions.

To a great extent, therefore, the architects of the post-apartheid order took to heart Adam Przeworski's argument that democratic consolidation requires the institutionalization of conflict. Broadly, the political framework has been explicitly geared to this. More narrowly, one encounters a host of structures and institutions set up to serve as fora for the arbitration and, hopefully, resolution of conflicts and differences – and for extending the juridical and social reach of newly won rights and liberties. In theory, as long as difference and conflict can be funnelled into such bodies – and as long as they retain legitimacy and trust – the prospects for further democratic consolidation are enhanced.

Likewise, the electoral system serves a similar role. At election time, the party political landscape seems healthily diverse – ranging from the dominant ANC to the smaller opposition parties and a menagerie of parties representing minority ethnic, regional and issue-specific interests. Meanwhile, the ANC's ongoing and startling ability to attract and serve as a gratifying abode for diverse groups, ideologies and interests is widely (and correctly) seen as one of the main pillars of stability.

These advantages and advances should not cloud appreciation of the central role played by South Africa's first democratically elected president. Nelson Mandela created a temporary recess in which a sense of unity or nationhood could sink a few tenuous roots. Mandela's historic feat was not only to have helped steer South Africa away from the brink of catastrophe but to have carved out a breathing space where pulses could settle, enmities subdue and affinities become recast. The grand authority and mythic stature attained by Mandela enabled him to 'float above politics' (in the manner of Charles De Gaulle), largely unencumbered by the realpolitik of his party and the attendant need to shore up power bases and juggle trade-offs.

His success lay in his ability to *traverse* many of the contradictions at play in South African society and the ANC – the 'modern' and the 'traditional', black and white, privilege and deprivation – a feat made possible by personal attributes and by the assiduously constructed myth that surrounds him. With Mandela's departure, South Africa emerged from what was a unique interlude and passed from the era of the statesman to that of the politician, from a dependency on the personal charisma of a leader to reliance on more conventional forms of politicking. With it comes more intrigue, conflict, uncertainty and contrariety.

At the same time, telling continuities still define democratic South Africa and its political management. South Africa corroborates James Baldwin's aphorism that 'people are trapped in history, and history is trapped in them'.[1] The success of a liberation struggle tends to insulate from scrutiny the strategic frameworks, decisions and traditions that steered the struggle toward victory. That these were, in some respects, problematic even in their historical contexts might be regarded as a piddling matter – for imperfect or not, they charted a comparatively victorious course. Yet, some of the conundrums and handicaps of the post-apartheid era have their origins in past decisions taken or shirked. An accumulation of historical currents have been inherited – the structural continuities that bedevil efforts at transformation, the ideological narratives that both propel and retard those endeavours, and the political alliances serving as vehicles into the future. Their utility for a project that dismantles the insider/outsider mould of society cannot be assumed. In many respects, they complicate the passage into the new.

Yet, South Africa is also a dynamic and bewildering hybrid of the old and the new. The modernizing thrusts that propel it through its transition might not be particularly novel, but they are being prodigiously blended with vintage conceptions, traditions and habits. The resulting resilience and flexibility accounts for much of the ANC's formidable and enduring stature, and the vigour of the dominant hegemonic project. This has been especially evident in the efforts to construct a new national consensus – a process that will continue indefinitely and that is also integral to the competing hegemonic works-in-progress, locked as they are in an increasingly uneven contest.

The main, advertised tasks of this quest are to defend the integrity of the nation-state, combat racist and ethnic-exclusivist legacies and trends, and to establish in South Africans' lives a sense of beneficial change, unity and common belonging while respecting their diversities. Forging such a national consensus around the principles of inclusivity and unity has required illuminating and inventing a range of commonalities that could abate the centrifugal dynamics at play in society. In broad outline, it has entailed attempts to design and supervise an expansive range of compromises around the principles of stability, 'realism', efficiency and patriotism. At one level, this enterprise can be called nation-state building, a highly contested but essential undertaking that occurs on the unruly turf of struggles that are not simply waged 'out there' beyond the encampments of the state, but inside *and with it*, too. Not a neutral entity to be entrusted with technical duties, the state itself is impregnated with many of the contending values and interests that necessitate nation-state building.

The venture seems to embody Jurgen Habermas' counsel that 'the nation of citizens does not derive its identity from some common ethnic and cultural properties, but rather from the praxis of citizens who actively exercise their civil rights' (1992). Its weakness is that it also serves as bedrock for a 'modernized' development path that is *both revising and reinforcing* imbalances of income, power and opportunity. Highlighted, in other words, is the need for sophisticated and effective forms of political, social and ideological management – much of which already is in evidence, as the previous chapter showed. But there are other fault lines that will have to be traversed with equal aplomb.

Resting on several pillars, the core foundations of the bid to build a nation-state reside in the terms and details of the political settlement, the post-apartheid political system and the rights and liberties inscribed in the constitution which, at the political-juridical level, establishes the principle of equality as the central axis of political and social relations. Buttressing them are specific compromises embedded in the settlement (the 'sunset clause', the protection of minority rights at local government level, guaranteeing the expression of cultural diversity), the nominally federalist character of the political system, acknowledgement of Afrikaners' right to seek self-determination, and the preservation of traditional leaders' authority. Also enlisted have been enterprises such as the TRC and the grand gesture upon which it was predicated: amnesty.[2] Its central role was to buttress political stability and to help engineer a psycho-social catharsis.

Truth and reconciliation

The Commission's origins lay in the final months of political negotiations, in 1993. It emerged as a compromise between the demand for justice (expressed by the democratic movement) and the demand for a blanket amnesty (made by the NP and its allies and functionaries). The choice, essentially, was 'to consolidate the peace of a country where human rights are protected today or to seek retroactive justice that could compromise that peace'.³ Struck during a period of intense political instability, the compromise was understandable. Its contours neatly matched those of the political settlement itself – defusing the threat of a counter-revolution by drawing opposing social and political forces into new forms of accommodation. Rhetorically, the TRC's role was described in psycho-social terms – of 'healing the nation'. 'The recognition of (past) guilt is a necessary part of the commitment to the future,' as (then deputy president) Thabo Mbeki told parliament in June 1997.

Victims had the opportunity to publicly air their experiences of human rights abuses; perpetrators were encouraged to disclose their actions in order to qualify for amnesty. The price of the enterprise was steep: full disclosure exempted perpetrators from criminal or civil action, thereby suspending the administering of justice.

The TRC's function, therefore, was to extend into the social sphere the consensual (or, at least, conciliatory) dynamics nurtured in the political realm, an approach that exalted 'inclusiveness and stability at all costs'. Ultimately, the Commission was burdened with the hope that truth-telling could beget reconciliation and, ultimately, help forge a unified nation.

Despite the prevarication and silences, a myriad of truths did emerge: mothers discovering the fate of their sons, activists describing the last moments of comrades, a policeman staring at the shallow grave of a guerrilla fighter who was executed after nine days of torture, saying only: 'God … she was brave'. The achievements of the TRC are perhaps best measured against the small certainties exposed in such moments, and in the chances it offered victims finally to release the grip of their tormentors. Former ANC guerrilla Tony Yengeni did this by ordering his police torturer to lower his paunch onto the floor and demonstrate his 'interrogation' techniques. So did Dawie Ackerman, left a widower by the 1993 St James church massacre in Cape Town, when he confronted his wife's three killers and demanded: 'Turn around and look me in the eye. Did you see my wife when you walked into that church? She was wearing the blue dress.' Yet ultimately, as one TRC commissioner has suggested, the process perhaps functioned better as a conduit for anger and anguish than as an instrument for healing and reconciliation.

The ambitious and essential undertaking was undermined by several flaws, none of which could be blamed on the Commission itself. Built on the testimony of individuals, the systemic character of the apartheid system was obscured. Political concerns enabled IFP leader Mangosuthu Buthelezi's role in the KwaZulu-Natal war to escape all but cursory examination. Like millions of their compatriots, the commissioners had to suffer the impenitence of self-confessed killers and endure the hush of thousands of human rights violators who steered a wide berth around the process. The shields of plausible deniability erected around former presidents

P.W. Botha and F.W. de Klerk and their inner circles were tested but not pierced. Those who shunned the process theoretically remain liable for criminal prosecution, but the potentially destabilizing effects of such recourse make it highly unlikely.

Some of this was caused by the disappearance of evidence (destroyed by apartheid officials or concealed within the nominally new intelligence services), by organizational, managerial and bureaucratic problems in the Commission, and by a lack of resources. The TRC had a budget of about R130 million ($22 million) with which to fulfil its task – 'the price of a can of Coca-Cola for every citizen', as one official lamented. In Johannesburg, a mere 12 investigators had to investigate 34 years' of human rights violations across four provinces. But the TRC also suffered a larger shortcoming:

> Truth recovery, and the work of the TRC, was simplistically viewed by many as the primary vehicle for reconciliation. As a result, and due to the intrinsic limitations of the TRC's remit of work, the fact that structural inequality was integral to genuine reconciliation was ignored … A cynical view would be that reconciliation between the oppressor and the oppressed was merely a façade (Hamber, 1998:12–13).[4]

The reconciliatory venture was hampered by other expansive compromises, not least the appeasement of capital. Not surprisingly, less than one week of the TRC's two-year life span was devoted to public hearings on the roles of business in the apartheid era. Built around individual testimonies of the perpetrators and victims of human rights abuses, the process did not penetrate the systemic nature of oppression and the corresponding benefits that the minority enjoyed. Not only did the TRC function in a broader socio-economic – and ideological – context that demonstrably reinforces existing inequalities, cleavages and antagonisms, but its remit prevented it from piercing the indifference of the privileged. Thus, individual remembrance was demanded, while collective amnesia was condoned in the name of reconciliation. The evasion of moral (and legal) culpability was sanctioned, most obviously in the case of corporate South Africa whose complicity in a devastated social landscape still is rarely, if ever, noted publicly. On the contrary, corporate interests stand conflated with the 'common' and 'national' interest.

Left largely untouched, too, has been white South Africans' ability to retreat into dens of clumsy prevarication, idle bitterness and nostalgia. Absent is contrition and the questioning (on any significant scale) of moral and social sensibilities, about the past and the present. In white South Africa, reconciliation has taken the hybridized form of denial and self-acquittal. Its arithmetic has remained exploitative, exacting sacrifices and humility from the oppressed, whilst indulging the arrogance of the privileged – a kind of existential analogy to the post-apartheid development path. In this sense, the TRC became a side-show in a larger drama that entrenches and rationalizes the inequalities of past and present. Its ultimate impact would be determined less by its own work than by other, more definitive forms of appeasement, chiefly the reluctance to more resolutely restructure the circuits whereby wealth and opportunity are distributed. Reconciliation remains, sadly, a chimera.

The modern and the traditional

Less obvious but as perilous is another stress line. Perhaps the most neg-lected contradiction in South Africa's quest for transformation is the ambiguous status and powers conferred on 'traditional' authority systems. While the democratic movement explicitly framed its struggle against apartheid in Enlightenment terms – hinging on civil and political liberties – the reality of tribal chieftaincies in rural areas represented a prickly coun-terpoint that was intellectually overlooked and strategically fudged.

South Africa now boasts a constitution that exemplifies many of the most hallowed political traditions of modernity. Yet, its political system increasingly has been embellished with efforts to incorporate traditional authorities into the political management of society. Some analysts argue that this amounts to a bid to reconcile two irreconcilable modes of political management:

> Chieftainship by its nature is an undemocratic institution. It confers rights and obligations on an individual merely on the basis of some accident of birth. No merit applies and no accountability is required. It is the antithesis of all tenets of democracy ... We now have a new system (of government) whose essence is equality before the law. We should therefore discard the old.[5]

In his book *Citizen and Subject*, Mahmood Mamdani (1996) contends that the cleavage between 'modern' and 'traditional' society ranks as the most fundamental, unresolved contradiction in much of post-colonial Africa, including South Africa. Millions of South Africans continue to live under the rule of local chiefs operating in the ambit of customary law. At the root of the chiefs' power is an admixture of ethnicized tradition, inherited authority and clientelism that fits uneasily with the principles of individual rights and democratic processes that underpin the new political system. The severely diminished status of women under traditional authorities is emblematic of this contradiction.

Several impulses encourage government's attempts to square this circle. The first is political. Traditional leaders stand at the hub of politicized ethnicity, most obviously in KwaZulu-Natal. If alienated, their counterparts elsewhere in the country could follow suit and become the backbone of other political parties' efforts to make inroads into ANC support in rural areas of the Eastern Cape, North-West and Northern Province especially.

Also featuring is the possibility that this could also take the form of de-stabilizing activities. Guiding the efforts to incorporate traditional author-ities into the new political order, therefore, is the *leitmotif* of post-1994 rule: stability.[6] The reward, though, could turn out to be the converse.

The conundrum of traditional authorities assumes political significance also in another sense – within the discourse of the African renaissance, which, among many other things, centres on a dynamic blend of 'African tradition' and values, and Enlightenment principles.

The second impulse seems based on personal sentiment. The systems and values of traditional authorities occupy an important place in the back-ground and philosophy of the older generation of African ANC leaders, including Nelson Mandela. In their personal lives, they appear to have har-monized these contradictory currents, a feat they believe can be replicated in political society. Mandela, for example, frequently has called on youth to respect chiefs; at the ANC's 1997 national conference he went as far as accusing critics of traditional authorities of displaying 'infantile radicalism'.

The third impulse is a mix of functional need and politics. The reality of chiefs' power in many rural communities, it seems, has to be calculated into the planning and implementation of development projects and local gov-ernment operations. Here, government appears particularly conscious of the disastrous attempts by FRELIMO to run roughshod over traditional authorities during the early years of Mozambican independence.

With traditional leaders' powers a highly charged issue inside the ANC, government at first avoided redefining their new status in decisive terms. Unable or unwilling to democratize traditional authorities – for fear of unleashing more destabilizing dynamics – the ANC in the early 1990s sought to embrace those leaders willing to align themselves to the anti-apartheid struggle. The formation of CONTRALESA sprung from that bid. Chiefs and kings have reacted to the ensuing equivocation by assem-bling a formidable lobby and adeptly exploiting the political concerns mentioned.

The upshot has been a growing series of compromises and concessions to traditional leaders. Although currently limited, the powers of the (national) Council of Traditional Leaders and provincial Houses of Traditional Leaders seems set to expand. While public service jobs are being cut and wage increases pegged lower than inflation, the government has decided that traditional leaders across the country would be paid hiked salaries, as well as pension and medical aid benefits – citing as one of the 'sad legacies of apartheid' the poor and unequal remuneration of traditional leaders.

Instead of being assimilated into and 'inoculated' in the new political system, traditional leaders have acquired greater leverage for demanding further concessions that both complicate and threaten efforts to translate basic rights and liberties into practice. CONTRALESA has demanded that the department of justice confer on chiefs the authority to try 'relevant criminal civil cases'. It also wants greater representation for chiefs on rural councils. In a memorandum presented to Mandela in 1998, the dangers of non-compliance were spelt out clearly: 'The great majority of traditional leaders ... decided to ignore and withhold co-operation from these rural councils. The result has been tension, divisions and a lack of service delivery in the rural areas.'[7]

There is a real danger that these multiplying gestures of accommodation could seriously upset the bid to achieve authentic and durable democratization. In Mamdani's view, South Africa could be headed for a situation he has termed 'deracialisation without democratisation':

> The real import of (the negotiated) transition to non-racial rule may turn out to be the fact that it will leave intact the structures of indirect rule. Sooner rather than later, it will liquidate racism in the state. With free movement between town and country, but with Native Authorities in charge of an ethnically governed rural population, it will reproduce one legacy of apartheid – in a non-racial form (1996:32).

Still lacking in these attempts to assuage chiefs and headmen is a formula that could blunt the contradictions between democratic governance and power exercised on the basis of traditional authority, leaving many millions of citizens caught in the to-and-fro between two modes of political management. Hardly less troubling is the possibility that the politicization of the traditional realm could acquire more hardy ethnic overtones. Pre-emptively or otherwise, central and provincial governments' prime recourse would be to dispense greater financial and developmental largesse, potentially recreating the clientelist relations that, in countries such as Zimbabwe, link the zones in which political modernity and traditional authority respectively hold sway. Hidden in such an outcome is a further danger: with rural power in large parts of the country organized along lines antithetical to the broader political system, progressive civil society organizations would then remain sequestered mainly in urban zones.

Radical as reality

Enormous changes have been wrought since 1994. The progress made at the superstructural level in many respects has been astounding: the constitution, new legislation, new policies and frameworks, overhauled state structures and refurbished state systems, are examples. Hitches and logjams identified inside government are constantly being addressed, with the power concentrated at the apex of the executive apparently intended to facilitate those efforts. Although inadequate in both quality and quantity, social delivery proceeds at a pace and in a manner unprecedented in most South Africans' lives.

Despite teething problems, post-apartheid South Africa's most resounding accomplishments reside in the deracialization of the political-institutional realm. Less decisive is the progress in fostering a national basis for consent or a national political consciousness in which the political potency of parochial identities is muffled. And much less definitive is the progress made towards deracializing and democratizing the economic system – not just in terms of grand ownership patterns but in the redistribution of opportunities to participate in it (as workers and entrepreneurs) and to share more equitably in the surpluses generated.

The efficacy of the institutional edifices and superstructural arrangements created depends ultimately on the ability to revise structural dynamics that sunder society into pockets of privilege and vast hinterlands of deprivation. These are being abetted and reinforced. Indeed, even the prospects of robust growth along the current path are questionable. As James K. Galbraith was forced to ask after reflecting on two decades of orthodox economic adjustment worldwide:

> Where are the continuing success stories of liberalization, privatization, deregulation, sound money and balanced budgets? Where are the emerging markets that have emerged, the developing countries that have developed, the transition economies that have truly completed a successful and happy transition? Look closely. Look hard. They do not exist (1999:2).

The development path embarked upon is already yielding what historian Colin Bundy has called 'a lop-sided structure – two nations disguised as one, a hybrid social formation consisting of increasingly deracialised insiders and persistently black outsiders' (1999:11). It is an outcome that bears scant resemblance to the visions of many millions who prosecuted the long struggle against apartheid. But it also hardly jars with an outcome many others – arrayed on either side of yesterday's barricades – quietly wished for.

Yet, as Chapter 8 argued, that dissonance does not augur doom for what has matured into a refined hegemonic enterprise. Its sophistication and likely longevity bears emphasis, particularly when confronted with a popular rival that remains ramshackle and woozy. The rapid maturation of that project – and the centrality of the ANC and the post-apartheid state in its prosecution – tempts the view that it constitutes an unfolding formative strategy. Yet this is not altogether clear. Without overstating the potential for flux under current conditions, it seems more accurate to see it as the crystallization of expectant accommodations, tactical adjustments and historically inflected judgements that heed, in the first instance, the imperatives of capital accumulation at the (interconnected) local and global levels. In such a reading, the avowal and pursuit of progressive socio-economic change is not rendered insincere, but is decisively subordinated to the extended reproduction of capital. Modest progress on the former front remains possible, but its scope and character are determined by the terms of the overarching class project that proceeds under the mantle of a nominally social-democratic experiment.

That, in turn, expresses a balance of forces that is profoundly unfavourable to a popular alternative project, the swift recovery of which is by no means guaranteed. It will require a long process of re-assessment, regrouping and rebuilding – all of which will have to occur on a terrain that includes but also transcends the geographic boundaries of South Africa – in other words, a revitalized popular project has to acquire a transnational character.

Inside South Africa, meanwhile, new benefits will continue to accrue to sections of the poor majority. These will occur on terms and amid conditions that recreate underfoot a society of insiders and outsiders. To what extent this will threaten social and political instability is impossible to predict. Tensions could be defused – though not resolved – as long the state is able to engineer and support a steady stream of development and upliftment initiatives, and constantly refurbish a political-ideological canopy of solidarity and trust. Yet that feat could be upset by unforeseen and uncontrollable events. A liberalized, developing economy such as South Africa that pursues deeper integration into a volatile world system enjoys no guarantee of a smooth ride.

Less unpredictable is the radical social dislocation and destabilization that looms as the AIDS endemic matures. South Africa has become the site of one of the fastest-growing HIV/AIDS epidemics in the world. In early 2000, the national HIV prevalence rate was 22 per cent. Projections show the country will be in the throes of an AIDS epidemic by the year 2005. By then, some 2,5 million people will have died of AIDS-related illnesses. By 2010, it is forecast that there will be at least a million AIDS orphans in the country. Already, statisticians have lowered South African's average life expectancy from 65,4 years to 55,7 years. In some estimates, that figure will drop to about 48 years by the year 2010. Other forecasts are even lower: 35–40 years.[8] Shocking as they are, these projections are not new. In 1996, an Old Mutual Actuaries and Consultants survey forecasted that the annual death rate in the workforce would rise from 5 to 30 in every 1 000.[9]

The 'miracle' of the new South Africa is doomed to be eclipsed by the failure to prevent this disaster, a failure that indicts all but a handful of structures and individuals, including the left.[10] Despite the existence of a comprehensive response programme (endorsed by the cabinet in 1994), it was not until five years later that government tried to throw its combined weight behind a national campaign. Even then, the commitment would be punctured by equivocation. Funding to AIDS service organizations was slashed (by 43 per cent in the 2000/1), state funding of AZT treatment for pregnant HIV-positive mothers was continuously denied and, in early 2000, the president would go as far as question the link between HIV and AIDS.[11] Somehow absent on this front has been the sophistication that has been the hallmark of politics and ideology in South Africa since 1994. The consequences defy comprehension. Their exact effects on the (thus far) successful attempts to make the centre hold remain to be seen.

All the while, South Africa will continue to witness and experience the emergence of new forms of popular organizations. Many of them are not only novel and perplexing but also impervious to easy categorization as 'progressive' or 'reactionary', 'transformative' or 'survivalist'. For the most part, they remain poorly researched and, therefore, understood. Blurred in them will be the line that ostensibly separates legality from illegality. Most will prevail in the shadowy recesses of society termed the 'informal sector', coalescing around distinct and often highly parochial sets of interests. They are the result of shifts that see people and 'communities' assuming and acting upon more specific, differentiated social identities, in contrast to the enveloping, homogenizing categories that served the anti-apartheid struggle. As a result, they call into question the legitimacy, representitivity and utility of some traditional structures, notably civics.

Their activities will increasingly define the country's cities and towns, where the bulk of people will continue to seek salvation. Their existence and growth will occur both because of and despite the overarching development path. In essence, they will come to constitute the netherworld of a post-apartheid South Africa that re-divides society into insiders and outsiders. They in turn will help shape the template on which the state acts and the realities in which people live.[12] They constitute neither a potential panacea nor the mere 'collateral damage' of a foreshortened voyage to a better life for all. They will feature prominently in any alternative to the prognosis painted in the preceding chapters – though exactly how and in what respects continues to elude the constituents of both hegemonic projects. It is cold comfort to remark that the rest of the world also offers few beacons on this front. But the fate of a popular project depends on incorporating this reality into its strategic vista.

For the left and the popular sectors in general there are, in other words, no blueprints, no pristine models to be dusted off. Neither can the efficacy of yesterday's strategies, tactics and practices be taken for granted. Lacking, too, is the luxury of a stable, familiar terrain on which to act. Required are new levels of invention, new forms of courage and a new appetite for risk. In an age when, as Colin Bundy once wrote, the left has 'no prospect of a quick victory or even a clear model of what that victory will look like' (1993:17), it can do worse than ponder the advice offered to a young Romanian poet in a Zurich café almost a century ago: 'One can never be radical enough; that is, one must always be as radical as reality itself.'[13]

Notes

1 *Notes of a Native Son*, 1955.
2 For a survey of the early debates surrounding amnesty, see Marais, H. and Narsoo, M. (1992) 'And justice for all?', *Work in Progress*, No. 85 (October) and Marais, H. (1993) 'The skeletons come out of the cupboard', *Work in Progress*, No. 91 (August/September).
3 As phrased in the Uruguayan context by former president Julio Maria Sanguinetti in 1986, cited in Marais and Narsoo, *op. cit.*, p. 9.
4 He attributes the 'cynical view' to Australian journalist John Pilger (1998).
5 Barney Mthombothi, 'Relics of the past', *Financial Mail*, 19 March 1999.
6 This concern was captured well in the remarks of a top ANC office bearer at a 1997 Alliance Summit meeting who warned of 'chiefs who were with us, beginning to fight against us, beginning to move away to join other forces. Are they a force to be forgotten, how do we deal with that, if you believe that you need to get rid of this institution, how do you deal with that, because if you are not careful, you could actually augment the forces against you.'
7 'Democracy's chief problem', *Financial Mail*, 12 June 1998.
8 Cited by Charlene Smith, 'Planning for AIDS needs to start now', *Mail & Guardian*, 5 March 1999.
9 'Economic cost of AIDS', *Mail & Guardian*, 31 January 1997.
10 For a study of South Africa's HIV/AIDS response, see Marais (2000).
11 The government invited several so-called AIDS 'dissidents' to address a panel coinciding with the World AIDS conference in mid-2000 in Durban, South Africa. The reason, according to presidential spokesperson, Parks Mankahlana, was that 'we humans know very little about HIV/AIDS'. See 'Government develops maverick AIDS theme, hits at drugs giants', *SouthScan*, Vol. 15, No. 6, 24 March 2000; Vol. 15, No. 5, 10 March 2000.
12 'People', rather than 'citizens', because millions of the country's inhabitants are globalized citizens, traversing the world in search of survival and opportunity – whom xenophobes call *amakwerekwere* (those 'from far away').
13 Lenin in early 1917, quoted by Alexander Cockburn in 'Radical as reality' in Blackburn (1992:167).

Bibliography

Adelzadeh, A. (1999) 'The costs of staying the course', *Ngqo!* (June), NIEP, Johannesburg.

Adelzadeh, A. (1996) 'From the RDP to GEAR: The gradual embracing of neo-liberalism in economic policy', research paper, Johannesburg.

Adelzadeh, A. & Padayachee, P. (1995) 'The RDP White Paper: Reconstruction of a Development Vision?', *Transformation* (February), Durban.

Adler, G. (1998) 'Social partnership: A dead end for labour', *SA Labour Bulletin*, Vol. 22, No. 1 (February), Johannesburg.

Africa Watch (1991) *The Killings in South Africa*, Human Rights Watch, New York.

African National Congress (1999) *ANC Election Manifesto*, Johannesburg.

African National Congress (1994) *Reconstruction and Development Programme: A policy framework* (base document), Umanyano, Johannesburg.

African National Congress Department of Economic Policy (1992) 'ANC policy guidelines for a democratic South Africa – as adopted at the National Conference' (28–31 May).

African National Congress National Executive Committee (1992) 'Negotiations: A strategic perspective', *African Communist*, No. 131 (Fourth Quarter), Johannesburg.

African National Congress Youth League (1996) 'Organisational and leadership issues in the ANC: A perspective of the ANC Youth League' (discussion document), Johannesburg.

Alexander, N. (1993) 'Nation-building: An interview', *Work in Progress*, No. 93 (November), Johannesburg.

Amin, S. (1998) 'The challenge of globalisation' (paper), Third World Forum, Dakar.

Amin, S. (1997) 'For a progressive and democratic new world order' (paper), Afro-Asian Solidarity Organization conference (April), Cairo.

Amin, S. (1996) 'Regionalisation in the Third World', Third World Forum document, Dakar.

Amin, S. (1993a) 'Social movements in the periphery' in Wignaraja, P. (ed.) *New Social Movements in the South: Empowering the People*, Zed, London.

Amin, S. (1993b) 'SA in the Global Economic System', *Work in Progress*, No. 87 (March), Johannesburg.

Amin, S. (1992) 'The perils of Utopia', *Work in Progress*, No. 86 (December), Johannesburg.

Amin, S. (1985) *Delinking*, Monthly Review Press, New York.

Amin, S., Arrighi, G., Frank, A.G. & Wallerstein, I. (1990) *Transforming the Revolution: Social Movements and the World-system*, Monthly Review Press, New York.

ANC/SACP/COSATU (1995) 'The need for an effective ANC-led political centre', endorsed Tripartite Alliance strategic perspectives paper published in *African Communist*, No. 142 (Third Quarter), Johannesburg.

Anderson, B. (1998) 'From miracle to crash', *London Review of Books*, Vol. 20, No. 8 (16 April), London.

Anon (1998) 'The current global economic crisis and its implications for SA', discussion paper approved at Tripartite Alliance summit meeting (October), Johannesburg.

Anon (1997) 'Compromising positions', *Development Update*, Vol. 1, No. 1 (June), Johannesburg.

Anon (1994) 'The RDP White Paper: Special feature', *RDP Monitor*, Vol. 1, No. 2 (August/September), Johannesburg.

Anon (1990) 'Prospects for a negotiated settlement', *African Communist*, No. 122 (Third Quarter), Johannesburg.

Arrighi, G. (1997) 'Globalisation, state sovereignty and the "endless" accumulation of capital' (paper), Fernand Braudel Center.

Baker, P., Boraine, A. & Krafchik, W. (eds) (1993) *South Africa and the World Economy in the 1990s*, David Philip, Cape Town.

Balibar, E. & Wallerstein, I. (1991) *Race, Nation, Class: Ambiguous Identities*, Verso, London.

Barrel, H. (1991) 'The turn to the masses: the African National Congress's strategic review of 1978–79', *Journal of Southern African Studies*, Vol. 18, No. 1 (March), York.

Barrel, H. (1990) *MK, the ANC's Armed Struggle*, Penguin, Johannesburg.

Barrett, J. (1993) 'New strategies to organise difficult sectors', *SA Labour Bulletin*, Vol. 17, No. 6 (November/December), Johannesburg.

Baskin, J. (ed.) (1996a) *Against the Current: Labour and Economic Policy in South Africa*, Ravan, Johannesburg.

Baskin, J. (1996b) 'Unions at the crossroads', *SA Labour Bulletin*, Vol. 20, No. 1 (February), Johannesburg.

Baskin, J. (1995) 'South Africa's new LRA', *SA Labour Bulletin*, Vol. 19, No. 5 (November), Johannesburg.

Baskin, J. (1991) *Striking Back: A History of Cosatu*, Ravan, Johannesburg.

Beaudet, P. (1991) 'Civics: A new social movement?' (paper), CIDMAA, Montreal.

Beaudet, P. & Marais, H. (eds) (1995) *Popular Movements and the Struggle for Transformation in South Africa*, Alternatives, Montreal.

Beaudet, P. & Theade, N. (eds) (1994) *Southern Africa after Apartheid?*, McMillan, London.

Bethlehem, L. & Makgetla, N. (1994) 'Wages and productivity in South African manufacturing', *SA Labour Bulletin*, Vol. 18, No. 4 (September), Johannesburg.

Beckman, B. (1993) 'The liberation of civil society: Neoliberal ideology and political theory', *Review of African Political Economy*, No. 58, Sheffield.

Bello, W. (1998a) 'The end of a "miracle": Speculation, foreign capital dependence and the collapse of the Southeast Asian economies' (paper), Third World Network, Penang.

Bello,W. (1998b) 'The end of the Asian miracle' (paper), Third World Network, Penang.

Bienefield, M. (1994) 'The new world order: Echoes of a new imperialism', *Third World Quarterly*, Vol. 15, No. 1, Oxfordshire.

Bird, A. & Schreiner, G. (1992) 'Cosatu at the crossroads: towards tripartite corporatism or democratic socialism', *SA Labour Bulletin*, Vol. 16, No. 6 (July/August), Johannesburg.

Blackburn, R. (ed.) (1992) *After the Fall: The failure of communism and the future of socialism*, Verso, London.

Bobbio, N. (1979) 'Gramsci and the conception of civil society' in Mouffe, C. (ed.), *Gramsci and Marxist Theory*, Routledge, London.

Bond, P. (1999) *Elite Transition: From Apartheid to Neoliberalism in South Africa*, Pluto, London.

Bond, P. (1996a) 'An international perspective on the "people-driven" character of the RDP', *African Communist*, No. 144 (Second Quarter), Johannesburg.

Bond, P. (1996b) 'The making of South Africa's macro-economic compromise' in E. Maganya (ed.), *Development Strategies in South Africa*, IFAA, Johannesburg.

Bond, P. (1996c) 'The making of South Africa's macro-economic compromise' in E. Maganya (ed.), *Development Strategies in South Africa*, IFAA, Johannesburg.

Bond, P. (1994a) 'Reconstruction and development during structural crisis', *African Communist*, No. 138 (Third Quarter), Johannesburg.

Bond, P. (1994b) 'The RDP, site of socialist struggle', *African Communist*, No. 137 (Second Quarter), Johannesburg.

Bond, P. (1994c) 'Election in South Africa', *International Viewpoint* (May), Paris.

Bond, P. (1991a) 'Theory of the economy', Pambile pamphlet series, Johannesburg.

Bond, P. (1991b) *Commanding Heights and Community Control: New Economics for a New South Africa*, Ravan, Johannesburg.

Bond, P., Pillay, Y. & Sanders, D. (1996) 'The state of neo-liberalism in South Africa: Economic, social and health transformation in question', *International Journal of Health Services*, Vol. 26, No. 4.

Bottomore, T. (1983) *A Dictionary of Marxist Thought*, Harvard University, Cambridge.

Bowles, P. & White, G. (1993) 'Central bank independence: A political economy approach and the implications for the South' (draft paper).

Brenner, R. (1998) 'The economics of global turbulence: A special report on the world economy, 1950–1998', *New Left Review*, No. 229, London.

Brittain, V. (1994) 'Africa, the lost continent', *New Statesman & Society* (8 April), London.

Budlender, D. (1997) *The Women's Budget*, IDASA, Cape Town.

Budlender, D. *et al.* (1992) 'Women and resistance in South Africa: Review article', *Social Dynamics*, Vol. 18, No. 1, Cape Town.

Buhlungu, S. (1997) 'Flogging a dying horse? COSATU and the Alliance', *SA Labour Bulletin*, Vol. 21, No. 1 (February), Johannesburg.

Bundy, C. (1999) 'Truth or reconciliation', *Southern Africa Report* (August), Toronto.

Bundy, C. (1993) 'Theory of a special type', *Work in Progress*, No. 89 (June), Johannesburg.

Bundy, C. (1991) 'Marxism in South Africa: Context, themes and challenges', *Transformation*, No. 16, Durban.

Bundy, C. (1989) 'Around which corner? Revolutionary theory and contemporary South Africa', *Transformation*, No. 8, Durban.

Bundy, C. (1987) 'History, revolution and South Africa', *Transformation*, No. 4, Durban.

Bundy, C. (1979) *The Rise and Fall of the South African Peasantry*, Heinemann, London.

Burbach, R., Nunez, O. & Kagarlitsky, B. (1997) *Globalization and its Discontents: The Rise of Postmodern Socialism*, Pluto, London.

Business Map (1999) *SA Insider: South African Investment Report 1998*, Johannesburg.

Cabesa, Quadro (1986) 'From ungovernability to revolution', *African Communist*, No. 104 (First Quarter).

Callinicos, A. (1992) *Between Apartheid and Capitalism*, Bookmarks, London.

Cargill, J. & Brown, A. (1999) 'Black economic empowerment – The next leg of the journey' in Business Map, *SA Insider: South African Investment Report 1998*, Johannesburg.

Carroll, W.K. (1992) *Organizing Dissent: Contemporary Social Movements in Theory and Practice*, Garamond, Toronto.

Casanova, Pablo G. (1997) 'The theory of the rain forest against neoliberalism and for humanity', AAPSO conference paper, Cairo.

Casanova, Pablo G. (1996) 'Globalism, neoliberalism and democracy', *Social Justice*, Vol. 23, No. 1–2, San Francisco.

CASE (1998a) *Upgrading Gauteng's Informal Settlements: First Follow-up Surveys at Eatonside, Albertina, Soshanguve South Extension 4 & Johandeo* (December), Gauteng Housing and Land Affairs Department, Johannesburg.

CASE (1998b) 'Who represents whom? Inside grassroots organisations in the Johannesburg mega-city', *Development Update*, Vol. 2, No. 1, Johannesburg.

Cassim, F. (1988) 'Growth, crisis and change in the South African economy' in Suckling, J. & White, L. (eds), *After Apartheid: Renewal of the South African Economy*, James Currey, London.

Castaneda, Jorge G. (1994) *Utopia Unarmed: The Latin American Left after the Cold War*, Vintage, New York.

Castells, M. (1998) *The Information Age: Economy, Society and Culture – Volume III – End of the Millennium*, Blackwell, Massachusetts.

Cawthra, G., Kraak, G. & O'Sullivan, G. (1994) *War and Resistance*, MacMillan, London.

Chomsky, N. (1998) 'Neoliberalism and global order: Doctrine and reality' (speech), Cambridge, Massachusetts.

Coates, D. (1996) 'Labour governments: Old constraints and new parameters', *New Left Review*, No. 219 (September/October), London.

Cole, J. (1987) *Crossroads: The politics of reform and repression 1976–1986*, Ravan, Johannesburg.

Coleman, N. (1999a) 'The basic income grant', *SA Labour Bulletin*, Vol. 23, No. 2 (April), Johannesburg.

Coleman, N. (1999b) 'The relevance of workfare to SA', *SA Labour Bulletin*, Vol. 23, No. 2 (April), Johannesburg.

Collins, D. & Ray, M. (1997) 'The September Commission: Confronting the future', *SA Labour Bulletin*, Vol. 21, No. 5 (October), Johannesburg.

Collins, D. (1994) 'Worker control', *SA Labour Bulletin*, Vol. 18, No. 3 (July), Johannesburg.

Community Constituency in NEDLAC (1996) 'Return to the RDP' (discussion document), Johannesburg.

Connell, D. (1995) 'What's left of the South African Left?', *Against the Current* (September), Detroit.

Cope, N. (1990) 'The Zulu petit bourgeoisie and Zulu nationalism in the 1920s', *Journal of Southern African Studies*, Vol. 16, No. 3 (September), York.

CORE, (1999) 'Study on the history of the non-profit sector in South Africa', research paper for the Johns Hopkins Non-Profit Sector Project, Johannesburg.

COSATU (2000) 'Public response by COSATU to the 2000/2001 budget' (March), Johannesburg.

COSATU (1998) 'COSATU's response to the 1998/99 budget' (parliamentary submission), 12 March, Cape Town.

Cottle, E. (1999) 'Jobs Summit fails to deliver', *SA Labour Bulletin*, Vol. 23, No. 1 (February), Johannesburg.

Crankshaw, O. (1993) 'On the doorstep of management', *SA Sociological Review*, Vol. 6, No. 1, Pretoria.

Creamer, K. (1998) 'A labour perspective on job creation', speech to Industrial Relations Association of South Africa (3 November), Cape Town.

Cronin, J. (1995a) 'The RDP needs class struggle', *African Communist*, No. 142 (Third Quarter), Johannesburg.

Cronin, J. (1995b) 'Challenging the neo-liberal agenda in South Africa', *Links*, No. 4 (January–March), Broadway.

Cronin, J. (1994a) 'Sell-out, or the culminating moment? Trying to make sense of the transition', paper presented to University of Witwatersrand History Workshop (July), Johannesburg.

Cronin, J. (1994b) 'The present situation and the challenges for the South African Left', discussion document (July), Johannesburg.

Cronin, J. (1994c) 'Towards a people-driven RDP', *African Communist*, No. 138 (Third Quarter), Johannesburg.

Cronin, J. (1992) 'The boat, the tap and the Leipzig way', *The African Communist*, No. 130, Johannesburg.

Cronin, J. & Naidoo, Jayendra (1994) 'Implementing and co-ordinating the RDP through government, the Alliance, democratic mass and community-based formations, and institutions of civil society' (paper), Johannesburg.

Cronin, J. & Nzimande, B. (1997) 'We need transformation, not a balancing act – looking critically at the ANC Discussion Document', *African Communist* (First Quarter), Johannesburg.

Davidson *et al.* (1976) *Southern Africa: The New Politics of Revolution*, Penguin, Harmondsworth.

Davies, R. (1997) 'Engaging with the GEAR', SACP discussion paper (March), Cape Town.

Davies, R. (1995) 'The international context', *African Communist*, No. 139/140 (First Quarter), Johannesburg.

Davies, R. (1992a) 'Integration or cooperation in a post-apartheid South Africa' (paper), Centre for Southern African Studies, Cape Town.

Davies, R. (1992b) 'Emerging Southern African perspectives on regional cooperation and integration after apartheid', *Transformation*, No. 20, Durban.

Davies, R., Keet, D. & Nkuhlu, M. (1993) *Reconstructing Economic Relations with the Southern African region: Issues and options for a democratic South Africa*, MERG, Cape Town.

Davies, R., O'Meara, D. & Dlamini S. (1985) *The Struggle for South Africa: A reference guide to movements, organizations and institutions*, Zed, London.

De Landa, M. (1991) *War in the Age of Intelligent Machines*, Zone, New York.

Department of Finance (1996) *Growth, Employment and Redistribution: A Macroeconomic Strategy*, Department of Finance, Pretoria.

Dexter, P. (1996) '75 years of the South African Communist Party', *SA Labour Bulletin*, Vol. 20, No. 4 (August), Johannesburg.

Dexter, P. (1995a) 'The big myth – sunset clauses and the public service', *African Communist*, No. 139/140 (First Quarter), Johannesburg.

Dexter, P. (1995b) 'The RDP: Ensuring transformation through the state and popular transformation', *SA Labour Bulletin*, Vol. 19, No. 4 (September), Johannesburg.

Dexter, P. (1994) 'Make the RDP make the Left', *Work in Progress*, No. 95 (February/March), Johannesburg.

Dlamini, K. (1999) 'Globalisation: Can unions reinvent themselves?', *SA Labour Bulletin*, Vol. 23, No. 1 (February), Johannesburg.

Edwards, C. (1998) 'Financing faster growth in South Africa: The case for reforming the financial sector', *Transformation*, No. 35, Durban.

Ela, J. (1998) 'Looking to a new Africa', *Le Monde Diplomatique* (October), Paris.

Ellis, S. & Sechaba, T. (1992) *Comrades against Apartheid: The ANC and the South African Communist Party in Exile*, James Currey, London.

Erwin, A. (1999a) 'Interview with Alec Erwin', *Global Dialogue*, Vol. 4, No. 1 (April), Johannesburg.

Erwin, A. (1999b) 'Address by Minister Alec Erwin: Trade and Industry Budget Vote', 9 March, Cape Town.

Erwin, A. (1994) 'The RDP: A view from the tripartite alliance', *SA Labour Bulletin* Vol. 18 No. 1 (Jan/Feb), Johannesburg.

Erwin, A. (1990) 'South Africa's post-apartheid economy: Planning for prosperity', *SA Labour Bulletin*, Vol. 14, No. 6, Johannesburg.

Erwin, A. (1989) 'Thoughts on a planned economy', *Work in Progress*, No. 61 (September/October), Johannesburg.

Esterhuysen, P. (ed.) (1994) *South Africa in Subequatorial Africa: Economic Integration*, Africa Institute of South Africa, Pretoria.

Etkind, R. & Harvey, S. (1993) 'The workers' cease fire', *SA Labour Bulletin*, Vol. 17, No. 5 (September/October), Johannesburg.

Everatt, D. (1999) 'Yet another transition? Urbanisation, class formation and the end of national liberation struggle in South Africa' (paper), Woodrow Wilson Institute, Washington.

Everatt, D. (1992) 'Consolidated CASE reports on the Reef violence' (paper), CASE, Johannesburg.

Everatt, D. (1991) 'Alliance politics of a special type: The roots of the ANC/SACP alliance, 1950–1954', *Journal of Southern African Studies*, Vol. 18, No. 1 (March).

Falon, P. *et al.* (1994) 'South Africa: Economic performance and policies', *Informal Discussion Papers on Aspects of the Economy of South Africa No. 7*, World Bank, Washington.

Fine, A. & Webster, E. (1989) 'Transcending traditions: Trade unions and political unity', *South African Review 5*, Ravan, Johannesburg.

Fine, R. (1992) 'Civil society theory and the politics of transition in South Africa', *Review of African Political Economy*, No. 55, Sheffield.

Fine, R. with Davis, D. (1990) *Beyond Apartheid: Labour and liberation in South Africa*, Ravan, Johannesburg.

Fine, R. & Davis, D. (1985) 'Political strategies and the state: Some historical observations', *Journal of Southern African Studies*, Vol. 12, No. 1 (October), York.

Forsythe, P. & Mare, G. (1992) 'Natal in the New South Africa' in Moss, G. & Obery, I. (eds), *South African Review No. 6*, Ravan, Johannesburg.

Foundation for Global Dialogue (1998) 'South Africa and Africa: Reflections on the African Renaissance', Occasional Paper No. 17, Johannesburg.

Frank, A.G. (1991) 'No escape from the laws of world economics', *Review of African Political Economy*, No. 50, Sheffield.

Freund, B. (1994a) 'The magic circle', *Indicator SA*, Vol. 11, No. 2 (Autumn), Durban.

Freund, B. (1994b) 'South Africa and world economy', *Transformation*, No. 23, Durban.

Friedman, S. (1999) 'Power to the provinces', *Siyaya!* (Autumn) Cape Town.

Friedman, S. (1993a) *The Elusive Community: The Dynamics of Negotiated Urban Development*, Centre for Policy Studies, Johannesburg.

Friedman, S. (ed.) (1993b) *The Long Journey: South Africa's Quest for a Negotiated Settlement*, Ravan, Johannesburg.

Friedman, S. (1991) 'An unlikely Utopia: State and civil society in South Africa', *Politikon*, Vol. 19, No. 1 (December), Durban.

Friedman, S. (1987a) *Building Tomorrow Today: African Workers in Trade Unions 1970–1984*, Ravan, Johannesburg.

Friedman, S. (1987b) 'The struggle within the struggle: South African resistance strategies', *Transformation*, No. 3, Durban.

Galbraith, James K. (1999) 'The crisis of globalization', *Dissent*, Vol. 46, No. 3 (Summer), New York.

Gall, G. (1997) 'Trade unions & the ANC in the "New South Africa"', *Review of African Political Economy*, No. 72, Sheffield.

Gelb, S. (1999) 'The politics of macroeconomic policy reform in South Africa', symposium (18 September), History Workshop of the University of the Witwatersrand, Johannesburg.

Gelb, S. (1994) 'Development prospects for South Africa', paper presented to WIDER workshop on Medium Term Development Strategy, Phase II, Helsinki (15–17 April).

Gelb, S. (ed.) (1991) *South Africa's Economic Crisis*, David Philip & Zed, Cape Town & London.

Gelb, S. (1990) 'Democratising economic growth: Alternative growth models for the future', *Transformation*, No. 12, Durban.

Gelb, S. (1987) 'Making sense of the crisis', *Transformation*, No. 5, Durban.

Gelb, S. & Saul, J. (1981) *The Crisis in South Africa*, Monthly Review Press, New York.

Ghosh, J. (1997) 'India's structural adjustment: An assessment in comparative Asian context' (seminar paper), Jawaharial Nehru University, New Delhi.

Gibson, B. & Van Seventer, D. (1995) 'Restructuring public sector expenditure in the South African economy' (paper), DBSA, Midrand.

Gill, S. (1999) 'The geopolitics of the Asian crisis', *Monthly Review* (March), New York.

Godfrey, S. & Theron, J. (1999) 'Labour standards versus job creation: The impact of the BCEA on small business', *SA Labour Bulletin*, Vol. 23, No. 5 (October), Johannesburg.

Godongwana, E. (1994a) 'Cosatu approaches a crossroads', *Southern Africa Report*, Vol. 9, No. 5 (July), Toronto.

Godongwana, E. (1994b) 'Industrial restructuring and the social contract', *SA Labour Bulletin*, Vol. 16, No. 4 (March/April), Johannesburg.

Godongwana, E. (1992) 'Industrial restructuring and the social contract: Reforming capitalism or building blocks for socialism?', *SA Labour Bulletin*, Vol. 16, No. 4 (March/April), Johannesburg.

Godsell, B. (1994) 'The Reconstruction and Development Programme: A view from business', *SA Labour Bulletin*, Vol. 18, No. 1 (January/February), Johannesburg.

Gordon, David M. (1988) 'The global economy: New edifice or crumbling foundations?', *New Left Review*, No. 168 (March/April), London.

Gorz, A. (1973) 'Reform and revolution' in *Socialism and Revolution*, Anchor, New York.

Govender, P. *et al.* (1994) *Beijing Conference Report: 1994 Country Report on the Status of South African Women*, Cape Town.

Government of South Africa (1994) *RDP White Paper*, Cape Town.

Gramsci, A. (1971) *Selections from the Prison Notebooks*, Lawrence & Wishart, London.

Gray, J. (1998) *False Dawn: The delusions of global capitalism*, Granta, London.

Greenfield, G. (1999) 'Who's unemployed now? Technocratic 'solutions' to the unemployment crisis' (paper), Hong Kong.

Greenfield, G. (1998) 'Flexible dimensions of a permanent crisis: TNCs, flexibility and workers in Asia' (paper), Hong Kong.

Habermas, J. (1992) 'Citizenship and national identity', *Praxis International*, Vol. 12, No. 2.

Habermas, J. (1986) *Autonomy and Solidarity*, Verso, London.

Habib, A. (1996) 'Myth of the Rainbow Nation: Prospects for the consolidation of democracy in South Africa', *African Security Review*, Vol. 5, No. 6 (working paper series), Pretoria.

Hall, S. (1996) 'Gramsci's relevance for the study of race and ethnicity' in Morley, D. & Chen, K. (eds), *Stuart Hall: Critical Dialogues in Cultural Studies*, Routledge, London.

Hall, S. & Jacques, M. (eds) (1989) *New Times: The Changing Face of Politics in the 1990s*, Macmillan, London.

Hamber, B. (1998) 'Who pays for peace? Implications of the negotiated settlement for reconciliation, transformation and violence in a post-apartheid South Africa' (paper), Johannesburg.

Hamber, B. & Lewis, S. (1997) 'An overview of the consequences of violence and trauma in South Africa' (occasional paper), Centre for the Study of Violence and Reconciliation, Johannesburg.

Hani, C. (1992) 'Hani opens up' (interview), *Work in Progress*, No. 82 (June), Johannesburg.

Hanlon, J. (1994) *Making People-driven Development Work* (report of the Commission on Development Finance for SANCO), Johannesburg, SANCO.

Hanlon, J. (1986a) *Apartheid's Second Front: South Africa's War against its Neighbours*, Penguin, Middlesex.

Hanlon, J. (1986b) *Beggar Your Neighbours*, James Currey, London.

Harris, L. (1993a) 'One step forward', *Work in Progress*, No. 89 (June), Johannesburg.

Harris, L. (1993b) 'South Africa's social and economic transformation: From no middle way to no alternative', *Review of African Political Economy*, No. 57, Sheffield.

Harris, L. (1990) 'The economic strategies and policies of the African National Congress', *McGregor's Economic Alternatives*, Juta, Cape Town.

Hart, G. (1994) 'The new economic policy and redistribution in Malaysia: A model for post-apartheid South Africa?', *Transformation*, No. 23, Durban.

Harvey, D. (1995) 'Globalization in question', *Rethinking Marxism*, Vol. 8, No. 4, pp. 1–17.

Harvey, D. (1990) *The Condition of Postmodernity*, Blackwell, Oxford.

Hassim, S. (1991) 'Gender, social location and feminist politics in South Africa', *Transformation*, No. 15, Durban.

Hill, G. (1999) 'The kwaito revolution', *Siyaya!*, No. 4 (Autumn), Cape Town.

Hindson, D. (1991) 'The restructuring of labour markets in South Africa: 1970s and 1980s' in Gelb, S. (ed.) *South Africa's Economic Crisis*, David Philip & Zed, Cape Town & London.

Hindson, D. & Morris, M. (1992) 'Political violence: Reform and reconstruction', *Review of African Political Economy*, No. 53, Sheffield.

Hirst, P. (1996) 'Global markets and the possibilities of convergence', paper presented to the Conference on Globalization and the New Inequality (November), Utrecht University.

Hobsbawm, E. (1996) 'Identity politics and the Left', *New Left Review*, No. 217 (May/June), London.

Hobsbawm, E. (1995) *Age of Extremes: The Short Twentieth Century*, Abacus, London.

Holloway, J. (1994) 'Global capital and the national state', *Capital and Class*, No. 52, London.

Horn, P. (1991) 'Conference on women and gender in Southern Africa: Another view of the dynamics', *Transformation*, No. 15, Durban.

Human Rights Commission (1991) *The New Total Strategy,* Human Rights Commission, Johannesburg.

Hussy, D. (2000) 'Where to now?', briefing document for the National Land Committee (February), Johannesburg.

IDASA (2000) 'Submission to the Portfolio Committee on Finance on the 2000/01 Budget', IDASA Budget Information Service (March), Cape Town.

ILO (1996) *Restructuring the Labour Market: The South African challenge* (ILO Country Review), Geneva.

INTERFUND (1999) *Annual Review: The Voluntary Sector and Development in South Africa 1997/98*, Johannesburg.

INTERFUND (1997) *Annual Review: The Voluntary Sector and Development in South Africa 1996/97*, Johannesburg.

Industrial Strategy Project (1994) 'Industrial strategy for South Africa: The recommendations of the ISP', *SA Labour Bulletin*, Vol. 18, No. 4 (January/February), Johannesburg.

Jacobs, S. (1999) 'An imperial presidency?', *Siyaya!* (Summer), Cape Town.

Jardin, C. & Satgar, V. (1999) 'COSATU and the Tripartite Alliance', *SA Labour Bulletin*, Vol. 23, No. 3 (June), Johannesburg.

Joffe, A., Kaplan D., Kaplinsky, R. & Lewis, D. (1994a) 'Meeting the global challenge: A framework for industrial revival in South Africa' in *South Africa and the World Economy in the 1990s*, Cape Town, David Philip.

Joffe, A., Kaplan D., Kaplinsky, R. & Lewis, D. (1994b) 'An industrial strategy for a post-apartheid South Africa', *Institute for Development Studies Bulletin*, Vol. 25, No. 1, Sussex.

Jordan, P. (1992a) 'Strategic debate in the ANC: A response to Joe Slovo', *African Communist*, No. 131 (Fourth Quarter), Johannesburg.

Jordan, P. (1992b) 'Has socialism failed? The South African debate', *Southern Africa Report* (January), Toronto.

Jourdan, P., Gordhan, K., Arkwright, D. & De Beer, G. (1997) 'Spatial development initiatives (development corridors): Their potential contribution to investment and employment creation', paper (January), Pretoria.

Kagarlitsky, B. (1999) 'The challenge for the Left: Reclaiming the state' in Panitch, L. & Leys, C. (eds), *Socialist Register 1999: Global Capitalism versus Democracy*, Merlin, Suffolk.

Kagarlitsky, B. (1995a) *The Mirage of Modernization*, Monthly Review Press, New York.

Kagarlitsky, B. (1995b) 'Letter to South Africa', *Links*, No. 4 (January–March), New Course, Newtown (Australia).

Kagarlitsky, B. (1989) *The Dialectics of Change*, Verso, London.

Kahn, B. (1991) 'Exchange rate policy and industrial restructuring' in Moss, G. & Obery, I. (eds), *South African Review No. 6*, Ravan, Johannesburg.

Kaplan, D. (1991) 'The South African capital goods sector and the economic crisis' in Gelb, S. (ed.) *South Africa's Economic Crisis*, David Philip & Zed, Cape Town & London.

Kaplan, D. (1990) 'Recommendations on post-apartheid economic policy', *Transformation*, No. 12, Durban.

Kaplinksy, R. (1994) '"Economic restructuring in South Africa: The debate continues": A response', *Journal of Southern African Studies*, Vol. 20, No. 4 (December), York.

Kaplinsky, R. (1991) 'A growth path for a post-apartheid South Africa', *Transformation*, No. 16, Durban.

Karis, T. & Carter, G.M. (eds) (1977) *From Protest to Challenge: A Documentary History of African Politics in South Africa, 1882–1964*, Hoover, Stanford.

Karis, T. & Gerhardt, G.M. (eds) (1977) *Challenge and Violence 1953–1964*, Vol. 3 of *From Protest to Challenge: A Documentary History of African Politics in South Africa 1882–1964*, Hoover Institution, Stanford.

Katz, M.M. (chair) (1994) *Interim Report of the Commission of Inquiry into certain aspects of the Tax Structure of South Africa*, Pretoria.

Keane, J. (1988a) *Civil Society and the State*, Verso, London.

Keane, J. (1988b) *Democracy and Civil Society*, Verso, London.

Keet, D. (1992) 'Shop stewards and worker control', *SA Labour Bulletin*, Vol. 16, No. 5, Johannesburg.

Kelly, J. (1999) 'Outsourcing statistics', *SA Labour Bulletin*, Vol. 23, No. 3 (June), Johannesburg.

Kentridge, M. (1993) *Turning the Tanker: The Economic Debate in South Africa*, Centre for Policy Studies, Johannesburg.

Khan, F. (1999) 'SANGOCO economics project base discussion document', paper prepared for SANGOCO, Cape Town.

Kraak, G. (1997) 'Coasting in neutral', *Development Update*, Vol. 1, No. 2, INTER-FUND, Johannesburg.

Kraak, G. (1996) *Development Update: An INTERFUND Briefing on the Development and Voluntary Sector in South Africa in 1995/96*, INTERFUND, Johannesburg.

Krugman, P. (1995) *Peddling Prosperity: Economic Sense and Nonsense in the Age of Diminished Expectations*, W.W. Norton & Co., New York.

Krugman, P. (1992) 'Towards a counter-counter revolution in development theory', *Proceedings of the World Bank Annual Conference on Development Economics*.

Laclau, E. (1990) *New Reflections on the Revolution of our Time*, Verso, London.

Laclau, E. & Mouffe, C. (1985) *Hegemony and Socialist Strategy: Towards a Radical Democratic Politics*, Verso, London.

Lambert, R. (1987) 'Trade unions, nationalism and the socialist project in South Africa', *South African Review No. 4*, Ravan, Johannesburg.

Legassick, M. & de Clerq, F. (1978) 'The origins and nature of the migrant labour system in Southern Africa', *Migratory Labour in Southern Africa*, UN Economic Commission for Africa.

Le Roux, P. *et al.* (1993) *The Mont Fleur Scenarios*, University of Western Cape, Cape Town.

Levin, M. (2000) 'Youth and the elections', *Development Update*, Vol. 3, No. 2, Johannesburg.

Lewis, D. (1991) 'The character and consequences of conglomeration in the South African economy', *Transformation*, No. 16, Durban.

Leys, Colin (1994) 'Confronting the African tragedy', *New Left Review*, No. 204, London.

Lipietz, A. (1989) 'The debt problem, European integration and the new phase of the world crisis', *New Left Review*, No. 178 (December), London.

Lipietz, A. (1987) *Mirages and Miracles: The crises of global Fordism*, Verso, London.

Lipton, M. (1986) *Capitalism and Apartheid: South Africa 1910–1986*, Aldershot.

Lodge, T. (1999a) *South African Politics since 1994*, David Philip, Cape Town.

Lodge, T. (1999b) *Consolidating Democracy: South Africa's second popular election*, Witwatersrand University, Johannesburg.

Lodge, T. (1989) 'People's war or negotiation? African National Congress strategies in the 1980s', *South African Review No. 5*, Ravan, Johannesburg.

Lodge, T. (1987) 'The African National Congress after the Kabwe Conference', *South African Review No. 4*, Ravan, Johannesburg.

Lodge, T. (1983) *Black Politics in South Africa since 1945*, Longman, Harlow.

Lodge, T. & Nasson, B. (1991) *All, Here, and Now: Black politics in South Africa in the 1980s*, David Philip, Cape Town.

MacEwan, A. (1994) 'Globalisation and stagnation' (seminar paper), Centro de Investigaciones Interdisciplinares en Humanidades, National Autonomous University of Mexico, Mexico City.

Macroeconomic Research Group (MERG) (1993) *Making Democracy Work*, Centre for Development Studies/Oxford, Cape Town.

Magdoff, H. & Sweezy, P. (1990) 'Investment for what?', *Monthly Review*, Vol. 42, No. 2 (June), New York.

Maharaj, G. (ed.) (1999) *Between Unity and Diversity: Essays on nation-building in post-apartheid South Africa*, David Philip, Cape Town.

Mamdani, M. (1996) *Citizen and Subject: Contemporary Africa and the Legacy of Late Colonialism*, Princeton University, Princeton.

Mandela, N. (1998) 'Address by President Nelson Mandela to parliament' (6 February), Cape Town.

Mandela, N. (1997) 'Address by President Nelson Mandela to the closing session of the 50th National Conference of the ANC' (20 December), Mafikeng.

Mandela, N. (1994) 'Inaugural address to a joint sitting of parliament' (24 May), Cape Town.

Mandela, N. (1991) 'Continuation lecture' (6 December), University of Pittsburgh, Pittsburgh.

Manuel, T.A. (2000) 'Budget speech' (23 February), Cape Town.

Manuel, T.A. (1999) 'Budget speech' (17 February), Cape Town.

Manuel, T.A. (1998a) 'Speech by Minister Trevor Manuel to parliament on the subject for discussion: Currency volatility and its effect on the South African economy' (22 July), Cape Town.

Manuel, T.A. (1998b) 'Address to Societe Generale Frankel Pollak 21st Annual Investment Conference' (24 February), Johannesburg.

Manuel, T.A. (1996) 'Speech by Mr T.A. Manuel, Minister of Finance', Bureau for Economic Research conference (8 October), Cape Town.

Marais, H. (2000) *To the Edge: An Examination of South Africa's National AIDS Response 1994–1999* (annual review), Centre for the Study of AIDS, University of Pretoria, Pretoria.

Marais, H. (1999a) 'Blinded by the light: The left in South Africa's transition' (seminar paper), Centro de Investigaciones Interdisciplinarias en Humanidades, National Autonomous University of Mexico, Mexico City.

Marais, H. (1999b) 'His masterful voice', *Leadership* (October/November), Cape Town.

Marais, H. (1998a) *Reinforcing the Mould: The character of regional integration in Southern Africa*, Third World Forum & Institute for Global Dialogue, Dakar & Johannesburg.

Marais, H. (1998b) 'Saving the Non-Aligned Movement from itself', *Global Dialogue*, Vol. 3, No. 3 (December), Institute for Global Dialogue, Johannesburg.

Marais, H. (1997) 'The Mbeki "enigma"', *Southern Africa Report*, Vol. 13, No. 1 (November), Toronto.

Marais, H. (1996) 'Who killed Bambi? The death of the RDP', *Weekly Mail and Guardian* (July 12), Johannesburg.

Marais, H. (1994a) 'Radical as reality', *African Communist*, No. 138 (Third Quarter), Johannesburg.

Marais, H. (1994b) 'The skeletons come out of the cupboard', *Work in Progress, No. 91* (August/September), Johannesburg.

Marais, H. (1993b) 'The new barbarians (The criminalisation of youth)', *Work in Progress, No. 90* (July/August), Johannesburg.

Marais, H. (1992a) 'The sweeping inferno', *Work in Progress, No. 83* (July/August), Johannesburg.

Marais, H. (1992b) 'What happened in the ANC camps?', *Work in Progress, No. 82* (June), Johannesburg.

Marais, H. & Narsoo, M. (1992) 'And justice for all?', *Work in Progress, No. 85* (October), Johannesburg.

Mare, G. (1992) *Brothers Born of Warrior Blood: Politics and ethnicity in South Africa*, Ravan, Johannesburg.

Mare, G. & Hamilton, G. (1987) *An Appetite for Power: Buthelezi's Inkatha and South Africa*, Ravan, Johannesburg.

Marie, B. (1996) 'Giants, teddy bears, butterflies and bees: Ideas for union organizing', *SA Labour Bulletin*, Vol. 20, No. 1 (February), Johannesburg.

Marie, B. (1992) 'Cosatu faces crisis', *SA Labour Bulletin*, Vol. 16, No. 5 (May/June), Johannesburg.

Marks, S. & Trapido, S. (1991) 'Introduction', *Journal of Southern African Studies*, Vol. 18, No. 1 (March), York.

Martin, H. & Schumann, H. (1997) *The Global Trap: Globalisation & the assault on democracy and prosperity*, Zed, London.

Marx, Anthony W. (1992) *Lessons of Struggle: South African internal opposition, 1960–1990*, Oxford University, Cape Town.

Maseko, S. & Vale, P. (1998) 'South Africa and the African Renaissance' in Foundation for Global Dialogue, *South Africa and Africa: Reflections on the African Renaissance*, Occasional Paper No. 17, Johannesburg.

Mayekiso, M. (1994) 'Taking the RDP to the streets', address to SANCO Southern Transvaal RDP conference (May), Johannesburg.

Mbeki, G. (1996) *Sunset at Midday: latshon' ilang 'emini!*, Nolwazi Educational, Johannesburg.

Mbeki, G. (1992) *The Struggle for Liberation in South Africa: A Short History*, David Philip, Cape Town.

Mbeki, T. (2000) 'State of the Nation Address at the Opening of Parliament' (4 February), Cape Town.

Mbeki, T. (1999a) 'Speech of the President of the Republic of South Africa, Thabo Mbeki at the 54th session of the United Nationals General Assembly', 20 September, New York.

Mbeki, T. (1999b) 'State of the Nation Address' (25 June), Cape Town.

Mbeki, T. (1998a) 'Statement of Deputy President Thabo Mbeki on Reconciliation at the National Council of Provinces' (10 November), Cape Town.

Mbeki, T. (1998b) 'Statement of the President of the African National Congress, Thabo Mbeki, at the 10th Congress of the South African Communist Party' (2 July), Johannesburg.

Mbeki, T. (1998c) 'Statement of the President of the ANC at the Meeting of the Central Committee of Cosatu' (23 June), Johannesburg.

Mbeki, T. (1998d) 'Statement of the Deputy President on the Occasion of the Debate on the Budget Vote of the Office of the Deputy President' (3 June), Cape Town.

Mbeki, T. (1998e) 'Address to NUM Congress' (28 March), Johannesburg.

Mbeki, T. (1997) 'Address to "Attracting Capital to Africa" Summit' (April 19), Chantilly (USA).

Mboweni, T. (1994) 'Formulating policy for a democratic South Africa: Some observations', *Institute for Development Studies Bulletin*, Vol. 25, No. 1, Sussex.

McGrath, M. & Whiteford, A. (1994) 'Disparate circumstances', *Indicator SA*, Vol. 11, No. 3 (Winter), Durban.

Meer, S. (1999) 'Election '99: How far have we come? A balance sheet of the transition', *Development Update*, Vol. 3, No. 1, Johannesburg.

Mercer, C. (1980) 'Revolutions, reforms or reformulations?', in Alan Hunt (ed.), *Marxism and Democracy*, Lawrence and Wishart, London.

Michie, J. & Padayachee, V. (eds) (1997) *The Political Economy of South Africa's Transition: Policy Perspectives in the late 1990s*, Dryden, London.

Miliband, R. (1996) 'The New World Order and the Left', *Social Justice*, Vol. 23, Nos. 1–2 (Spring–Summer), San Francisco.

Miliband, R. (1983) *Class Power and State Power: Political essays*, Verso, London.

Mills, G., Begg, A. & Van Nieuwkerk, A. (1995) *South Africa in the Global Economy*, SAIIA, Johannesburg.

Moll, T. (1991) 'Did the apartheid economy "fail"?', *Journal of Southern African Studies*, Vol. 17, No. 2 (December), York.

Moll, T. (1990) 'From booster to brake ? Apartheid and economic growth in comparative perspective' in N. Nattrass & E. Ardington (eds), *The Political Economy of South Africa*, Oxford University, Cape Town.

Morley, D. & Chen, K. (1996) *Stuart Hall: Critical Dialogues on Cultural Studies*, Routledge, London.

Morris, M. (1993a) 'The legacy of the past' (paper) (December), University of Economics, Prague.

Morris, M. (1993b) 'Who's in, who's out? Side-stepping the 50% solution', *Work in Progress*, No. 86, Johannesburg.

Morris, M. (1993c) 'Methodological problems in tackling micro and macro socio-economic issues in the transition to democracy in South Africa' (paper) (May) Slovak Academy of Sciences, Bratislava.

Morris, M. (1991) 'State, capital and growth: The political economy of the national question', in Gelb, S. (ed.), *South Africa's Economic Crisis*, David Philip & Zed, Cape Town and London.

Morris, M. (1976) 'The development of capitalism in South Africa' *Journal of Development Studies*, Vol. 12, No. 3.

Morris, M. & Hindson, D. (1992) 'Political violence: Reform and reconstruction', *Review of African Political Economy*, No. 53, Sheffield.

Morris, M. & Padayachee, P. (1989) 'Hegemonic projects, accumulation strategies and state reform policy in South Africa', *Labour, Capital and Society*, Vol. 22, No. 1.

Moss, G. & Obery, I. (eds) (1991) *South Africa Review No. 6*, Ravan, Johannesburg.

Moss, G. & Obery, I. (eds) (1987) *South Africa Review No. 4*, Ravan, Johannesburg.

Murphy, M. (1994) 'A shaky alliance: Cosatu and the ANC', *Indicator SA*, Vol. 11, No. 3 (Winter), Durban.

Murray, R. (1971) 'The internationalisation of capital and the nation state', *New Left Review*, No. 67 (May/June), London.

Mzala (1990) 'Is South Africa in a revolutionary situation?', *Journal of Southern African Studies*, Vol. 16, No. 3 (September), York.

Mzala (1987) 'Towards a people's war and insurrection', *Sechaba* (April).

Mzala (1981) 'Has the time come for arming the masses?', *African Communist*, No. 102 (Third Quarter), Johannesburg.

Narsoo, M. (1993) 'Doing what comes naturally: A development role for the civic movement', *Policy: Issues and Actors*, Vol. 6, No. 2 (June), Centre for Policy Studies, Johannesburg.

Narsoo, M. (1991) 'Civil society – A contested terrain', *Work in Progress*, No. 76 (February), Johannesburg.

National Institute for Economic Policy (1994) *Making the RDP Work: Draft Submission for the RDP White Paper*, NIEP, Johannesburg.

Nattrass, J. (1988) *The South African Economy: Its Growth and Change*, Oxford University, Cape Town.

Nattrass, N. (1996) 'Gambling on investment: Competing economic strategies in South Africa', *Transformation*, No. 31, Durban.

Nattrass, N. (1994a) 'Economic restructuring in South Africa: The debate continues', *Journal of Southern African Studies*, Vol. 20, No. 4 (December) York.

Nattrass, N. (1994b) 'The limits to radical restructuring: A critique of the MERG report', *Third World Quarterly*, Oxfordshire.

Nattrass, N. (1994c) 'Politics and economics in ANC economic policy', *African Affairs* (July), London.

Nattrass, N. (1991) 'Controversies about capitalism and apartheid in South Africa: An economic perspective', *Journal of Southern African Studies*, Vol. 17, No. 4 (December), York.

Nattrass, N. & Ardington, E. (eds) (1990) *The Political Economy of South Africa*, Oxford University, Cape Town.

Nel, P. (1999) 'Conceptions of globalisation among the South African elite', *Global Dialogue*, Vol. 4, No. 1 (April), Johannesburg.

Netshitenze, J. (1998) 'The state, property relations and social transformation', ANC discussion paper, Pretoria.

Nicolau, K. (2000) 'Digging deep', *Ngqo!* (NIEP bulletin), Vol. 1, No. 2 (February), NIEP, Johannesburg.

Nicolaou, K. (1999) 'Pandora's box', *Ngqo!* (NIEP bulletin), Vol. 1, No. 1 (June), NIEP, Johannesburg.

Niddrie, D. (1990) 'The duel of dual power', *Work in Progress*, No. 67 (June), Johannesburg.

Nkuhlu, M. (1993) 'The state and civil society in South Africa', conference paper (August), Cape Town.

Nyawuza (1985) 'New "Marxist" tendencies and the battle of ideas in South Africa', *African Communist*, No. 103 (Fourth Quarter).

Nzimande, B. (1997) 'The state and the national question in South Africa's national democratic revolution' (paper), Harold Wolpe Memorial Trust conference, Cape Town.

Nzimande, B. (1992) 'Let us take the people with us: A reply to Joe Slovo', *African Communist*, No. 131 (Fourth Quarter), Johannesburg.

O' Meara, D. (1983) *Volkskapitalisme: Class, capital and ideology in the development of Afrikaner-nationalism 1934–1948*, Ravan, Johannesburg.

Osborne, P. (1991) 'Radicalism without limit? Discourse, democracy and the politics of identity' in *Socialism and the Limits of Liberalism*, Verso, London.

Padayachee, V. (1995) 'Debt, development and democracy, The IMF and the RDP', *Review of African Political Economy*, Sheffield.

Padayachee, V. (1994a) 'Can the RDP survive the IMF?', *Southern Africa Report*, Vol. 9, No. 5 (July), Toronto.

Padayachee, V. (1994b) 'Dealing with the IMF: Dangers and opportunities', *SA Labour Bulletin*, Vol. 18, No. 1 (January/February), Johannesburg.

Paine, G. (1999) 'Dark side of a hot idea', *Siyaya!* (Summer), Cape Town.

Panitch, L. (1994) 'Globalization and the state' (paper), Universidad Nacional Autonoma de Mexico, Mexico City.

Pellicani, L. (1981) *Gramsci: An Alternative Communism?*, Hoover Institution, Standford.

Petras, J. (1997) 'Intellectuals: A Marxist critique of post-Marxists', author's draft paper (February), New York.

Phillips M. & Coleman, C. (1989) 'Another kind of war: Strategies for transition in the era of negotiation', *Transformation*, No. 9, Durban.

Pilger, J. (1998) *Hidden Agendas*, Vintage, London.

Pityana, B., Ramphele, M., Mpumlwana, M. & Wilson, L. (1991) *Bounds of Possibility: The legacy of Steve Biko and Black Consciousness*, David Philip & Zed, Cape Town & London.

Polanyi, K. (1944) *The Great Transformation: The Political and Economic Origins of our Time*, Beacon, Boston.

Postman, N. (1992) *Technopoly: The Surrender of Culture to Technology*, Vintage, New York.

Poulantzas, N. (1978) S*tate, Power, Socialism*, Verso, London.

Poulantzas, N. (1976) *The Crisis of the Dictatorships: Portugal, Greece, Spain*, New Left, Manchester.

Przeworksi, A. *et al.* (1995) *Sustainable Democracy*, Cambridge University, Cambridge.

Price, R.M. (1991) *The Apartheid State in Crisis; Political Transformation in South Africa, 1975–90*, Oxford University, London.

Rapoo, Thabo (1995) *Making the Means Justify the Ends: The Theory and Practice of the RDP*, Centre for Policy Studies, Johannesburg.

RDP Office (1995) *Key Indicators of Poverty in South Africa*, Ministry in the Office of the President, Pretoria.

Reitz, M. (1995) 'Divided on the "demon": Immigration policy since the election' (paper), Centre for Policy Studies, Johannesburg.

Rifkin, J. (1995a) *The End of Work: The decline of the global labour force and the dawn of the post-market era*, Putnam, New York.

Rifkin, J. (1995b) 'The end of work?', *New Statesman & Society* (9 June), London.

Rodrik, D. (1999a) *The New Global Economy and Developing Countries: Making Openness Work*, John Hopkins University, Baltimore.

Rodrik, D. (1999b) 'Making openness work', speech (18 March), Overseas Development Council, Washington.

Rodrik, D. (1997) 'Sense and nonsense in the globalisation debate', *Foreign Policy* (Summer), Washington.

Rodrik, D. (1996) *Why do more open economies have bigger governments?*, Working Paper 5537 of the National Bureau of Economic Research, Cambridge, Massachusetts.

Rudin, J. (1997) *Challenging Apartheid's Foreign Debt*, Alternative Information and Development Centre, Cape Town.

SACP (1999) 'State, reform and revolution', document presented at the Special Strategic Conference (3–5 September), Johannesburg.

SACP (1998) *Forward to the SACP 10th Congress!* (Draft Programme Discussion Documents), Johannesburg.

SACP (1997) 'New confidence on the left' (editorial), *African Communist* (Third Quarter), Johannesburg.

SACP (1996) 'Let us not lose sight of our strategic priorities', Secretariat discussion document (October), Johannesburg.

SACP (1995) 'Strategy and tactics document', Ninth SACP Congress, Johannesburg.

SACP (1994) 'Defending and deepening a clear left strategic perspective on the RDP' (discussion document), *African Communist* No. 138 (Third Quarter), Johannesburg.

SACP (1962) 'The road to South African freedom: Programme of the South African Communist Party', *African Communists Speak*, Nauka, Moscow.

SACP & COSATU (1999) 'Trade unions and day-to-day struggles to build socialism' (paper), Johannesburg.

SAIRR (1992) 'Race Relations Survey 1991/92', Johannesburg.

SANGOCO, Commission on Gender Equality & SA Human Rights Commission (1998) *The People's Voices: National Speak Out on Poverty Hearings – March to June 1998*, Johannesburg.

Sassen, S. (1997) 'The global economy: Its necessary instrumentalities and cultures' (paper), University of California.

Sassen, S. (1996) *Losing control? Sovereignty in an age of globalization*, Columbia University Press, New York.

Satgar, V. (1997) 'Workplace forums and autonomous self-management: A perspective on transformation from below', *African Communist* (Third Quarter), Johannesburg.

Saul, J. (1994a) '(Half full) Or half empty? Review of the RDP', *Southern Africa Report*, Vol. 9, No. 5 (July), Toronto.

Saul, J. (1994b) 'Thinking the thinkable: Globalism, socialism and democracy in the South African transition' in Ralph Miliband & Leo Panitch (eds.), *Socialist Register 1994*, Merlin, Toronto.

Saul, J. (1993) *Recolonization and Resistance in Southern Africa in the 1990s*, Between the Lines, Toronto.

Saul, J. (1992) 'Structural reform: A model for revolutionary transformation of South Africa?', *Transformation*, No. 20, Durban.

Saul, J. (1991) 'South Africa between barbarism and structural reform', *New Left Review*, No. 188, London.

Saul, J. & Gelb, S. (1981) *The Crisis in South Africa: Class Defence and Class Revolution*, Monthly Review, New York.

Schneider, F. & Frei, Bruno, S. (1985) 'Economic and political determinants of FDI', *World Development*, Vol. 13, No. 2, Washington.

Scholte, J.A. (1997) 'Global capitalism and the state', *International Affairs*, Vol. 73, No. 3.

Schreiner, G. (1994) 'Restructuring the labour movement after apartheid', *SA Labour Bulletin*, Vol. 18, No. 3 (July), Johannesburg.

Schreiner, J. (1993) 'Breaking the mould', *Work in Progress*, No. 93 (November), Johannesburg.

Schrire, R. (ed.) (1992) *Wealth or Poverty? Critical Choices for South Africa*, Oxford University, Cape Town.

Secombe, W. (1999) 'Contradictions of shareholder capitalism: Downsizing jobs, enlisting savings, destabilizing families' in Panitch, L. & Leys, C. (eds), *Socialist Register 1999: Global Capitalism versus Democracy*, Merlin, Suffolk.

Seekings, J. (1997) 'SANCO: Strategic dilemmas in a democratic South Africa', *Transformation*, No. 34, Durban.

Seekings, J. (1993) *Heroes or Villians?*, Ravan, Johannesburg.

Seekings, J. (1991) 'Trailing behind the masses: The United Democratic Front and township politics in the Pretoria-Witwatersrand-Vaal Region, 1983–1984', *Journal of Southern African Studies*, Vol. 18, No. 1 (March), York.

Segal, L. (1991) 'The human face of violence: Hostel dwellers speak', *Journal of Southern African Studies*, Vol. 18, No. 1 (March), York.

Sender, J. (1995) 'Economic restructuring in South Africa: Reactionary rhetoric prevails', *Journal of Southern African Studies*, Vol. 20, No. 4 (December), York.

Shubane, K. & Madiba, P. (1992) *The Struggle Continues?: Civic Associations in the Transition*, Centre for Policy Studies, Johannesburg.

Sikwebu, D. (1999) 'June 2nd aftermath: Defining a role for Cosatu', *SA Labour Bulletin*, Vol. 23, No. 4 (August), Johannesburg.

Simkins, C. (1987) *The Prisoners of Tradition and the Politics of Nation Building*, SAIRR, Johannesburg.

Simon, R. (1991) *Gramsci's Political Thought*, Lawrence & Wishart, London.

Simone, A. (1994) *Local Institutions and the Governance of Community Development in South Africa* (author's draft), Foundation for Contemporary Research, Cape Town.

Slovo, J. (1992) 'Negotiations: What room for compromises?', *African Communist*, No. 130 (Third Quarter), Johannesburg.

Slovo, J. (1990) 'Has socialism failed?', *SA Labour Bulletin*, Vol. 14, No. 6 (February), Johannesburg.

Slovo, J. (1976) 'South Africa – No middle road' in Davidson, B., Slovo, J. & Wilkinson, A. (eds), *Southern Africa: The New Politics of Revolution*, Penguin, London.

South African Government (1994) *White Paper on Reconstruction and Development: A Strategy for Fundamental Transformation* (September), Pretoria.

SouthScan bulletin (various issues), London.

Sparks, A. (1994) *Tomorrow Is Another Country: The Inside Story of South Africa's Negotiated Revolution*, Struik, Johannesburg.

Stadler, A. (1987) *The Political Economy of Modern South Africa*, David Philip, Cape Town.

Stanners, W. (1993) 'Is low inflation an important condition for high growth?', *Cambridge Journal of Economics*, No. 17, Cambridge University, Cambridge.

Stein, H. (ed.) (1995) *Asian Industrialisation and Africa: Studies in policy alternatives to structural adjustment*, St. Martin's Press, London.

Stiglitz, J. (1998) *More Instruments and Broader Goals: Moving Toward the Post-Washington Consensus*, WIDER annual lecture (January 7), Helsinki.

Suttner, R. (1992) 'Ensuring stable transition to democratic power', *African Communist*, No. 131 (Fourth Quarter). Johannesburg.

Suttner, R & Cronin, J. (1986) *Thirty Years of the Freedom Charter*, Ravan, Johannesburg.

Sweezy, P.M. & Magdoff, H. (1992) *Globalization – To What End?*, Monthly Review, Vol. 43, No. 9 (February), New York.

Swilling, M. (1991) 'The case for associational socialism', *Work in Progress*, No. 76 (February), Johannesburg.

Swilling, M. & Phillips, M. (1989a) 'The emergency state: Its structure, power and limits', *South African Review No. 5*, Ravan, Johannesburg.

Swilling, M. & Phillips, M. (1989b) 'State power in the 1980s: From "total strategy" to counter-revolutionary warfare' in *War and Society: The Militarization of South Africa*, David Philip, Cape Town.

Theron, J. (1999a) 'Labour standards versus job creation: The impact of the BCEA on small business', *SA Labour Bulletin*, Vol. 23, No. 5 (October), Johannesburg.

Theron, J. (1999b) 'Terms of empowerment', *SA Labour Bulletin*, Vol. 23, No. 1 (February), Johannesburg.

Toussaint (1988) 'On workerism, socialism and the Communist Party', *African Communist*, No. 114 (Third Quarter).

Trevor, A. (1984) 'The question of an uprising of the people as a whole', *African Communist*, No. 97 (Second Quarter).

Tsoukalas, C. (1999) 'Globalisation and the executive committee: The contemporary capitalist state' in Panitch, L. & Leys, C. (eds), *Socialist Register 1999: Global Capitalism versus Democracy*, Merlin, Suffolk.

UNCTAD (1999) *World Investment Report 1999*, New York.

UNCTAD (1997) *World Investment Report 1997: Transnational Corporations, Market Structure and Competition Policy*, New York.

UNDP (1998) *Poverty and Inequality in South Africa*, Pretoria.

Vadney, T.E. (1987) *The World Since 1940*, Pelican, London.

Various authors (1970) *African Communists Speak: Articles and documents from the 'The African Communist'*, Nauka, Moscow.

Vilas, Carlos M. (1996) 'Neoliberal social policy', *NACLA Report on the Americas*, Vol. 29, No. 6 (May/June), New York.

Vilas, Carlos M. (1993) 'The hour of civil society', *NACLA Report on the Americas*, Vol. 27, No. 2 (September/October), New York.

Vilas, Carlos M. (1989) 'Revolution and democracy in Latin America', *Socialist Register 1989*, Merlin, London.

Virilio, P. (1978) *Popular Defense and Ecological Struggles*, Semiotext(e), New York.

Von Holdt, K. (1997) 'The September Commission: Shaping congress debates, stimulating activism', *SA Labour Bulletin*, Vol. 21, No. 6 (December), Johannesburg.

Von Holdt, K. (1996) 'David or Goliath?: The future of the unions', *SA Labour Bulletin*, No. 20, No. 4 (August), Johannesburg.

Von Holdt, K. (1993) 'Cosatu Special Congress: The uncertain new era', *SA Labour Bulletin*, Vol. 17, No. 5 (September/October), Johannesburg.

Von Holdt, K. (1992) 'What is the future of labour?', *SA Labour Bulletin*, Vol. 16, No. 8 (November/December), Johannesburg.

Wade, R. & Veneroso, F. (1998) 'The Asian crisis: The high debt model versus the wall-treasury-IMF complex', *New Left Review*, No. 228, London.

Wade, R. & Veneroso, F. (1998) 'The gathering world slump and the battle over capital controls', *New Left Review*, No. 231, London.

Wade, R. (1996) 'Japan, the World Bank and the art of paradigm maintenance: The East Asian miracle in political perspective', *New Left Review*, No. 217 (May/June), London.

Walker, C. (1982) *Women and Resistance in South Africa*, Onyx, London.

Wallerstein, I. (1996) 'The ANC and South Africa: The Past and Future of Liberation Movements in the World-System', address to South African Sociological Association, Durban (7 July), Durban.

Watkins, K. (1994) 'GATT: A victory for the North', *Review of African Political Economy*, No. 59, Sheffield.

Watts, M. (1994) 'Development 11: The privatization of everything' (workshop paper), University of California, Berkeley.

Webster, E. & Adler, A. (1999) 'Towards a class compromise in South Africa's "double transition": Bargained liberalisation and the consolidation of democracy', symposium paper (September), History Workshop of the University of the Witwatersrand, Johannesburg.

Weiss, L. (1997) 'Globalisation and the myth of the powerless state', *New Left Review*, No. 225, London.

Whiteford, A. & Van Seventer, D. (1999) *Winners and Losers: South Africa's changing income distribution in the 1990s*, WEFA Southern Africa, Pretoria.

Whiteford, A., Van Zyl, E., Simkins, C. & Hall, E. (1999) *Labour market trends and future workforce needs*, HSRCl, Pretoria.

Wolpe, H. (1988) *Race, Class and the Apartheid State*, James Currey, London.

Wolpe, H. (1984) 'Strategic issues in the struggle for national liberation in South Africa', *Socialist Review*, Vol. 8, No. 2, London.

Wolpe, H. (1980) 'Towards an analysis of the South African State', *International Journal of the Sociology of Law*, No. 8.

Wood, Ellen Meiksins (1995) 'Editorial', *Monthly Review* (July/August), New York.

Wood, Ellen Meiksins (1990) 'The uses and abuses of civil society' in Miliband *et al.*, *Socialist Register* 1990, Merlin, Suffolk.

World Bank (1996) *World Development Report 1996*, Washington.

World Bank (1994) *Reducing Poverty in South Africa: Options for equitable and sustainable growth*, Johannesburg.

World Bank (Southern Africa Department) (1993) *South Africa: Paths to Economic Growth*, Washington.

Zarenda, H. (1994) 'The inconsistencies and contradictions of the RDP', address to the Johannesburg Branch of the South African Economics Society, 4 October 1994.

Zita, L. (1995) 'The RDP: Towards a working class approach', unpublished paper, Johannesburg.

Zita, L. (1994) 'The limit and possibilities of reconstruction', unpublished paper, Johannesburg.

Zita, L. (1993a) 'Unity of the Left', *African Communist*, No. 134 (Third Quarter), Johannesburg.

Zita, L. (1993b) 'Moving beyond the social contract', *African Communist*, No. 133 (Second Quarter), Johannesburg.

Zuege, A. (1999) 'The chimera of the Third Way' in Panitch, L. & Leys, C. (eds), *Socialist Register 2000: Necessary and Unnecessary Utopias*, Merlin, Suffolk.

Index